W9-CBO-841

BY VED MEHTA

Face to Face
Walking the Indian Streets
Fly and the Fly-Bottle
The New Theologian
Delinquent Chacha
Portrait of India
John Is Easy to Please
Mahatma Gandhi and His Apostles
The New India
The Photographs of Chachaji
A Family Affair
Three Stories of the Raj

CONTINENTS OF EXILE
Daddyji
Mamaji
Vedi
The Ledge Between the Streams
Sound-Shadows of the New World
The Stolen Light
Up at Oxford

CONTINENTS OF EXILE

U P

AT

OXFORD

Main Quadrangle, Balliol College, Oxford. Ca. 1959. CREDIT: CAS OORTHUYS,
THE NETHERLANDS PHOTO ARCHIVES

VED MEHTA

CONTINENTS OF EXILE

UP

AT

OXFORD

W.W. Norton & Company

NEW YORK / LONDON

Parts of this book appeared in The
New Yorker, The American Scholar, *and*
The American Oxonian.

Printed in the United States of America

First Edition

Continues the Series, Continents of Exile, which includes:
Daddyji, 1972; Mamaji, 1979; Vedi, 1982; The Ledge Between the Streams, 1984; Sound:
Shadows of the New World, 1985; and The Stolen Light, 1989.

The text of this book is composed in Garamond #3.
Manufacturing by The Maple-Vail Book Manufacturing Group.

Library of Congress Cataloging-in-Publication Data

Mehta, Ved, 1934–
Up at Oxford / Ved Mehta.
p.   cm. — (Continents of exile)
1. Mehta, Ved, 1934– . 2. Blind—United States—Biography.
3. College students—England—Oxford—Biography. I. Title.
II. Series: Mehta, Ved, 1934– Continents of exile.
HV1792.M44A3   1993   362.4'2'092—dc20 [B]   92–42491

ISBN 0-393-03544-1

W.W. Norton & Company, Inc.
500 Fifth Avenue, New York, N.Y. 10110
W.W. Norton & Company Ltd.
10 Coptic Street, London WC1A 1PU

1 2 3 4 5 6 7 8 9 0

To Natasha

Putting this particular book to press gives me special pleasure. In my autobiographical series, "Continents of Exile," it is the first to be set in Britain, my third spiritual home—the two others being India and America. I am deeply indebted to the Fellows of Balliol, who elected me a visiting Fellow for the academic year of 1988–89, and so enabled me to spend a year in Oxford reviving my memories and checking them against the college archives. As I finish the book, I think of my amanuenses, Danielle Clarke, Violet Lutz, and Melissa Burkhart, who, in addition to helping me much as Milton's daughters helped him, provided inestimable editorial suggestions. I think of Jasper Griffin and how his hours of evocative conversation helped me recall our Oxford days. I give warm thanks to him and to Sir Richard (R.W.) Southern and Christopher Hill, to Hilary Rubinstein and Donald Lamm, and, as always, to the late William Shawn, Eleanor Gould Packard, and my wife, Linn, all of whom read the manuscript and offered invaluable criticisms and suggestions. Many other friends—too many to name here—were generous with their time and their memories; fortunately, all of them figure in this narrative, and the reader will meet them in due course. It goes without saying, however, that I alone bear full responsibility for everything in the book. Although the writing of the book is done, I will go on lovingly remembering all the people who gave a hand—for their love, as the poet says, "rememb'red such wealth brings / That then I scorn to change my state with kings."

V.M.

New York
February 1993

CONTENTS

CONTINENTS OF EXILE

U P

AT

OXFORD

I

A EUROPEAN PRELUDE

OXFORD IS AUTHORITATIVELY DESCRIBED IN MY 1901 edition of Baedeker as "on the whole much more attractive than Cambridge to the ordinary visitor," so the traveller is instructed to "visit Cambridge first, or to omit it altogether if he cannot visit both." Certainly the University of Oxford was much better known than the University of Cambridge in the British India of my childhood. Indeed, my father's friends who had studied at Oxford used to say that without going there one could have no idea of its place in English literature, British history, and British philosophy—in British society. They spoke of Oxford as the home of clever people, the training ground of the governing class, the nursery of Prime Ministers. It was as though Oxford were, in its way, like the Hardwar of the Hindus, the Mecca of the Muslims, the Golden Temple of the Sikhs—the holiest of the holy places of pilgrimage. Even when I was a child, there was no place I wanted to go to more than Oxford. Instead, when I was fifteen I came to America for education, and when I finished high school in Arkansas I ended up as an undergraduate at Pomona College, in Southern California. But there Pomona and its associated colleges were spoken of as the Oxford of the Orange Grove. Half a dozen of my professors at Pomona had studied at Oxford, and so had Pomona's president, E. Wilson Lyon. They all spoke about Oxford, making me even more determined to go there. But how was I to get there? At Pomona, I was being supported almost entirely by scholarships and grants, and sometimes even being able to finish college seemed impossible. At one point, my college was planning to nominate me for a Rhodes scholarship. But it turned out that as an Indian citizen I was ineligible to enter the American competition, and, at the same time, as one studying in America I was ineligible to enter the Indian competition for the single Rhodes scholarship available to all of India each year.

Nevertheless, in the spring of 1955, my third year at Pomona, I began to try for admission to Balliol. One of my history professors, John Gleason, had gone to Balliol and was a great champion of my going there. Founded in the thirteenth century, it was thought to be the oldest college at the university. It was also the most international, and was reputed to have been the first Oxford college to admit "blacks and wogs," in the nineteenth century. It was the birthplace of the Indian Civil Service and the alma mater of a number of India's leading civil servants, and, like some other Indians, I had grown up thinking that it was the whole university, rather than one college among more than a score of Oxford colleges. In May, I wrote a letter to the Master of Balliol, Sir David Lindsay Keir, inquiring about my chances of admission, and I soon got a letter back from K. J. Dover, Senior Tutor. "The Master has passed on to me your letter of May 30th, as I deal

4

with applications for admission to the College," he wrote. Saying that the college would be able to give me its decision before February 1st, he concluded, "Would you please send me (before January 1st, 1956) three testimonials from those who have seen most of your work at Pomona."

At my suggestion, my father, who happened to be in Europe, had made several trips to Oxford, had stopped by Balliol, and had called on, among others, Mr. Dover and T. H. Tylor, Fellow and Tutor in Jurisprudence, who was one of two blind tutors at Oxford. Mr. Tylor had immediately taken an interest in my application to Balliol. "Mr. Tylor said that at any one time there are three or four blind undergraduates at Oxford and that there has been an unbroken tradition of blind students at Oxford for half a century," my father wrote me in June. Admission to a college was handled primarily by the tutor (or tutors) of the subject that the applicant proposed to read, and the senior tutor took it for granted that if I came to Oxford I would be reading law. That was what most blind people read. (I had been blind since I was almost four.) Indeed, Tylor assumed that, like him, I would go on to do the advanced law degree, the B.C.L., and that afterward I would teach law in India. It never occurred to my father to question the assumption, because most of the Indians he himself knew who had studied in England were successful barristers at home. He couldn't imagine a better qualification than law for any career in India.

Soon after I received my father's letter, I was on my way to Harvard, where I was to attend the summer school, beginning in July. I was studying at Harvard for the first time, and I was much excited. I threw myself into work, taking a course in the twentieth-century American novel and one in short-story writing, with a view to perfecting the skills I needed to finish an autobiography that I was working on with the guidance of Edward Weeks, the editor of the *Atlantic*.

At Harvard, I also wrote a stream of letters to American,

British, and Indian organizations, telling them I expected to be admitted to Balliol and inquiring whether they had grants for which I might be eligible. At the same time, Dr. Lyon at Pomona, Mr. Tylor at Balliol, and other friends wrote on my behalf to their friends at various foundations. (I applied for admission and scholarships to Harvard, Yale, and Princeton, too, but merely as a fallback.) All the letters got the same sort of reply—that I did not fit the classification for the organization's scholarships. It seemed that there was indeed no scholarship that was designed for someone like me—someone who, as it were, fell between two continents and wanted to study on a third, and was also blind.

As it happened, my application to Balliol was specially discussed at a college meeting in October, and I was notified immediately that I had been admitted, provided that I could obtain six hundred pounds a year in financial support. But November, December, and January came and went, and I seemed no closer to getting to Oxford. I had all but given up hope of ever getting there. Even people I knew well to whom I had written, seeking to advance my cause, had stopped answering my letters, as if I were making a nuisance of myself, as if I were asking for the moon.

Then, in February, I received a letter from Mrs. G. J. Watumull, the head of the Watumull Foundation, in Honolulu, who was one of many family friends I had appealed to. She said that she had not answered my letter for nearly four months, because she had been working behind the scenes: that she had sent my appeal to Paul Braisted, the president of the Hazen Foundation, in New Haven, Connecticut; that, although Braisted had agreed to present my case to his board of trustees, he had not been very hopeful; and that then the board-of-trustees meeting had been postponed.

I didn't want to write any of this to you [she wrote], so I decided to bide my time instead and await a report of the meeting of the Board of Trustees in January. This morning's mail brought the letter, and I enclose a copy because they will grant you a fellowship.

I can't tell you how happy I am over this decision. I have waited with great anxiety for this date, and I can assure you it is a very rewarding one. The Hazen Foundation has been interested in students from India and in the readjustment of Indian students, after study abroad, to their homeland. I also know Paul Braisted personally and I must say I did my best in pleading your cause. That it was effective gives me great pleasure and satisfaction.

Now I hope you'll forgive me for not writing for such a long time.

I was elated. A scholarship from her foundation had helped me to get to Pomona; soon a scholarship secured through her efforts would get me to Oxford. Now there is no question—I'm actually going to Oxford, I thought. I'm actually going to study in Matthew Arnold's "sweet city with her dreaming spires."

IT was marvellous to be in Europe with my parents and finally to be on my way up to Oxford. I was constantly struck with wonder as I visited places I knew from books, tried out my college French, and listened to French conversations in the streets; I thought that people spoke as if words were bonbons.

And my mother in Paris! Just the thought of it made me smile. But then for my parents and me to be having a holiday in Europe was itself extraordinary. In Paris, my father took us to famous restaurants to which he had gone with Mrs. Clyde—Ethel Clyde, who was his and the family's benefactress. My mother had never been to the West; in fact, she had been out of India only once, and then only to Ceylon. She had hardly ever stayed in a hotel. The prices of things in Paris worried her. Whenever we were in a restaurant, she tallied up the number of cigarettes and glasses of wine that people around us were consuming, and claimed that if my father had lived like a Frenchman she would have been out of house and home practically on the day of her marriage. She could not understand why the French people were always sitting in restaurants and cafés, drinking and smoking, wasting good money that they might have used to rear children—to buy them clothes and shoes. (I was one of seven children.) As far as she could see, France was a nation of spendthrifts.

We were in Paris for only a week, but, as always, my mother proved able to adapt herself to her surroundings. She ate sausages, meatballs, chops. She never asked what was in them but just said "Ram, Ram," bit her tongue, and bravely ate them. A friend of hers who had gone to England had practically fasted the whole time she was there, because everything that was put before her—yogurt, fruitcake, ice cream, cauliflower—seemed to her to smell of beef. But my mother didn't fret about eating beef. She told herself that only Indian cows were sacred.

My father had not done anything really touristy in the West for thirty-six years—not since he was a student in London, in 1920—and he had made up his mind to treat us to a real holiday. We stayed in a hotel on the Place de l'Opéra. We took a guided tour of Versailles, had lunch at the Café de la Paix, walked along the Champs-Élysées, went to the Lido and the Folies-Bergère. We visited the Tuileries and the Luxembourg Gardens, the Eiffel Tower and Notre Dame. My mother was interested in everything, but she also dropped remarks like "There are no comforts like home comforts," leaving us in no doubt that she would rather have been saving the money for the children's clothes and shoes.

"Here in Paris, we should pretend we are not spending real money," my father would say. "Not the kind of money we earn in India with the sweat of our brow."

The money he was spending in Paris was what he had earned by serving as a companion physician to Mrs. Clyde, who was a friend of people like Eleanor Roosevelt, Margaret Sanger, and Norman Thomas, and was a longtime contributor to what were then unconventional causes, among them birth control, school integration, and nudist camps. She was also a hypochondriac and something of a globe-trotter. For four years, she had been employing my father on short-term assignments. The job was a godsend for him, since we had lost everything in the Partition of India, in 1947, and, on top of that, three years later he had turned fifty-five, which was the age of mandatory retirement for all government officers. He had been given a year of extension, after which his thirty-year career in India's health departments came to an end. It was thanks to Mrs. Clyde that he could finally keep a promise he had made to my mother at the time of their marriage—that one day he would show her the West. The assignment with Mrs. Clyde was all found, so he had been able to save the salary she paid him—seven hundred dollars a month. True, the amount she paid him for a few months' service was a fraction of what she would have had to pay an American doctor for comparable service, but he thought of it as found money. And, of course, at that time seven hundred dollars could buy a lot in many parts of the world. Hence our holiday.

MY father, my mother, and I were walking along a street. I was so intent on taking in everything around me that I became aware of my mother's absence only when she joined us again.

"So what did you do?" my father asked, laughing in his usual open, kindly manner.

"I refused," she said, trying to suppress a laugh.

"No!" he exclaimed. "How did you get in?"

She ignored the question. "When the children were growing up, you used to tell them how much better things were in the West, but you never told them of the inhuman customs—that you have to pay for what is a God-given right of every person."

"But what did you do?" my father pressed.

"An old French lady put in a coin, and I went into the stall."

"No doubt she thought you didn't know one French coin from another," my father said.

"I don't," she said, and she added, jokingly, to me, "Son, at home your daddy used to boast that when I came out to the West he would fill my purse with foreign money and I could hold my head high, like a queen. But see—my purse is empty."

Right there on the street, my father put some franc notes in my mother's purse and set about explaining the different coins, holding out various franc and centime pieces for her to see.

"*Monsieur, Madame, un moment, s'il vous plaît,*" an elegant-sounding man said, darting out of a doorway. He fell in step with us as if he knew us. "Is the sah-ree that Madame is wearing Kashmiri silk? It is *très joli.*" His pronunciation of English words with a thick French accent and his mixture of French and English words put me in mind of Charles Boyer, and so to me he sounded irresistible. "You want to *changer* some mo-nee?"

"He's an Arab," my father said, in Punjabi, and we quickened our steps.

"Twice the official rate, brother," the Arab said, following us. "I'll give you twice the bank rate."

"We're not interested," my father said. But the Arab stayed right with us.

My father turned around. "My friend, I'm a doctor from India. I'm a government officer. I don't engage in hanky-panky."

"Doctor, Doctor, you must be new to Paris," the Arab said.

"That we certainly are," my father said.

"Give him a couple of rupees and get rid of him," my mother said, in Punjabi.

My father laughed. "He's not a beggar. He's a money changer. He's offering twice the official rate for dollars."

"Three times for you, Doctor," the Arab said, as if divining my father's Punjabi. I was amazed at his brazenness, since it was daylight and we were on a fairly crowded street.

"Tell him to go away," my mother said, in Punjabi. "After the Partition, we are just beginning to have some clothes on our backs, and now here is another Muslim wanting to take them off."

My father stopped and said to the Arab, "Let us alone, friend. But no hard feelings." He put out his hand.

It is typical of him to want to shake hands, even with a crook, I thought. In his opinion, "Manners maketh the man" was a saying second in wisdom only to "When in Rome do as the Romans do."

"The Doctor has honored me by calling me his friend," the Arab was saying ingratiatingly. "I want to do you a friendly service, nothing more. You can check up. No one uses banks. You can check with Thomas Cook & Son."

We turned onto another busy street. It struck me that the illicit money changer could not be plying his trade in public unless the practice was indeed generally accepted.

My mother must have had a similar thought, because she said, "What's the harm? With the extra money, I can buy handbags for the girls."

My father also had a change of heart, though whether it was due to the Arab's reference to the respected Thomas Cook & Son or to my mother's mention of handbags for my sisters I never found out.

My father stopped and turned around. "How much can you change, my friend?"

"Any amount the Doctor would like," he said.

"A hundred dollars?" my father asked.

"Yes, for sure."

My father reached for his wallet. He imagined that the money would change hands in the street, so infectious was the Arab's bravado.

"Not here," the Arab said, taken aback. "Put that back in your pocket. You have to come with me in *un taxi.*"

Before we knew what he was doing, he had flagged down a taxi and was holding the door open.

I had always thought of my father as a great man—magnanimous, courageous, honest, a prince among men, free of base motives and concerns. He was everything I felt I was not. Every servant we had in my childhood had pointed to him as an Indian who could be an Englishman, above bribes and petty jealousies. I was about to protest at the idea of an illegal transaction—and in a foreign country at that. But car horns were honking all around, and the taxi driver was talking in fast, incomprehensible French, no doubt berating us for holding up the traffic.

"*Venez,* so we can continue our *conversation,*" the Arab said. He jumped in beside the driver, all the while urging us "*Vite.*"

Then things happened so quickly that later I wasn't sure of the sequence. Like an automaton, I tried to get into the taxi, but I neglected to bend down. I hit my mouth hard against its roof. Where there had been an artificial front tooth there was a gaping hole. Doors slammed. The taxi sped away. The Arab disappeared. My father all but dropped his money, stuffing it back into his pocket. My mother was on her knees in the street looking for the dental bridge. Tears ran down my face uncontrollably.

Some time later, when I had recovered a bit, I reflected that perhaps, just as psychologists say, there are no accidents in life. It occurred to me that in some part of my mind I might indeed have wanted to have the accident, in order, perhaps, to take the bloom off my arrival at Oxford; even if I could somehow afford to have a new tooth made, there was no way I could get it in time to make a good first impression on my tutors and fellow-students. Certainly, during my first, nervous days at Oxford, I would have trouble enunciating my dentals, at the very least—and that in a place that was legendary for setting the standard for the King's English. Then why had I brought the accident upon myself? One possible explanation was that it had something to do with the pain my parents had endured at the hands of another kind of hustler, who had thoroughly fleeced them before I joined them on the Continent.

❦

I HAD arrived in Frankfurt from Boston, where I had just finished my young autobiography and submitted it to the publishers, three weeks before the trip to Paris. It was late August, but the Frankfurt air already had a touch of autumn in it. Indeed, there was more than a hint of a season of change. I felt light-headed and almost hopped down the shaky plane steps.

I was twenty-two. I was setting foot on the Continent for the first time. I was about to see my mother, whom I had not seen in seven years. I had finished high school and college in America, where I had gone because the handful of schools for the blind in India catered more to orphans and ragamuffins than to someone like me, interested in receiving a formal education. The plan was for my parents and me to spend six weeks together in Germany, Italy, Switzerland, France, and England before I went up to Oxford, in the second week of October.

"Hello," my mother said now, greeting me at the bottom of the plane steps. "Youngster, your mother is in the West. She is a mem." She pulled me down by a lapel of my jacket and tried to kiss me on the cheek, in the manner of a Westerner. She succeeded in planting a kiss very low on my cheek. (She was at least six inches shorter than I was.)

I winced. I could feel a drop of blood forming on my cheek. It took me a moment to realize that she had taken to wearing a nose ring and I had been nicked by its point. The idea of my mother's wearing a nose ring irritated me. To my Western sensibility the piercing of the nostril seemed a sort of mutilation.

I unobtrusively dabbed at the blood on my cheek with a

handkerchief, as if I were wiping away a tear.

"Then give your mother at least a hug, like a good Punjabi," she said. Feeling guilty, I embraced her.

"You're supposed to be waiting in the terminal," I said, giving her a little shove. I felt embarrassed at her being there. I had travelled from America to Europe alone, and her coming right up to the plane to receive me seemed to imply that I couldn't get around without assistance.

"The young German hostess from Air India gave me permission to come up to the plane when I told her that my blind son was coming," she said. Oh God, I thought, she hasn't changed. She's still asking for pity, as if I were a helpless, uneducated little boy in her care.

"I'm not blind," I said petulantly, and then, sobering, added, "Not in the way you think."

"What did you say?" my mother asked.

"Never mind."

Since I had not seen my mother for seven years, I had imagined in the plane that I would be warm and affectionate with her, babble about my school and college experiences, about how I had missed her. But now that I was with her I was tongue-tied.

We started walking toward the terminal.

"Why do you wear a nose ring?" I asked abruptly.

"Youngster, I have always worn a nose ring. You've forgotten."

"I never remember being stabbed by it," I said.

"Stabbed by it!" she exclaimed. "How you talk! It's true that when your father got some money I bought myself a new nose ring, with a diamond. You probably don't like my nose ring because ladies don't wear them in America. Well, let me tell you, I'm much prettier and younger than your daddy's Mrs. Clyde."

I couldn't help noticing that my mother was hanging on to my arm as if she were the seventy-seven-year-old Mrs. Clyde rather than my forty-eight-year-old mother. (She was thirteen years younger than my father.) Though my mother was extremely active and looked youthful, she had been in indifferent health for as long as I could remember.

We were inside the terminal, and my father was waiting for us. He put a large hand on my shoulder. I discreetly disengaged my arm from my mother's grasp.

My mother tried to take hold of my hand. I was a small boy again, a handicapped child, who was not going to school, as her other children did: she would take me on her errands, talking to friends or haggling with street venders and shopkeepers along the way, not caring how bored I was.

I disengaged my hand and stepped closer to my father. Our arms touched, making, I thought, a solid, manly front against the feminine world of trivial concerns.

In the taxi—nothing less than a luxurious Mercedes—my father directed the driver to take us to Bad Nauheim.

"I thought that was a spa for old people," I said. "Why are we going there?"

"Dr. Langreuter, the director of a special allergy clinic for asthma there, thinks that he might be able to cure your mother of her asthma," my father said. My mother had been asthmatic since she was twenty-three. "Dr. Langreuter has become a good friend of mine."

In the course of the drive, my father told me that earlier in the year he had flown to Frankfurt from New Delhi to work for Mrs. Clyde on a three-month assignment. After seeing her off for New York, where she lived, he had rushed to Geneva to receive my mother, flying in from New Delhi.

"I almost didn't get off from Delhi," my mother said, and she explained that Ashok, my younger brother, had come down with diphtheria. Before she knew it, the family had put her on the plane, and its door had closed behind her. Throughout the journey, she had recited *gayatri* mantras, and she had kept saying to herself, "I shouldn't have left a sick child behind." At the

Geneva airport, she didn't even pause to catch her breath before asking my father for news from home. He told her that he had had a call saying that Ashok was fine.

Our taxi was humming along the autobahn. The road was smooth and straight. We could have been anywhere in the world, but the comfort of the ride was distinctly Western.

My mother said that after she had a chance to collect herself in Geneva she looked around. Switzerland seemed so clean, so neat, so orderly. It looked golden. Everything was golden—the hotel, the bathroom, the dining room. It was a heavenly change from the dust, soot, and heat of India.

My father, to his great delight, had on his arm his wife—his "one and only," as he liked to jokingly refer to her—and that was a great change from escorting Mrs. Clyde, who was constantly arguing with him, contradicting him, and challenging him. My mother was fascinated by Geneva's shops and bought handker-chiefs, tablecloths, chocolates, and a watch. My father had planned to take her straight from Geneva to Bad Nauheim for asthma treatments, but instead, on an impulse, he decided to make a detour to Baden-Baden, the famous German spa in the Black-Forest. He had gone there with Mrs. Clyde, and he thought he had worked out a mathematical system for winning at roulette.

My mother was stunned by the casino; she had never seen so many lights going on and off, and had certainly never seen so many people gambling at roulette tables. My father explained to her how to bet, and gave her fifty marks to play on her own. She lost thirty and was devastated. She felt as if she had pawned her favorite piece of jewelry. As for him, before the evening was over he had won a hundred and fifty marks.

During the taxi ride, I came to realize that my parents didn't sound like themselves. I had dismissed the idea at first, thinking that coming out of a plane after a long flight made everything sound different. But now it struck me that my parents seemed to be talking as if they were missing some teeth.

"Has something happened to your teeth?" I asked.

"Don't ask," my mother said, breathing hard. "There is always someone or other waiting to ensnare your father." She laughed.

I remembered that my mother had a habit of laughing at everything, and also that she wheezed when she laughed. Her laugh had at times grated on my nerves.

"What are you talking about?" I asked.

"Dentist," my mother said, under her breath. "Luckily, I'm ensnared only to the extent of my lower teeth, but your daddy is getting new upper and lower teeth."

"I thought you came to Bad Nauheim for your asthma," I said.

"Don't mention it," my mother said. "Everything has had to be put aside, because your daddy and I are involved in tooth construction, which will take at least three more weeks."

I was appalled. In all the years I had spent in America, I had hardly taken a holiday, and I imagined that my parents and I would make the grand tour of Europe, in the manner of nineteenth-century English travellers. I thought that my father would know where to take my mother and me, what to show us; he had been crisscrossing the Continent with Mrs. Clyde off and on for four years. So far, I knew the Continent only through books. I was eager to get to know it with my boots.

"You can't mean this about the dentist," I said.

"Son, we have a lot of dental treatment ahead of us," my father said. "What can't be cured must be endured. You see, we got trapped."

❦

THEIR first morning in Baden-Baden, as the story was told to me, my mother woke up and complained of pain in her gums. My father examined her mouth. The gums of her lower jaw were inflamed. "It looks like an allergic reaction to something you ate," he said. By breakfast time, her gums were bleeding.

They cut short their visit to Baden-Baden and took an express train to Bad Nauheim, where my father had good medical connections because of the time he had spent there with Mrs. Clyde.

His friend Dr. Langreuter quickly arranged to have a Dr. Ata, whom he spoke of as the best-known dentist of the spa, examine my mother in the hotel room.

Dr. Ata, who was a short, thin, nearly bald man in his late fifties, diagnosed my mother's condition as gingivitis. He applied some kind of paint to her gums, and it gave her immediate relief.

"I've done the teeth of world-famous people," Dr. Ata said as my father was showing him to the lift. "The king of Saudi Arabia was so pleased with my teeth that he presented me with a Cadillac with solid-gold fittings."

"What do you mean when you say 'my teeth'?" my father asked.

Dr. Ata launched into a long explanation, which caused him to miss several lifts. He said that soon after the First World War he heard that a German dental surgeon in Berlin had developed a technique for capping teeth which made them look perfectly white and even, and that film stars and politicians from all over the world were flocking to him. Dr. Ata had made his way to Berlin and managed to become the great surgeon's apprentice. "I was a smart young man, and, with the surgeon's help, I eventually got myself registered as a dentist in Germany and set up practice in Berlin."

During the Second World War, Dr. Ata was forced to flee to Turkey with, he said, "just the clothes on my back." ("The phrase, echoing, as it did, our plight during the Partition, struck a sympathetic chord in me," my father said.) When the war was over, he returned to Germany and set up a clinic in Bad Nauheim, which was famous for its rich clientele. He invited my father, as one doctor to another, to visit his clinic.

My father, who, for some reason, had never heard of Dr. Ata on his earlier visits, accepted the invitation.

That afternoon, Dr. Ata picked my father up in his Cadillac, which was indeed equipped with gold fittings, from the dashboard all the way to the back window. The clinic, too, my father was astonished to see, was fitted out with gold. Peering down from the walls were people who looked like celebrities, every one of them smiling and showing dazzling, even teeth.

Dr. Ata took him around the laboratory, which had furnaces, where the caps were prepared. "You see how beautiful the teeth are," Dr. Ata said, putting one in my father's hand. "I hear from Dr. Langreuter that you lecture in America. My teeth could do wonders for you."

Although my father had listened to Dr. Ata with growing interest and curiosity, he said, "My teeth are fine. I don't need to have anything done to them."

"But look over there in the mirror," Dr. Ata said, pointing to a large mirror decorated with gold leaf. "Your teeth don't show very much. They have been worn down by age. Their enamel is thin."

My father was surprised at how worn down his teeth looked; until that moment, he had never taken a close look at his teeth in a mirror.

"I could fit my teeth on top of your teeth and improve your appearance one hundred per cent," Dr. Ata said. "Also, you will have my teeth as long as you live, with no cavities, exposed dentine, or broken teeth."

My father noticed that Dr. Ata had a hypnotic voice. That should have put him on his guard. Instead, he imagined that Dr. Ata could make him and my mother, too, look like those celebrities. Anyway, the process of transformation seemed very easy, for he got the impression that Dr. Ata filed down only a bit of the natural teeth and fitted his caps on top of them.

My father returned to the hotel room full of impressions of

his visit to Dr. Ata's clinic. "Now that we are in Bad Nauheim, it may be a lifetime's opportunity for both of us to get our teeth done," he told my mother.

My mother's gums had recovered so quickly under Dr. Ata's paint that she thought of him as almost a magician. She said she would like to visit his clinic.

The next day, they both went to the clinic. My father asked Dr. Ata what it would cost them to have their teeth done.

Dr. Ata said that it would cost a lot of money if my father were an ordinary patient, but that since he was a fellow-doctor and a friend he could have the work done at a special price. "Your cost will be exactly seventeen hundred dollars," he announced.

"How lucky that I should have the money in my pocket," my father said to my mother, in Punjabi.

Indeed, he had three months' salary from Mrs. Clyde—twenty-one hundred dollars—intact, for his Baden-Baden winnings had covered practically all their expenses so far. He had hoped to show my mother the Continent, give her a break from bearing and rearing children. He had planned to revisit, with her, the London haunts of his student days, and to take her to Venice and Florence. She was very observant and had a good eye for color and design, so he believed she could appreciate the art treasures of Western Europe. He thought he would enjoy taking her to the Scandinavian countries to see their mountains and fjords. And then there was Paris. No Indian was really sophisticated who had not made a pilgrimage to Paris. And why stop there? There was plenty of money to take in Rome and Vienna, Lisbon and Barcelona as well. Anyway, he could easily supplement the money by visiting casinos in Nice and Monaco. In fact, his idea had been to take her to every town and hotel he had visited with Mrs. Clyde, so that thereafter she could at least visualize what he did in Europe while she sat at home in India. He had even toyed with the idea of taking her, in the autumn, to America, where he was scheduled to make a two-month lecture tour of the Midwest.

But now, intoxicated by Dr. Ata's talk, they decided to forgo all those travel plans in favor of the new teeth. What better use could they make of the money than having their teeth done— teeth that would see them through old age? They rationalized that living in a hotel in Bad Nauheim was in itself a fine holiday.

❧

MY first Continental night was spent on a cot, which, to save money, had been set up for me at the foot of my parents' bed in Bad Nauheim. Now I was sitting with them in the hotel dining room, having my first Continental breakfast—a phrase that sounded romantic to my ears. There were almost a dozen varieties of breads and buns, along with honey and packets of all kinds of jams.

My mother took a sip of tea and observed that it was the first time in weeks that she had been able to have anything hot.

"Your mother likes her tea boiling hot," my father said. "She'll never like tea in America. Not only do they make it with tea bags but they drown it with cold milk. Even in the best hotels and restaurants, they have never heard of hot milk. No matter how often I asked for it, I was always served cold milk with my tea."

"The days of my ever drinking American tea are gone," my mother said. "Dr. Ata's bills have seen to that."

"Money comes and money goes," my father said. "As long as my hands and feet work, money will come."

Bells began to peal somewhere in the distance. They seemed to go on and on, ringing change after change.

"What are those bells?" I asked.

"They're church bells," my father said. "On the Continent, you can hardly go anywhere without hearing them. Don't you like them?"

"They're haunting," I said.

"They seem to ring these bells whenever someone gets married or dies," my mother said. "But you can't tell from the bells which it is, so you never know whether you are supposed to be happy or sad."

I hadn't heard any church bells in America. I had read in history books that in the Middle Ages monks did their tasks to the peals of bells. I was charmed and thrilled.

"What are we going to do today?" I asked.

"You can follow the daily regimen of the spa with us," my father said. "We can all go and have a mineral-water bath and drink some mineral water. We can have some mouth and nose inhalations of atomized air. They have certainly been giving your mother some relief from her asthma. In the afternoon, we can have massages and nap. And in the late morning and early evening there are concerts in the park. We never miss those. You'll see. The day just disappears."

"Don't forget our teeth appointments," my mother said.

The more they talked, the more claustrophobic I felt. I wanted to go to the ruins I had read about in history books, experience the Continent, practice my French, do a hundred other things. But now it seemed that instead of travelling through the Continent I would be stuck in a hotel for elderly Germans.

"When we go for our teeth appointments, you can read," my father said.

"I wish we'd never heard of Bad Nauheim," my mother said. "I wasn't enthusiastic about having my teeth done. I think, from the very start, Ata typed your daddy as a person who wears his heart on his sleeve, whom anyone can take advantage of."

My father began reproaching himself for his gullibility, but he couldn't be glum for very long. Always irrepressible and ebullient, he spun a fantasy about teaching Dr. Ata a lesson. "I'll frog-march him to the top of a mountain. I'll make him stand at the edge of a cliff. I'll threaten him with a vigorous kick squarely on his behind. I'll make him beg for mercy. I'll make him promise to go back to Turkey, where he comes from."

We all laughed.

In our different ways, we had all been on edge. But now I, for one, realized that I couldn't allow myself to feel angry at my parents for getting me stranded in Bad Nauheim. After all, what was my plight compared with theirs? Besides, I was savoring the feeling of being an only child instead of one of seven, as at home. I was revelling in the chance to have the complete attention of my parents at last. (Parents' love is not divisible, but their attention is.) I was in Europe, and my brothers and sisters, stranded in India, were missing out even on the experience of having Europeans—the world rulers of our childhood—actually wait on our family in the hotel.

THE next installment of the story had it that at one point during one of the first sessions, when Dr. Ata stopped the drilling to allow my father to gargle, my father ran his tongue along the tooth being prepared. Then he examined it in the mirror over the basin and felt it with his finger. "You've drilled away most of my tooth!" he cried. "Haven't you filed it down too far?"

"I must make sure that the cap fits perfectly," Dr. Ata said. He had started referring to his "teeth" as "caps" now. "We can't have the tooth showing under the cap. You must trust me."

My father glanced at the smiling faces on the walls around him and felt reassured.

Each day, after the Novocain wore off, my parents could scarcely eat or drink. Anything, cold or hot, solid or liquid, that touched the exposed tooth was excruciating. A good part of the time, they stayed in bed. It was as if they were two people marooned on an island. (Apparently, it never occurred to them to call a halt to the procedure; once started, it seemed to have a momentum of its own.) They became dependent on room service. They ministered to each other. They regularly cursed Dr. Ata, ruing the day they had ever allowed him to look into their mouths, but they tried to keep their spirits up with professions of confidence in him.

❧

ONE morning, my father skipped his dental appointment with Dr. Ata and took a train to Frankfurt to consult, on the sly, an assistant professor at the university dental clinic. When the professor removed a couple of the temporary caps that Dr. Ata had put on my father's teeth, he asked, "What kind of teeth did you have before this?"

"Strong, healthy ones," my father said.

"Mein Gott! Then you've said *auf Wiedersehen* to most of your healthy teeth. They are now reduced to stumps. An Indian dentist has done this to you?"

"No, sir. It is the work of Dr. Ata, of Bad Nauheim," my father said.

"Mein Gott! Why did you ever allow Dr. Ata to get his hands on your teeth?" the professor asked. "He's not properly qualified. He only talked himself into getting registered and licensed. That was after the Second World War, when the government machinery was *kaputt* here."

"Then why haven't the authorities done something about him?" my father asked, even as he knew he was grasping at straws.

"Once someone is registered and licensed, the authorities can do little about it. That is what we've learned."

"What should I do now about my teeth?" my father asked, in a sinking voice.

"You have no choice but to get him to finish the job. You have this consolation—that you'll have very nice permanent dentures. You may not have needed them for many years, but a great many old people need dentures sooner or later."

When Dr. Ata had at last finished his work, my father examined and reëxamined his new teeth and observed that they were indeed little more than glorified dentures.

☙

AFTER paying Dr. Ata, my father was on a short financial leash, so we cut short our travels on the Continent and flew to London, stopping only in Paris. Luckily, on one of his earlier visits to London my father had become a member of the Royal Over-Seas League, a club off St. James's Street, which had cheaper rooms and some better amenities than many hotels. There we got a couple of poky rooms in an annex, without baths, for a guinea each, which included a cooked English breakfast. My father pointed out that we needn't spend much time in our rooms, since the League had several excellent public rooms, and that if we had a good breakfast we could give lunch a miss.

The atmosphere of the League was redolent of the Raj. There was a display of regimental ties in the lobby, and one could often detect the accents of ex-colonials in the English spoken there, for the membership was drawn largely from the Commonwealth. For me, it was a special pleasure to be again among people who spoke English in the British way. Indeed, I felt I had not heard English spoken so beautifully since I was a child. Even the accents of the ex-colonials sounded splendid to my ears.

Almost as soon as we had settled into the League, my mother asked, by no means for the first time, "What am I going to do when you both go away?" Within a couple of weeks, my father was to fly to America for his lecture tour and I was to go up to Oxford. "Ram, Ram," she said. "The life here is too expensive. I should go back home. My only consolation is that I don't cost you very much."

"How many Indians can live just off St. James's Street, a stone's throw from Buckingham Palace?" my father asked. "You are living like a queen."

"It's only for ten days," my mother said. That was as long as a member was permitted to stay at the League on a single occasion.

"And, just think, we are sitting in the center of London, right by some of the best shops in the world," my father went on.

"London suits your Mrs. Clyde best," my mother said. "She has the money in her purse to go into the shops. I have Ata's new teeth as my memento of a visit to Europe."

"You should stay on in London," my father said. "After I get some money from my lecture tour in America, we'll have our real holiday. There are so many places on the Continent I would like to show you."

"I think she should go home to India now," I said. "If she stays on here while you are in America, I won't be able to look after her."

As I said this, I was torn, pulled this way and that. It seemed to me that even if my father could afford to pay for my mother for the two months he was away she could not stay in a hotel in London. That required the self-reliance of a Western woman. Therefore, she would probably have to live in some bed-and-breakfast place in Oxford, near my college. But what would she do there all day? Who would be there to speak Punjabi with her? Whom would she have her meals with? It seemed to me that, willy-nilly, I would become her mainstay. But just the idea of taking responsibility for her—taking care of her if she got sick, for instance—was unsettling; it seemed as if my glamorous Oxford life would be compromised even before it got under way. In America, I had grown so used to thinking only about my own needs that I could not bring myself to think about anyone else's— not even my mother's. The truth was that I felt very differently about my mother from the way I wanted to feel. Her poor English and her lack of competence at things that Western women took for granted—driving a car, holding a job, talking to men as equals—depressed me. During the years of separation, I had started imagining her as a tranquil, restful person, with a light voice, like the mothers of my American friends, or like the American girls I had got to know. I had completely forgotten that my mother didn't have a light voice—that attacks of asthma had long since cracked her voice. I was trying to get used to her wheezing and panting, gasping and yawning, her frequent throat clearings and fits of coughing—all part of her asthmatic condition. I would tell myself that for her taking each breath was not only a source of life but also a source of terror. Yet, however much I commiserated with her intellectually, the sounds of her asthma set me on edge. For that matter, some of the relatively comforting sounds she made were sometimes off-putting: the clink and chink of her gold bangles and her dangling earrings, the clicking of her knitting needles, the pop and snap of her medicine bottles. For as long as I could remember, she had taken all sorts of pills for her asthma and to build up her weak health. The sounds disturbed me, because at school and college I had lived alone and had come to depend on complete quiet for study and reflection. She seemed to be always shivering and saying "Brrr." But even as I dwelt on her shortcomings I would tell myself that she had qualities many Western women didn't have. She could cook and sew, knit and embroider. Everyone marvelled at her taste in clothes and at her beauty and her youthful appearance. (My father claimed that asthmatics always retained their youthful looks.) But in my heart of hearts I didn't think she lived up to the mothers of my American friends. So I was racked by guilt.

"Son, rest assured, she will not disturb you in Oxford at all," my father was saying, in his most understanding way. "I'll arrange for some Indian family here in London to take her in as a paying guest."

That afternoon, when we were walking along Piccadilly Circus, my mother suffered a severe attack of asthma. My father hailed a taxi, and we drove straight to the clinic of Dr. A. W.

Frankland, in Harley Street. He was a leading specialist in allergies whom my father had sought out on an earlier visit, with a view to having him, in due course, examine my mother and advise him on her condition. The two doctors had become fast friends.

Dr. Frankland saw my mother immediately. He examined her for some time and then called us in. "I'm going to put your wife on a new medicine, which she will have to take for three weeks," he said, and he wrote out a prescription and gave my father some details about it. "After that, I'd like to see her again."

"That's settled things, then," my father said to my mother as we left Dr. Frankland's clinic. "You'll have to stay in England until I get back from America."

"What God wishes, so it will be," she said, still breathing hard. "Your Dr. Frankland is a saint. He has saved my life."

WE were unable to find any place in London where my mother could stay. Then, suddenly, my father remembered the Chowdharys, and said he thought that they might be able to give us a lead, if not take in my mother themselves. He explained that Mrs. Chowdhary was a relative of Satya, his niece by marriage, and recalled that my brother-in-law Gautam had stayed with Mrs. Chowdhary in London right after he met my sister Umi in Bombay. Mrs. Chowdhary had asked Gautam then, "Have you thought about marriage?" He had said, "I've just met a girl. If she will have me, I will marry her. Otherwise, I will remain single for the rest of my life."

"However much I love Satya, she's not a blood relative," my mother said. "And who knows what relation Mrs. Chowdhary is to her? That Gautam story is seven or eight years old. We have good reason to remember it, because Gautam is our son-in-law, but why should Mrs. Chowdhary remember it?"

"But we have a claim on the Chowdharys' friendship as fellow-Punjabis," my father said.

"When people do well in England, what reason do they have to remember their Punjabi ties?" my mother asked.

"But Chowdhary is also a fellow-doctor," my father said. "I remember Gautam's telling me that Dr. Chowdhary has a good general practice in Laindon, Essex, and that the Chowdharys have been settled in England for over twenty years."

My father obtained the Chowdharys' telephone number from Directory Inquiry, and Mrs. Chowdhary answered the phone. He spoke to her in Punjabi and invited her and her husband to dinner at the Indian Service Club, on South Audley Street.

After he hung up, he said, "Mrs. Chowdhary warmly accepted my invitation for Thursday. In fact, she says that Dr. Chowdhary likes to go to that very club every Thursday, for his evening out in London. But she insists that first we come out to their house for an Indian lunch, this Sunday. She says that Indian friends, Indian students, and even Indian travellers just passing through London often gather at their home for Sunday lunch, and it's no imposition. She left me no choice but to accept." He turned to me. "Their son, Vijay, is studying at Oxford, so you'll be able to get a good few tips from him about Oxford life. It all sounds propitious."

That Sunday, we took a taxi to Fenchurch Street Station, in the City, and caught a closed-carriage train to Laindon. The train was so grubby and old that we could almost have been in the Punjab. The whole venture, I thought, struck a discordant note. As I knew from my reading, Sunday lunch was a British institution, and it somehow seemed inappropriate to eat spicy Indian food in the middle of the day.

The Chowdharys' house, which stood in a small garden and had consulting rooms for Dr. Chowdhary's practice, was spacious, well heated, and full of pungent curry smells. Both the

Chowdharys seemed like typical Punjabis—warm-hearted and outgoing. Yet, oddly, Mrs. Chowdhary was wearing a frock and stockings, and Dr. Chowdhary soon let drop the fact that he was a Freemason—indeed, the master of a lodge.

At the table, Mrs. Chowdhary, like a typical Indian, talked about food, as if the purpose of living were to eat.

"Our friends are always complaining about the poor English diet of fish and chips and boiled vegetables," Dr. Chowdhary said at one point.

"To me, nothing tastes better than fish and chips off a page from a tabloid," my father said. "It takes me right back to my student days in London. But all of us like Indian food."

"My daughters and I like it spicy, and the Long-Lived One and my sons like it mild," my mother said. Being a typical Hindu wife, she always referred to my father by epithets rather than by name.

"Did you know that I have written an Indian cookbook?" Mrs. Chowdhary asked, piling more rice on my plate despite my protests.

"Mummy, you shouldn't boast," Vijay said abruptly. Though he was very English in manner, he seemed like an Indian in that he was given to long silences, as if he thought that the main point of social life was not conversation but a sort of physical nearness. But then his silences might have been only a reaction to his parents' volubility.

"What's wrong with taking a little pride in one's work, darling?" Mrs. Chowdhary said. Calling a grown son "darling"—or, rather, "dahling"—sounded odd in the Indian setting. "Since Vijay went to Oxford, he looks down on our Punjabi ways," she told us, with a laugh.

"What do you think of my son's book?" my father asked Mrs. Chowdhary. It developed that a couple of days before, without telling me, my father had sent the Chowdharys a typed copy of my autobiography. Such a move by anyone else might have seemed calculating, as if he were laying the groundwork for asking a favor. But my father was just as likely to press the manuscript on a stranger in a train. That was simply his way. Still, I felt embarrassed.

"I looked through it last night," Mrs. Chowdhary said. "Your son is a very well-informed young man. I like the person in his autobiography immensely. He's a great scholar with no eyesight. God has taken his sight away but given him other senses in compensation."

I could feel blood rushing to my cheeks. I was far from being a scholar; I was going up as a freshman to Oxford. And the business about sight and compensatory senses was something I'd grown up hearing Indians say, as if the notion relieved the guilt they felt at having sight.

Vijay, perhaps sensing my discomfort, asked me if I would like to go for a walk. As we were on our way out, he put on a felt hat and picked up a rolled-up umbrella. I decided that his thoughtfulness and gentleness, like the hat and the umbrella, were part of his Oxford sophistication. His voice was very English, and he spoke without a trace of Indian accent. He came across as a person tightly held in by bands of steel.

"We'll see a lot of each other at Oxford," he said on the walk, and then suddenly fell silent, as if he felt he had assumed too much. By asking him a series of direct questions—to which he gave shy, staccato answers, as if he at once felt that I was invading his privacy and thought that I was asking things I should already know—I discovered that he had gone up to Queen's College, Oxford, from Brentwood, a public school (in England, of course, the phrase means "private school"), in 1953. Although he was a year younger than I was, he was a graduate; he had taken Schools, the final degree examinations, in physiology that summer. He was staying on to do a course in pathology and pharmacology before continuing his medical studies in a teaching hospital in London. He wasn't sure that he wanted to be a doctor, but his father was very keen to have him follow in his footsteps.

"Do you like to go to pubs?" he asked, as if trying to change the subject.

"I've never been to one—though, of course, I've read about them," I said.

"I go for lunch to the Chequers. I'll take you there sometime."

I'd come across Chequers as the name of the Prime Minister's country residence and had trouble imagining that a pub might have the same name, but I said nothing. I was in awe of his already being an Oxford graduate, and was afraid of sounding gauche.

We walked through the quiet English town and back to the house. My parents and the Chowdharys were now having tea. Sitting with them was the Chowdharys' other child, Shakuntala—Vijay's younger sister, who had just turned eighteen. She was ignoring the general conversation, and was half singing to herself and carefully painting her nails.

"She hasn't done well enough to go to the university," Mrs. Chowdhary was saying. "She doesn't mind about it in the least—do you, darling?"

"None of my girlfriends are going to the university," she said.

"You see, she has a happy, uncomplicated nature," Mrs. Chowdhary said, with a laugh. "In that way, she's completely English."

I joined them for tea, but Vijay excused himself and went out to the garden, and Shakuntala went upstairs. I remember thinking what a contrast the sister and the brother were. Shakuntala's bubbly personality seemed only to set off Vijay's grave, almost solemn nature.

At one point, my father said to Mrs. Chowdhary, "I think of you as a sister."

The spontaneous remark was probably intended as nothing more than a simple expression of affection, but Dr. Chowdhary, a Punjabi gentleman with a certain nobility of character, took it in another spirit. He left the room and returned with a *rakharhi*—a little silken bracelet that, once a year, on Rakharhi, a Hindu sister ties on the wrist of her brother.

"Did you know that it's Rakharhi today?" he asked my father.

"No, I didn't," my father said, surprised. "Here in England, it's very difficult to keep up with our lunar calendar."

The Chowdharys had been out of India a score of years or more, yet they knew the exact date of Rakharhi, while my parents, who had been out of India only a few months, had completely lost track of when it was. I was again struck by how punctilious the Chowdharys were in their observance of Indian customs.

At Dr. Chowdhary's prompting, Mrs. Chowdhary tied the *rakharhi* on my father's wrist and put an Indian sweetmeat in his mouth. He completed the ritual by immediately pulling out a five-pound note and handing it to her.

Until I went away to America, each of my sisters had tied a *rakharhi* on my wrist on Rakharhi and put a sweetmeat in my mouth, and I had given her five rupees from my pocket money. My father's sister had performed the same ancient Hindu rite with him—symbolizing a sister's abiding love for her brother and his abiding protection of her—as had my mother's brothers with her. Now here we were in Britain, at the table of a Freemason, and my father was taking part in the ancient rite with a woman who was wearing a frock and stockings. The whole episode was at once touching and bizarre.

Some time later, my father confided to Dr. Chowdhary my mother's medical need to stay on in England.

"She can come and stay with us," Dr. Chowdhary said spontaneously. "What's the problem? She should think of our house as her own house. Anyway, I'm scheduled to go to visit my mother in East Punjab soon. Mrs. Mehta will be a good companion for Savitri."

Dr. Chowdhary was very respectful to my father, who was both an older colleague and an older man (Dr. Chowdhary was fifty-four, and my father was sixty-one), and I wondered if he really meant what he said.

"I keep wondering if Ma should stay in England without you," I said to my father.

"I'll have my ticket in my pocket," my mother said. "If I'm unhappy in England, I can always get on the plane and go home."

I ascribed her bold assertion to her wish to be finally rid of asthma—something she imagined that Dr. Frankland might actually bring about. Her friends in India with similar chronic conditions were always dreaming of going to London for treatment; they were convinced that British doctors could perform miracles that were beyond the ability of their Indian counterparts.

"If you stay on here, don't count on me for anything," I said.

"I'll be completely independent," she said, in English.

Mrs. Chowdhary hesitated in seconding her husband's invitation. She said that lately she had decided to become a writer and had begun her autobiography—that, in fact, she had been saying to Sheel (her referring to her husband by his first name, like a Westerner, struck yet another discordant note) that she wanted to cut down on her social commitments, and not just write but live like a writer, become more "solitary." "And, to give me more time to myself, I've been looking for a housekeeper," she said.

Well, then, my father said, forgetting his natural delicacy in a burst of enthusiasm, my mother could help out around the house, relieve Mrs. Chowdhary of household chores, allow her to become more solitary. Mrs. Chowdhary might not see it in that light right away, but that was only because she didn't know what my mother could offer her.

"Now that you've tied a *rakharhi* on Dr. Mehta, Savitri, you must do your duty by his wife," Dr. Chowdhary said. "She is now your sister."

"Sheel is always right," Mrs. Chowdhary said, her voice full of the devotion of a Punjabi wife. "He always sees to the heart of things. He has the wisdom of a man born in a Punjabi village."

Soon Mrs. Chowdhary herself was putting forth arguments for my mother's staying with them while my father was away, saying that she would need company once Vijay went to Oxford and Dr. Chowdhary went to India, and that my mother could not only be a help around the house but also perhaps teach Punjabi and Punjabi customs to Shakuntala. So far, Shakuntala, for all her parents' efforts, had refused to learn anything Indian.

Mrs. Chowdhary did still harbor some reservations, however, as I learned years later from reading her diary. "It may work out all right, but I cannot help feeling anxious," she wrote. "Two months is a long time. In India, it does not seem much to stay with somebody, but it is different here."

My mother, too, had some reservations. On the train, as we were returning to London that evening, she said, "Mrs. Chowdhary is all right, but we can never be like sisters."

"Why not?" my father asked.

"Well," my mother said, hesitating, as if she feared a reprimand from my father, "how can an Indian woman who speaks so sweetly come to the table in a frock and stockings?"

"The Chowdharys live in England and no doubt have English passports," my father said. "Why shouldn't Mrs. Chowdhary wear Western clothes? Anyway, if you yourself lived here you might find wearing Western clothes a boon. They are warmer, and they allow your arms and legs more freedom than our clothes do. Certainly, if you lived and worked here, you would have to wear Western clothes."

"Ram, Ram, never," my mother said. "And she calls her lord and master by his first name."

"The beauty of England is that the sexes are considered equal here," my father said. "You can call me by my first name if you like."

"After thirty years of marriage—Ram, Ram," my mother said.

My father and I both laughed.

❦

OUR Sunday lunch with the Chowdharys was on September 30th, and on October 11th—the day before my mother went to stay with them, and two days before my father left for America—I packed my suitcase for Oxford. Vijay came in from Laindon specially to see me off. He seemed to be taking a proprietary interest in me, perhaps because of our families' sudden closeness, or perhaps because of his firsthand knowledge of Oxford. Whatever the reason, my parents bade me goodbye at a bed-and-breakfast place we had moved into near the League, and Vijay and I went to the station without them. My father's parting words were "It's appropriate that a fellow-Oxonian should be seeing you off." It's just like my father to defer to Vijay, I thought. And maybe he's right about a fellow-Oxonian. Although I felt like a hick, I also thought of myself as an Oxford man. I was already trying to walk and talk as I imagined that Oxford men did: to discipline my casual Southern California step and to put a certain crispness—in the manner of Vijay—into my speech, which was an amalgam of Raj, Arkansas, and Southern California English.

At Paddington Station, Vijay insisted on carrying my suitcase right into the train, finding a seat for me in the compartment, and lifting the suitcase up onto the luggage rack. I walked back onto the platform with him and took leave of him there; he himself was not coming up to Oxford for two or three more days. I got into the train again and took my seat.

Feeling that I was finally alone—free of the strange new country and the disorienting new impressions and friends—I slumped down in my seat and gave myself up to reverie about the new life that awaited me in Oxford. Everything about it seemed quaint and mysterious. "Laundry should be sent in a separate parcel addressed to the Domestic Bursar, Balliol College, Oxford, with your name clearly indicated inside it," the College Secretary had written cryptically to me in California. What did she mean by "laundry"? It was inconceivable that the college would have wanted me to send ahead my shirts, socks, and underwear, which were what I understood "laundry" to mean. After much rooting about among Oxford men at Pomona, I had bought some sheets and pillowcases (I had never owned any before, because linens had been provided by both the school and the college), made a parcel, and posted it to the Domestic Bursar, wondering who he was and what part he would play in my Oxford life, but I continued to fret over whether I had done the appropriate thing.

The train lurched and began pulling out of the station.

"Goodbye, then!" Vijay called out, his voice fading in the *clackety-clack* of the train. I realized, with a shock, that he had been standing at the half-open window of the compartment all the time, no doubt expecting me to stand on my side of the window and talk to him. He must think I'm a churl, I thought. I'm not fit to be an Oxford man.

II

SCHOLARS AND GENTLEMEN

A**T OXFORD STATION, I TRIED TO PRESS ON THE PORTER** two half crowns. After all, he had carried my suitcase and escorted me from the train through the ticket barrier and out onto the street. He would not accept the money.

The coins felt heavy in my hand. A porter was turning down a tip from me because I was blind. I was touched but irritated by his misplaced kindness. "Go on, have a drink on me," I said, trying to put the monetary exchange into a sociable context. I wanted the business to be over with quickly. I was sure that people were watching.

"Ta, ta," he said, pushing away my outstretched hand. He added, in a kindly tone, "No porter will accept money from a person who can't see."

In America, the dollar is almighty, I thought, but here the custom is different.

"I am Geoffrey Slater," a youthful-sounding man said, coming up to me. "I'm a lawyer. Mr. Tylor asked me to meet you at the station."

Slater's introducing himself as a lawyer confused me, and I asked him if he was a lawyer for the college.

"No, I'm in my third year of reading jurisprudence," he said. It dawned on me that at Oxford by the mere act of reading a subject one became, in a sense, a man of the profession.

We got into a taxi. I was so overwhelmed at finally being at Oxford—trying to imagine what we were passing, from the little reading I had done about the place—that we rode mostly in silence. At one point, I asked Slater, "Are we going to the college?"

"Yes, to college," he said.

I must remember that "college" doesn't take an article here, I thought. It's like going "to church."

I walked through Balliol in a daze, haunted by one thought— that I was going to be part of a college that was nearly seven hundred years old. *Seven hundred* years old. I asked Slater if there were any buildings surviving from the Middle Ages.

"I don't think so," he said. "The college didn't become important until the nineteenth century, so most of the buildings date from the Neo-Gothic period. Magdalen, Christ Church, and New College have much older and more beautiful buildings, but Balliol is intellectually the most distinguished."

For a moment, I felt sad that I hadn't gone to a more beautiful college, but then I conforted myself with the thought that the body is merely a temple for the soul.

"Here we are, at Staircase XVI," Slater said. I was familiar with a "stairway" and a "stairwell" but not with a "staircase." The word sounded to me like something straight out of a historical romance.

He showed me to the door of my room, at the bottom of the staircase, and said, "Would you like to come round for a sherry before hall?"

"Sherry" rang a bell. I must have come across it in P. G. Wodehouse or in one of Dorothy Sayers' Lord Peter Wimsey novels. I wasn't sure whether sherry was wine, ale, or spirit, but I was loath to admit that to Slater.

"Yes, I would love to. How kind of you." I wondered if I sounded too effusive—too much like an uncouth American—and if the English response would have been casual and understated, like "Till sherry, then." One had to be oneself, but what if one preferred the vision of a more cultivated self? A dreadful thought entered my head: What if I weren't able to get the stuff down? If I did, what if I weren't able to hold my drink? I had scarcely ever tried liquor. In fact, I had only recently trained myself to drink coffee, in preparation for going to Oxford.

"Shall I meet you at the porter's lodge?" I asked. "Do you have a favorite pub?"

"Since you don't know the way to my room, I'll come and collect you."

Damn it! I must have read about people having friends to drinks in their rooms, I thought. How could I have forgotten it? He must think I'm a hick. Rightly so. After all, at Pomona no drink was allowed on campus. If I'm not careful, I won't get many invitations.

"I'll be round for you at six," Slater said, and he left.

I closed the door after him. I felt terribly alone. I examined the furnishings: a big cupboard, a large, clunky affair, rather like a Jacobean chest stood on its end, with a heavily carved door; an old, battered desk and a straight chair under the only window; a hard single bed against the wall; two wooden armchairs with removable foam-rubber cushions for the seats and backs, placed in front of an unlit gas fire; and a small built-in bookcase. The floor was covered with thin carpeting.

I had never seen a gas fire before. While I was fumbling around trying to light it, I heard the door open behind me, without a knock. I started.

"It's only George Gibbons, your scout, sir. May I light the fire for you?" a voice said.

"Yes, please," I said, standing up and stepping back. I had read that Oxford scouts—college servants who looked after students and dons—were the most obliging men in Europe, but I couldn't remember how scouts were addressed.

As if reading my mind, he said, "Some scouts like to be called by their last name, but I like to be called by my Christian name, if it's all the same to you, sir." He seemed to be waiting for a response.

"By all means, George," I said.

He showed me how to turn on the gas tap and light the fire, and left unceremoniously. I have my own Jeeves, I thought, and he's real.

The gas fire made a wonderful bursting sizzle as it caught, and settled into a cozy hissing sound of gas flowing. But the heat of the fire reached little beyond the grate. I sat with my chair drawn up against the grate and with my feet resting on top of the fire.

❧

"Sweet or dry sherry?" Slater asked.

I didn't know one sherry from another, but, thinking that dry sherry sounded more sophisticated, I asked for it.

"Sherry is the oil of the academic life," Slater said, pouring me a glass.

"Not port or Madeira?" I was about to ask, but checked myself. Perhaps port was drunk only by dons, and Madeira by sailors.

My knowledge of Oxford seemed shakier than ever.

Slater handed me the glass. It was so small that I almost dropped it. It is like the dosage glass in which we children used to be given medicine, I thought, raising it to my lips. The drink smelled like a mixture of wood shavings and tincture of iodine. I held my breath and tossed it down in one gulp. The liquid suffused me with inner warmth. I suddenly realized that I had been shivering for hours—ever since I got to Oxford. The air was heavy and damp and seemed to cling to one's skin like wet, clammy clothes. In earlier centuries, people at Oxford must have dressed as warmly for staying inside as they did for going out, I thought. Perhaps that is also the reason that people have such elaborate meals and quantities of drink in English novels.

Thinking that a compliment was in order, I said, "Great stuff." No sooner was the phrase out of my mouth than I felt horribly self-conscious. "T" was about the hardest consonant for me to enunciate without my front tooth, and the phrase came out sounding like "Grea-ss-uff." Somehow, around the Chowdharys I hadn't felt so self-conscious about my missing tooth. It had been like being around family. But now I was chatting over sherry with a real English undergraduate.

"What say?"

I said nothing.

"So you're going to work with Tylor," Slater said, pouring me another glass.

When I applied to Balliol, I had been so bent upon gaining admission that I hadn't stopped to think whether reading law made sense for me. After all, Tylor had taken it for granted that that was what I would do, and successful blind people everywhere were lawyers. Quite early, Tylor had impressed upon me that, since Roman law formed the basis of English law, he expected me to have an adequate knowledge of Latin before coming to Oxford. As a result, I had spent some of my senior year studying Latin. Around the time of graduation, however, I began to have second thoughts about reading law. I learned that at Balliol, for law, I would essentially have only Tylor as my tutor. During the Pomona years, I had scarcely met a blind person, and the thought of being beholden to a blind tutor for my further education seemed like a backward step—like returning to a school for the blind.

I began to fret about what kind of teacher Tylor might be. From Slater I learned that he had published little or nothing; in contrast, my best teachers at Pomona were those who had published a lot—had proved their ideas in the intellectual marketplace, beyond the college gate. On top of these misgivings, while I was finishing my young autobiography I had come up against the question of where I should settle—in India or in America—and discovered that I had more conflicts about that than I had previously imagined. (At the time, the idea of settling in Britain, the country of India's erstwhile rulers, was unpalatable.) I therefore felt that I should postpone the decision about law until I had resolved the question of where I would settle. If I was to be a lawyer in America, I would eventually have to go to an American law school; if I was to be a lawyer in India, I could always read for the bar in London after graduating from Oxford. Finishing the book also opened up the possibility of my straying from the beaten path of law and striking out for a different career. In that event, the best use I could make of Oxford would be to get more general education. I had aired my reservations about reading law to my father as soon as we met in Europe. He had immediately said, "Forget about law. Now that you have written a book and are going to Oxford, there are indeed other careers open to you." But I was going to Oxford in a little over a month, and we both thought it best to leave well enough alone until I could talk things over with Tylor on the spot.

I now asked Slater what, exactly, Tylor was like.

"He is—well, clever," Slater said slowly, as if to bring out every nuance of the word. The words seemed to conjure up a man with an agile, almost athletic brain.

In America, my question would have been the occasion for a flood of impressions of Tylor's quirks and habits, I thought, but maybe in England they aren't interested in personal details. Still, I thought I should try to find out as much as I could about him before I risked telling him of my change of heart about law.

"What is Tylor really like?" I pressed.

"He's a very interesting character," Slater said, taking some more sherry and warming to the subject. "In the thirties, he came in second in the British Chess Championship, and last year he was made British chess master for life. He's a bachelor and lives with his mother and sister. Many present judges were once Tylor's pupils, and whenever they return to the college for meetings of the Younger, or law, Society, Tylor is apt to come at them as if they were still his pupils, saying, 'Good God, what kind of judgment was that one you made six weeks ago?' It is said that the judges quail before him as they defend themselves."

I laughed nervously, and asked, "Is he a good tutor?"

"He doesn't prepare one for Schools, if that's what you mean," Slater said. "He sets topics for tutorials which are not really examination questions. I suppose he believes that university education should be broader than just preparing undergraduates to do well in final examinations. Anyway, lawyers at Balliol as a group don't seem to do as well in Schools as lawyers in other colleges."

"Do you get on with him?"

"Well enough," Slater said. "People say that he was a great tutor between the wars but he has gone off somewhat since then. He's still good at cross-examining and finding out the extent of our knowledge and ability, but if he has made his mind up on a particular point in law he regards that as the final word. In this he may be no different from a lot of tutors who have reached their fifties and think that they've given a lot of thought to a particular issue and solved it to their satisfaction, and who tend, therefore, to be a little impatient with anyone who challenges them. Certainly, if one disagrees with Tylor, he comes back very vigorously, and he gives the impression of being very put out. So, in the end, one comes away with respect for him but, I suppose, not affection. In fact, we are all terrified of him."

The more Slater talked, the more anxious I grew about being forced to study with Tylor. (After all, he had admitted me, and, for all I knew, my admission was only for reading law.) He seemed the antithesis of a good tutor—of a tutor who made his students feel that they were partners in a search for truth. Also, Tylor seemed very rigid—a quality I associated with the blind generally. Since the blind achieved mastery of the world with difficulty, they ordered it in their minds and were therefore inordinately preoccupied with order. Indeed, he might even be like the many blind people who rejected new information and new ideas for fear of being overwhelmed by them.

I confided to Slater that I was no longer sure that I wanted to read law.

Slater was taken aback. "I wouldn't have thought you could change your mind like that," he said. "Tylor is expecting you to be his pupil."

"In America, people change their majors all the time," I said. "When do people here decide on their subject?"

"We have to decide almost at the age of thirteen what direction we are going to go in, and then stick to it," he said. "We are prepared accordingly for O levels, for A levels, and for Oxford and Cambridge entrance exams." Ordinary levels and advanced levels, he explained, were national examinations that schoolboys and schoolgirls took at the ages of sixteen and eighteen. People who wanted to go to a university had to do A levels, and those who wanted to go on to Oxford or Cambridge had to take their entrance examinations before the age of nineteen.

"Fortunately, none of that applies to me, since I already have a degree," I said.

"True enough," he said. "In any event, Tylor has arranged a

tea at his home tomorrow afternoon for you to meet other law-yers. He'll collect you from your room half an hour before, at three-thirty, so that you can get to know each other. What are you going to do?"

"What are his teas like?" I asked, stalling. The sherry had gone to my head. I felt inert.

"His teas? I only went to one, as a freshman. It was a pretty formal affair. Someone had played an awful trick on us, though. There was an ugly little dog running about. She seemed to be the only free thing in the room. I think she was something like a Jack Russell. We'd been told that the dog was called Puggy and that the only way to get into Tylor's good graces was to be nice to Puggy. So a lot of us unfortunate freshmen patted the dog on the head and said, 'Come here, Puggy,' 'Nice Puggy'—and then we heard Tylor boom across to his sister, 'Puggy!' "

Slater spoke in a very different way from Americans. There was a certain irony in his tone. He seemed to be aware of the nuances of the words he used, and to make an effort to bring them out. For me speech had always represented the look in the eye, the bone structure of the face, the complexion of the skin. I now felt I was hearing speech in its full magnificence for the first time.

TYLOR stopped by my room a half hour before tea, just as Slater had said he would.

"How are you getting on?" he asked.

"All right, sir," I said, offering him a chair. I should have avoided saying "right," I thought. But the only alternative I could think of, "O.K.," sounded American and colloquial, not at all in keeping with the Lord Peter Wimsey ambience.

"I have an old dear who has been reading to me for some years," Mr. Tylor said, remaining standing. "She has some extra time, and I've arranged for her to read to you. She didn't go to university, but she has a good heart and charges two and six an hour."

Tylor came across as a retired colonel, talking in an essentially inflectionless, emphatic way, in a sort of "broadcasting voice," which blind people who are not socially well adapted sometimes develop in compensation for lack of eye contact and spontaneous gestures. I wanted to make a clean breast of my decision not to read law, but his authoritative voice stopped me. Anyway, he was waiting for my response to his offer of a reader.

"I prefer readers who are university graduates," I said timidly, trying to enunciate my "t"s as clearly as I could. "They are more expensive, but, in the long run, I find they save me money, because they are faster and more efficient."

I feared he would take umbrage, but he said, "The old dears I use are anything but efficient. They often fall asleep reading to me." He laughed. I thought it was princely of him to be so reasonable—not to press me to adopt his arrangements.

"Let's go along to tea," he said. "Puggy is waiting for us in the car at the back gate."

We set out for the back gate. Just as I was on the verge of telling him about my decision, he started telling me about himself. He said that he had been blind from birth but he had some perception of light, which helped him to get around. His father, a successful architect in Bournville, Birmingham, had sent him to Worcester (the best school for the blind in England, I knew). From there he had come up straight to Balliol to read law in 1918, when he was eighteen. "I got my First and stayed on for a B.C.L. Although I got a Second in it, that didn't get in the way of my staying on at Balliol and teaching. I'm hoping you will be able to pull off a First and do a B.C.L." The Oxford honors degrees were ranked from First through Fourth, and very few students of any subject in any year were awarded Firsts.

He has been at Balliol for thirty-eight years, I thought. His life seems so straightforward in contrast to mine. For a fleeting moment, I was tempted to follow his example and read law. Who knew? If I did well, I might one day succeed him. But I recoiled from the thought even as I was tempted by it.

We were at the back gate, and, thinking it was now or never, I blurted out, "I don't think I want to read law."

He stood still and remained unnervingly silent for a moment or two, and then asked "Why not?" I could detect in his booming voice a note of disappointment and annoyance.

I hesitantly gave him one or two reasons, fully expecting him to shout at me and ask me why I hadn't thought of them before I sought admission to Balliol in his subject. Instead, he said, in a matter-of-fact way, "Law is particularly suited to blind people."

"I'm not blind," I said. Then, realizing how foolish that sounded and that I'd made the same remark to my mother earlier, I quickly added, "I mean, reading law makes no sense for me unless I know where I'm going to live—India or America. I would rather read Philosophy, Politics, and Economics—P.P.E. seems to have the kind of general syllabus that would be useful no matter where I lived."

"I'll sound out the P.P.E. tutors and see what they think," he said.

Miss Tylor, who had a manner that I associated with Red Cross volunteers in India, drove us to their house—a Victorian house in North Oxford.

"I have only one eye," she said apologetically in the car, as if to establish her membership in the kingdom of the blind.

"We have only one good eye between us," Tylor joked. He explained that soon after Miss Tylor's birth the doctors diagnosed his condition and that of his sister as hereditary, and their parents decided not to have any more children.

In the Tylors' sitting room, a dozen or so lawyers were gathered. Mr. Tylor deftly split the guests into two groups, making one group sit with Miss Tylor on one side of the room and the other group sit with him on the opposite side. I was directed to sit at Miss Tylor's right; he seemed to have worked out in advance exactly where each guest was to be placed.

Miss Tylor turned to me and started talking about her brother, as if his concerns were her whole life. She was not only his chauffeur, his housekeeper, and his social secretary, she said, but also his companion when he travelled to play in chess tournaments, although she herself had no interest in the game.

I asked her what she was interested in. She would have enjoyed decorating her own house, she said—the house we were in had been decorated by her mother—but there was no likelihood of her having the chance. She had never got married. She gave the impression of being home-loving and quite dedicated to her brother, and of living for the few social occasions, like the tea, that gave her a chance to see other people.

When we had finished the savories and Miss Tylor had spoken as long to the person on her left as she had to me, Mr. Tylor called out "Half time!" and we guests shifted sides.

I was now seated on Mr. Tylor's right, and the arrangement accentuated my feeling that I was there under false pretenses—that I would have been low man on the totem pole, or possibly not at the tea at all, if Tylor had been apprised earlier of my hesitation about reading law. But Tylor talked to me as if my being there in an honored place were perfectly natural.

When it was time for sweets, Mrs. Tylor, a quiet, reserved, mild-mannered woman—she was a Quaker, I learned later—who seemed to rule the roost from behind the scenes, brought out and served to us a very rich, creamy cake.

The atmosphere of the whole tea was that of holding court. I had fallen so deeply under the spell of the British and the Oxford mystique that, although Mr. Tylor was clearly very different from me, I thought I had never been present at such an impressive, well-planned, and well-orchestrated occasion.

The Tylors asked me if I would stay back for a sherry after

the other guests had left. That seemed to be part of their plan to welcome me to Oxford, and I did.

Over sherry, the subject of what I would do for my holidays came up. (Oxford was in session only six months of the year, for three eight-week terms: Michaelmas, beginning in October; Hilary, beginning in January; and Trinity, beginning in April. The presumption was that people would use the six-week Christmas and Easter breaks and the long summer break for reading on their own.) "You should probably stay at Oxford and read through the vac," Tylor said. ("Vac" is Oxford for vacation.) "That's what blind undergraduates generally have to do, since reading with readers and in Braille is so slow." He was no doubt right, but I found the remark a little irksome. I'd had dreams of travelling around the Continent, or, at least, seeing something of England— perhaps by staying in country houses, as I'd heard that foreign students often did. Miss Tylor may have sensed my irritation, because she said, "Most undergraduates spend their vacs working on their subject." Of course, they must, I thought. After all, there is only one examination, the dreaded Schools at the end, and everything depends on one's performance on it. I asked the Tylors if they toured in Europe or England during their holidays. Miss Tylor said that they generally went to a particular hotel on the Dorset coast, near Poole. The hotel had many permanent boarders, and over the years she and her brother had developed a whole circle of friends who had nothing to do with college or the university. At the hotel, they played bridge and did a little swimming. Tylor said that he had mastered a particular path from the hotel down the cliffs to the shore. There he would trail his wrists in the cold water to adjust the temperature of his body to the water, then wade in and swim. He liked water, he said. In his day, he had been a good oarsman and had rowed a skiff single-handed—with someone else steering for him, of course. At Oxford, he mostly worked out on a stationary bicycle. Every morning, he pedalled furiously for a half hour.

As Tylor talked, I reflected that his life had the rigidity of a conventional English upbringing. Even as there was something oppressive about the idea of a brother and sister living together, and working as a team, like husband and wife, there was also something touching about the relationship. Both gave the impression of being pleased with themselves, yet one detected in him a little impatience with her, and in her a little resentment of him because she hadn't had a chance to shine on her own. That seemed to be par for the course; after all, married couples weren't free from such irritations. The two were like a couple in an English novel who had renounced the pleasures of lesser mortals for a higher existence.

The day after the tea, Tylor stopped by my room and told me that at lunch in the Senior Common Room he had spoken to the half-dozen tutors who taught P.P.E. and they were more than amenable to my reading it.

I thanked him.

"I'm still of the opinion that blind chaps should read law," he said as he was leaving. "But there have been one or two who have read Modern Greats, and they haven't done too badly for themselves."

The remark was a bit unsettling, but I told myself that I should be pleased, because I had got my way.

III

FLOREAT
DOMUS DE
BALLIOLO

I HAD GONE TO OXFORD EXPECTING TO BE EXTREMELY impressed by the place, thinking that it would be sublime, .and wishing that something marvellous would happen to me the moment I reached it. Maybe Oxford wasn't quite as impressive or sublime as I had expected, but at first blush it seemed to me to be so. Certainly my first impressions of Balliol were much more positive than Vijay's of Queen's. He had told me he found his college "cold and off-putting." From the first day, I thought that Balliol had something of a welcoming atmosphere. The very shabbiness of the architecture, though a little disappointing, made me feel at home. After America, the lavatories and other facilities seemed primitive, but then they were in the Balliol tradition of "plain living and high thinking." Anyway, I told myself, a certain amount of mortification of the flesh was a good thing. My first week in Oxford was about the most exciting time I had ever spent. Onto my mantelpiece cascaded cards inviting me to gatherings of people I had scarcely met, to meetings of a dazzling variety of clubs and societies. Every time I went out of my room, I encountered someone new and, often, from a different part of the world. I felt that I was among some of the world's liveliest minds, in one of the most beautiful spots on the planet. The place was full of lore and history. Right outside the college, on Broad Street, was a cross set into the road surface, which was said to mark the exact spot where Bishops Latimer and Ridley and Archbishop Cranmer were burned at the stake as heretics during the reign of Bloody Mary. The college porter quoted to me Latimer's remark to Ridley when both were at the stake, "We shall this day light such a candle, by God's grace, in England as I trust shall never be put out," and told me how Cranmer, when asked to recant at the stake, had steadily held his right hand in the fire—the offending hand that, contrary to what was in his heart, had, under duress, penned recantations—and cried out, "I see Heaven open and Jesus on the right hand of God!" Indeed, my historical consciousness seemed to increase daily by the mere fact of my living in Oxford. I was constantly being lifted up by a feeling of awe at having arrived there.

I got my first real view of my contemporaries in hall, at the Freshman Dinner, at the start of the Michaelmas term. In reality, the freshmen were of various ages: there were eighteen-year-old boys who had come up straight from school, twenty-year-old soldiers demobbed (the year 1956–57 was the first since the beginning of the war to have no compulsory military service), and twenty-two-year-old Scots and foreigners like me, who already had a degree.

Two freshmen sitting on my left were carrying on a conversation as if they were alone at the table.

"All Irish writing is boring," one said.

"What about Yeats?" the other asked.

"I don't like poetry," the first one said.

"And Beckett?" the other asked.

"Pointless drivel," the first one said.

"Joyce?" the other asked.

"Stylistically a tour de force, no doubt, but really no insight into the human heart, and that is, after all, what the critics celebrate him for," the first one said.

Their self-confidence was striking. No doubt they would modify their opinions in time, but the fact that they had such bold, unconventional opinions, and were not afraid to voice them, impressed me.

As was required, I had on, over my tweed jacket, my commoner's gown—a jacket-length, sleeveless black cotton affair with a turnover collar and with a streamer on each side of the back which hung the full length of the gown. Although the gown was an adaptation of the everyday dress of an earlier period, I felt ridiculous wearing it. The wretched thing had no buttons or ties, and seemed to float about me. I couldn't imagine that I would ever get used to wearing it for dinners in hall; and we were also required to wear our gowns for tutorials, lectures, and other formal functions. At the same time—rather inconsistently—I was proud of my gown, and even coveted the longer gown of a scholar; I felt as if I were folded into the distinctive cloak of a medieval clerk.

A freshman named Jasper Griffin, who had the room next to mine on Staircase XVI, and who had gone to Christ's Hospital, a renowned four-hundred-year-old public school, was sitting across

from me. He introduced me to his neighbor at the table, Roger
Tomkys. They had both come up to read in the Honours School
of Litterae Humaniores, the study of the ancient Greek and Latin
languages and literature, ancient history, and ancient and modern philosophy. The first examination in the faculty was called
Classical Honour Moderations, or Mods, and the final School was
known as Greats. Men reading Greats, as the whole School was
commonly called, tended to be the most learned of the undergraduates.

Jasper and Roger were soon engaged in a rather abstruse yet
lighthearted discussion of the distinction between the spiritual
and the physical. They quoted Plato, Aristotle, and Virgil, in
Greek and Latin, and threw out definitions and manipulated words
and phrases as if they were playing table tennis. Such discussions
could take place only at Oxford, I thought. It's so English. People here are so intelligent. Although anyone would have been
impressed by their ability to coruscate with ideas, I was bedev-
illed by dark thoughts of my own inferiority. I could more or
less understand some of the Latin, but the Greek was lost on me,
and I felt that no matter how hard I worked I could never catch
up—never meet the English standard. And the frightening thing
was that both Jasper and Roger were only nineteen. Not only
that but Roger had done two years of National Service, so he
must have learned all this at school by the time he was seventeen.

Yet in the course of dinner I discovered that I could tell Jasper and Roger almost anything—that I had gone to college with
cowboys, for instance—with a straight face and they would believe
me. Also, they both seemed very easily shocked, as they were
when I spoke of a particular part of my college campus where
undergraduates went to neck. Indeed, Roger, only a little less
than Jasper, seemed to find almost anything about the outside
world strange. That, I concluded, was probably due as much to
their English character as to their inexperience. Both seemed
endearingly innocent and fresh. Undergraduate life was going to

be livelier than I had imagined in my wildest dreams.

I took a few sips from my wineglass and, now and again, fingered a small glass next to it, wondering what it was for. I asked Jasper and Roger about it. "Port," Jasper said cryptically.

"Yes," I said, trying to put on a knowing air.

"You'll be drinking the health of the Queen and the college," Roger said.

"He knows all that," Jasper said to Roger. "After all, he grew up in the Empire."

The truth was that I didn't know any part of the ritual, but I felt I had already overstepped the bounds of propriety by asking about the little glass. I now began to wonder who was more worldly—they or I.

Later, after the scouts cleared the pudding dishes, the port was passed around, and, from the head table, the Master, whom I knew only as a distant, lordly figure, rapped the gavel and said, "Gentlemen, the Queen."

The entire hall stood up from the benches as one man and said, "The Queen."

The Master said, "Gentlemen may smoke." And we all sat down.

In a rather halting and flat yet emotional voice the Master gave a little speech. He said he wished to remind us that Balliol was a thirteenth-century foundation and was therefore the oldest college in Oxford. Merton men made a similar claim for their college, and so did men from University College, but we were to disregard their claims, for, as a constitutional historian, he could assure us that ours was the oldest foundation. He proposed the health of our college, and the hall again stood up, and, this time, said in unison, *"Floreat domus de Balliolo."*

We remained standing while a loving cup was passed clockwise from the head table along all the tables, around the hall. When the cup, a large silver affair with handles, got to me, it almost slipped out of my hands; it was nearly as heavy as a full bucket.

I started to take a sip, but Jasper, from across the table, stayed my hand. Following his whispered instructions, I bowed as best I could to the gentleman on my right, then to Roger, opposite, and to the gentleman on my left, not knowing whether I was supposed to incline my head or bow from my waist. Nor did I know how big a sip I was supposed to take. In my confusion, I got barely enough of the liquid into my mouth to discover that it was hot and highly spiced. (In due course, I found out that it was mulled claret.) Relieved, I started to hand the cup on, only to be directed by Jasper to bow all over again.

I was astonished that Jasper, whom until the dinner I had found unapproachable, seemed to be taking an interest in me, like a friend. Also, I had never been part of a toast before; I'd only read about such things in English novels. Perhaps because I was totally unprepared, I found the toasts, the Master's speech, and the "communion" very affecting. Maybe the ritual has gone on for hundreds of years, I thought. I'm being raised to the company of great men. I recalled that Matthew Arnold, Arthur Hugh Clough, Gerard Manley Hopkins, and Arnold Toynbee had gone to the college.

My reverie was interrupted by a thunderous rap of the gavel: the dinner was adjourned.

Jasper and I and some others went for coffee to the room of Tom Braun, a second-year Greats man. As he put the coffeepot on a gas ring, he painted a picture of Oxford life for the benefit of us freshmen. "One needs a lot of sleep at Oxford," he said. "So it's a pleasant aspect of the university that it is so structured that one needn't get out of one's bed till noon. One undergraduate I knew got a First in mathematics by either staying in bed or playing poker." Tom had an elaborate way of putting things, and spoke in smoothly flowing sentences.

"What did the mathematician do for food and books?" I asked.

"Food and books?" Tom said, as if taken aback by the question. "Oh, well, the chap probably had a lot of cheese and biscuits lying about, and his friends must have brought him books, if he ever felt the need to read one."

"What about lectures?" I asked, incredulous.

"You're not in America," he said. "No one here need attend lectures."

"How does one manage, then?" I asked.

"Manage?" he said. "Well, there are books, aren't there? And I suppose that by the time people come up to Oxford they've learned to read." He seems to be afraid of behaving like anyone else, I thought. Perhaps he finds it too ordinary or boring.

The people in the room were getting restless. They must think that I don't know the first thing about the art of conversation, I thought. They must think that I'm an uncouth foreigner who believes that conversation is only a matter of questions and answers. But I can't help it.

"What about tutorials?" I asked.

"Well, that can't take more than an hour or two a week, can it?" he said, as if he felt that I was needling him. He added wryly, "But if you find your tutor snoozing in bed when you arrive for your tute, don't begrudge the chap his sleep."

"What are you supposed to do, then?" I asked, ignoring the general mirth around me.

"Oh, well, you can gently knock, and withdraw to the J.C.R. He'll come and get you when he's ready for you." (The J.C.R., I knew, was the Junior Common Room.)

"How eccentric," I said. "How long is that kind of thing likely to take?"

"Tutors are known for getting into their trousers fast," he said, laughing. He abruptly turned away and began talking to Jasper.

"You make it sound as if one didn't have to do much work here," I said.

"Well, there's only one real examination at the end, after all," he said, turning back to me.

"But the class of degree you get entirely depends on it," I said.

"But I've never known anyone to fail, actually," Tom said flippantly. "If one works hard in the final year, one should be able to do decently in Schools even if one is a clod and a troglodyte." He yawned.

I was beginning to feel the effects of the wine at dinner and the port following it. I gulped down my coffee, excused myself, and started toward my room and bed. Jasper walked out with me.

"Tom certainly makes Oxford sound like a breeze," I said.

"Well, that's old Tom," Jasper said. Tom inspired such affection that he was already "old Tom" to us. "He was having you on. 'Here is an innocent chap,' he must have said to himself. 'Let me have some pleasurable diversion at his expense.' You walked into the trap like a lamb into an abattoir."

I could only reflect on my earlier assessment of Jasper's gullibility.

EACH of us freshmen had to be interviewed by the Master. I felt extremely intimidated, recalling that I would be talking to someone who wore the mantle of Benjamin Jowett, the great Master of Balliol in the nineteenth century. Jowett had set Balliol on its course of world eminence; had instituted educational reforms that helped to lay the foundations of modern, secular Oxford and of the Indian Civil Service, which he opened to competition; had established the tradition of Balliol men succeeding in Schools and going on to fill the tutorships and headships of other colleges and take prominent places in both houses of Parliament and at the bar; had left a permanent mark on English scholarship and theology; and had made translations of Plato that became English classics. A contemporary of Jowett, Henry Charles Beeching, voiced the esteem in which Jowett was held, writing:

> First come I; my name is Jowett.
> There's no knowledge but I know it.
> I am Master of this college:
> What I don't know isn't knowledge.

On the appointed day, I knocked with trepidation at the door of the Master's lodgings, and was received by the Master himself—Sir David Lindsay Keir, the author of the standard "Constitutional History of Modern Britain" (since 1485), which had gone through half a dozen editions since it was first published, in 1938. In contrast to the American practice, where the head of a college tended to be a fund-raiser, selected by a group of businessmen serving as trustees of the institution, the head of an Oxford college tended to be an important scholar, elected by its Fellows, who, acting together, formed its governing body. Keir was known wherever British government had influence or was studied. The mere fact that everyone, from the pantry lad to the Senior Fellow, addressed him as "Master" was awe-inspiring.

As soon as I sat down, the Master asked me a question. I didn't catch a single word. He spoke like someone who had had a throat operation. "I beg your pardon, Master," I said, in my most polite manner. He repeated the question. I still didn't catch it. I strained to hear what he would say next.

"What games do you play, Mr. Mehta?"

"Games, Master?" I exclaimed, taken aback. I don't know quite what I had expected from the interview, but I had imagined that it was his way of welcoming a new member to the college and of putting a name to a face—that, at most, he would ask me something about my Indian background and my American schooling.

"Yes. Cricket? Rugby? Tennis?" He spoke in a monotone, with a heavy Scots accent.

I could scarcely believe my ears. Perhaps he asks questions of freshmen by rote, I thought. "Such games are not suitable for a blind person," I said.

"Then what games do you play?" he asked.

I was surprised by his insistence. "I play no games, Master," I said. The atmosphere of the interview was so formulaic that it didn't occur to me until later that I could have mentioned that I liked to fly kites and to bicycle, and that I rode and swam a little.

"You play no games?" he echoed. His voice was so flat that it was almost sepulchral. "What are your plans for afterlife?"

"Afterlife, Master?" I repeated stupidly. I couldn't believe that he was interested in my fantasies about immortality.

"Yes, afterlife," he said. And then, perhaps thinking that because I was a foreigner my English was weak, he added, "Your life after Balliol."

"Oh, that! I don't know, Master." That part of my life seemed so distant.

"Mr. Tylor thinks that you might get a First in jurisprudence," he said. "If you do, that should certainly help you to do well in your afterlife."

"With Mr. Tylor's permission, Master, I've switched to P.P.E."

"What say? This is a surprise to us, since everyone is admitted to read a particular subject." Without waiting for me to explain, he went on, "I don't think you've told me what your ambition for afterlife is."

I almost blurted out, "Prime Minister, Master." My father was sure that with an Oxford degree I could become Prime Minister of India. But then when my oldest sister played through "Give Me Five Minutes More" on the violin for the first time he had also thought that she would be another Paganini.

"I don't know about my afterlife, Master," I said.

I reflected afterward that "Prime Minister" would have been just the answer. For one thing, the few Indians who were able to come up to Oxford all secretly harbored that ambition—and, indeed, an Oxford or Cambridge degree was a royal road to high office in newly independent India, just as it had been in British India. For another thing, I was later told by an Australian friend, Father Julian Miller, who was ordained a Catholic priest before he came up to Balliol, that when he was confronted with the same question by the Master he had gained much kudos with him by saying that in afterlife he planned to become pope. And, Julian reported, he had proceeded to sketch out for the Master's benefit the basis for his expectations: that the cardinals would have to look for a pope outside Italy one day; that they would be afraid of electing a pope from a dominant country, like America; that internal rivalries would prevent them from electing a pope from another European country; that they would therefore have to turn to a neutral, non-European country; and that Australia would be the natural candidate. In the meantime, Julian had gone on to say, thanks to his degrees from Rome and from Oxford, to his family connections, and to the help of an Australian bishop whose patronage he enjoyed, he would have risen to the position of cardinal and would be ready for the calling. The Master had been much impressed, and had applauded his "noble ambition for afterlife."

"I'm sure you're aware, Mr. Mehta, that three Balliol men in their afterlife became viceroys of India," the Master was saying.

As an Indian from the Empire, I knew all too well that fifteen viceroys had come from Oxford and that three of them—the Fifth Marquess of Lansdowne, Lord Elgin, and Lord Curzon—were Balliol men. "Yes, Master," I said.

"Thank you. This has been an agreeable conversation."

I went to my room shaking from the meeting. I had always

basked in the good opinion of my teachers and of the heads of institutions that I attended, but, for some reason, I had got off on the wrong foot with the Master, and I felt that there was no way I could rectify the situation. When I calmed down, however, I realized that not being in the Master's good graces gave me little to fear except the reproaches of my conscience.

Subsequently, some people told me that after Sir David was elected Master he had had a minor stroke, which had affected his spirits; others said that, like many brilliant English scholars, he had pushed himself so fast in his youth that by the time he became the Master he was somewhat burned out; still others said that people elected to high college office had often done their major scholarly work and had passed their prime. (The Master was sixty-one.) In my second year, I had the Master for constitutional history, and I was much impressed by his legal acumen. Still, his politics were so extreme—he was a royalist by persuasion—and his speech and mannerisms were so pompous that he was a constant source of amusement to undergraduates; they took great delight in imitating him.

MY first Oxford tutorial was in philosophy, and it was with John Patrick Corbett, who taught in the library tower, on the front quadrangle. Holding on to the wrought-iron rail, I nervously climbed the flights of well-worn stone steps. Another Tylor, no doubt, I thought. Yet I reasoned that I should be able to acquit myself better in a tutorial in philosophy than in a tutorial in jurisprudence, for while I was an ignoramus in law I was acquainted with a diverse body of philosophical thought, through philosophy courses I had taken at Pomona.

Halfway up the steps, I met an American friend who had just finished his tutorial with Corbett. "Good luck," he said, and he paused to tell me, "When I first started doing my tutorials with

Corbett, I hadn't done any philosophy. I couldn't imagine that anyone could be worked up about things like where the mind ends and the body begins. It all seemed to me like common sense. One day, after I finished reading my essay—I believe it was my fourth tutorial—Corbett said to me, 'I feel that I'm being hit over the head from all sides. I don't know where it's coming from.' I said, 'I felt the same way when I was writing it.' I must have lost fifteen or twenty pounds in my first term of philosophy."

I continued up the treacherous steps and, trying to control my nervousness, knocked at Corbett's door.

"Come in!" The invitation came across almost as a shout. Either the great man has been interrupted in the middle of a thought or he doesn't realize how his voice carries, I reflected.

I felt weak in the knees, but I walked in, gently closing the door behind me. The room was warm and comfortable and had a pleasant smell of pipe tobacco. Corbett was standing near the gas fire, rolling back and forth on the balls of his feet, as if he were trying to grapple with a particularly recalcitrant thought.

"Ah, Mehta, you found your way to my room," he said suavely. He had a pipe between his teeth.

It was my first meeting with Corbett, and I put out my hand. He didn't so much as take a step toward me. The Master had shaken my hand, but maybe that's not done in tutorials, I thought. Feeling uncouth, I dropped my hand.

"Do sit down," Corbett said kindly.

I took a chair. It was identical to the one in my room, right down to the foam-rubber cushions, as if there were something distinctive, though not necessarily distinguished, about Oxford furniture.

"What ph-philosophical works have you read? Or perhaps I should ask, rather: Have you done any philosophy?" Corbett inquired, taking the pipe out of his mouth, and continuing to roll back and forth. He had a little stammer, which seemed to be not so much a speech impediment as a mannerism. (I had noticed that some people at Oxford actually cultivated a stammer, as if to underscore the transition from thought to speech.)

"I studied philosophy with W. T. Jones," I said proudly. He was perhaps the most distinguished scholar at my college in America, and I felt sure that he would have a reputation in Oxford.

Instead of sounding impressed, Corbett said, "Never heard of the chap—who is he?" His voice was very English, and he had what I imagined was a perfect Oxford accent—plummy but clear. His voice radiated self-confidence and a sense of well-being, and had the timbre and range of a musical instrument.

"You must know W. T. Jones," I said.

"I don't know any Jones in the first rank of philosophers anywhere," he said flatly.

"But he was a Rhodes scholar and did a B.Litt. at Oriel College."

"That degree is for Americans," he said, in a "That's for the birds" tone. "B.Litt. is not an examination degree. It's a low-level research degree. Many Americans choose to do it, because they can't stand the rigor of Schools." Corbett himself had read P.P.E. and had got a First in Schools, which was a sine qua non for teaching at Oxford.

"But he wrote a big book on the history of Western philosophy," I persisted. "It's a textbook used in a lot of American colleges."

"I d-despise textbooks," Corbett said. "It's a p-packaged form of education that is a substitute for thinking."

"But the Master's 'Constitutional History' is a textbook."

"That's different," he said. "That's like a legal casebook."

"Dr. Jones's book isn't a typical textbook—it gives you big chunks of quotations from the philosophers themselves," I said.

"*Reader's Digest* of philosophy, eh?" he said, with a big laugh.

"Jones doesn't condense philosophers—he gives extracts from them," I said, still trying to rally to the defense of my old teacher and mentor.

"Extracts, eh?" Corbett said, with another big laugh. "And why do you think extracts are better than condensation? You aren't saying less is more, are you?" He began pacing, as if he'd finished with the subject and wanted to get on to something else.

Next to my father, Dr. Jones was perhaps the man I admired most. But part of my admiration for him was that he seemed quintessentially Oxford. Here was Corbett, however, telling me that Jones wasn't: that, in fact, Jones knew the Oxford tutorial method and the Oxford system of impersonal examiners—which he had always held up as a model for education—only at second hand.

"You still haven't told me what ph-philosophical works you've read," Corbett went on.

"I've read in the works of many ancient and modern philosophers."

"Yes," he said distantly, as if he were trying to imagine my California education.

"I take it, then, that you don't at all approve of a historical approach to philosophy," I said.

"I don't know that it matters what I approve or don't approve. What I think is irrelevant. Would you not agree that reading philosophical works merely in a historical context reduces them to the domain of historical ideas?"

"Then how does one do philosophy? How is philosophy done here?"

"We do problems of philosophy, the way you might do problems of mathematics. 'Are there universals?' is addressing a philosophical problem that philosophers, in one way or another, have been grappling with since at least the time of Plato. Would you like to do an essay on 'Are there universals'? What I am interested in is your own ideas about the question, so don't trot out what this philosopher said and what that philosopher said, à la an American term paper."

For me, writing about problems in philosophy was a whole new way of looking at philosophy. Jones's philosophical approach and, by extension, his philosophical textbook suddenly seemed parochial. I wondered if he had presented a shortcut to philosophical education, whereas Corbett was introducing me, at that very moment, to the Socratic method—the heart of philosophical education and, by analogy, of the tutorial method. With the zeal of a convert, I was quick to criticize the old in the light of the new. (In later years, I read several new books by Jones and rediscovered my admiration for him.) The prospect of writing the essay was exhilarating.

"Do you have any suggestions for readings?" I asked.

"Well, you might want to look at . . ." He rattled off names of authors.

I tried to slow him down by asking him for the first names of the authors and the titles of their books. "Any particular book by Laserowitz?" I asked at one point. He obliged, but my questions seemed to make him impatient. It appeared that for him all the authors were members of a scholarly family, and everyone in the community was expected to know them. The upshot was that for the essay I should consult A. D. Woozley's "Theory of Knowledge," David Pears' "The Nature of Metaphysics," H. H. Price's "Thinking and Representation," Locke's "Essay Concerning Human Understanding," and Morris Laserowitz's articles.

I was afraid that if I asked him which parts of the books I should read the question would invite derision. And yet the idea of getting someone to read aloud half a dozen philosophical works within a week for one of two weekly essays I had to write (the other was in economics) seemed a near-impossibility. Indeed, I felt I could spend a whole week studying just Locke. So I found myself asking him if he wanted me to read particular chapters in the books.

"Just look at the books and read what catches your interest," he said.

Look at the books. That was a visual command, no doubt asking me to skim them. But there was no way for an ordinary reader to do such a thing for me. I thought he would understand that. At the same time, I didn't want him to make any special concessions for me. I always wanted to be treated like anyone else. So I said, rather lamely, "Catches my interest?"

"Just get hold of their arguments."

I may have been a convert, but now I found myself being a backslider, and hankering after my old teacher, who not only would have written the full names and titles of the books on the blackboard but would have directed us to the exact pages containing the gist of the arguments, or to a textbook. And later he would have recapitulated the arguments in a lecture, almost making the reading optional. (Oxford lectures were usually not summaries of published material but, rather, the results of research and thinking, often on very narrow or recondite topics.) It now seemed to me that the American system of education, built around textbooks and lectures, was particularly well suited to someone in my situation, who had to take in most information by ear. But I consoled myself with the thought that the Oxford system promised to make me a true scholar.

There was a knock—another pupil at the door. "Well, we have to stop now," Corbett said.

I automatically put out my hand, but then stuck both hands deep in my pockets and hastily made my way out.

❧

"MAY I have a word with you?" I asked, running after Mr. Tylor in the quadrangle. I had tried several times to see him in order to ask him how I could use the Bodleian, the university library, but each time I put my ear to his door he had been either giving a tutorial or talking on the telephone.

"You're an extraordinary chap," he said, in his broadcasting voice, as he stopped to talk to me. "How did you know who I was?"

If the remark had come from a sighted person, I would have regarded it as patronizing. Now I simply asked myself: How could a fellow blind person be so unenlightened? Still, the few educated blind people I'd met in England had made me realize that they were much less socially adept than their counterparts in America—as if they had developed their minds at the expense of training their other faculties. In any event, I felt indebted to Tylor for my admission to Balliol and was disinclined to entertain critical thoughts about him for long.

"I know your step, sir," I said. I didn't want to be drawn into a discussion in which I might have to say something uncomplimentary about his way of walking—he had a thud of a footstep—so I quickly got to the business at hand. "I was wondering if you could tell me whom I should talk to about getting a room in the Bodleian."

"Why do you need a room in the Bodleian?" he asked.

I was speechless. At college in America, I had always been able to obtain a room in the library to work in; after all, I needed a place where a reader could read aloud to me and I could type my notes without disturbing anyone. Also, American libraries routinely lent books. In contrast, no book could leave the Bodleian premises except by special leave of the curators and convocation of the university; in fact, it was said that the Bodleian authorities had refused to lend a book to Charles I and had used that precedent in refusing to lend a book to Oliver Cromwell.

"I need some way of using the Bodleian," I stammered.

"I don't think I've ever had to use the Bodleian," Tylor said.

I could scarcely believe my ears. The other Oxford dons lived and breathed for the Bodleian. It was said, for instance, that when Eduard Fraenkel, the emeritus professor of Latin, arrived at

Oxford as a German refugee in the thirties he had turned up at the Bodleian at seven o'clock in the morning and discovered, to his horror, that the library didn't open until nine. Later, he had moved from a comfortable house to a less comfortable one because the latter was closer to the Bodleian.

"How do you manage, then?" I asked weakly.

"The Royal National Institute for the Blind is very helpful with Braille books," he said. "I'm sure they will do everything for you. I'm the vice-chairman of its council."

"I've been in touch with them," I said, feeling desperate. "They are well equipped with law books but don't seem to have many recent works in philosophy or economics."

"Well, you talk to Quinn," Tylor said, continuing on his way. "He'll sort you out. He's the college librarian." While the university had the Bodleian, each college had its own library.

Although I was wearing ankle-high boots lined with sheepskin, which I had just acquired from Ducker & Son, in Turl Street, I was chilled to the bone from standing outside. At the same time, I was sweating from the effort of talking to such an imposing Englishman. I asked myself—not for the first time—whether because of my Raj childhood I always conducted myself as if the English were my superiors and I were their inferior. "Damn it! I'm at Oxford," I told myself. "I should be able to feel on an equal footing with them." Yet, compared with the sweeping flow of Tylor, Corbett, et al., my English sounded like a cryptic, almost foreign tongue. How could I hold my own with them?

❧

THE college librarian, E. V. Quinn, had a self-effacing manner that belied my stereotypes of the English. Even for a librarian, he spoke in exceptionally hushed tones, so that one had to strain to hear him. Moreover, his speech was hesitant and shy, as if he worried that he might give offense. What little he did say he covered up with eruptions of a nervous laugh. On the one hand, I thought that I had found in him a friend: his obliging nature was all too evident. On the other hand, I didn't want to ask anything of him: he had the air of someone who was much put upon. In response to my questions, Quinn gave a series of hesitant answers that added up to "I wish I could say otherwise, but there's no place for you to read in the college library. But, like any college member, you are free to take books to your room. It's true that certain set texts that are required for individual Schools are in great demand, but I can see to it that you always have the books you need. That holds for volumes of bound periodicals, too. I would be glad to look up anything for you in the catalogues. You need never bother about interrupting me. It should be possible to do Schools just using the college library. The P.P.E. School is a very popular one, and the syllabus consists mostly of recently published books. The college library is bound to have almost everything. I am, of course, speaking from memory, and might be completely off. If there should be gaps in our P.P.E. books, I'm sure we can turn to people in the Bodleian. I'm not saying that you could consult any book you wanted to in Duke Humfrey"—the original part of the Bodleian, one of the oldest libraries in Europe—"but that is by no means the whole of the Bodleian. Besides Duke Humfrey, there is, after all, the New Bodleian. It's a modern building, and I believe that it even has some offices. The people at the Bodleian could surely find some place there where you could work with your reader. Of course, I can't speak for them, but I'm sure there must be a room that can somehow be made available to you for the time you need it— perhaps an office not in use just then."

Quinn astonished me with his gentleness, much as Tylor had with his fierceness, and I was left with the thought that I would always be in awe of the English, whatever their stripe.

As things turned out, I had to do all my work in my room,

except when the books I needed to consult were not in the college library. Then I was allowed to use an office in the New Bodleian. The arrangement proved to be less daunting than I had feared.

❦

IN the quadrangle, I was hailed by the college chaplain and dean, the Reverend Francis Leader MacCarthy-Willis-Bund. It was a matter of some amusement to the undergraduates that in 1950, by royal license, he had added Willis-Bund to his name. That was his mother's family name, which he had been required to add to his father's name as one of the conditions of his inheriting a property in Herefordshire from his maternal grandfather. The older members of the college sometimes called him MacCarthy, as if they were still adjusting to the change.

"How goes it?" he asked, as if he wanted to detain me in conversation.

"I'm settling in, Dean," I said. I was touched that he was taking an interest in me. In a surge, I felt glad that I'd come to Balliol. There is coziness here amid the cold, I thought. Though it was one of the largest Oxford colleges, with about four hundred students and thirty Tutorial Fellows, it had the feeling of a small, cloistered society.

We stood in awkward silence, which was all the more awkward because the dean's stomach was rumbling the whole time. "Yes," he said, as if he were waiting like a father confessor.

Now that I had the ear of the dean, it occurred to me that perhaps I should ask him one of the questions about college rules which had been worrying me. That morning, I had heard a porter turn away a mother who had come to see her freshman son, saying that women were not allowed in college between 7 P.M. and noon. At first, I hadn't paid much attention to the contretemps. Oxford was, by and large, a monastic university, where, I imagined, women were considered a distraction to the basic goal of scholarship. But then I had remembered that I would have to have readers in my room. I had often had women readers, and had found the contact with them nurturing—perhaps because, for reasons that were not completely clear to me, I didn't have any close women friends. I wondered what, exactly, the rules about women in college were. There was no orientation program for the freshmen. The college, no doubt, expected one to learn the rules by a sort of osmosis.

"Dean, are women not allowed in college in the morning at all?" I asked.

"I suppose not," the dean said. "Why do you ask?"

"I was just wondering," I said, taken aback both by the equivocation of his answer—he was supposed to enforce the college rules—and by the directness of his question. I didn't know how to go about phrasing the problem about women readers, so I asked, with my pulse quickening, "Why have such a rule?"

"Why not?" the dean asked.

"I'm wondering, sir, how I can have women readers in my room in the morning," I said. I stumbled through the explanation.

"I expect you'll be having elderly ladies, like Tylor's. Is that right?"

"Not necessarily," I said. "I might have young women."

"You know, there's a college rule that no one is supposed to be outside college after midnight," he said vaguely. "But if you ever are, there is a window on the ground floor of Staircase X. Any undergraduate can show you how to climb in."

The dean then walked away, as if he had suddenly remembered something.

❧

IN my cold, Spartan room, I lit the gas fire and huddled my thin, chilled body in a chair in front of it. The meeting with the dean had left me bemused. Even if he was only underscoring the fact that the rules at Oxford were made to be broken, the comparison between a woman reader walking into college in full view of the porter in the morning and an undergraduate climbing through a window in the dark was hardly illuminating. And, in any case, I thought, I'll have to work with a reader in this hole. But, after all, Oxford undergraduates have been working in one kind of hole or another since the Middle Ages. The grandeur of life here surely has more to do with the traditions and the style of the place than with accommodations—at least, at Balliol.

I went over in my mind the meeting with Quinn. However sympathetic and well-disposed he was, I couldn't forget that in America I had always been able to do most of my work in the library and so to function like a normal person in my room; friends had been able to drop in on me as they might on anyone else, without regard to the presence of a third party or to my time with a paid reader—or, indeed, to my special need to have a reader at all. In Oxford, my attempt to separate my working life from my private life was bound to be futile. Yet my wish to compartmentalize them was, if anything, stronger. I'd heard that the most delicious part of Oxford life went on in the rooms over coffee or a drink, with undergraduates casually dropping in. Certainly Oxford conversations were legendary; some Oxonians claimed that they had learned more from other undergraduates than they had from their tutorials. The thought that my room might be passed up because I was likely to be working with a reader there— that I might miss what Pope once called "the sweeter banquet of the mind"—was dispiriting.

The gas fire hissed, as if mocking what I'd imagined Oxford to be, from the distance of America. My front was nearly baked, but my back was freezing. I turned around in my chair so that my back could get some of the heat. I rested my head against the cushion. I was besieged by all kinds of morbid thoughts. I had

read somewhere that parents rued the day when the colleges substituted modern gas fires for the ancient coal fires, because, with
the changeover, an undergraduate had at his fingertips the means
of taking his life: he had only to turn on the gas. I tried not to
think about the hiss. I momentarily nodded off.

At Oxford, especially during the first days, I felt sleepy all
the time, and that was maddening, since there was so much to
do. I fretted that my sleepiness was due to depressed spirits, but
then someone told me that people in Oxford generally felt like
sleeping more, because the air was heavy and damp, and that
though Oxford wasn't as cold as, say, Cambridge—where the
wind swept in from the North Sea across the Fens—its cold was
more penetrating. Even hardy Yorkshiremen, coming from the
cold North, were laid low by the damp Oxford cold, which was
no doubt a consequence of the town's being situated in a river
valley. No one could imagine what the rationale was for founding
a great university in the valley. It may have happened that people
simply congregated there and, in time, clusters of buildings were
put up.

The walls of my room felt damp to the touch, and the damp-
ness made the room feel permanently cold. Besides, my room
didn't get any sun; even when the sun came out, it was blocked
by big trees in the quadrangle. I was never able to keep my hands
and feet warm, and I couldn't stop shivering in my light clothes;
I didn't yet have money to buy proper warm English clothes. I
seemed to be always climbing on top of my gas fire and scorching
the bottoms of my trousers. (By the end of the first term, I had
scorched the backs of all my trouser legs, and if I hadn't had a
keen sense of smell I would probably have set my legs on fire.
Indeed, an American undergraduate burned her legs on the electric fire in her room, and had to be hospitalized for ten days.)

I wanted to splash some cold water on my face, so I headed
for the lavatory. Jasper and I had the two ground-floor rooms,

and the lavatory was just outside our doors, across a little passageway. Exasperatingly, it was occupied.

❧

IN all the years that I had been bathed in the romantic glow of Oxford, I had not had so much as a glimmering of its discomforts and hardships, of how the place would restrict and circumscribe me.

For the whole staircase, which contained ten bed-sitters and the college law library, there was a single lavatory, which had the only toilet and the only basin. (In at least one college, scouts still carried basins of hot water to undergraduate rooms.) It was hard to get into the lavatory, particularly in the morning, and the passageway was so small that there was no place to stand and wait one's turn. Consequently, people were forever thudding up and down the stairs and trying the door. I remember that when I woke up I would tarry in bed, listening for the lavatory door to open. The moment I heard the rattle and bang of the bolt and the creak and squeak of the door swinging open, I would grab my shaving things and towel and dash in. The lavatory was a small, unheated room with a single window, which was set high in the outer wall, facing St. Giles, one of the busiest thoroughfares in central Oxford, and was always left open. Hence the lavatory was so cold and so noisy that I felt as if I were out on the street. There was the whoosh of coaches braking and disgorging tourists, and, during lulls in the traffic, the click and scrape of shoes on the pavement. Sometimes I could even hear snatches of conversation. And, despite the open window, the lavatory had a noxious smell. The basin was so filthy that I shrank from using it to mix water—there were separate taps for hot and cold water. Brushing my teeth, shaving, and washing involved a certain amount of juggling: holding my nose, cupping a hand to catch hot and cold water, and rinsing my mouth or splashing my face before the water could leak out between my fingers. It seemed that I was always either scalding a hand or numbing it with freezing water.

The facilities for showers and baths were also inadequate, and since, in addition, they generally required a trek in the open air, most undergraduates went through the term without bothering about either. The college's single set of showers was four staircases away from me, in an unheated basement. The closest bathtub to me, which was three staircases away, was also situated in an unheated basement, and was grimy and full of tide marks. In fact, I often had the impression that the dons and the undergraduates were so preoccupied with the life of the mind that the preoccupation became a sort of wall, which prevented them from noticing their surroundings. We were being equipped, without knowing it, to enjoy physical comforts when we had them but not to miss them when we didn't. Perhaps that's why people from Oxford could live anywhere in the world, however primitive the conditions.

Hall, too, was oppressive, in its way. Although I was always awake in the morning by eight or eight-fifteen, I seldom, if ever, made it to hall for breakfast, because the hall doors were closed promptly at a quarter to nine. I either didn't get into the lavatory in time or cherished the extra few minutes in bed. More often than not, I stayed away deliberately, and got through the morning on the strength of coffee and gingersnaps. In hall, one sat at a long table on a bench without a back. There were never amenities like tablecloths or napkins. The stale smell of Brussels sprouts was so pervasive that it overwhelmed even the smell of kippers, on the rare occasions when they were part of the breakfast fare. On top of all that, breakfast was unappetizing. Nor were lunches or dinners any better. They consisted mostly of a sliver of fatty meat served with overcooked Brussels sprouts or cabbage and with potatoes as hard as rocks, followed by a nondescript pudding. Also, at breakfast in hall people didn't seem particularly friendly.

The meal was eaten in silence, and if one attempted conversation one was put in one's place. The atmosphere made me feel a little like the new officer in Evelyn Waugh's novel who comes into the mess and greets his colonel cheerfully with "Good morning," only to be squashed by his superior's retorting, "Good morning, good morning, good morning—I hope that will do you for three mornings." Anyway, whatever the meal, the undergraduates often sat in groups, as if they had known one another at school and were happiest being part of a gang. They also talked more at each other than to each other, as if they were used to having conversation not with any particular person but with a group that shared their backgrounds and assumptions, speech mannerisms and slang. Unless one was bold and self-confident enough to butt in, one was simply ignored. In short, the atmosphere in hall at most meals was very different from the festivity of the Freshman Dinner.

I could have put up more easily with the college's physical shortcomings if only I hadn't had to surrender the freedom to move around independently outside the walls of the college. Everywhere at Oxford, one was confronted with the disorder of winding paths and lanes, oddly placed buildings and trees, roaring lorries and cars, weaving bicycles and scooters. Either there were no sidewalks or what sidewalks there were would be taken up by scaffolding, standing bicycles, lampposts, gutters. After all, Oxford was a historic town, with accretions of buildings; the colleges and business establishments, streets and lanes had grown up higgledy-piggledy through the centuries, and the result was a palimpsest of an ancient medieval town and a modern industrial city. With a sinking heart, I realized that there was no way I could get to lectures by myself—something I had been able to do not only at Pomona but also at Harvard and at the University of California in Berkeley, where I had once attended summer school. Lectures were given all across Oxford—in halls and lecture rooms of various colleges and in Schools, a building on High Street where university examinations were also held. The lectures were said not to be an essential part of the curriculum, as they were at Cambridge, and undergraduates certainly skipped them, but I imagined that they would be especially useful for me, since I took in so much information by ear. Anyway, there was a difference between choosing not to go to the lectures and being, as it were, disabled from going to them. The thought that outside the college I would always have to go around with a friend or in a taxi was galling. Tylor and Rupert Cross—the other blind tutor at Oxford—were led around with no apparent injury to their vanity, but I felt that I was different. Perhaps because I had grown up in the Raj, where respectability counted for much more than money, I was overweeningly proud, and would rather pass up doing something than ask for help. Besides, I had lived in America, and there, once I had mastered the layout of a town, I could go anywhere I liked, since towns tended to be generally orderly, with wide pavements, and traffic lights at major intersections, and often had a gridiron pattern, with regular blocks. Indeed, in the New World I had learned to travel everywhere by myself, crisscrossing the continent almost as if I could see.

LATE one morning soon after I arrived at Oxford, Vijay turned up at my door. He came without warning, and, as it happened, my little room just then was like a railway station. A chap had barged in to solicit my membership in the Labour Club; a curiosity-seeker who had heard that I'd written a book was skulking in a corner waiting to talk to me; Jasper had just emerged from his room on his way to the Buttery—a small college store that also sold drinks—and wanted to know if I would like to join him for a pint; and a retired Army officer, Major John Bottomley, who was my reader, was bustling about as if to make it obvious that he didn't approve of such interruptions.

Vijay, in an overcoat and bowler hat, stood around awkwardly, tapping his umbrella. I felt flustered—I didn't know which way to turn—but I did my best to make him feel welcome. Jasper, noticing my discomfort, went off to the Buttery by himself. I cleared out the other people who had dropped in, and arranged a new hour for Major Bottomley. Vijay proposed lunch at the Chequers, and we set off.

Vijay was the only person at Oxford who actually knew my family, and I was eager to improve my acquaintance with him. Our parents are from the same Punjabi caste group, I thought. We could be cousins. And yet he's so English. Once, when I rang my mother up from the porter's lodge—on the only telephone undergraduates could use—she had told me, laughing, "Whenever he wants to come home for a weekend, he rings up his mother and says, 'Mummy, may I come home this weekend?' He even rings up if he wants to come home for just a Sunday lunch. An Indian son would come home as a matter of birthright and demand to stay as long as he felt like it. He would lord it over everyone as if he were the master of the house. But Vijay is as meek as a mouse, and with his own mother."

Vijay and I crossed Broad Street and walked along Turl, across the High, to the Chequers. Along the way, I tried to make bright conversation with him, as I had heard English undergraduates do, railing against Anthony Eden's Conservative government, and quoting Swift: "Whoever could make two ears of corn or two blades of grass to grow upon a spot of ground where only one grew before, would deserve better of mankind, and do more essential service to his country than the whole race of politicians put together." To myself, I sounded appropriately impressive.

"I admire Eden," Vijay said. I felt like a balloon whose air had suddenly whooshed out.

The Chequers was an old pub in a twelfth-century house. As we gave our orders to the publican, in a noisy, smoke-filled room, I suddenly felt a little miffed: now I would probably have to shell out half a crown or more for myself and also pay for Vijay's lunch. After all, it was only right that I should pay for him, since my mother was staying with his family. I told myself that I shouldn't begrudge the extra expense.

Standing at the bar, I ate my first cheddar-cheese sandwich and drank my first glass of cider. I voiced my thrill.

"Don't tell me that you've never tasted cheddar or cider before!" Vijay exclaimed.

"No, I haven't," I said, wishing that I could hide my ignorance, and, at the same time, feeling glad that I was exposing it only to Vijay, who was really a fellow-Indian. I pointed to a relish that was served with the sandwich. "What is this?"

"A gherkin," he said.

The name conjured up in my head a sweet confection, but the taste of the little pickled cucumber was so sharp that I almost coughed it up.

"You see, I'm more Indian than you are," Vijay said. "I like spicy food."

"Another round, sir?" the publican asked.

"Yes, another round, please," I said enthusiastically.

"Maybe you would like to try sausages or a Scotch egg," Vijay suggested.

"The works," I said, trying to sound worldly.

Vijay laughed. "Are you sure you'll be able to manage all that?"

Catching on to the fact that sausages and a Scotch egg were two separate, filling dishes, I decided to pass up a second sandwich and the sausages, and ordered a Scotch egg; the name had an exotic ring.

"Here you are, sir," the publican said, setting a plate and another glass of cider in front of me.

The Scotch egg—a boiled egg wrapped in sausage meat—was so delicious that I thought I could happily have it for lunch every day.

"I prefer pub food to any other," I said, feeling very jolly. The cider was going to my head.

❦

WHEN people heard that I was doing P.P.E., they would say, "God help you! You'll have Balogh." Thomas Balogh, a refugee Hungarian economist, was notorious for setting his own rules for what he called "the tutorial game." It took me the first couple of weeks of the term simply to find him. When I finally caught up with him, in his room, he said, "Well, well, my little poppet, what have you come here to do?"

"P.P.E.," I said, trying not to smile at his way of talking. Anyway, I wasn't sure if "my little poppet" was an affectation or a translation of a perfectly ordinary Hungarian phrase.

"What economics have you read, darling?" he asked.

"Paul Samuelson's 'Economics,' among others."

"That's not nearly enough," he said. "Go read some more, and then come for a tutorial."

Balogh wouldn't deign to tell me what to read, but he gave me a time, a date, and the name of my tutorial partner, who was an American. "He's a real donkey—you'll be well matched," he said wryly.

During my first tutorial with Balogh, my partner read aloud an essay he had written on the accounting of national income. During the reading, Balogh lay before the open fire, or sat in a chair next to a huge pile of mail. He would pick up a letter from the pile, noisily open it, read it, crumple it up, and toss it over his shoulder. At one point, he actually got up and visited the lavatory, leaving the door open and insisting over his shoulder that the reading should proceed.

In the middle of the discussion of the essay, he excused himself to go to the porter's lodge and, when he returned, feigned surprise that we had not continued with the argument.

"But you weren't here to listen to the argument," I said.

"Well, well, my little poppet, you won't do well in Schools if you take that attitude," he told me. "The examiner will be interested in your views, not mine. Keep your eyes fixed on results in Schools, darling, and you won't go wrong."

The mention of Schools struck terror to my heart. He may be a brilliant, if eccentric, economist, but is he going to be any help in preparing me for Schools?

"What did you think of my essay?" my partner asked him boldly.

Balogh proceeded to tell him what was wrong with the "American animals"—the authors of the book that my partner had based his essay on.

"I don't think you've read this book, Mr. Balogh," my partner said.

" 'Tommy,' please. You're right—I couldn't stand to read those two asses."

In the remaining five minutes of the tutorial, Balogh gave a brilliant disquisition on the accounting of national income. His remarks on authorities were, by turns, irreverent, scornful, and impish, with flashes of humor. Just as they say, Oxford is full of queer birds, I thought, and this bird is full of suppressed fury— a kind of wild energy that is very engaging. Maybe the best education, by its very nature, is idiosyncratic. The corollary to the Oxford system of impersonal examiners, however, was a responsible, conscientious tutor. Balogh, who was known to be a good husband and father—something that was important to me—had been a Fellow of the college for fifteen years and had a good professional reputation. But if he doesn't keep his antics under control he is bound to make a hash of the tutorials, I thought.

At the end of the tutorial, to my great relief, he said to me, "I like Indians, Mehta. One day, we will get on like a house afire. But I think it's best that for your first term of economics you go to Paul Streeten. He's a sober chap—just right for you."

In the end, I was never taught by Balogh. We did, however, become good friends later in life, when he was Lord Balogh and, together with another Hungarian economist, Nicholas Kaldor, was celebrated for having been an economics adviser to Prime Minister Harold Wilson in the sixties.

❧

I DID several essays for Streeten, an Austrian refugee, who was the other economist at Balliol. I enjoyed doing economics with Streeten, an extremely poised, charming man, who had a much steadier hand on the tiller than Balogh did. It turned out that I had a considerable aptitude for the subject. But there was a rub: my readers literally fell asleep reading the economics material.

Employing competent, intelligent readers had always been difficult, but I soon discovered that at Oxford the problem was compounded, because ordinarily I could not engage fellow-students to be my readers. Not only was there no tradition at Oxford of combining work and study but students husbanded their time in pursuit of their own interests during the short, intensive university terms, and deserted the place during the long breaks in the academic year. I was therefore compelled to seek readers from outside the university, and that involved placing advertisements in local newspapers. After a long search, I was able to find only two good readers—Major Bottomley and a young divorcée, Elizabeth Lumsden, who had two small children. Neither of them was able to handle the economics material; for one thing, it was extremely mathematical, and, for another, understanding it depended a lot on graphs.

Streeten and I reached the same conclusion—that, since there was no way for me to work through graphs and mathematical formulas with readers, economics would remain my weak suit in P.P.E., and therefore I should perhaps read in some other school.

I felt crushed, for I had done several essays for Corbett in philosophy and was enjoying the subject hugely. But there seemed to be no alternative.

❧

I DECIDED to talk to John Bryson, and explore the possibility of reading in the Honours School of English Language and Literature. So few people read English at Balliol that he taught the whole syllabus himself. Bryson was sixty years old and had the reputation of being a real gentleman, who didn't like to exert himself; he was the only Fellow who had a personal servant. He was a bachelor, and so was in the tradition more of the old dons, who lived and breathed for college, than of modern dons, who tended to be married, to have families, and to live in houses outside college. He was also old-fashioned in that he did not feel the need to publish; he had not written a single book. I was told that he was a notable collector of Pre-Raphaelite drawings and also of some oils, and was said to be interested more in his art than in teaching. I wrote him a note and got an appointment.

I now knocked at his door. He invited me in and offered me a chocolate. I declined, worrying about the chocolate sticking to my new dental bridge, which had just been made for me by an Oxford dentist known for his "crown and bridge" practice.

I explained to Bryson my problem with economics and told him that I was thinking about switching to English.

"But why do you want to read English?" he said. "People should go to university to learn things they can't learn on their own. But anybody can enjoy literature. Did you know that until the twentieth century you couldn't read English literature at a university in England? It's really a school for women."

"But you read English."

"I was probably too lazy to read anything that required effort, and I knew from quite early days that I wouldn't have to work very hard for my keep. Lord David Cecil is a much better scholar than I, and he read Modern History." Lord David was the Goldsmiths' Professor of English Literature at Oxford.

"But I'm interested in writing."

"There are lots and lots of writers who didn't read English literature," Bryson said, and he added, with heavy irony, "I don't think Chaucer or Shakespeare read English. If you look at the authors on the syllabus of the English Honours School, I doubt if many of them read English. As you can imagine, English is not a school that has much of a following at Balliol. Since Jowett's day, Balliol undergraduates have been interested in becoming leaders of men."

I felt that any man would want to be a "leader of men." Also, I was leery of doing anything that might be thought feminine, and I was conscious of the fact that after Oxford I would have to earn my keep. At the same time, I didn't want to be blocked from changing over to English from P.P.E., and said as much to Bryson.

"I'll, of course, be glad to have you read English," Bryson said. "Would you like to write an essay on Milton for me for next week?" That's rushing things, I thought. I'll have to get permission from Corbett and Streeten to change over to English. "Term is flying by. If you want to read English, you should get started."

Bryson was right. As a graduate, I would be doing Schools in two years. (Undergraduates ordinarily did them in three years.) There was no time to lose. So I said that I would think about writing an essay on "Paradise Lost."

"I should mention to you that a third of the school's syllabus is concerned with learning and reading Anglo-Saxon. Many Americans find that a stumbling block to reading English at Oxford. They prefer to read English at Cambridge, where there isn't the scholarly emphasis on the Middle Ages that there is here."

I asked him how it was that Anglo-Saxon was such an important part of the English syllabus.

" 'Beowulf,' " he said. "The English attach great importance to 'Beowulf.' It's the national epic."

I began to wonder whether it would make any sense to spend my valuable Oxford time learning Anglo-Saxon just so that I could read "Beowulf." I began to despair. Every school I thought of reading seemed to present formidable hurdles. I also wondered whether there were any Braille books for learning Anglo-Saxon.

"Do you know of a blind person who has read English to whom I could talk first about Braille books in Anglo-Saxon?" I asked.

He said that he knew of one such person, a John Higgins (that is not his real name), and told me where to find him, adding, "He's been pestering me for years for pupils. He can't be all that good. I believe he got a Second."

HIGGINS lived in one small, shabby room—digs scarcely suitable even for most undergraduates. He spoke so softly, with so little energy in his voice, that I had to make an effort to hear him. "Anglo-Saxon in Braille, you ask?" he said. "I had trouble, but I managed. English literature? Don't read it. There's no future in it for blind people. You can see for yourself how I live. I haven't had a job since I came down."

He sounded so defeated that I thought he almost fitted the stereotype of the helpless blind man. I couldn't understand how an Oxford graduate with an Honours degree could be reduced to such a pitiable state, and asked him why he was having trouble finding a job.

"It's the system," he said. "No Oxford college would give me a job, because I got a Second. I've had to make ends meet as best

I can by privately tutoring undergraduates, and they are not easy to come by, because college tutors don't like to send pupils to private tutors. If a college tutor doesn't have the time or can't tutor in a particular subject, he'll farm the pupil out to a colleague in another college."

"Did you try to get a teaching position somewhere other than Oxford?"

"Once you lose your footing on the academic ladder, you're finished. Anyway, I could never have got on the ladder, because I got a Second. The galling thing is that I'm as intelligent as a lot of my contemporaries who are now teaching at top Oxford colleges. If I could see, I would have got a First. As you know, taking in information through one's ears and fingers is just not the same as taking it in through one's eyes."

"Have you thought of becoming a schoolmaster?"

"No. Schools require a schoolmaster to play games. I can do nothing but live on the fringes of Oxford and hope for an early death."

He seemed to be full of excuses, and it was hard to assess whether he was a victim of "the system" or of his own passivity. Whatever the case, the meeting cast a pall over my wish to read English.

Just about then, I was waking up to the fact that England, compared with America, was a poor country. In pubs and in rooms of friends, I was meeting poor scholars who had done brilliantly at Oxford or Cambridge but were now barely making a living by eking out any academic work they could get with odd jobs like washing plates in restaurants or working as publicans.

My new reader, Alastair McCann, was a case in point. He had responded to my advertisement in the *Oxford Mail,* and I had told him I could give him only part-time work as a reader, which paid very little—three and six an hour—and had asked him about himself. He had hemmed and hawed, as if the question gave him a great deal of trouble, and finally said that he had read Classics at Cambridge. It turned out that, in his late thirties, he was unemployed. It seemed to me extraordinary that someone with a Cambridge degree should be jobless. I asked him how he would make ends meet. "But I'll enjoy it," he said, evasively, coughing—he was a heavy smoker. I asked him in turn if he had thought of teaching, publishing, or proofreading, though as I did so I dreaded that he would look for a better job than reading to me, but he ruled out everything I mentioned. He couldn't be a schoolmaster, because he couldn't teach sports, and he didn't want to work in any office or be forced to join a union.

❧

WHILE I was in my room recovering from my encounter with Higgins, I heard thunderous footsteps in the staircase entry.

"Mehta!" Tylor said, bursting into my room. "I've been a Fellow of Balliol for twenty-seven years, and I have never heard of such ungentlemanly behavior as yours."

"What have I done, sir?" I asked, jumping up from my chair and standing at attention. I rapidly went through in my mind everything I had done since arriving at Oxford, but I couldn't imagine what he was talking about. Dr. Johnson's words flashed into my mind: "When a man knows he is to be hanged in a fortnight, it concentrates his mind wonderfully."

"I was just having lunch in the S.C.R.," Tylor was bellowing. "Everyone there seemed to think that you were reading his subject. Balogh said that you've done a tutorial with him. Both Streeten and Corbett think you're writing essays for them. Bryson thinks you're writing an essay for him. And the Master is sure that you're reading law with me. In the history of the college, we've never had a situation like this. People are admitted to read a given subject, and that's what they read. I made allowances for you, because you came from America, and now you've given me some of my most vexing moments. I can forgive anything but ungentlemanly behavior. How did you think that you could go and read English without informing the P.P.E. tutors?"

"I'm not writing an essay for Bryson—or, rather, I don't think I will be reading English literature," I said, feeling chastened.

"Why does Bryson think so, then?"

"I don't know. We discussed it, but . . ." I couldn't go on. The explanation seemed too involved.

"You simply cannot be at Oxford for most of the Michaelmas term and give that inane answer. You can't go and read English without getting the permission of your P.P.E. tutors, and you can't now go back to reading P.P.E. without making it up with Bryson. It's two o'clock now. By six o'clock, you must apologize to all the tutors that you have put out by your behavior, and settle with them what you can read." He stormed out.

I felt shattered. Never in my adult life had anyone spoken to me as Tylor had. But was there anything that I could have said to Tylor in my defense? It was true that technically I was still in the P.P.E. school. It was also true that, while I'd gone to Bryson in a spirit of exploration, I could have left him under the impression that I might—indeed, would—be reading English. I certainly had not forthrightly objected to writing the essay on Milton. In fact, through him I had gone to see Higgins. And the worst of it was that I was no closer to making up my mind about what I should read than I had been when I first got to Balliol. Maybe the accepted wisdom that blind people should read law was right, I thought. But read law with Tylor? I wished there were someone old and wise I could talk to—someone who knew the problems of the blind, and who could advise me about studying in England and about earning a livelihood in India or America. The natural person would have been my father. But he had such exalted ideas about my abilities and my future that he could not be of much help. Anyway, he was in America.

I staggered out of my room without knowing where I was going or what I should do. In the quadrangle, I was accosted by the medieval-history tutor, R. W. Southern. I had met him in passing once, and his book "The Making of the Middle Ages" had impressed me deeply. I had recently learned that he wrote it while he was in the hospital recovering from tuberculosis, with his wife and his friends carrying books back and forth for him. (According to one story, his bed had been pointed toward natural light, which was considered healthful but made reading difficult, and, moreover, he had had to hide his books from a particularly vigilant Sister Barker, and sometimes the collection of books under his blankets had reached from his ankles to his shoulders.)

"Mr. Mehta, you look troubled," he said. His voice had none of the broadcasting power of Tylor's, or the formidable presence of Corbett's, or the half-seductive, half-mocking tones of Balogh's, or the natural elegance of Bryson's. It was gentle, but was not meek, like Quinn's. On the contrary, it was remarkable for a steely determination.

I nodded. I was in a welter of emotion, and I feared that if I opened my mouth I would dissolve into tears. I finally got out, "It all has to do with what I'm to read at Balliol."

"You look like a historian to me," he said.

The idea took me aback. Although I'd taken a lot of courses at Pomona in philosophy and English literature, in the end I had majored in history, and I had thought for a while of getting a Ph.D. in the subject; in fact, I had been awarded a four-year fellowship at Harvard for that purpose. Yet once I was admitted to Oxford I had hoped to do something different. I don't know if I can cope with the demands of the Oxford history school, I thought. There will be a lot of reading, a lot of skimming. Just to write one essay, I may have to read in a dozen books. But then everything has its drawbacks. Now history suddenly seemed like a possible answer.

"I did history in America," I said.

"Maybe, then, you can do a D.Phil. in history. You should talk about that with Rodge." A. B. Rodger was the senior tutor

in history. "But I should say that people who do an undergraduate degree here get the most out of Oxford."

"Before I do anything, I have to apologize to the P.P.E. and
English tutors, and, yes, Tylor," I said, trying to hold back my
tears. "How will I explain to them my switching subjects for the
third time?"

"You can tell them that the historians will be glad to have
you read Modern History." He asked, with a preoccupied air, "By
the way, Mr. Mehta, which way was I going?"

"You were coming from the S.C.R., sir," I said.

"Then I've had my lunch," he said. He continued on his way.

❦

A. B. RODGER—Rodge, as he was known—was the son of
an Edinburgh minister. He had become a Fellow of the college
in 1924 (five years before Tylor and thirteen years before Southern), but, like Bryson, he had never published a book or an article.

"Yes, my boy," he said when I went to see him on the afternoon of my *crise*. "Sit down. Sit down." He himself remained
standing, jingling the coins in his pocket and whistling under
his breath.

I started to tell him about my conversation with Southern.

"Dick Southern has resolved your problem," he said. "Isn't
that right, my boy?"

I said that that was not quite right.

He resumed his jingling and whistling.

I told him as quickly as I could that I was wondering if I
should do a D.Phil. or an undergraduate degree.

He sat down and began to enumerate the pros and cons of
both. He said that a D.Phil. from Oxford was very useful, especially in America. Indeed, it had been specifically devised, early

in the century, for American Rhodes scholars. But I should be aware that postgraduate education at Oxford was very different from what it was at an American university. In America, postgraduate students were put through a lot of course work, the purpose of which was to make them into college teachers. Graduate schools there were like professional schools. At Oxford, in contrast, it was assumed that if one wanted to teach at a university one got trained for it as an undergraduate. In fact, most dons had just read in an Honours School, obtained a First, got themselves elected Fellow and Tutor, and settled down to teaching, as he had. The reason an English university could function that way was that the work done by boys in English schools was of a much higher standard than that done in comparable American schools; English schoolboys coming up to Oxford knew more about their subjects than did Americans who arrived with college degrees. The truth was that postgraduate education was simply not taken seriously at Oxford. There was no specific program or provision for it. Students were just left alone to get on with their research and theses. They had to satisfy no requirements—had no examination save for the defense of the thesis. And writing a D.Phil. thesis was just like writing a book. Since I had written a book, I was, no doubt, used to doing a sustained piece of work, and therefore the writing of a thesis shouldn't present me with a problem. But he couldn't emphasize strongly enough that anyone doing a postgraduate degree at Oxford plowed a lonely furrow. Consequently, he, like Southern, would advise me to do a second undergraduate degree. That way, I would get the most out of Oxford. And many people who arrived at Oxford with foreign degrees—from America, Australia, India—did exactly that. It was the best way of entering the stream of Oxford education and English life. In fact, the great thing about an Oxford undergraduate education was that one learned as much from one's contemporaries as one did from one's tutors.

"My boy, let me have your answer. Will you read Modern History or do a D.Phil.?" he demanded, getting up from his chair.

"Do you want to know that right now?" I asked.

"Right now, my boy."

He redoubled his whistling and the jingling of his coins while marching around the room. There was something military in his manner. (He had fought in both wars and had been wounded several times.) "Yes, my boy?"

A D. Phil. will give me a leg up in the American academic world, I thought. That will enable me to teach at a university and have a certain amount of security and comfort. It seemed like a sensible route. But it didn't hold the promise of making me an Oxford man in the way that Southern was, and Rodge and Tylor were.

"The heart of Oxford is the tutorial system. And that's only for undergraduates, my boy," he said. Jingle, jingle.

He was right. If I was only going to do research in history and write a book, there was no need for me to be at Oxford. I could do that anywhere.

Jingle, jingle.

I'd been speaking English for only seven years, and I wrote it like a foreigner, without an innate sense of language or style. What could be better training for thinking and writing than being required to come up with two essays every week and having them scrutinized by the likes of Southern—or, come to that, Rodge, who might not have a reputation outside Oxford but had a wonderfully concise way of putting things? Still, I wavered.

"Which is it to be—Dr. Mehta or Mr. Mehta?" he asked.

That settled the question, for the sound of "Dr. Mehta" sent shudders through me. That's my father's name, my father's title, I thought. What am I, and what is he? He is Hyperion to little more than a satyr.

"I'll read Modern History," I said.

"Then, my boy, you'll be a real Oxford man," he said. "I thought you were a sensible chap."

By six o'clock that evening, I had called on Corbett, Balogh, Streeten, and Bryson, and made my apologies. They were extremely friendly and wished me well—as, indeed, did Tylor, my last port of call.

❦

MY first essay for Southern, which I submitted more than halfway through the Michaelmas term, was about the Saxons in England in the sixth century. I had spent the whole past week reading or consulting half a dozen books and taking notes on them, and had stayed up half the night outlining in my head and typing out the essay. (Later, I began dictating my essays, because that way I could not only revise the text but also consult and quote sources.)

Southern had decided to tutor me on my own (generally, history pupils were taken in pairs), and since I wasn't able to read my essay to him he read it to himself. At one point, he read a sentence aloud. The experience of hearing my words read aloud by one of the leading medievalists in the world was devastating. The sentence sounded like gobbledygook, and I feared that the whole essay was no better.

"It's dreadful," I said.

He laughed, but in a kindly way. "I don't like 'motivation' in the sentence. It sounds like jargon. And don't you think it's jarring to come upon it in a discussion of the sixth century?"

"What about 'impulse'?" I asked.

"Yes, better," he said.

He's just on the third page, I thought. He hasn't got even halfway through the essay. He's not going to read on. Why should he? It must be tedious—boring for him to read my feeble effort to explain something that he knows so well. But he resumed reading.

Southern finally put down the result of my week's labor and said, distantly, "Yes." Then, fastening on one seemingly minor point in the essay, he asked me if I was right in assuming, as I had, that between half a million and a million Saxons had crossed over to England. How many ships did I think that such a host would need for transportation? Where did I suppose that the invaders would get the timber to build the ships? How long did I imagine that it would take them to build each ship? How long did I think the stretch of water was that they had to cross? How much did I think was the rate of increase in the Saxon population once they had settled in Britain? What would I estimate was the total population of Britain at that time?

I tried to address his questions. Each time, he easily disposed of my answers by referring me to a source at hand; his large desk was stacked with tomes. He would reach for a book and read aloud a passage or describe a picture, always in the spirit of sharing information rather than of correcting me. He knew not only where each book was but also where anything in a particular book was to be found.

When the tutorial was over, he stood up and opened the door for me. As I was leaving, he said, "By the way, you don't have to exhibit your reading in your essay. It should just be a point of departure."

God, even the facts are gratuitous, I thought. How am I to write my next essay? "I'd like to improve my writing," I said.

"I think you might find reading the 'Oxford Book of English Prose' a help," he said.

I left my first history tutorial feeling at once depressed at having been shown up as an ignoramus and exhilarated at being on the threshold of a new order of study. I reflected that history was not just facts to be memorized—names, dates, battles—but a matter for judgment, speculation, and imagination. It was a bit like doing detective work, or marshalling evidence in a court-room, or going deep-sea fishing. History tutorials will be very stimulating, but they will also require a lot of slogging work, I thought.

In the quadrangle, I ran into Tom Braun and told him about my tutorial with Southern. "If all my tutorials are like that, I'm not going to have much leisure to enjoy Oxford," I said.

"You look like a nice chap to me," he said. "You don't look to me like one of these awful troglodytes, whom all good chaps shun much as Christians must have shunned Lazarus."

"Oh, Tom, for God's sake!" I said.

He became sympathetic. "Once you get the hang of writing essays, you'll be able to toss them off. Maurice Keen is a top medieval historian in the making, and I can't say that I've ever seen him laboring over anything very long or hard. In fact, I just saw him in the Buttery with a large glass of whisky in his hand."

"But it's not twelve yet," I said.

"Actually, he looked as if he'd just got up. No doubt he has whisky to start the day. That's what makes him such a good historian."

In subsequent weeks, I handed Southern essays on the follow-ing questions: "The Character and Extent of Anglo-Saxon Influ-ences on the Continent in the Eighth Century"; "The Aims of St. Dunstan, St. Ethelwold, and St. Oswald"; "How Far Do the Existing Anglo-Saxon Laws Help in Forming a Picture of the Classes in Society and Their Changing Relations Between ca.600 and 1066?"; "Which of the Sources Give Us the Best Picture of Alfred?"; "Compare the Position of the King in English Society in the Reigns of Edgar, Canute, and Edward the Confessor"; "The Prelude to an Inevitable Collapse—Can This View of Edward the

Confessor's Reign Be Defended?"; and "Does the Reign of Stephen Show That the Baronage Had No Political Aim Beyond Their Individual Personal Advantage?" To make up for the lost time, I was doing two essays a week for him.

I would arrive at Southern's room for a tutorial, and he would have his nose in a book. He would look up and say, "Oh, Mr. Mehta. Do come in." After I sat down, he would ask "Have you got an essay?" and then sound almost surprised that I did have one. Sometimes during a tutorial, Sir Maurice Powicke, who was the *éminence grise* of Medieval History, a diminutive man in his late seventies, would stick his head in, and, in his rather quiet voice, would go through some elaborate apology to the effect that he couldn't accept Dick's offer to take him for a drive, because the Dean, who had a larger and more powerful car, had also offered to take him for a drive the same afternoon.

Southern, like some of the Anglo-Saxon saints he introduced me to, was gentle and dedicated to learning. Although I felt that I was learning a lot and was writing better, I grew restive about the Oxford history school, especially the study of the so-called Dark Ages. My grasp of Latin was too weak for me to appreciate the original documents. In any case, the period was too remote, the documentation too fragmentary, the reading material too intractable to get me passionately involved, for all Southern's luminous intelligence. In part because of Southern's stature among the Balliol history tutors, Medieval History had an important place in the study of British history. And the study of British history formed the spinal column of the Modern History school, although only three out of ten examination papers were strictly concerned with it. Not only were we required to know British history continuously from the fifth century to the First World War but many of the optional papers we could offer were directly or indirectly connected with it. (Two of the examination papers were in our assigned "special subject," and the only special subject that dealt with India was "Great Britain and India in the Age of Warren Hastings.") I had no trouble imagining the rationale for this concentration on British history: we were at an English university; much of the syllabus was based on the study of documents, and most of the documents that were available and accessible were in English or in related languages; the methods and tools we acquired in our study of Britain could easily be applied to the study of any other country; and so on. Yet I found the emphasis on British history oppressive. Had my mother country and my adopted country fought for their independence only to have me knuckle under to British history, I wondered.

I so venerated Southern that I was tongue-tied in his presence, but when I had done half a dozen tutorials with him I aired my reservations to him, going as far as to say that I had doubts about continuing in the history school. "Maybe I should do the D.Phil. after all," I said.

"Studying at Oxford is rather like joining the church," he said distantly, in the manner of a priest talking to a parishioner. "You know that the university has been here for centuries and that countless generations of undergraduates have benefitted from studying here. You have to take it on faith that since the system worked for them it will work for you."

His simple remark made me remember a few lines from Browning:

> All we have gained then by our unbelief
> Is a life of doubt diversified by faith,
> For one of faith diversified by doubt:
> We called the chess-board white—we call it black.

IV

THE
SWEETER
BANQUET
OF THE MIND

R OBERT OAKESHOTT, A THIRD-YEAR GREATS MAN, WAS
one of the most engaging men at the college. He was
quixotic, funny, serious, and a bundle of class contradictions. Outwardly, he had all the trappings of an establishment figure, if a rather eccentric one. His father, a
Balliol man who had also read Greats, had been the

headmaster of a top public school, Winchester College, and was now the Rector of Lincoln College at Oxford. Robert had gone to Tonbridge, the school where his father was reared, and, like many public-school men, he moved around with a gang so close-knit that its members could almost have passed for a mythical animal. They had a sort of group personality, as if each were always in need of an audience; it was hard to imagine any one of them talking to just one person. All the members of the gang were public-school men who came from professional or upper-class backgrounds. They were known for strutting about—for constantly getting in and out of taxis, for hard drinking, for exchanging jokes and witticisms in loud voices. Indeed, they conducted themselves as if they belonged to the governing class, and the place were part of their inheritance—as if the majority of undergraduates, who were non-public-school men and were being supported at Oxford on state subsidies, were interlopers. The public-school men seemed so confident of their class and position that some of them paid no attention to their dress. Robert was one of the scruffiest dressers in college, and it was said that he often didn't brush his teeth for weeks at a time. But his clothes did not disguise a very proper school voice or a rather ironic manner. I was extremely intimidated in his presence until his Hungarian-revolution caper, which led me to discover that he had another dimension. As he later told the story, the day he heard that a revolution had broken out in Hungary he had an essay due for Russell Meiggs, his Ancient History tutor, but he couldn't think of anything to say. So he decided to skip the tutorial and try to go to Hungary instead, and see the exciting events for himself. But how was he to pay his way? He came up with the stratagem of writing a newspaper article, although he had never done any journalism. He went across to the porter's lodge and put through a call to the *Observer*, the most intellectual of the Sunday papers. He asked to speak to David Astor, the editor, and explained to Astor's secretary that he was an undergraduate at Balliol (Astor was a Balliol man) and that he knew Astor's niece (he had met her at a students' international conference). He said that he wanted to go to Hungary and write a piece about the revolution for the *Observer*. Could the *Observer* provide him with two airplane tickets to go there? He felt sure that Astor would like the Hungarian revolution to have "the benefit of the fair wind from Balliol." Astor's secretary said that Mr. Astor was in a meeting but she would get back to him. A little while later, she rang back and said that the *Observer* was sending him the two tickets, and that Mr. Astor looked forward to reading whatever Oakeshott wrote.

One ticket was, of course, for Robert himself, but he hadn't stopped to think who should use the other ticket, because he knew that there would be no shortage of claimants for it in his gang. He put the air ticket up to the gang in a game of chance with matchsticks. (Robert was famous for all kinds of boyish games that involved nothing more costly than a matchbox.) The person who drew the broken matchstick was to be his companion on the trip to Hungary. Ian Rankin, who was at Christ Church, drew the broken matchstick.

The next morning, the gang gave Robert and Ian a big send-off in the Buttery, and the two flew to Vienna. They spent the evening there, drinking with Tatyana Orlov, who had been at Oxford with them, and, as it happened, had gone to Vienna to recover from unrequited love for Ian. That night, Robert and Ian hitched a ride into Hungary. In Budapest, they got the news that the Russians were coming in tanks, and Robert helped to drive some Hungarians to freedom. He never wrote the newspaper article, but he got a lot of publicity for the revolutionary cause and helped to establish a Balliol Hungarian Refugee Fund.

Both Hungary and Suez were preoccupations of many undergraduates in the Michaelmas term of my first year. Everywhere, undergraduates were going at it hammer and tongs over the latest reports in the newspapers: the R.A.F. bombing of military targets in Egypt; Anthony Eden's speech on the radio defending the

British action; Aneurin Bevan's speech in Trafalgar Square against the Suez action; the ceasefire, and the agreement of Israel to withdraw from Egypt. *Mutatis mutandis,* Hungary. For a lot of left-wing undergraduates, Suez was a disgraceful, not to say criminal, attempt to revive colonialism. Hungary, however, was something they preferred not to talk about. Any who were forced to express an opinion tried to make the event seem different from what it was, or defended it, or candidly agonized over it: How could the Russians have done it? Quite a few of these left-wing undergraduates trundled along as if Hungary had changed nothing, and some argued that there was nothing shocking about the event. They continued to talk about nationalizing the means of production as a panacea for social ills everywhere. It was a rare left-wing undergraduate who saw Hungary as a brutal act, in line with other brutal acts of the Soviet Union. The right took the view that in Suez the British had been betrayed by the Americans, because Washington had stopped Britain and France from finishing the job, and that Hungary was a terrible thing—the smashing of a country by brute force. They were sure that the use of brute force would perpetuate the Soviet empire and the Soviet menace for centuries. (In retrospect, neither of the views seems very perceptive: Suez now seems like an Anglo-French attempt to stop the Middle Eastern countries from functioning with complete independence; and, of course, the use of brute force in Hungary did not save the Soviet empire from disintegration.) Also, the Cold War was very much in the air. The most vocal people were generally those who took the view that there was no need to have the Cold War—that, on the one hand, the "socialist powers" were unduly suspicious of the West, and, on the other, Churchill and Dulles, the Cold Warriors, were unnecessarily trying to force the world into an aggressive campaign against the socialist powers. The truth was, however, that neither the left nor the right, for all their heat and invective, were breaking heads over serious issues, for the fifties at Oxford, as elsewhere, were a period of decorum. Both dons and undergraduates wore ties and tweed jackets. In most respects, that period—unlike the twenties or the thirties—had no distinctive character that we were aware of. Perhaps because the forties had been split down the middle by the Second World War, it didn't occur to most people in the fifties that a decade could have a character. Insofar as we perceived the fifties as a decade at all, it seemed like a "between" period. We all had a feeling that something was likely to change, but none of us had any definite idea about what that change might be.

In postwar Oxford, no fewer than seventy per cent of the undergraduates were supported by state scholarships, thanks to the Labour Government's socialist reforms. Still, many of us, whatever the source of our support, equipped ourselves like gentlemen—that is to say, without handling money very much. In fact, during term time we all lived a charmed life, in the town as in the college—that of people living on credit, who don't expect the day of reckoning ever to catch up with them. In addition to buying tins of biscuits, packets of coffee, college stationery, bottles of wine, and other necessities from the Buttery, we bought books from Blackwell's, shoes from Ducker & Son, clothes from Shepherd & Woodward—all on credit. Large bank overdrafts were routine. In term, we didn't pay a single bill; we carried money only for going to pubs.

At Balliol, the fifties were a particularly good intellectual period, in the sense that many people got good results in Schools and swept up university prizes. Indeed, the college was the flagship of the university in classics, and possibly in P.P.E. and in Modern History, too, although in those two schools it had competition from Magdalen. As always, the fate of a college rested with the schoolmasters who decided where their brighter boys should go; at that particular time, their choice, by and large, was Balliol.

Since the time was the fifties, before the sexual revolution, we lived, to all intents and purposes, in a male society. We drank in the Buttery with men. We took our meals in hall with men. We dropped in to one another's rooms for coffee and tea. We shone in conversation, performed dazzling intellectual feats, set off fireworks of wit—all for the benefit of men. When we saw women, they seemed like creatures from another planet.

The ideal Oxford man of the fifties not only was brilliant but also did well at everything effortlessly and with a certain panache. Very few people could live up to that ideal. Perhaps as a consequence, it took hold of people in different ways. Tom Braun, who became a fast friend of mine, was a good example. One could hardly step out into the main quadrangle without encountering him. He had an idiosyncratic way of standing and walking—holding his head well forward. He definitely let it be known that he was repelled by many of his Greats contemporaries, who, though brilliant, were on the dour side and, in his phrase, lived the lives of troglodytes. (I myself had more in common with his studious Greats contemporaries than with him.) He reacted to them by becoming increasingly flippant and eccentric. The Oxford ideal of panache had apparently gone straight to his head, for he seemed to find it humiliating to be seen doing any work at all. He seemed to be always hanging around the Junior Common Room looking for amusing company, and it was hard not to be detained by him in conversation. No one could ring more changes on a theme than he could, and the astounding thing was that he was seldom boring, even when he was being his most obsessive self, and banging on about, say, the evils of the proposed road through Christ Church Meadow as a means of relieving traffic congestion on High Street. He could talk about the scheme endlessly, seeing in it an example of the villainous behavior of politicians, the ravages of industrialism, man's feckless nature, the defilement of natural beauty, the town's war on the gown, and a hundred other things, until it seemed the most important issue of the day. He was on show in the J.C.R. by lunchtime, and at twelve or one or two at night one could still find him wandering about from staircase to staircase, making witty remarks and telling stories. (He must have done a lot of slogging work secretly, even later at night, and slept through mornings without giving a thought to lectures, for he got a very good First, with high marks on many of his papers, in Greats and went on to become a Fellow and Tutor in Ancient History at Merton.)

✿

TOWARD the end of my first term, Ralph Spence came up to Jasper and me in hall and asked us to a party in his room. In America, I would have shunned a college party. The mention of a party would have conjured up in my mind men with good looks dancing with girls wearing corsages or fraternity pins. There had been no way that I could compete in that setting—the battle was lost before it started. I used to console myself with the thought that being different was better than being conventional. But what was valued at an Oxford party was conversation and wit—the play of the mind. People at Oxford cultivated their eccentricities; being different was regarded as a hallmark of strong character. In any event, I was flattered to be taken notice of by Ralph, because, among other things, he was a second-year historian who had gone to Rugby, a public school in the first rank. At the same time, I was intimidated by the invitation from an establishment chap. Ralph, however, was more outgoing and friendly than many public-school boys, and I also took heart from the fact that Jasper, who could hold his own with anyone conversationally, would be there, and that no one would be dancing. (I had once asked Jasper if people danced at Oxford parties, and he had said cryptically, "Intellectuals don't dance.")

When I arrived at the party, I found that some of the second- and third-year men came with women on their arms. I didn't know any of the women. I joined a little group of men around Roderick Allison, a Greats man in his second year who was from

Manchester Grammar, the top grammar school. (Grammar schools, unlike public schools, were supported by the state.) "One day, a German undergraduate was taking some people around Oxford," Roderick was telling the group. "In High Street, he pointed to Oriel College and said, *'Das ist Worcester College.'* A passer-by stopped and said, 'Excuse me, but this is Oriel.' To which the German replied, 'Vot is that to me? I am a Balliol man.' "

There was general laughter. Many in the group, no doubt made edgy by the presence of women, appeared to relax, as if they were reassured at being reminded of the "effortless superiority" of Balliol men. Tom Braun came over to the group. "Is it true that in India a poor beggar who's a Brahman can lord it over a rich man who's not a Brahman?" he asked me.

"A Brahman does belong to the highest caste," I said. "But what do you have in mind?"

"Well, just imagine if the porter at the lodge were a Brahman—he could walk into the Master's lodgings and order the Master to clean his boots!" There was general laughter.

"It's not that simple," I said. "Poor people in India can't order anyone around."

"But what a wonderful society, where the shopkeeper caste can be rich and Brahmans poor," Tom said, and he added, a little mischievously, "I'm sure you're a Brahman."

"I'm not," I said reluctantly. So important were the subtlest class distinctions that I felt sure the group I was standing in would think less of me for not being a Brahman. I drew myself up proudly and added, "I belong to the Kshatriya caste, the caste of princes and rulers." That sounded pretentious even to my ears, but I told myself that I was in England, where everyone gave himself airs.

"I wish I were a prince, like you," Tom said, a little ironically.

I felt deflated. "Tom, you know perfectly well that that's not what I said!" I cried.

"I wish we had the Indian caste system here, instead of our class system, with the public-school chaps and the débutantes and the Queen," Tom said.

"You'd complain bitterly if we had any such thing here, Tom," Jasper said.

Although Tom himself was not of English parentage (his parents were German), and was not your ordinary upper-class type (he was a conscientious objector, and had fulfilled the requirement for National Service by serving in the Friends' Ambulance Unit), he was preoccupied with the trappings of the English upper class, and with upper-class speech. He was always catching me out for saying "*Au*gustine" instead of "Au*gu*stine," or "K*a*nt" instead of "K*e*nt," or for using the bourgeois word "bathroom" instead of the upper-crust word "lavatory." In the beginning, I argued with him that there could be no one correct English pronunciation of the names of a Latin father and a German philosopher, and that I sometimes called a lavatory a bathroom because the latter was a literal translation of the Hindi word. But I soon came to rely on Tom as an authority on everything English—except, perhaps, the Oxford accent. (I privately dismissed that as a myth, for Balliol itself was a babel of accents.)

I got myself another drink and joined another group. "What's your college?" I asked a woman standing next to me.

"St. Hugh's." She aspirated "Hugh's" so that it sounded almost like a whistle.

My heart skipped a beat. She's just the kind of well-bred English girl I knew I would meet at Oxford, I thought.

"What a splendid white dress you have on, Jane!" Ralph said, coming over to her.

So that's her name, I thought. At Oxford, no one seems to bother with introductions—it's as if we were all members of a family. Maybe I can walk her back to her college at the end of the party.

"There are really only two classes—U and non-U—and you can tell which class a person comes from by his speech," Jane was saying in response to someone else's remark. In England, class was always in the air.

Everyone joined in the discussion. People started producing whole sentences as examples of U and non-U speech. "They've a very nice house" was U; "They have a lovely home" was non-U. "I'm going to have my bath" was U; "I'm going to take my bath" was non-U. "Have some more tea?" was U; "How is your cup?" was non-U. "Are we going to change?" was U; "Shall we wear evening dress?" was non-U. "I was sick on the boat" was U; "I was ill on the boat" was non-U. The examples made my head whirl. The whole business sounded nonsensical, but I felt the pain of being excluded—excluded from Jane's friendship, from, as Rodge had put it, "the stream of Oxford education and English life" itself. I felt as if I were being buffeted in a storm at sea and would never develop my sea legs.

I turned my full attention to a test that Jane was giving on U and non-U words. I was too shy to speak up, but I kept a mental score. My spirits improved, for I correctly identified all the U words: "bike" for "bicycle," "lunch" (meal in the middle of the day) for "dinner," "vegetables" for "greens," "mad" for "mental," "lavatory paper" for "toilet paper," "rich" for "wealthy," "false teeth" for "dentures," "spectacles" for "glasses," "telegram" for "wire." I thought that I was passing the test with flying colors. Then someone brought up "England," and everyone agreed that "England" was U and "Britain" non-U.

" 'England' and 'Britain' mean different things," I protested, coming out of my shell.

"Yes, they do," Jane said. "But a U Englishman would know instinctively that 'England' is the preferred usage. He would not, in any case, say 'Britain' but, rather, 'Great Britain' or 'United Kingdom.' "

I felt depressed again.

"What about 'Scotch' or 'Scottish'?" Roderick asked, joining us.

" 'Scottish,' " Bob Walters said. Like Roderick, he was a second-year Greats man.

"Wrong," said Roderick. "It's 'Scotch.' "

"That's a tricky one, but 'Scotch' is right," Jane said.

Roderick preened himself for coming up with a tricky example and for scoring over Bob. Boys from Manchester Grammar School liked to score over boys from lesser grammar schools, and Bob was from Bristol Grammar School, a notch below Manchester.

" 'Sweet' or 'pudding'?" Jane asked, pressing on with the game.

" 'Sweet,' " said Bob and Roderick in unison.

" 'Sweet,' " I chimed in.

"Wrong," said Jane.

"But 'pudding' is a specific thing," Roderick objected. "It wouldn't do to call compote a pudding."

"But 'pudding' is right," Jane said. "I've proved my point—that a non-U speaker can never become a U speaker. One word or phrase will always betray him, brand him an impostor. You see, U speakers never make mistakes." She took fiendish delight in knowing what was right, as if she had been born with U speech and everyone else present had only acquired it. She must be from Roedean School or from Cheltenham Ladies' College, I thought. (They were the two top public schools for girls.) I felt so intimidated that I had difficulty controlling my trembling.

"Balderdash!" Jasper said, joining the group with a drink in his hand. His voice never failed to sound dramatic. "It's fashionable for a lot of U speakers to use non-U words to give their speech color or a joky flavor. Anyway, all these examples are straight out of 'Noblesse Oblige.' So, in a sense, it's nothing more than the view of Nancy Mitford and her sources of what is U and what is non-U."

His pronunciamento stunned everyone into silence, as if he'd spoken ex cathedra; the citation of chapter and verse seemed to deflate the whole business of U and non-U speakers. But I wasn't totally reassured, for, although Jasper spoke with a certain elegance and polish, a certain natural assurance and authority, he wasn't upper crust. He had gone to a public school, but it was not one of the top rank. His parents had not been in a position to pay for his public-school education, so he had been supported by a scholarship. Indeed, he came from a working-class area of Southeast London, and during one school vacation he had worked as a porter in Waterloo Station. Perhaps as a consequence, he had a touch of Cockney accent, which gave his speech a slightly raffish quality. But I'm sure that Jasper's vocabulary is pure U, I thought, Mine certainly is not. I'm well aware that my pronunciation is non-U. I can no more change my Indian voice and American experience than a leopard can change its spots, and Jane knows that.

It was getting near eight o'clock, the hour when women had to be out of Balliol and inside the gates of their own colleges. The thought of taking Jane home and entering her college made me feel shy. I was reminded of "Alice in Wonderland," in which a great Oxford experience is represented by Alice's vain attempts get into various gardens—either she's too big or too small or she can't find the key.

All around me, people were smoking, making the air stuffy and miasmic. I felt tired. I began fretting that Jane thought I was a blank-faced, non-U bore, and that she would find someone else to take her home from the party.

I gulped down my drink—a big glass of gin-and-tonic. I thought that I had never liked anything as much as its distinctive juniper smell and its bittersweet taste, which seemed to be only accentuated by the sparkle of the tonic water.

The room started thinning out as people flocked to the bedroom to collect their coats. (Ralph was one of a few lucky Balliol undergraduates who had separate little bedrooms.) Boldly, I walked over to the bedroom door and maneuvered myself next to Jane, who was waiting to collect her coat. I tried to gather my courage to ask if I might take her home. As I hesitated, I suddenly wondered how I would get back from St. Hugh's by myself. Just then, I heard Murray Forsyth, a friend who was a freshman and a historian, ask Mary, another St. Hugh's girl, if he might see her home. I'll walk back with Murray, I thought.

"I'll take you home, Jane," Ralph said.

Within moments, the rooms were practically empty. All the men who I imagined were desirable to women as friends and escorts were gone.

I had looked forward to my first Oxford party with as much excitement as I had felt before my first tutorials. But I had failed miserably. All the accumulated difficulties of my Oxford life, among them the damp climate, the poor living conditions, the bad food, the frustration of not being able to go everywhere by myself, the problem of finding good readers, the strain of work, the worry over money, the foreign sensation of the new dental bridge, the constant struggle to find my footing on the English class ladder, the adjustment to a whole new country—all these things, which until now had been held in check by the spell of being in a legendary place, suddenly overwhelmed me. I wanted to go to bed, to be alone.

I was almost paralyzed with drink. A neophyte to alcohol, I had not yet mastered the difference between table wine and sherry, sherry and gin. In fact, I'd been knocking back gin-and-tonics as if I were drinking plain tonic water. I decided to leave. So, it seemed, did the other people left behind at the party—Jasper, Bob Walters, and someone whose voice I now had difficulty identifying.

The four of us went into Ralph's bedroom to get our coats. As we were picking them up from the bed, we heard a clink and rattle from under the bedclothes.

"Oho! What lies here in the master's absence?" Jasper cried out.

Bob yanked off the bedclothes. In the depression of the mattress were four unopened bottles of gin.

"He must have hidden the leftover booze, so that we wouldn't find it and drink it up," Bob said.

"Let's show him!" the man with the hard-to-place voice said thickly.

I didn't quite catch the meaning. The floor was now rising and falling like a wave, now bouncing like the end of a seesaw. The bed and the bedside chair seemed to lean and slant and turn. The walls themselves seemed about to be wrenched out of their moorings. My head spun like a top.

"Show what? Show—show him to what?" I asked, trying to get my tongue around the words.

"Show him that he can't hide booze and get away with it," Bob said.

In my mental haze, I thought for a moment that he was suggesting that we make away with the bottles. "We can't—can't steal his gin," I said.

"Who suggested such a thing?" Jasper said, with some exasperation.

"Come on, let's drink up the gin and leave the empties in his bed and cover them up, just the way he left them," the mysterious man said.

At Oxford, rooms were not locked. Bottles of liquor—and, indeed, everything else—were left out in the open. It was the fact that Ralph had wanted to hide the bottles from us that goaded us on.

As one man, we four unscrewed the tops of the bottles and put them to our mouths. There was a lot of confused talking and laughing. We weaved and stumbled around the room, singing sixteenth- and seventeenth-century tavern songs with lewd lyrics.

(To give a little life to my room, I had recently acquired a combination gramophone and radio, and one of my few records was these tavern songs, sung by Alfred Deller and the Deller Consort. I had played it often for my friends who dropped in on me for coffee after lunch or dinner. The lyrics of the catches and glees, rendered in tenor and countertenor voices, were very easy to memorize, and the record had become a favorite among my friends.) We began singing:

> Man is for the woman made
> And woman for the man.
>
> As the spur is to the jade,
> As the scabbard for the blade,
> As for digging is the spade,
> As for liquor is the can,
>
> So man is for the woman made,
> And woman for the man.

Then someone started us on another song:

> Wine does wonders every day,
> Makes the heavy light and gay,
> Throws off all their melancholy,
> Makes the wisest go astray,
> And the busy toy and play,
> And the poor and needy jolly.

Even before we had finished this, we were on to another song:

> Once, twice, thrice, I Julia tried,
> The scornful puss as oft denied,
> And since I can no better thrive,
> I'll cringe to ne'er a bitch alive.

> So kiss my Arse, disdainful sow!
> Good claret is my mistress now.

And this trailed off into still another song:

> Such a lass, kind friend, and drinking
> Give me, great Jove, and damn the thinking.

At some point, Ralph and some other friends returned from seeing the women to their colleges. I went right around the room shaking everyone's hand and saying, "I love the world!" My conduct seemed to provoke general mirth, which I was at a loss to understand.

Then a bottle was passed around like the loving cup at the Freshman Dinner. I remember bowing a lot to my neighbors and repeatedly saying to Ralph, "You can't play go-hide-and-seek, Ralph! You just can't do that with the bottles, Ralph."

Perhaps the fact that drink tastes good and makes one feel good is a justification in itself for drinking—at least, for ordinary social drinking. Some drinking may even be part of the process of growing up. A university is a place for experiencing things—however foolish they may be. Indeed, there may be no better place than a university for excesses. Anyway, wherever there are highly intelligent young people living in a community there will probably be a certain amount of drinking and antics, if for no other reason than to oil the wheels of friendship. Besides, we at Oxford were certainly under intense intellectual pressure, and drink provided a sort of refuge from it. Or, at least, that's the best explanation or apology I can offer for our conduct.

I went around the room again, shaking everyone's hand and saying in the most English voice I could summon, "You are a splendid bloke!"

All at once, I felt something rising inside me, as if I were a volcano about to explode. I shot out of Ralph's room, didn't so much run down as drop down the stairs, almost a flight at a time, and reached my own staircase and my room in a flash.

The room was cold and clammy. I thought of lighting the fire and changing and getting into bed, but my limbs suddenly felt limp, as if I'd lost control over them. I'll lie down just for a moment and then get into my pajamas, I thought, and threw myself on the bed face down. I made a feeble attempt to get under the bedclothes, but I was no more capable of doing so than a jellyfish. It was freezing. I rolled over to the far side of the bed and pulled the bedclothes over me as best I could.

I was wrapped up, mummy fashion, my face mercifully shrouded. I was the toast of the freshman class. I was walking with Jane, hand in hand. "I have an Englishwoman as a friend!" The voice wouldn't come out. I screamed—still the voice wouldn't come out. *You get tangled up with a forungy, and you're finished. You'll never be Prime Minister.* The towpath seemed to go on and on. I slipped, and fell into a swimming pool. Whichever way I pulled the towel, it felt wet and viscid. I drew up my legs, coiled and folded myself as small as possible, but there was no dry patch. The river overflowed and inundated its banks, drenching me in its turbid waters.

I woke with a splitting headache. The blankets and mattress were soaked right through. I felt that I'd be soiled for the rest of my life. I would certainly be sent down in disgrace, be snubbed everywhere—be a pariah.

I looked at my watch and realized that my scout, George, was due soon, to draw the curtain and light the fire. I didn't know how I would face him. I dragged myself out of bed. Slowly, I peeled off my clothes and got into my dressing gown. Then, towel over arm and soap in hand, and with my head bowed, I walked to the showers in the back quadrangle, feeling like a condemned man. I stood under the hot shower for what must have been forty-five minutes, scrubbing and re-scrubbing, but still I fancied that I smelled stale gin from every pore of my body. Dejectedly, I started back to my room.

I practically fainted when I met George on the way. He hurried past me, saying, "You didn't sleep in your bed last night, sir." I had imagined that he had long since gone to hall and was busy serving breakfast.

As I was going into Staircase XVI, Jasper was coming out. "You look green," he said. He, too, rushed past me.

I staggered into my room, and for a moment I thought that, by mistake, I had wandered into someone else's. It smelled fresh, and the bed—mattress and all—had been changed. The clothes of the evening before were gone (George always saw to it that my laundry and dry cleaning were sent out), and clean clothes were ready for me.

GEORGE never referred to my gin binge (from the day of the party to this moment, I've scarcely been able to drink gin) or to the mess he had to clean up. He did that job as he performed all his scouty duties—silently, discreetly, cheerfully. I don't remember hearing him complain once about anything. College was his life, and he was devoted to his undergraduates as a pastor is to his parishioners.

Once, I asked George, who was exactly twice my age, about his family.

"I have a wife and children, sir," he said.

"How many children?" I asked.

"A lot, sir. And *a lot* of them are girls." He said that as if "a lot" were a number, like nine or eleven, and as if somehow the number were larger when it was applied to girls than when it was applied to boys.

"I'm sure they all have lovely names," I said, rather stupidly, wanting to prolong the conversation but not knowing quite how.

"All the girls' names begin with 'J,' sir," he said.

"Why is that?" I asked. "Do you have a particular liking for 'J' names?"

"Can't say I do, sir," he said. "Mrs. and I think that when they go courtin' it'll be easier that way. They'll all be just 'Miss J. Gibbons.' "

Why that would be easier he didn't make clear.

Unlike many scouts, George was not very chatty with his undergraduates. But he was a real presence in our lives. Every morning at around eight, he would wake me up with the greeting "Top of the morning to you, sir." He would pull back the curtain on the single window, light the gas fire, clear away the cups and glasses of the night before, and take them across the hall to the lavatory for washing. I was a heavy sleeper (in America, I had hooked up a particularly loud doorbell to an electric timer to wake me up), and sometimes, lying half-awake on my hard bed in the cold room, I imagined that George's ritual appearance was only a dream, that his actual coming was still in the future. He was quick to grasp my need to catch a little extra sleep. Once he had arranged the clean dishes on the bottom shelf of the bookcase, he would make sure that I was actually sitting up before he left.

Shivering, I would dress in front of the gas fire, which always seemed to hiss more than to throw off heat, and I would tell myself that my trials were nothing compared with those of George. Dressed in gray flannels, a sports jacket, a white shirt, and a tie, he arrived at college on a bicycle at a little after seven and, following the same ritual of curtains, fires, and dishes from room to room, awakened all the students on Staircase XVI—his bailiwick. Then he changed into a white jacket for hall, served breakfast, and helped to wash up. After that, he returned to his staircase to make the beds and tidy up the rooms. He didn't have much time for general dusting—my mantelpiece often felt gritty to the touch—but after he had finished with the room it always had a clean smell of polish.

George got a little breathing time between eleven and twelve or twelve-thirty, but apparently it wasn't long enough to let him go home. There was no common room for scouts, so, more often than not, he, along with other scouts, haunted the White Horse, wedged between the two parts of Blackwell's, on Broad Street, or else the King's Arms, on the corner of Holywell and South Parks Road, or the Roebuck, on Market Street—all pubs within easy reach of college. He was not a great drinker (none of the scouts were), so he mostly sat over a pint of bitter and chattered away the time until he had to get back to college to serve lunch to us. After we finished lunch, George and all the other scouts would sit down to their lunch in hall. I remember noticing that they always took their places in order of seniority, the oldest scout at the top of the table and the youngest lad at the foot. Everything in England was hierarchical.

In the afternoon, George helped around the kitchen and the college. In the evening, he returned to our rooms to close the curtains and wash up any cups and glasses we had used. His work wasn't done until he had finished serving dinner in hall. Everyone dined in, because everyone was charged for dinner (people paid for lunch only if they ate in hall); since hall was not large enough to accommodate everyone, there were two sittings—first hall at a quarter to seven, and second hall at half past seven. I reckoned that it was a rare evening when George got home before nine.

By piecing together information from George and other scouts, I learned that scouts earned about ten pounds a week and counted on perks, like getting free college meals and a free college house nearby, or, more often, inexpensive Council (government) accommodation. They also relied on getting a tip of a pound or two from each undergraduate at the end of the term and on being left the odd thing, like a used teakettle, when an undergraduate went down. (One of the scouts, I heard, had sold the same teakettle three times.) In term time, the scouts worked seven days a week. It was said that their long weeks compensated for their having the vacs off. But the scouts didn't get paid when they didn't work, so for them the vacs were really a form of layoff. During some vacs, they found temporary work in college, looking after conferees (sometime after the First World War, the college had started renting its facilities to conferences), but during many of the vacs they had to make do by working as casual laborers in Lord Nuffield's Morris Motors, which was in Cowley, just a few miles outside Oxford, or as waiters in resorts like Scarborough. Once a year, there was a college picnic for all the scouts and their families in a seaside place, like Weymouth. That was the high point of the scouts' year.

AT Oxford, the ringing of the tower bells and church bells was always in the background of our consciousness. Every evening, at five minutes after nine, Great Tom, which was at Christ Church and was the loudest and most deeply revered of Oxford's bells, would be rung a hundred and one times, to commemorate the original number of scholars at the college. Sometimes the bells were disruptive and intrusive. On Sunday morning, no one could either sleep or study, for the peals of various church bells seemed to end only to start up again. On Wednesday evening, those of us who lived on the west side of the college couldn't converse, or even think, for two hours while the bell ringers at St. Mary Magdalen practiced the ringing of changes. Jasper's one small window, set high, was directly across the street from the church, and in his room the sound of the ringing bells was so loud that his room might as well have been inside the bell tower.

The most that one could do during the practice session was to marvel at the art and the science of change ringing, which, I had read, had come down from the seventeenth century. It was said to be a purely English art form, but it didn't seem particularly aesthetic to my ear. On one level, change ringing was so mathematical that it seemed less like playing a musical tune than like solving a chess problem. There were combinations of bells, and each possible combination had to be gone through a certain number of times in a particular pattern; some changes at St. Mary Magdalen must have run into four figures, and to go through the whole sequence must have required a lot of concentration, even if the result was monotonous to the listener. On another level, change ringing seemed to have to do primarily with athletics. In the case of St. Mary Magdalen, there were eight bells, and since one person was required at each bell rope, eight student types were kept ringing away for a whole evening, as if change ringing were a very competitive sport. (On the Continent, changes are rung without any physical exertion—on a carillon, which has a keyboard, like a piano.) If one was in on bell ringing, the changes were no doubt exhilarating. For the bell ringers, even the names of particular changes, like "Treble Bob Hunt," must have been magical. I, however, was all but driven out of my mind by hearing rising scales for two solid hours: *tee-tee-da-da, tee-tee-da-da, tee-da-da, tee-da-da.* The cacophony was not only preëmptive but also triumphant.

On the whole, though, the bells gave structure to our day, calling us to tutorials and hall and vespers. (The evensong at Magdalen and at New College was thrilling.) They also had pleasant literary associations:

> Oft, on a plot of rising ground,
> I hear the far-off curfew sound

> Over some wide-watered shore,
> Swinging slow with sullen roar.

The curfew bells—the signal to extinguish all lights and fires—that Milton is recalling here were probably introduced in England even before the time of William the Conqueror. The bells reminded us of the customs and glories of the Oxford past even as they marked our progress toward the vague, unknown future.

V

DERVORGUILLA AND HER BENEFICIARIES

T HE LAST FRIDAY IN NOVEMBER OF THE MICHAELMAS
term, I went to the railway station to receive my mother.
She was coming up from Laindon for the first time, to
spend the weekend with me. She got off the train with a
little overnight bag and a crude, unwieldy gallon-size
tin—the kind of tin in which Dalda ghi is sold in common bazaars throughout India.

"Why are you bringing ghi to Oxford?" I asked irritably, in Punjabi, as I took the tin from her on the platform.

"Who said it has ghi in it, youngster?" she retorted. She took my free arm affectionately as we set off.

Lugging the Dalda tin, I felt a little like Caliban in the enchanted regions of Oxford.

"It's filled with *pinnis,*" my mother said after a while.

"*Pinnis!*" I cried, recalling the Indian sweetmeats in the form of small balls that were made with chick-pea flour. She has forgotten that I don't like Indian sweetmeats, I thought. Even before developing a Western palate, I had found them heavy and oversweet.

"Your mother can't come empty-handed to see her son at Oxford," she said. "You and your friends will enjoy them."

Jasper's mother would have brought a chocolate cake, I thought. And everybody would have enjoyed sharing it. But *pinnis?* Still, I mustn't be too harsh. God knows what lengths she has gone to in order to find *pinnis* in London.

Sitting beside her in the taxi, I felt tongue-tied. She seemed such an alien presence in Oxford. At college, everyone categorizes people by their speech, I thought, and Mamaji can barely speak English.

"What do you make of Suez?" I ventured, as much to break the silence as to provoke discussion. For weeks now, that had been the hottest topic of discussion in the newspapers and among the undergraduates.

"What did you say, youngster?" she asked distractedly.

"Suez. Have you heard about it?"

"It's a Muslim issue. I'm glad that the British are finally siding against the Muslims."

She talks as if she were still in India, I thought.

"This is a very pretty city, youngster," she said suddenly. "I see why you people get charmed by it, like snakes by a snake charmer's pipe."

Her observation surprised and delighted me, and it helped me to relax.

We got out of the taxi in front of a nineteenth-century house on Walton Street, where I had rented a room for her for the weekend. "This is a very famous street," I said. I started to explain to her that the Oxford University Press was down the road, and St. Sepulchre's Cemetery, where Benjamin Jowett was buried, was up the road. Then I remembered that she had no acquaintance with Oxford lore. The Press and Benjamin Jowett are all one to her, I thought, and I quickly said, "Never mind."

After I established her in her room, we walked the short distance to my college—the wretched Dalda tin knocking against my side. It seemed that at every step I had to avoid bumping people with it.

In my room, I started to make tea. I filled the electric kettle with water from the lavatory, and plugged it in. Just as I was taking down the cups and saucers from the bookshelf, there was a familiar knock at the door, and Jasper walked in. I introduced him to my mother.

"Here, sweeten your mouth," she said, offering him a *pinni* and explaining that it was one of the favorite sweetmeats of the Punjabis.

I could feel the blood rushing to my cheeks.

"Grew up eating *pinnis,* eh?" Jasper said to me, more kindly than ironically. He obligingly took a bite. "Mm, it's very exotic," he said politely. He left with the half-eaten *pinni* in his hand.

"He is a real English sahib, even though he is a beard-wallah," my mother said, laughing.

I was annoyed by her carrying over the Indian notion of the sahib, bearded or not, to Oxford. "He is a friend—he lives next door," I said, trying not to sound sharp.

My mother made the tea—a cup with hot milk for her and a cup with lemon for me.

I asked after the Chowdharys.

"Did you know that Dr. Chowdhary did, after all, get off to India to see his people in the Punjab?" my mother said. "He flew on November 5th, despite the news that England was bombing Egypt."

"No, Vijay hasn't said anything about it," I said. I had spoken to her many times on the telephone, but never for very long (telephone calls were expensive), and had kept in touch mostly through Vijay. "How is Mrs. Chowdhary doing?"

"There is a lot to tell, youngster," she said, laughing. "I was determined to prove to your daddy and to you that I am capable of living by myself in England, so I tried my best to settle into the routine of the household. In the beginning, I would have breakfast with Dr. and Mrs. Chowdhary, even though they eat breakfast in silence, looking over the post and the morning newspaper, like real England-wallahs. When we talk, she still calls me 'Mrs. Mehta.' Even if sometimes 'Sister' slips out of my mouth—that is what I would call her at home—I always correct it to 'Mrs. Chowdhary.' "

"When I was there, I had the impression that it was a very Punjabi household," I said.

We were finally talking easily, like mother and son.

"By and large, it is," she said. "Punjabis are always arriving at the house straight from the plane, with an introduction to the Chowdharys, and expecting to be put up and looked after. Just yesterday, one gentleman arrived with 'B.A.' printed all over his luggage. Mrs. Chowdhary welcomed him by giving him a glass of milk. That reminded him so much of home that he started to cry."

"What does she do with all of them?" I asked.

"Many of them are Punjabi boys. She hopes that one of them will take an interest in Shakuntala and marry her. She arranges for the boys to take Shakuntala on country walks or to the cinema."

"How is Shakuntala?"

"Oh, she is her smart self. I look after her like my own daughter. We are always laughing about my impressions of England and her impressions of India." Shakuntala had spent a short time in India.

"Does she go to school?"

"She drives up to Basildon New Town to take lessons in Latin, but quite a lot of the time she is at home. She spends hours in front of the mirror, touching up her eyes, cheeks, and lips. She is always cutting, filing, and polishing her nails. She likes me to do up her hair. She is a real child—a real *bachcha.*"

My mother poured us some more tea, and I asked how she occupied herself at the Chowdharys'.

"Dusting and helping with the laundry, tidying up and doing the flower arrangements. I also attend Mrs. Chowdhary when she goes shopping, and carry things out to the car. On Tuesdays, I'm not able to help her as much as I'd like to, because I keep my fast, as I do at home. Anyway, she seems to be impressed that I always sense what I am expected to do. Dr. Chowdhary likes Indian food, so in the evening I always cook an Indian dish for dinner. It always astonishes me that Dr. Chowdhary enjoys washing the dishes. He calls it his duty. One of us ladies dries them, and the other stacks them in the cupboard."

"So it seems you are getting along well with the Chowdharys."

"You would think so, youngster, but in life there are no roses without thorns. One morning, after Dr. Chowdhary left for the clinic Mrs. Chowdhary said to me, 'It would be nice, Mrs. Mehta, if you waited until Dr. Chowdhary has left before coming down for breakfast.' I said, 'That suits me. I can stay in bed a little longer.' She said, 'Another thing, Mrs. Mehta. I want to really settle down to my writing work. Can you look after yourself during the day?' I said, 'Of course. I am perfectly capable of amusing myself. Anyway, Dr. Frankland has told me that I should take long walks—that might help my asthma.' Ever since that conversation, I have come down late and had breakfast by myself. When the clock on the mantelpiece says eleven, I go out for a walk. As your daddy instructed me, I always have money in my purse to treat any acquaintance I meet to tea, bus fare, or the like. Sometimes I stop in at a shop. I am astonished at how shop-keepers here keep customers waiting. At home, they offer ladies of a good family a chair, perhaps a cup of tea, and, at the very least, address them as 'Mother' or 'Sister.' Also, they don't even haggle over prices here. Everything has a fixed price.'"

"Have you made any friends?"

"I have become great friends with Miss Mayo, Mrs. Chowdhary's occasional English maid. She invited me for tea at her house, and I went there with a cake. She has a big house, and wonderful things in it—a refrigerator, an electric stove, an electric iron, silver teaspoons, and a big double bed with a beautiful bedspread. I was shocked to discover that she lives alone. I said to her, 'Sister, you are so attractive. How is it that you never got married?' She said, 'I was married. I have a very handsome son, who works in an office in London. He is married and has a son.' She didn't say whether she was a widow or divorced, and I didn't think it was right for me to pry, but I said, 'How is it that you don't live with your son, then?' She said, 'When I got married, one week my parents would come and have tea with me, and they would bring a cake, and the next week I would go and have tea with them, and I would bring a cake. My son and I have the same arrangement. That's the way we do things in England.' The next time I went to Miss Mayo's for tea, I took along a present of a pound of wool, so that she could make a sweater for herself. Like me, she is much interested in knitting. I visit her often now, in the afternoon. In the morning, I work as a volunteer in the old people's canteen.'"

"Old people's canteen?" I asked, with some surprise.

"Yes. One fine day, Mrs. Chowdhary said to me, 'I would like to spend more time on my writing work. Why don't you take over my job at the old people's canteen?' She had been doing volunteer work in a canteen for old people who are living off meagre pensions—they come every day to get free tea and biscuits. I hesitated, because my English is so poor. I was afraid that the old people would speak to me and I wouldn't be able to answer them. But then I decided that I was in England and your daddy would want me to give it a try, so I said yes. The canteen is a homy place, with a sink, a gas stove, a counter, and some benches along the wall. Whoever drops by is given some tea and two biscuits. We volunteers try to engage everyone in a 'chat-up.' Then we wash up the tea things, wipe the counter, and scrub the gas stove. Every day, I walk to the canteen and work for a few hours. I find it refreshing to get out of the Chowdhary household and make English friends. I find that I know more English than I thought. I have become very popular. My picture has even appeared in the local newspaper. And I have become fast friends with one Mrs. Brown. We often take a bus together to London. I always pay the bus fare and treat Mrs. Brown to tea and cakes. You'd be amazed at how well I can get around London by myself."

There was another knock at the door, and Tom Braun walked in. My mother insisted on giving him a *pinni*.

"Mrs. Mehta, if you don't mind, I won't eat it now," he said, in his most mellifluous, ingratiating voice. He put it in his pocket and left.

Contrary to my misgivings, I later learned that my mother had made a great impression on Jasper and Tom—indeed, on anyone who met her. People spoke of her as "dignified," "mysterious," and "beautiful."

THE Balliol Junior Common Room was a long room, extending from Staircase XIV to Staircase XV. Its atmosphere was very much that of a London club. At each end were writing desks, with plenty of crested Balliol paper and envelopes; a long table, piled with newspapers and magazines, stretched almost half the length of the room; and all around were deep leather armchairs. People were constantly coming and going, and standing around or sitting around, talking or reading.

The porters at the lodge—the gatekeepers of the college—thought that the lodge was the hub of the college, but R. V. North, who was the steward of the J.C.R., thought that the J.C.R. was the college itself. He had taken to heart Jowett's remark "The College is for the young men," and imagined that the J.C.R. was their home away from home. And he thought that in later life the J.C.R. would be the place they would revisit as old members.

On one side of the room was a hatch opening into the pantry. Usually, the hatch was kept shut, but at three-thirty in the afternoon it would be opened, so shortly thereafter all of us would break off whatever we were doing and head for the J.C.R. for tea. There would be a great rush as we formed a queue in front of the hatch, through which North and his assistant, Mrs. Pether, were handing out tea while the pantry boy, the third member of the team, worked around the sink and the stove. At a terrific rate, they produced tea in big, steaming mugs, which were just the right size to warm one's hands on, and plates of sandwiches, buns, cakes, and the like. (One of the favorite sandwiches was gentleman's relish—anchovy paste.) The armchairs were always taken quickly, so most of us would stand, balancing our plates on top of our mugs. That had the advantage of keeping the steam from escaping, and so prolonging the pleasure of drinking hot tea; not only one's hands but also one's insides needed warming.

The ritual of afternoon tea in the common room was new to me. It seemed wonderfully civilized and civilizing, something out of novels—quaint and romantic. At the same time, the tea provided a much needed supplement to the poor meals in hall. Everything in the J.C.R. was basic and very cheap, and, in any case, the teas were charged to our battels—the Oxford term for the accounts covering all college expenses. (When I first came across the word, I was much taken with it. It sounded like school slang that divided the insiders from the outsiders, and seemed especially charming because its root was a French word meaning "to fatten.") The J.C.R. pantry provided everything at cost, not even allowing anything—so North used to boast—"for breakages."

North had been hired as a J.C.R. steward, with his wife as his assistant, just after the war. From his very first day, he had been the guiding spirit of the J.C.R. By the time we were undergraduates, it was hard to imagine the J.C.R. without him. He would arrive at half past seven in the morning. He and "the lad," as he called the pantry boy, would sweep around the chaps lying about—they had been to various late parties and were sleeping it off—or ease them out of the way. He would put out the newspapers and replenish the supply of stationery. By the time undergraduates came in to read the morning papers, at eight-thirty, he would have the J.C.R. completely picked up and in order. The J.C.R. was technically run by a president, a secretary, and a treasurer, who were elected by students of the college. North used to say that, rather as the lady of the house in an Edwardian country place made a daily pro-forma appearance in the kitchen, the J.C.R. treasurer or secretary would look into the pantry once a day to go over some detail. Otherwise, he was left alone to run the place as he saw fit.

Our J.C.R. was known throughout the university as one of the most active, both socially and politically. A few reticent people hid behind newspapers, but most of them carried on conversations—facetious, ironic, or quite impassioned—at all hours of the day and night. Conversations with the J.C.R. officers and a "Mr. Food" were carried on by other means, however—through three notebooks that were labelled in ink "Mr. Food's Book," "The President's Book," and "J.C.R. Suggestions Book." The books were generally kept on the long table, and in the morning North could often be observed looking at them—to see, he said, "which direction public opinion is blowing in." One complainant wrote in Mr. Food's Book:

Sir,

Would you ask the chef not to use such old shepherds in his shepherd's pie?

Mr. Food disposed of the complaint with one French phrase:

Sir,

Bon appetit.

The complainant came back with the following grouse:

Sir,

The chicken I had in Hall last night was so old and tough that I'm sure it was glad to have died.

Mr. Food responded with a deft turn on the original complaint:

Sir,

At least it wasn't a shepherd.

Food was also on the mind of a complainant writing in the President's Book, who charged into a controversy about an abstract painting in the room:

Sir,

May I say hurrah? I have, after some small cerebration, contrived to solve the problem presented by the Hitchins over the J.C.R. fireplace. It is, of course, a picture of the chef's Brussels sprouts or perhaps the cabbage which we receive so often in Hall. And could it, perhaps, be surrounded by macaroni pudding?

The president entered into the culinary spirit of the complaint, and wrote this curt reply:

Sir,

How about the top left-hand corner as the chef's creamed cauliflower?

Not all the effusions in the J.C.R. books were complaining or whimsical. One undergraduate wrote this in the President's Book:

Sir,

May I express my appreciation of the work North does? Today (Sunday), having to entertain some people to tea at very short notice, having no food, and finding all the shops closed, I went to North with a large number of highly unreasonable demands, all of which were fulfilled. Please convey my thanks.

The president replied in the same complimentary tone:

Sir,

North will, I am sure, appreciate your very noble tribute. Members of the J.C.R. cannot reflect too often how much they owe to him in every way. Thank you for voicing your thanks.

The Suggestions Book, in which some remarks were also directed to the president, was essentially the J.C.R.'s own broadsheet. It furnished an excuse for writing anything about the college, the university, or the world. One undergraduate sounded off on Philip Toynbee, a cultural Pooh-Bah:

Sir,

Mr. Philip Toynbee's speech at the Union, which, as you heard, advocated a sort of children's crusade to Hungary, seems to me the apotheosis of petitionism. May we please decide once and for all that petitions, of whatever cause, be banned from the J.C.R. Whenever anything of political significance occurs there springs up a rash of petitions, whose only value is to instill a feeling of smugness into those who sign. What influence can these miserable bits of paper have? Their only result is to make the petitioners fallaciously believe that they have done their duty. Enough, sir, of this signing and countersigning.

The president was nothing if not judicious in his reply:

Sir,

(i) Petitions are already banned from the J.C.R.

(ii) I don't think one can *entirely* discount the influence of petitions on those whom they are intended to influence.

(iii) I don't either think that they should altogether replace any other action. But—*vide* the meeting this evening—other forms of action aren't always easy to decide on.

Not surprisingly, the pages of the Suggestions Book filled up rapidly. When we were on our second book of the Michaelmas term, an undergraduate wrote:

Sir,

Surely "volume two" should appear on the title page of this book. Yours, in the tradition of German scholarship.

To this the president's riposte was

Sir,

It has appeared.

Later in that term, a fourth book was started—a Betting Book, in which bettors offered challenges like "You can't walk from Oxford to the end of Banbury Road backwards" or "You can't poach an egg in a teakettle." I don't remember whether anyone took up the challenge of walking backward, but I know that an undergraduate did "prove" he could poach an egg in a teakettle: he broke the egg into a teacup and used the teacup as a lid for the teakettle.

❦

ONE evening near the end of the term, I attended a college party in Murray Forsyth's room. At a certain stage, the English undergraduates started doing party pieces about the Silver King, the popular nickname for the Master—inspired by his graying hair and regal bearing. Sending up the head of the college was a general pastime at Oxford parties, but at this one people threw themselves into the diversion with unusual gusto, as if it gave them a certain release from the tension of the term. Anyway, the Master's demeanor provided good material for caricature. The Master, who generally wore a dark three-piece suit, a subdued tie, and well-polished shoes, and sometimes sported a homburg, was known for his majestic walk. Tom Braun imitated the Master's walk, moving around deliberately, in a stately manner. Then, speaking in the Master's ponderous voice, which suggested a judicious weighing of every word uttered, he treated us to the Master analyzing the problem of games in the college. Like the Master, he paused after every phrase, as if he were collecting his thoughts: "There is a problem . . . about the amount of time . . . undergraduates are devoting to games. . . . This is not so. . . . When you analyze the question . . . it appears there is no problem. . . . Let us analyze it. . . . First, we have the undergraduates who are members of the Boat Club. . . . They are no problem. . . . They are necessary. . . . Second, we have the cricket team. . . . They are no problem. . . . Thirdly, we have . . ." Tom managed to imitate so accurately the Master's slow, methodical style of speaking—which made one want to push him along—that by the end of his analysis one couldn't bear to hear another word about the matter.

Several people who liked to ham wanted to get into the act and do their party pieces, but Tom was not ready to yield the stage. "I had a very distinguished career," he continued, over the general commotion. "But then I came to this college . . . and, for reasons that nobody has ever adequately explained to me . . . I became slow of speech and slow of thought. . . . What is there about this college that lays great men low?"

Like everyone else, I laughed at Tom's impersonation, but it also gave me pause. The Master was perhaps the most isolated person in the college. Life at the top must be especially lonely for him, I thought.

The very next day, I received a handwritten note from the Master, asking me to come and see him about "a grave matter that has come to my attention." The phrase terrified me.

"MR. MEHTA," the Master said as soon as I sat down in a chair across from him.

"Yes, Master," I said.

There was a long pause.

He looked for a piece of paper on his desk, and went on, in a heavy monotone, "What do you do with the gas?"

"Gas, Master?" I repeated stupidly, and quickly added, "I have a gas fire in my room."

"But what do you do with it?"

"What do I do with it, Master?"

"In my memory this complaint has never come up."

"What complaint, Master?"

"The Domestic Bursar has called my attention to your battels."

"Yes, Master," I said, filling up the pause.

"I doubt if anyone in memory has paid more for his gas fire than for his college fees."

"Do you mean the charges for my gas fire, Master?"

"Your gas charges for the Michaelmas term are, as I think I have already pointed out, more than your college fees. I would be interested to know how your charges can be so high."

The explanation was simple: I left the gas fire on when I was out of the room. Even so, it did little to dispel the permanent Arctic chill that hung about the room. The chill seemed to me to press home the point that comfort was an enemy of good scholarship, that character was formed by shivering, much as it might be by the itching from a penitent's hair shirt. But, while I embraced this philosophy with my mind, my body was another matter.

"I feel the cold very much, Master," I said.

"I trust, Mr. Mehta, you will not give me an occasion to bring up this subject with you again."

"No, Master," I said.

"Thank you," he said. He stood up.

I never gave the Master another occasion to call me on the carpet, because that very day I renounced the little luxury of keeping the gas fire on to blunt the edge of the chill I felt when I walked into the room. Whenever I got the cold shivers, I thought of the scholars at the medieval university living on hard bread.

LIKE some other foreign undergraduates, I kept hoping that I might get an invitation for Christmas from an Oxford friend, but no such invitation was forthcoming. The foreigners who were Rhodes scholars, however, talked as if they intended to spend their Christmas vac going from one grand house to the next.

They seemed to have lined up invitations from romantic-sounding seaside resorts, like Bournemouth, or cathedral cities, like Canterbury, or country houses in Wiltshire or Kent. I eventually discovered that there was a Rhodes and Dominion Fellowship Trust, which undertook to introduce Rhodes scholars to English gentry. Every year, when a new crop of Rhodes scholars had settled in at Oxford the members of the Trust had them to tea at Rhodes House, looked them over, and, in the light of their interests and personalities, made suitable arrangements for their vacs. "It's a wonderful network," an American friend who was a Rhodes scholar told me. "It's a way of getting to know an England different from Oxford's—a kind of England that a lot of old English families live in. I'm sure if you go and see the Warden of Rhodes House he can plug you into the network."

I called on the Warden, E. T. (Bill) Williams—a formidable man, with whom I had had some dealings as an aspiring Rhodes scholar. Although he was not a career soldier, he had served on the general staff of Field Marshal Montgomery during the Second World War and had achieved the rank of brigadier—something of a feat for a civilian. His rank in the Army had been so grand that he might have had expectations grander than his present position. In any case, he had the air of a disappointed man— something I found I could identify with.

I told him that I longed to visit an English family for part of my Christmas vac.

"You might have been a Rhodes scholar, but you are not," he said. His manner was not unkind but matter-of-fact. "There is no way that I could put you on the vac network of people who like to have Rhodes scholars stay with them—even if I wanted to. It would not be fair to those people. After all, they extend hospitality to Rhodes scholars, and they would be none too pleased if a might-have-been scholar were wished on them."

I was about to get up and leave, but he seemed to feel the need to clarify the point further. "You will not be invited to any

Rhodes scholars' parties," he said, "because I have no such category as honorary Rhodes scholar."

I got his point—that Rhodes scholars were a closed society, like so many clubs and societies in England.

❧

SOME of my English friends were making plans to go to Spain or Portugal, France or Italy for Christmas vac. Will they be taking books with them, I wondered, or are they going there to improve their languages? It was often said that people used the term for living the Oxford life and the holidays for swotting away at the books.

"Are you going to work in the vac?" I asked Tom Braun, who I had heard might be going to the Mediterranean. We were standing in the queue for tea in the J.C.R.

"My dear man, you don't go to the seaside with your books— they would just get wet. What American ideas you have! I took you to be a high-caste Hindu." He turned away from me, as if I were one of the college drudges.

He has the most charming way of putting people in their place, I thought. I resolved on the spot to go to the Continent and acquire some panache, like him. I made discreet inquiries at the college office. How did one go about finding a family to live with on the Continent? (At Oxford, such a question, it seemed, had to be posed in an impersonal way.) I was put in touch with an agency in London which found French families who were interested in taking in students as paying guests. The people at the agency wanted to know about my command of French. I wrote them that I had American college French. They asked where I would like to go. I wrote back that I would prefer to go to Paris, but that I was flexible.

The agency sent me a packet of brochures about possible families. One particular brochure seemed irresistible. It contained pictures of no fewer than seven girls, ranging in age from seventeen to twenty-six. They all looked ravishingly pretty to my reader's eyes. And they were all unmarried daughters of M. and Mme. de la Chapelle. (I've changed the surname.) The family lived in a seventeenth-century château in the Loire valley, near Tours. M. and Mme. de la Chapelle invited applications "only from gentlemen from the ancient universities in Great Britain." With so many young single girls at home, they can't be too careful, I thought. The brochure noted that their château was known for its excellent table and wine, and that gentlemen could supplement their French conversation in the château with formal lessons in the language at the university in town. The rule of the house was that everyone had to speak French only.

The château sounded like something out of a fairy tale. But there was a catch: the rates for paying guests at the de la Chapelles' were three times those asked by any other family in the agency's packet of brochures. I felt, however, that I had no choice: visions of seven girls danced in my head like sugar plums. I had planned to go to Paris for a month, but I decided that instead I would go to the de la Chapelles for ten days, reasoning that by living with a relaxed aristocratic family in the countryside I would have a more intensive exposure to better French, and learn it faster, than I would with a busy bourgeois family in Paris. The agency required a non-refundable prepayment, and I quickly sent it off.

In due course, I got my tickets, and wrote a letter to M. and Mme. de la Chapelle, telling them the date and time of my arrival.

It was the last day of term, and, drawing back the curtains, my scout said, "You'll be having your Handshaking today, sir."

"That's right," I said, turning over and trying to catch a little extra sleep.

"I had a gentleman from your parts in this staircase last year, sir. At Handshaking, he went around the table trying to shake hands, and he says to me, 'George, no one took my hand, and yet they call it Handshaking. You English are a funny lot.' "

"No! He actually tried to shake hands at Handshaking?" I said, sitting up in bed in feigned surprise. The truth was that that's what I myself would have done, but I had long since learned that at Oxford one didn't expose one's ignorance, even to one's scout. At my last tutorial, Southern had simply asked me to show up at the Old Common Room—a sort of second clubroom for the Fellows—at a particular time. I had not given the matter much thought, imagining that it was some kind of formal leave-taking—that is, until George brought up the subject.

"Well, that's exactly what my Mrs. said to me when I told her about it. I says to her, 'How was the gentleman to know, coming from Bronx, in America?' "

"*The* Bronx," I said, trying to sound knowledgeable.

George had already lit the fire and collected the tea things and was on his way out. I had to detain him somehow if I was going to find out just what one was supposed to do at Handshaking. But I hesitated, and he was gone.

At the appointed time, I put on my gown and went over to the Old Common Room. Because I had never before had any occasion to go to the building, I approached it with an uncertain step. The most junior history tutor, John Prest, called me in, and pulled out a chair for me at the foot of a long table, at which the four college history tutors and the Master were gathered.

Southern turned to the Master, who was at the head of the table, and said, "As you know, Master, Mr. Mehta came to history rather late in the day. But it would appear from the few essays he has written for me this term that he is hardworking, and has a mature historical judgment."

The Old Common Room had terrible acoustics. Although Southern always spoke clearly, I had to strain to hear him—I couldn't be sure whether he had said "a mature" or "immature" historical judgment. But he talked on, and from his comments I surmised that Handshaking was an evaluation of a term's work— a sort of check on a student's progress, like end-of-term examinations elsewhere.

Suddenly, I woke up to the fact that the Master was saying something to me. In addition to contending with his Scotch accent and his throat affliction—or whatever it was—I now had to cope with the terrible acoustics, and the result was that I couldn't make out much of what he said. Yet the way he raised his voice indicated that he was asking me a question. I had to think fast, and tried to imagine what that might be. It must be about my work, I thought, so finally I said—I feared, rather stupidly— "I'm enjoying reading history very much, Master."

Christopher Hill, who was sitting next to Dick Southern, sniffed. (Hill would be my history tutor in the following term.) I had seen him around the college, and had noticed that he sniffed often. I imagined that he did so out of shyness; he was an extremely clever man, and said everything he had to say much more rapidly than the people he was talking to could take it in—a habit that inevitably led to long pauses. But his sniff that particular day sounded to me louder than usual, as if it were directed at me, and as if it said, "I expected something better from you."

Rodge, who, as the senior history tutor, was seated to the Master's right, now spoke, saying something to the effect that, although I had gone from honor school to honor school before settling down to read history, I was not fickle—quite the contrary.

Since the senior history tutor had spoken, I thought that the ordeal was over. I half stood up to go, but then the Master seemed to direct another question at me. What can he possibly be asking me now, I wondered. I couldn't imagine what, but the four history tutors and the Master seemed to be waiting for an answer.

"I plan to spend the Christmas vac in France, learning French—or, rather, improving my French," I said, wildly guessing at the question.

The Master said something else. It could have been anything. Suddenly, without knowing what I was doing, I bowed to the tutors on my right, to the Master, opposite, and to the tutors on my left, much as I had to fellow-freshmen at the Freshman Dinner when we were passing the loving cup. Then, thinking that everyone must consider me mad or demented, I almost ran to the door, only to fumble for the door handle.

Christopher Hill jumped up and opened the door for me. He stepped out of the room with me. "Everybody has trouble understanding the Master in that room," he said.

"What did he say?" I asked, relaxing a little.

"Only nice things, repeating your tutors, in the usual Keir manner," he said, with a sniff, and he added, without much conviction—almost ironically—"You'll get used to Handshaking with the Master. Have a marvellous time in France!"

In a rush of gratitude, I put out my hand.

I expected to meet his warm, humane hand, but instead I was greeted by his little finger. In my confusion, I almost fell against a fellow-freshman, Michael Mockridge, who was waiting to go in for his Handshaking.

Although I found the ritual of Handshaking oddly inspiring—indeed, it made me work harder in the vac than I had in the term—still, whenever I thought about encountering Christopher Hill's little finger I felt my face turning red. I could understand that at Oxford—in contrast to Holland, say, where people shook hands even if they saw each other several times a day—people didn't shake hands, perhaps because we were all considered part of a family. But the thought of having been extended a little finger by my future tutor on the last day of my first term continued to haunt me, as if that, rather than anything said at the actual Handshaking, were the verdict on my beginnings at Oxford.

❦

I SAT in the dining car in the boat train, over an entrecôte and a glass of Beychevelle, on my way to Tours. Tom Braun would approve, I thought. Then I got to wondering what scenery we were passing, and wished that I were travelling with a girlfriend, like the witty young man at the next table. Maybe then I could see everything through her eyes, I thought. There was so much to learn, and it was so hard to learn it by myself. I didn't even know what a boat train was—a train that was taken on a boat or a train that took passengers to a boat. In Oxford conversations, there were many references and allusions that I didn't understand, but I was loath to let on, for fear of seeming uncouth and being found wanting in the ubiquitous game of one-upmanship; I just patiently waited for the context to illuminate the meaning. I should have looked up "boat train" in the dictionary, I now thought, but then remembered that there had been the fear of revealing my ignorance to my reader. For the benefit of my fellow-passengers, I put on a cheerful expression to mask my sinking feeling of ignorance. *Clackety-clack. Clackety-clack.* At least, I was going somewhere, and wasn't stranded in an Oxford bed-sitter feeling envious of fellow-undergraduates who were hobnobbing with the English gentry or sunning themselves in European resorts.

I could have asked my father about the boat train, I thought. He had recently returned from his lecture tour in America, and he and my mother had seen me off at the station in London. We three had spent Christmas Day together at the Overseas League, but he had been preoccupied by an accident my brother Om had suffered in the port of Yokohama. In fact, as soon as I heard about the accident I, too, could think of little else. It seemed that about six months earlier, while brother Om was working on the boiler in the engine room of his steamship—he was a fourth engineer in the Indian merchant marine—the boiler had exploded in his face. He had sustained first-degree burns on his hands and wrists and second- and third-degree burns all over his body; his eyes had barely escaped. He was evacuated to a hospital in Yokohama and was under treatment for several months. Then he was shifted to a hospital in Madras. After two months there, he was discharged, and he had recently come home to Delhi. The members of the family had written to my father about the accident and had told him that, except for his hands and wrists, which would probably be scarred for life, his skin had completely healed but seemed a little darker.

"I wish I had known about the accident," I said.

"None of us knew about it," my father said. "Anyway, what could we have done? I was boxed in by my lecture commitments, your mother was stuck here, and you had your studies to think of."

We booked a call to Delhi in order to talk to brother Om, and spent hours waiting for it to come through. Finally, we did speak to him, but his voice kept fading out. (In those days, there was no cable connection between Europe and India; the telephone traffic was handled by radio.)

"At least, we heard Om's voice," my father said. "He sounded like himself."

"It's Ram's mercy that he is still here," my mother said. "Just think about lying in a hospital where you don't know a soul, don't know the tongue, don't know whether you will live or die."

"But he has pulled through," my father said. "We should look on the bright side of things."

We all tried to do so, and at the station my parents seemed in good spirits, perhaps because they were savoring the sense of adventure I felt in travelling to the Continent by myself.

Now the conductor walked through the dining car, pinging and clicking his ticket puncher. He announced that the disembarkation point would be Dover. Ah, Dover beach, the "darkling plain, swept with confused alarms of struggle and flight," I thought. So we will get off the train, bag and baggage, and get on an actual boat. Of course, that's what a boat train has to be.

The wine was beginning to have its effect. I felt light-headed, even happy. I thought about the girls—how they would roll French "r"s on their tongues—and about the château, wondering whether my room would be in a stone tower, up a steep, winding staircase.

At the terminal, I got a porter, and he helped me through the immigration formalities and onto the boat. After a stormy crossing, there was another train, to Paris; a taxi from the Gare du Nord to the Gare d'Austerlitz; and yet another train. Later, there was a further change, but, thank God, to a train on an adjacent platform, which I was able to manage on my own, by following the other passengers. At dusk, when we were finally approaching Tours, the train began to slow down and my heart to speed up.

The thought of the girls from the distance of Oxford had been enticing, but now that the meeting was at hand I felt apprehensive and shy. I imagined that I'd be met at the station by the whole de la Chapelle family—that's how we would have received a guest at home—and that I would be enfolded in the family warmth and driven in an old but elegant car to the château. The girls would pile into the back, as best they could, some sitting with their shoulders forward, others with their shoulders against the back—perhaps even taking turns bending forward and leaning back, just as we did at home. Like my father, M. de la Chapelle would take the wheel, and he would probably put me in front, between him and Mme. de la Chapelle. No doubt there would be a lot of chatter among the girls. Would they have difficult names? Would I be able to tell their voices apart right away? What would they all talk about? Would I be able to follow their tongue? What would I say to them in my indifferent French? How could I win a place in their hearts—or, actually, in the heart of one girl, who might become my guide in Tours, and show me around the university and the town?

Tours was château country. On the drive, would they point out châteaux along the way, and then leave off, thinking that the subject could be of no interest to me? I will make them understand that it is, I resolved. I'll make them realize that I can see things through my mind's eye. Then I wondered how I would make them realize that, and I was overwhelmed by a feeling of hopelessness—a feeling that I wouldn't know what to say in the car, any more than I would know what to do once I got to the château, and that the de la Chapelles would soon get busy with their own lives and tire of me, leave me alone in my room. Damn it, I'm paying them, I thought. I have rights. I'm here to learn French. I won't let them treat me like an unwanted guest. But even as I thought this I remembered that I didn't have the benefit of eye contact, that language was about the only way I could reach anyone, and that, with my indifferent French, I would be doubly handicapped with the de la Chapelles. I would be discounted and patronized—and in French.

The train pulled up at the Tours railway station. I got out, with my suitcase, and stood on an unbelievably cold, windswept platform, my teeth chattering as I idiotically turned my head this way and that, trying to look alert, listening for excited voices greeting me. I felt impatient with the bustle of the platform and the distracting noise of the train pulling out. Suddenly, I was standing alone on the open platform. They are late, I thought. All big families are late. I remembered that when we were going somewhere we would all be in the car with the engine running, and my mother wouldn't be there. Finally, she would come hurrying. She would get in the car, and my father would start to drive away, but she would remember something she had forgotten to do, like bringing her medicine, locking her cupboard, or giving an order to a servant. My father would back up the car, and the wait would begin again.

A man with a heavy footfall walked toward me. *"Ah, M. de la Chapelle,"* I said, smiling and putting out my hand. I wanted to be the first to greet him, in order to put him at ease and to start our relationship on a note of bonhomie. There was no response. *"M. de la Chapelle, n'est-ce pas?"*

"Non."

"Connaissez-vous M. de la Chapelle? M. et Mme. de la Chapelle sont les parents de sept jeunes filles."

"Je ne les connais pas, Monsieur. Je suis chef de gare."

I was at a loss as to what to say or do, but told myself that I must keep my wits about me. *"Avez-vous un téléphone?"*

The stationmaster showed me to a rickety old telephone on the outside wall. I had committed to memory the de la Chapelles' address and telephone number, and, standing in the cold, I dialled the number of the château. A very old-sounding man answered the phone. I tried to speak in my best French, but there seemed to be no way I could make myself understood. I shouted into the phone. I tried a one-word approach, and finally got him to understand that I was the guest that the de la Chapelles were expecting.

"Ici M. de la Chapelle," he finally said. *"Prenez un taxi."* That's as much as I understood.

The old buzzard is deaf, I thought. It would be just my luck to find a deaf man to learn French conversation from. Then I reminded myself about the *jeunes filles* and cheered up. He must be the *grandpère,* I thought.

The stationmaster helped me to find a taxi.

I got in it and gave the address, and we set off. It was a five-mile drive to the château.

As soon as I had got out and paid the driver, he drove off. An English taxi driver would have waited to see that I was safely in, I thought. The French are a tribe unto themselves. Once more, I was standing out in the French cold with my suitcase, expecting that seven twittering, fluttering girls would swoop me up, but all I heard was what sounded like a lot of French street children playing somewhere in the grounds. I began to worry that I had been dropped in the wrong place. But an elderly lady with a lot of jangling keys in her hand came out and greeted me. *"Ah, M. Mehta, d'Angleterre."*

Yes, this was the de la Chapelle château. Yes, she was Mme. de la Chapelle herself.

Inside, there was a spiralling stone staircase with a wrought-iron rail, and we climbed up and up and up. At the top, I was shown to my room, and it turned out that I was sharing it with a Canadian undergraduate from Oxford, whom I knew slightly.

"What the hell is this place?" I asked as soon as Madame had left.

"Je ne comprends pas anglais," he said, adding, with a smirk in his voice, *"Ici."*

With some exasperation, I repeated my question in French.

"Vous voudriez faire la connaissance des jeunes filles?"

"Oui, certainement," I said.

"Moi aussi."

I tried my best, but I couldn't get him to tell me any more about the place.

We went down to dinner. Gathered around a big table were perhaps twenty French men and women, and at a smaller table nearby lots of children were finishing their dinner. There were cursory introductions, and I noticed that most people had family names other than de la Chapelle. I was placed near M. de la Chapelle, between the Canadian and another Oxford undergraduate, who also spoke bad French with me.

After we sat down, I made bold to ask Mme. de la Chapelle, at one end of the table, about her daughters.

"Elles sont toutes ici," she said.

"*Mais, le cahier de l'agence . . .*"

One of the other women at the table finally understood, and said, in English, "Oh, that's an old picture of us—that picture was taken before the war. We are now all mothers and—who knows?—maybe grandmothers soon."

MY ten days in Tours passed pleasantly enough. The Oxford undergraduates, after the initial coolness, accepted me as one of them, and every morning we would go to the university for our French lessons and then have lunch in a café, drink the excellent local wine, laugh about the goings on at the de la Chapelles', and talk about "if"s and "can"s of history: What if Charles Martel had not defeated the Saracens in 832? Would Tours and Poitiers— perhaps all of Western Europe—have become Muslim? We talked about Louis XI, who introduced the silk industry to Tours; the Franco-Prussian War, during which Tours was the seat of government of the national defense; and Balzac, who was born in Tours. In the afternoon, we might troop like eager tourists to the Cathedral of Saint-Gatien, to the churches of Saint-Julien and Notre-Dame-la-Riche, to the Hôtel Gouin, or to the Château Villandry, which had beautiful gardens, where Charles Perrault supposedly conceived his "Sleeping Beauty." Sightseeing was not my forte, but I picked up considerable information from my fellow-undergraduates and from a couple of tour guides. In the evening, whether or not we wanted to, we joined M. de la Chapelle at the bridge table—fortunately, I had my Braille cards along and knew how to play. He seemed to consider the bridge table a sort of lectern for teaching us conversational French, and his doing that, of course, was the reason for our being his paying guests in the first place. Especially when he was the dummy, he would tell us stories, in the pure French for which Tours was famous, about his ancestors, who were great royalists and great patriarchs.

I returned to England much poorer but with a good deal of confidence in my French, and spent the rest of my vac holed up in dingy little digs (during the vacs, the college turned out foreign and British students alike) swotting at the books.

☙

I HAD an introduction to Vivian Galbraith from John Gleason, one of my Pomona professors, who had studied with him, and soon after the start of the Hilary term I dropped him a line. I heard from him by return of post, asking me to his house for tea that very afternoon.

Galbraith turned out to be like virtually no one else I had met at Oxford. He did not have a trace of pretension, pomposity, or cant, although he had read both Greats and Modern History at Balliol. (He had got a Third in Greats, and had turned around and read history in one year and got a First.) Right then, at the age of sixty-seven, he was serving his last year as Regius Professor of Modern History at Oxford. He had acquired a recording of "My Fair Lady" shortly before I came to tea, and the whole time I was there he played it at high volume, and tried to talk above it, the rhythm of his speech a little like Eliza Doolittle's before it was refashioned by Professor Higgins' labors. Yet, even while "My Fair Lady" was blaring in the background and Mrs. Galbraith was serving tea, he managed to put me onto an Oxford legend about Christopher Hill, who was to be my tutor on Tudors and Stuarts that term.

Christopher had come up to Balliol to try for a scholarship in 1930, when he was eighteen. Galbraith, who was then Fellow and Tutor at the college, and another history tutor, Kenneth Bell, had interviewed him. Christopher totally collapsed at the interview. He was an inarticulate and callow public-school boy from St. Peter's School in York, and when he did manage to speak he had a stutter. He was barely able to answer yes or no to the provocative questions that the two tutors put to him. In the evening, after the interview, while he was sitting dejectedly in the chilly Balliol room assigned to him, there was a knock at the door, and Galbraith and Bell burst in. Christopher was confused and terrified, and became all the more so when the two tutors sat down and embarked on a furious argument about religion. Their argument became so heated and desperate that at one point Galbraith bellowed, "What good thing ever came out of the Church of England?" Christopher, who had been sitting there silent, depressed, and skeptical, could hold back no longer. "Swift," he broke in. The two tutors appeared to think that that was the most brilliant remark they had ever heard, and they set about dissecting it and closely examining him on it. Soon the dialogue turned into a three-way argument, and Christopher had his real interview after all—thanks to the instincts of his future tutors, who, it was said, in good Balliol tradition had looked past appearances. He won the scholarship, went on to get a First in Modern History, and was elected one of the two prize Fellows of All Souls, who are chosen annually, on the basis of competitive examinations in one or another of the traditional subjects—history, politics, economics, philosophy, classical languages, and law. There was no prize more glittering for someone who had just taken Schools than to be elected to All Souls. As a Fellow of All Souls, he could look forward to being almost automatically reëlected, and taken care of for the rest of his life. In time, Christopher Hill's name was added to the roster of Balliol's great historians.

As it happened, I always went to Christopher Hill right after my tutorial on the Middle Ages with Southern. The contrast between the two tutorials—one clerical, the other secular—was so great that I felt I was going from one chamber of a Turkish bath into another, and the impression was strengthened by the fact that Southern's room, being in a newer part of the college, was warm and snug, while Christopher's seemed to be always cold and damp.

I would climb right to the top of Staircase XIX, which was next to the back gate, with my essay for Christopher Hill in hand, and knock at the great man's door. "Come in!" he would call out—with the emphasis on "come." He had a cavernous room, furnished with dingy college tables and chairs and lined from floor to ceiling with books. Prominent in the room was a portrait of Oliver Cromwell, with whom, I soon discovered, Christopher had a love/hate relationship. A gas fire would be hissing in the background, and Christopher, in a tweed coat and slacks, his black hair unruly and his blue eyes inquisitive, would be sitting in a wing chair, his feet tucked under him. Although he was in his mid-forties, he came across more as an older graduate student than as a historian with an international reputation. As soon as I got to know him, I realized that his giving me his little finger after the Handshaking was only a sign of shyness—that he must have been taken aback by my putting out my hand as if I took Handshaking literally.

I was in the habit of addressing all adult Englishmen—tutors, shopkeepers, tailors, or dustmen—as "Sir." That was my Raj upbringing. The very first time I called Christopher "Sir," he came down on me: "Please, not 'Sir'—just 'Christopher.'" It required some time, but I was eventually cured of the habit, at least in respect to him.

My tutorial partner and I would take turns writing essays for him. Generally, undergraduates were required to read their essays aloud to their tutors, and my tutorial partner would read mine to Christopher. He would listen with deep concentration, hardly ever interrupting. At the end of the essay, he would never say whether it was good or bad. Instead, he would say "Thank you" or "Thank you, that was interesting" or "Thank you very much; that was most interesting"—variants that we soon learned meant "Satisfactory" or "Good" or "Very good," respectively. If he asked us, as he only rarely did, to cite a source for a point that was unknown to him, we could take the request to mean "Excellent."

CHRISTOPHER was singular among dons for being so egalitarian and fair-minded that all distinctions of degree, rank, and age were repugnant to him. He was devoid of race prejudice of any kind, and was so far ahead of his time that he treated women no differently from men, without a hint of condescension. Because he said everything he had to say in the fewest possible words, there were long pauses in the tutorials, and they were made all the more disconcerting by his nervous habit of sniffing.

Unlike other tutors, Christopher never directly contradicted us. He would merely shift around in his chair and say something like "That's not really an answer, is it?" or "Come on, what about thus and so?" to call to our attention a fact or an idea we had overlooked which made nonsense of our argument. Also, other tutors might summarize the salient points of the topic, or give their own conclusions, and one would note them down in the hope of trotting them out in Schools. Christopher took the opposite approach. He would only ask questions—very difficult questions, which made us do all the thinking and talking. At his gentle prodding, we found ourselves demolishing accepted interpretations, always with reference to specific evidence, and standing established authorities on their heads. He would play the role of devil's advocate even more vigorously if we parroted arguments he had presented in his extremely influential books and articles. After such a performance, it was hard to believe that he himself had actually once put forward the very opinions he was attacking. He also had other ways of bringing out the best in his pupils. He would discover what our interests and strengths were, and set us essay topics accordingly. I remember that at one point he got wind of the fact that for some time I had been working through "Paradise Lost," with the help of the classic six-volume biography of Milton by David Masson. He assigned me an essay on the topic of "Paradise Lost" and Milton's eventual disillusionment with the Puritan revolution. Writing an essay on the connection between the two was intoxicating.

I WENT to Christopher for several terms (he also prepared me for examination papers in my special subject, the Commonwealth and Protectorate from 1647 to 1658), and after I had known him for some time I discovered that he had been a card-carrying Communist and still held many Communist views. It was said that, like many of his contemporaries in the thirties, he had joined the Party as an undergraduate. But, unlike many of them, who had abandoned Communism when it proved inconvenient for getting ahead in the world, he had remained faithful to his principles— indeed, had remained a Party member even after the 1956 Hungarian uprising and its repression. The discovery staggered me— someone who had come from California, the Nixon country of the Cold War, where people had been blacklisted and could not get jobs if they had ever flirted with Communism, and where even my young readers had been required to take an oath affirming that they had never belonged to a Communist organization and were loyal to the United States. I had no trouble imagining someone's being a Communist in the early thirties. Distinguished intellectuals on both sides of the Atlantic had been taken in then by the Soviet experiment. But it was hard for me to understand how someone as highly intelligent as Christopher could have remained a Communist through the purges, through the Nazi-Soviet Pact, through the Cold War, through the events in

Hungary—and, moreover, could have continued to work at Oxford all the while. I had, of course, encountered extreme-left-wing undergraduates, but, as I saw it, there was all the difference in the world between their youthful enthusiasm and the considered views of someone who was not only a teacher I esteemed highly but also an internationally known scholar.

Christopher was an extremely guarded person, not one who would easily let his hair down. But once, after I had come down from Oxford and we had become good friends, I tackled him on the subject of Communism. His remarks were illuminating, if in his characteristically terse, elliptical, ironic way. "I was brought up as a Nonconformist," he said. He paused, and sniffed. "I learned to question authority when I was very young. When I was six, I had a schoolmistress—I remember she had a hole in her stocking, rather high up. I didn't want to eat something, because I was sure it would make me sick. She insisted that it wouldn't. I ate it, and in fact was sick." Pause. Sniff. "My parents had a strong sense of fairness. To them, the whole idea of one race being superior to another was repugnant. I heard my first anti-Semitic joke when I was twelve or thirteen, and I didn't get the point. When it was explained to me, I was shocked." Pause. Sniff. "The moment I got into Oxford, they decided that my sister must go there, too—that she shouldn't be discriminated against because she was a girl. She was seven years younger than I, but eventually she came up to St. Anne's." Pause. Sniff. "In my undergraduate years, poetry was very important to me. Whenever there was a new book of Auden's or Eliot's, I bought it. I was very excited by metaphysical poetry, and Eliot's essays on the metaphysicals stimulated a desire to understand seventeenth-century England, whose conflicts and tensions had produced them. That was one reason for my fascination with seventeenth-century English history and for my interest in Marxism. It was not the only reason, but I turn it out to people who expect me to give political reasons for these two interests. Still, each reason is part of the truth, I

think. At Balliol, the classicist Norman O. Brown, two years my
junior, was a great influence on me. He pushed me to the left,
telling me it was my moral duty to join the Communist Party,
though I don't think he did so himself. I was very active in left-
wing politics—particularly in the October Club, and in the peace
movement, where I first met Dick Southern, who had come up a
couple of years earlier. Actually, being a Fellow of All Souls confirmed me in my Communism. The college had a lot of money
that the Fellows just spent on leading the good life. A lot of
junior Fellows felt, as I did, that the college was just a place of
privilege. In the college, there were as many anti–All Souls people as there were pro–All Souls people." Pause. Sniff. "A librarian tipped me off that Russian historians were producing interesting
work on seventeenth-century England. I started learning Russian
with the help of gramophone records, and so on, and, with All
Souls' financial support, went to Moscow for a year of further
study. I lived as a lodger with the wife of a kulak who was doing
time in Siberia for speculation. She was carrying on the business
by taking me in as an illegal lodger. While I was living there,
her husband turned up. He was in the bloom of health, from
which I concluded that kulaks could not be having as bad a time
in concentration camps as foreign reports said." Pause. Sniff. "You
asked about the purges. I was there when the purges began, in
1936. An English engineer working in Russia—not a Communist—remarked to me about the victims, 'This time, even the
Soviet government can't save them.' He was convinced that they
were guilty. I rationalized the 1938 purges in a similar way. In
any case, I was always skeptical of what the English papers said
about the Soviet Union. I had long experience with the whoppers
of the English press. I was, of course, shocked by the Nazi-Soviet
pact, but I blamed Chamberlain for it. My friends and I had for
some time been advocating that Chamberlain make a pact with
Stalin against Hitler. For the last two years of the war, I was in
the Foreign Office, and I found that many of my colleagues were

pro-Russian. We all hoped for an Anglo-Soviet alliance after the war. I really didn't become disenchanted with Stalin until 1953, when Khrushchev made his anti-Stalin speech. I finally left the Party in 1957, because the Communist Party in England was still trying to justify the invasion of Hungary."

"But your books and tutorials were free of Communist rhetoric," I said, and then added that his youthful book "Lenin and the Russian Revolution," which I had happened upon late in the day, was the only exception.

He sniffed, and said, "I dropped the Marxist vocabulary because of a remark of Tawney's about 'Lenin and the Russian Revolution.' " R. H. Tawney, who, in the twenties, wrote the widely acclaimed "Religion and the Rise of Capitalism," was one of the most widely admired left-wing historians. "He said, 'Hill is good, but I wish he wouldn't sing the doxology at the end of every chapter.' If Tawney, with whose ideas I was sympathetic, thought that of my book, I wondered, then what must others think? Thereafter, I avoided the doxology."

"Did you ever encounter any professional difficulties because you were a Communist?"

"Luckily, I had tenure at Balliol, or I would have been thrown out in the fifties. There were a lot of historians then who simply couldn't get a job at a university or anywhere else because of their politics. In England at that time, if you remember, there was what one might call a cold purge, conducted in a discreet and gentlemanly English way, so that people victimized politically seemed to be passed over for other reasons."

Christopher himself, defying the fate of other left-wing scholars, served as Master of Balliol from 1965 to 1978.

WHEN I was up at Oxford, some of us used to debate which college was the oldest and therefore the foundation of the university. Balliol, University, and Merton all vie for this honor. University was the first to have a benefactor (a bequest was made in 1249); Balliol was the first to acquire an actual site for its community of scholars (tradition puts the date at 1263); and Merton was the first to have statutory existence (its original statutes date from 1270). In any event, colleges in the thirteenth century were founded by men who, because they had a university education—in Paris, for instance—had risen to the top of the royal and ecclesiastical hierarchy, and wanted to prepare the way for other talented men: their relatives first and foremost, but also poor and able men from their dioceses or the counties of their birth.

The origins of Balliol have been traced to Walter Kirkham, the Bishop of Durham, and a penance he imposed on a notoriously rapacious and violent baron named John de Balliol. The Balliol family was one of the ranking families in northern England, owning lands in both England and France, and Balliol himself married into an eminent Scottish family, thereby substantially increasing his holdings. In fact, his wife, Dervorguilla, was a noblewoman who was descended from Scottish kings (and one of her sons made claim, for a brief time, to the Crown of Scotland), and she moved easily and grandly in the high society of both England and Scotland.

Around 1255, John de Balliol and some of his retainers seized the church at Long Newton, in the diocese of Durham, and forcibly occupied it. He and Bishop Kirkham had for some years been quarrelling over certain family lands of Balliol's, which in the previous century had apparently been pledged to the bishop of that time as security for a loan, and also over the Baron's tardiness in doing homage to Kirkham himself. In the words of one chronicler, Bishop Kirkham was "a man mild and pure in heart, small in stature, but most liberal and pious in disposition, who preferred to sing psalms, rather than to hunt in the woods," but, in his way, he was as strong-willed as the Baron, and he now appealed to the King, Henry III, and the King ordered Balliol to make reparation to the Bishop. Balliol had no choice but to obey. According to this chronicler, the Bishop "with a confident spirit wisely reduced his fugitive son to agree that he should solemnly come to the door of Durham Cathedral, and while all the people looked on, should be whipped by his hand; and that he should assign a sum for the maintenance of scholars in Oxford which should continue in perpetuity." Historians think this account may be somewhat embellished, since it is improbable that a nobleman of Balliol's rank could ever have been publicly whipped, but it does seem that soon after the King's order Balliol, as a penance for his violation of the church's sanctity, started paying a few scholars at Oxford eightpence a week each. According to tradition, this payment was instituted as a foundation in 1263, some three years after the death of the Bishop. Balliol, however, seems to have made no provision for continuing it "in perpetuity." He died in 1268 or 1269, and the responsibility for its survival passed to his wife, Dervorguilla.

Dervorguilla's devotion to her husband was extraordinary in a time when life was particularly unsettled, changing, fierce, and cruel. Upon his death, she had his heart removed from his body, embalmed with sweet-smelling spices, and laid in a specially made ivory casket, and the casket was then locked, enamelled, and bound with silver. She probably chose to preserve the heart because in the thirteenth century people were beginning to take a scientific interest in the body, and regarded the heart as the seat not only of physical vitality but also of love. In any event, throughout the Middle Ages saints' relics were thought of as talismans; large relics were enshrined in churches, and small ones, such as bits of bones, were kept by individuals for private veneration. Of course, Balliol was far from being a saint. Dervorguilla, for the twenty-one years of life remaining to her, treated the heart with reverence, as if her beloved were constantly there with her. Whenever she sat down to eat, she had the casket next to her, and the food left over from her meals was distributed to the poor in his memory.

For some years, Dervorguilla was preoccupied with making permanent arrangements for the heart. She was not a member of one of those great families whose ancestors had endowed monasteries, where the heart could be tended to in perpetuity, nor was she rich enough to endow an entire monastery herself. So in 1273, after long negotiations with the General Chapter of the Order of Citeaux, she founded a Cistercian abbey on her own land in Dumfriesshire, which came to be known as Sweetheart Abbey, and she directed in her will that she should be buried there with the heart between her breasts.

When Dervorguilla finally turned her mind to the Oxford foundation—to which she had continued her husband's payments from year to year—she saw in it a way of providing for the well-being of her husband's soul and the perpetuation of his name, or so it appears from her first set of statutes for the scholars, issued in 1282, which begins, "Desiring with maternal affection to provide for the well-being of our sons and Scholars dwelling in Oxford, we direct, ordain, and prescribe that they observe punctiliously all that is hereinafter written." Her statutes provided that the scholars should attend Mass on Sundays and on the greater feast days, that they should hear sermons, that they should study by following the university statutes and proctors appointed by her, that they should speak Latin and hold weekly disputations, and that they should say three Masses a year for the soul of her husband, and also for the souls of her children, her friends, and her proctors, and for her soul. She seems to have felt particularly strongly about two additional matters. First, no rich scholar was to conduct himself so as to be a burden to his poorer brethren; the food left over from the common table was to be given to a poor student designated by her proctors. Second, the scholars were never to pawn, sell, or otherwise dispose of the missal she had vouchsafed to them in her husband's memory. She clearly did not give much thought to the details of an actual college. "Her earliest statutes have the charm of a half-formed idea," Southern writes. "Even the number of students is not specified."

Dervorguilla appointed Walter of Fotheringhay, a native of one of her residences who was also one of her executors, to serve as the principal of her Oxford scholars, and Father Richard of Slikeburne, a Franciscan from a village on her estate in Northumberland, to serve as their adviser. The two men started buying small tenements, and in time they collected most of what now forms the front quadrangle of the college.

Dervorguilla died in 1290, at the age of eighty, and was buried according to her wishes. (At least we Balliol men remembered her as the woman who established Oxford, a male bastion until 1920, when women formally became members of the university.)

Balliol had modest aims from the very beginning. If its scholars wanted to pursue higher degrees, they had to move either to Merton or, later on, to other colleges. Also, the stipend remained fixed for some time at eightpence. At Merton, it seems, scholars were paid twelvepence. The college came into its own in the fourteenth and fifteenth centuries. John Wycliffe, the great religious reformer, served as its Master around 1360. A few of its Fellows are known to have studied on the Continent. Among them was William Gray, who died in 1478 and bequeathed to the college his library, consisting of a hundred and eighty-one manuscript volumes and one printed book. It became the basis of the college's present library. In the late sixteenth and early seventeenth centuries, the university prospered, and so did Balliol. More men wanted to attend the university, and the college, because it wanted to supplement its income, began to admit more of them. The college did well by its undergraduates and established lectureships in subjects ranging from rhetoric and mathematics to poetry. During the English Civil War, however, the college had difficulty collecting battels and got into financial straits so severe that it had trouble even paying its bills to the bakers who baked its bread and the brewers who brewed its ale. For the remainder of the seventeenth century and throughout the eighteenth century, the college, like the university, was a sleepy place.

Modern Balliol is said to date from the time of John Parsons, who was Master of the college from 1798 to 1819. Among other things, he helped to institute the Honours Examination Statute, which initiated the system of competitive examinations. Parsons' successor, Richard Jenkyns, threw open most of the scholarships to competitive examinations. (Previously, scholars were nominated individually by the Master or by Fellows.) It was during his mastership that Matthew Arnold and Benjamin Jowett came to the college. The ancient requirements that the Fellows be ordained and that everyone attend chapel were abandoned, and around the middle of the nineteenth century Fellows gradually stopped automatically taking holy orders, as they had always done. Thus the college acquired its secular character. Benjamin Jowett, who was elected a Fellow in the eighteen-thirties, while he was still an undergraduate reading Greats, was Master from 1870 to 1893. He probably had a more profound influence on the college than anyone either before or since. Under him, the teaching of undergraduates came first and scholarly contributions by the Fellows second. He got outstanding scholars to teach in the college, instituted weekly tutorials for all undergraduates, and developed the library so that it had one of the best collections of books for taking Schools.

IT was Easter vac of my first year, and I found digs for a few weeks in a pleasantly shady street, with a landlady who was the charming young wife of an inspector of income tax. I was soon deeply immersed in documents for my special subject, the Commonwealth and Protectorate from 1647 to 1658—for which I would be going to Christopher Hill in the Trinity term—and grappling with the problems presented by Oliver Cromwell's character and Charles I's execution. It was at once challenging and frustrating to read material written in the style and idiom of another period and to try to glean the meaning and intention of various remonstrances, addresses, petitions, and letters. I also began working through Aristotle's "Politics," Hobbes's "Leviathan," and Rousseau's "Contrat Social" sentence by sentence. These were the set texts for my political-science paper, and I would be given gobbets from them to comment on in Schools.

I was particularly lucky to have Alastair McCann as one of my readers, not only because he seemed to have no other commitments and was available for seven or eight hours a day but also because he would go through extremely dense and difficult documents as if he had read them over in his own time in preparation for reading them to me. He seemed to sense which passages I might have difficulty with and often reread them without my having to say anything to him. When I was trying to puzzle out the meaning of an especially abstruse passage, he would discreetly help me by finding key words or key sentences and reminding me of passages we had read in an earlier session. With anyone else, this might have been intrusive or irritating, but not with him. He was so circumspect and threw himself into the work with such energy that he could almost have been my teacher. Also, as a person, he was so considerate that if the landlady dropped in to see me he would almost make himself invisible, retreating to the window with a book or stepping out to have a cigarette. And the minute I was alone again he was there, reading from the exact place where we had left off.

Every now and then, he would stop and take tablets. At the

time, I did not know what they were, and I felt too shy to ask him anything personal. (I was still so uncertain about what was done and not done in England that I was always on my guard.) Later, he told me that the tablets were heavy doses of amphetamines.

❧

ONE evening near the end of the Trinity term, I went to the railway station to receive my father. It was his first visit to Oxford since I had come up, and I was excited at the thought of showing him around my university. His visit had been put off several times. First, he had been busy lecturing in America; then he had gone home to India to look after the family; and, most recently, he had been travelling on the Continent with Mrs. Clyde. As a rule, when I saw my father during his travels with Mrs. Clyde it was hard for us to get any time to ourselves, because she was always around, but he had just written me from Frankfurt that he and Mrs. Clyde would soon be in London and he had got leave to come see me for a weekend.

Mrs. Clyde enjoyed visiting practically every country in Europe except England. She didn't like its cold, damp climate, and she was irritated by certain customs of the English, such as constantly saying "Thank you." She would complain, "You step in the elevator, and the operator says 'Thank you.' You get off the elevator, and the operator says 'Thank you.' The porter opens the door, and he says 'Thank you.' The commissionaire opens the door of the taxi, and he says 'Thank you.' " My father would explain to her that the English were simply polite people, and he and she would have a laugh over the custom. But the next time he proposed including England in their travels she would say, "No, *thank you!* I don't want to go there, shiver, and be thanked all the time. You only like England because you were a student there."

When we children were growing up, my father used to talk so much about England that I imagined he had spent half his life in the country. When I finally discovered that he had spent barely a year there, as a student, in 1920, I wondered how the country could have made such a deep impression on him. Now here I was, also with less than a year in England and already an irrepressible Anglophile.

I was excited at the thought of having my father all to myself in Oxford. I imagined that we, father and son, would saunter through ancient colleges, around the Magdalen Deer Park, and along the Christ Church Meadow, and talk about all the great Englishmen who had come out of Oxford. But, to my astonishment, he got off the train reciting Urdu couplets: *"Gardish main hon agar ham, rehtaa hai dil vatan main. Sumjho hamain vaheen peh, dil ho jahaan hamara."* ("If voyager be I, remains the heart in homeland. Understand I am there, wherever my heart is.") No sooner had he finished reciting these than he launched into some others, apparently oblivious of the people on the platform: *"Hazaaron Khwahishain aisee, keh har Khwahish peh dam niklai. Bahot niklai merai armaan, laikin phir bhee kam niklai."* ("A thousand wishes are such that for every wish I would expire. Very many such longings I have plumbed, but still they are all too few.")

In spite of myself, I was moved at hearing the couplets. When I was growing up, my father's recitations—usually prompted by a chance remark—were a part of every family gathering. To my child's ear, his voice, like the couplets, had seemed to contain the wisdom of the ages. But now, as I thought of the English people at the station, I felt embarrassed. I was afraid that they might take us for wogs who couldn't speak English.

"I trust you had a pleasant trip," I said, in my best King's English.

My father, however, said in Urdu, speaking as the nightingale invoked by the poet: *"Nah tarapnai kee ijaazat hai nah faryaad kee hai. Dam ghut kai mar jaoon yeh marzee maire sayyaad kee hai. Ataa hai yaad mujh ko guzraa hooa zamanaa, woh jharian chaman kee woh mairaa ashianaa, woh saath sab kai urnaa woh sair aasmaan kee, who baagh kee habaarain who sab kaa milkai ganaa."* ("Neither do I have the freedom for a heartbeat, nor for making a request. Choking off my breath and dying in my cage, that is the wish of my jailer. How I cannot help remembering the bygone time, those shrubs with flowers, that funhouse of mine, flying with all the world, touring the skies, enjoying the blossoms, singing with all the world.")

"They are beautiful couplets," I said, in English, picking up his suitcase and stepping along. In a surge, I felt proud to have my father in Oxford—proud to be walking in step with him out of the Oxford station, the backs of our hands slightly touching as we threaded our way through the evening rush-hour crowd to a queue for taxis. "I remember the couplets from my childhood. But what is the occasion—or situation?"

" 'Situation' is the right word," my father said, finally talking English. "It's my situation with Mrs. Clyde."

"You talk as though you were her prisoner rather than her doctor," I said. "Anyway, you've worked for her now for many years."

"I've done it out of necessity," he said.

The job with Mrs. Clyde had, in a manner of speaking, fallen into his lap not long after his retirement, and he had grown dependent on it, for in India the income, while not very much in Western terms, went a long way. Still, he had never stopped looking for an alternative type of work. At one time, he had thought that lecturing in America might fill the bill, but he didn't have a name as a lecturer, and he wasn't able to get himself a good lecture agent. A friend who was the president of the Knife and Fork Club, a society something like the Rotary Club, had arranged the lecture tour for him the previous year. It involved travelling on buses and little planes to small towns in the Midwest as part of a sort of debating group, the other members being a French politician, an English journalist, and an American editor. The four of them were billed as a "miniature United Nations Security Council," and were required to stage debates on world issues of the day at dinner meetings of the club. The atmosphere was a little like that of a travelling circus, he told me, and the debates had to be couched in artificially simplistic terms to make them palatable to the audiences. Furthermore, after expenses, the money from the lecture tour was minimal, and could do little more than supplement what he earned from Mrs. Clyde.

"In good conscience, how much time can I spend taking her pulse, keeping track of her weight, and prescribing her supplementary medicines?" my father said now. Then he lapsed into Punjabi to say, "I wish your mother were here with us."

"Please speak English," I whispered. "What will all these English people think?"

"Did you know that my job has become a joke with Daulat Ram and company?" he said, in English. Daulat Ram was his next-to-youngest brother and the one closest to him. "Everyone says, 'Brother goes away every year to dance attendance on an old American lady.' How I wish I could say with the English poet, 'It matters not how strait the gate, how charged with punishments the scroll, I am the master of my fate: I am the captain of my soul.' "

"You should tell Daulat Ram and company that, thanks to Mrs. Clyde, you have made the entire Western world into Lahori Darvaza," I said. That was the name of one of the main gates to the bustling old walled city of Lahore, and my father's childhood home, outside the city walls, was near the gate. My father was fond of quoting a saying of *his* father, Lalaji: "I'll send one son after another to England for education until I make London into Lahori Darvaza."

My father laughed, in his usual open, unrestrained way.

❦

AFTER putting my father's bag in the college guest room where I had booked him for the night, we set out for my room. In the main quadrangle, some undergraduates were playing croquet. The sound of mallet hitting ball announced that summer had come to Oxford and soon we would all be leaving for our long vac. My first Oxford year was about to close, and I already felt carefree. In my room, we drew the two armchairs closer to the gas fire. I poured two glasses of sherry from a bottle on the mantelpiece, and handed one to my father. We loosened our ties, took off our shoes, and sat down, resting our feet on the fender.

"Cheers, son," my father said. "Even Lalaji, far-sighted though he was, would never have dreamed that one day father and son would be sitting at Oxford and sipping sherry like Englishmen."

I asked after my mother.

"Now that she's England-returned, she has got a lot of self-confidence," my father said. "You should hear the stories she tells about Laindon and Oxford and London and Bad Nauheim and Frankfurt. You'd be very much impressed."

At one point, the subject of Mrs. Clyde and my father's job with her came up again. "Her medical problems don't amount to much," he said. "Her only complaint this summer has been a sore foot. She soaks it every day, and I massage it and then put a new elastic bandage on it. No sooner does the foot get better than she bangs it on something and the regimen of soaking and massaging has to start again. Anyway, whatever her complaints are, they don't require the services of a medical man."

"You certainly don't seem happy with Mrs. Clyde," I said.

"She's good—too good—to me," he said. "If I as much as sneeze, she tells me to rest in bed. She's always very solicitous. But I can't tell you how possessive she is. When I arrived in Frankfurt in April, she was already at the hotel. I felt a little grimy from the long flight from Delhi, so after greeting her I went to take a bath. Because there was no soap in the bathroom, and I had to call down for it, the bath took longer than it should have. When I came out to the common room of our suite, I could tell that she was out of sorts for having been kept waiting. I apologized, and within a moment she was her old good-humored self. The trouble is that there is no time that I can call my own."

"Can't you just tell her that you need some time to yourself?" I asked.

"At the different places we stay, she does encourage me to go out by myself, but whenever I do I come home and find her sulking, and then I'm the one who feels out of sorts. And now there is another problem. Just the other day, she said, 'I don't feel comfortable calling you Dr. Mehta.' So I said, 'You can call me Mehta.' She said, 'But that's what someone would call a servant. What do your friends call you?' I said, 'A.R.' She said, 'That's no name. What is your first name?' I explained to her that my first name was Amolak, but it was always used with the second name, Ram, and that only my mother and my elder sister had ever called me that. She said that that name was a mouthful, so could she just call me Molak? That's what she calls me now. I don't like it, but what can I do?"

"I wonder if from her point of view it wouldn't be better to simply have a close friend as a companion."

"She tried that for many years. But either a friend wouldn't stay with her or a friend didn't have the time to pick up and go when she felt like it. It seems it's easier for her to pay me to be with her. Also, I'm sure her friends get tired of arguing with her. One of the problems is that no matter what you say to her it becomes an argument."

"How so?"

My father said that his Indian background was a constant source of argument. There were so many things about him that she, as a Westerner, couldn't grasp. For instance, almost every day new names of his relatives would come up in conversation. The occasion might be the receipt of a letter from his grand-nephew Sudeep asking for a mouth organ, or from his niece Vidya requesting a pressure cooker. These relationships would have to be explained to her. She saw his obligation to his family and relatives as unending, and would say that every time she helped to make him solvent by giving him "work" he would go and squander the money on presents for his relatives. One of their continuing and more frustrating arguments, he said, was about the grand wedding he had recently held for my second-oldest sister, Nimi, because, try as he might, he could not get Mrs. Clyde to understand that in India, where marriages were arranged, a father had to celebrate a wedding in a manner commensurate with his position in government and society. He said that she would cry out, "You're a poor man! Why do you have to spend money on a wedding?" He would say, "She's my daughter—I have a duty to settle her in life. I have a certain station that I must maintain. My relatives and colleagues expect that of me." For days, she would keep bringing up the subject, and each time he would have to explain to her all over again the importance of the Indian family and its role in society.

"Sometimes our arguments get so heated that we don't speak for an entire day," he said. "The truth is, what she really needs is a valet, who can pack bags in a hurry and be ready to change hotels and countries at a moment's notice. One day this summer, we went to a Bavarian village in order to hear its orchestra practice there. The next morning, she woke up and said, 'Let's go to Heidelberg—it has a great university.' I telephoned for accommodations there, and we left that day. But when we arrived in Heidelberg she got a bad attack of hay fever and insisted that we leave the same day for a place with a low pollen count. Sometimes she doesn't decide where we are going until we are in a taxi."

"I hope there are some enjoyable moments with her," I said.

"Yes, of course. We do some good things together. The other day, we went to 'The Merry Widow,' and just the day before yesterday we saw the movie 'It's Great to Be Young.' Sometimes I meet interesting people. When we were in Geneva, I met Mrs. Clyde's nephew, Marshall Hill Clyde, Jr. A large, jovial man, he lives on his inherited wealth like a maharaja. He has two yachts, which he sails on Lake Geneva. His wife, Jackie, is really interesting. She studies Indian philosophy and is interested in Vedanta. So we had a lot to talk about."

I poured a little more sherry for myself. My father was still nursing his, and I remarked on how odd it was that we should spend our little time at Oxford together talking about Mrs. Clyde. "But then, of course, it is because of her that you and I are sitting here," I said. And I reflected that she had helped to pay for my education.

My father said that, for all the difficulties of the relationship, he hoped that she would ask him back for the following year. "You know, I like her immensely," he added, his voice warm with sherry. "She's a remarkable lady. No one could have done more for us—the job with her has put our family on its feet."

The bell for hall was striking, so we pulled up our ties, put our shoes back on, and set off for dinner.

On the way, I told him that because I had got such a late start in reading history, and because I wanted to take a couple of literature courses at Harvard that summer, I had decided to take three years over my degree instead of two—and, luckily, the Hazen Foundation had agreed to cover the extra year. "This also means that next Oxford term I can read English," I said. "This way, I can eat my cake and have it, too. And, by the way, this also means I will be in America to help launch my book this August."

"Wonderful," my father said. "I'll certainly see you in the States, because Mrs. Clyde is going back home for a little while."

How different his visit already is from Mamaji's, I thought. In many ways, he is much more Oxford—a cosmopolitan world traveller—than I'll ever be.

VI

TIME, THE

SUBTLE

THIEF OF

YOUTH

O NE DAY TOWARD THE END OF THE TRINITY TERM OF my first year, I received a letter from John Barron, the secretary of the Leonardo Society, inviting me to be a guest at the society's next biweekly meeting. "The society will meet in the rooms of Jeremy Knowles, on Staircase XIII, at 8:15 on the evening of Friday June 7th," the letter said. I was interested. I had heard a little bit about the society from Jane Shelden Davis, one of my readers, who was going out with Jeremy Knowles. It consisted of fifteen self-selected, high-powered undergraduates who met every second Friday in term to read and discuss papers on the sciences or the arts, with a lot of mulled claret to oil the tongue. I went along to Knowles's rooms on the appointed evening. The sitting room was warm and welcoming, and smelled of pipe tobacco, like a well-used study. John Barron, a polite man in his final year of Greats, poured me a glass of mulled claret from a jug at the door and moved on. I froze, not knowing what I was expected to do, but was immediately cheered to discover that three friends of mine—Anthony Leggett, Peter Gregson, and Roderick Allison, all second-year Greats men—were in the room. They were talking about Aristotle's notions of science—a matter about which I knew next to nothing. I stood among them biding my time until I could enter the conversation gracefully.

I had seldom held a glass of steaming wine before. I warmed my fingers on it, much as I would on a J.C.R. tea mug. Barron had only half filled the glass, so I got the full benefit of the aroma of the mulled claret: wine, cloves, cinnamon, cardamom, and raisins. It seemed a little feast in itself. I took a sip and felt warm all over.

Knowles, a second-year chemist, joined the group and started holding forth on the subject of wine tasting.

"You should do a paper about it for the society. And bring a lot of wine," Peter Gregson said.

"By gosh, I will," said Knowles.

"Knowles, how can you taste any wine? You are always puffing on a pipe," Roderick said. He had an ingenuous way of asking questions that the rest of us were too discreet to ask.

"You must be confusing cigarette smoking with pipe smoking," Knowles said, blowing an extra bit of smoke at him.

I swirled the claret around in my glass and took another sip.

I held the liquid on my tongue to get its full flavor. This is the good life, I thought. This is Oxford.

We all sat down wherever we could find seats, and Barron read the minutes of the previous meeting. It told of Richard Snedden's paper, entitled puzzlingly "Ki Kuy Hoi to Kitty Hawk," which he had apparently illustrated with facsimiles of drawings and photographs of the Wrights' airplane. Barron noted that Snedden had invoked the name of Leonardo da Vinci, the eponymous hero of the society, who had tried, through scientific research, to give substance to his dream of flying.

The minutes are written with a light touch, which makes them tantalizing, if disconnected, I thought.

They were approved by a motion, and then Anthony Leggett read a paper on "Science and Sophistry." The paper was extremely impressive. His sentences were limpid. His thoughts had the rhythm of music. Anthony had just turned nineteen, and his voice sounded even younger. The effect was rather like hearing a violin prodigy in short pants give a virtuoso recital. Anthony had had a Catholic education, no doubt with Jesuits for teachers. He was marked to get a First in Greats, and was planning to read physics after that. When he finishes degrees in Greats and physics, he will be three years younger than I am now, I thought. I may be sitting in a room with the future Lindemann, or possibly even Einstein.

But, when Anthony finished, Barron said, a little derisively, "Society's need for science is overrated. The ancient Greeks developed the hypothesis of the atomic swerve purely by a-priori reasoning." He got up and, moving about the room, suavely filled glasses from the jug.

"There is also the example of Zeno. Without the aid of science, he came up with the idea of the impossibility of perpetual motion," Roderick said.

It seemed to me that Barron and Roderick were flaunting their lack of knowledge of science; as typical English arts undergraduates, they seemed to have done even less science than I had done at Pomona. I therefore said something tentative about how one shouldn't underrate science. To my gratification, my remark met with approving noises, especially from Peter Gregson.

"One shouldn't overrate ancient philosophy, either," Peter said. "For instance, the ancient philosophers were foxed by Zeno's conundrum of the race between Achilles and the tortoise."

"The ancient philosophers had trouble with the problem because they didn't take into account the fact that speed implies time," I said, trying to make a good impression as a guest. There are only about a dozen of us, I thought. We are disciples of some ancient mystery, gathered to renew our vows of allegiance, to rededicate ourselves to a common search for truth.

"The ancient philosophers also neglected to realize that a point has no dimensions," Barron said, as if to inject a light note into a discussion that he felt was getting too serious.

Anthony demurred. He vigorously cited examples of ancient philosophers who did realize that a point had no dimensions.

The English think nothing of flatly contradicting one another, I thought. They don't seem to take personal feelings into account in intellectual arguments.

Peter and Roderick weighed in with more citations from ancient philosophy.

In my turn, I gave some citations from Greek philosophy— taken from my philosophy and history courses at Pomona—which argued that a point has no dimensions.

"The Greeks certainly thought that an atom has no dimensions," Roderick said hazily. I thought he was switching to Barron's point of view, but then he said, "Yet if, when an atom is multiplied, it has mass, which is divisible, doesn't that imply that an atom indeed has dimensions?"

"Good thinking," Barron said, still ambling around the room filling people's glasses.

Roderick was by no means alone in sounding a little hazy.

"Can one really speak about a void—something in which there is no atom, something in which there is nothing?" Ray Ockenden said, out of the blue, somewhat ironically. He was a second-year man reading Modern Languages.

"Every bit of space has some matter in it," I said. "There is no such thing as empty space. But, to get back to the question about the dimensions of a point, are the modern philosophers, in their theories about points, influenced by their ancient predecessors?"

"Anaximenes has had a lot of influence," Ockenden said in response to my question. He added facetiously, "He said that air was the prime substance out of which the world was made. He probably meant hot air."

"The Greeks have very little to teach us," Richard Snedden said. Until then, he had been silent. He was a second-year man reading P.P.E. "They were unscientific."

"But what about the clepsydra? What about Empedocles leaping into Aetna to test his theories?" Knowles said. Knowles's references to a water clock that was probably used in Egypt in around 2000 B.C. and to the ending of the Greek philosopher's life, which I had never heard about, impressed me, especially coming, as they did, from a scientist.

"But there is such a thing as a void," Jeremy Collier said. Like Snedden, he seemed to have just waked up. He had taken his Schools in chemistry the year before and had got a First. He was staying on and doing some postgraduate work. Collier said he would create a void for us, and he fetched a glass half full of water from the washbasin in Knowles's bedroom, put a postcard over it, turned it upside down, and removed the card, to demonstrate how the vacuum held back the water. But it held back the water only momentarily, and Snedden got doused. There was a hubbub. Snedden was none too pleased. Anyway, no one seemed to be sure what the experiment was supposed to prove. But it was acknowledged all around that it was diverting and that it moved the philosophical discussion right into the twentieth century.

"I think we're at the end of our intellectual powers for tonight," Barron said. He adjourned the meeting, saying that the private business meeting would reconvene "almost immediately."

Paul Smith—a second-year historian, who, like me, was a guest—and I were bidden goodbye. It was 10:45 P.M. Going down the stairs, I asked Smith, "What do they do in a private business meeting?" Since he was a year senior to me, I thought that somehow he would know.

"Probably decide if they would like us as members," he said.

"I wish I had known that. I would have tried to speak more intelligently."

Smith, a very shy man, who had said hardly anything during the meeting, now cryptically said, "Yes."

The following day, I was thrilled to receive a note from Ray Ockenden, the new secretary-elect, informing me that Smith and I had been elected members of the society.

❧

In June, I went to my first dinner of the society; it dined once a term, with a distinguished invited speaker. We met in the Massey Room, a great, heavily furnished room in a small independent building near the back gate of the college, where many dinners and drinking parties of college clubs and societies were held. Around three massive teakwood tables arranged in a horseshoe shape were massive chairs of wood and red leather, which resembled those at the High Table, perhaps even those in the House of Lords. The room would comfortably seat thirty, and, with tables and chairs pushed against the walls, could probably accommodate a hundred for drinks.

We all gave our orders for apéritifs to the scouts who were on hand to serve the dinner, and gathered around our distinguished speaker, Neville Coghill. An affable but rather vain and theatrical man in his late fifties, he was Fellow and Tutor in English Literature at Exeter College, and Merton Professor of English Literature designate.

"Why does Chaucer need to be turned into modern English at all?" Ockendon asked, needling Coghill. Coghill had achieved considerable notice in the country at large for his edition of Chaucer's "Canterbury Tales" in modern English.

"He doesn't," Coghill said. "It's only his spelling that needs to be modernized, for lazy modern readers."

"But your edition has made you a pretty penny," Barron said.

"It keeps me in the style to which I've become accustomed," Coghill said smoothly.

Dinner was announced, and we all finished our drinks and sat down for a leisurely five-course meal. Scouts had to bring each course directly from the hall kitchen to the table—often at a run, to keep it hot. (The Massey Room had only a little pantry.) We were served onion soup Macafferty, lobster mayonnaise, roast duck and mandarin oranges, strawberries and cream, and mushroom savory, each course with its own wine—sherry, white wine, red wine, sweet wine, and port, respectively—and all the wines were of good vintage. (The charge for the dinner was put on our battels.) Once the table was cleared and the port passed around again, clockwise, Coghill spoke, with feeling, for fifteen minutes or so about the role of "aesthetic slogans"—titles, epithets, catch-phrases, and the like—in literature. His remarks were followed by a lively discussion roaming over the centuries, and touching on everything from the songs of medieval troubadours to television jingles for new cars.

I felt very grand, eating and drinking, and talking to Coghill as if he were one of us.

After Coghill departed, there was a short loo-break, and then we reconvened in Knowles's sitting room for the private business meeting.

"The first order of business is the election of the new secretary," Barron said, calling the meeting to order.

Ockenden's election was made official. He immediately started taking minutes.

Snedden now launched into a good-natured harangue against Barron, the outgoing secretary. "You broke the society's long-standing tradition, sir, when you allowed the sweet to be served before the savory," he said at one point. "I move that the new secretary make certain that at future dinners the members of the society eat cheese and biscuits, or whatever, before they eat their sweet."

"I second the motion," Jeremy Collier said promptly.

"But that would mean that the sweet wine would be immediately followed by a second round of port, without any food to clear away the sweetness from the palate," Ockenden said. "I therefore strongly object."

Despite Ockenden's protests, Snedden's motion was carried.

"How did the odd tradition of eating the savory before the sweet get started, anyway?" I asked Snedden during a lull—he was sitting next to me.

"The members, in their wisdom, could perfectly well decide to have port with their soup," he said quickly. That didn't answer my question, but he turned away in order to propose another motion—that Ockenden be instructed to find out from Ernie if the number on the society's premium government bond was lucky.

Collier again seconded Snedden's motion.

"Who is Ernie?" I asked Collier, who was sitting on my other side.

"Oh, ERNIE is an acronym for Electronic Random-Number-Indicator Equipment," Collier said. "It's a device used to hold a lottery of government securities. It actually selects the winning number for cash prizes."

This motion, too, was carried over an objection by Ockenden;

clearly, the new secretary didn't want to go to the bother of finding out and reporting on the matter. Then, pleading that he had a party he had promised to look in on, Ockenden left, asking Snedden to take the minutes for him.

Peter Gregson now launched into a speech about the Black Russian phenomenon, without explaining whether he was talking about tobacco, drink, or a gun. It soon became clear, however, that he was sending up dons who rode their hobbyhorses without ever explaining the context or the framework of their research.

"I find the tobacco fumes in Knowles's room choking," Peter said abruptly. He coughed in an exaggeratedly racking way, as if to say that the word "choking" wasn't sufficiently emphatic.

"I think Gregson should be issued a smog mask," Knowles retorted, puffing on his pipe more furiously than ever.

"Hear, hear!" the other smokers cried.

"Shame, shame!" the nonsmokers cried.

"My lungs are all furred up," Peter said, standing up and coughing harder.

"I don't think it's fair to criticize my room on the occasion of the society's dinner," Knowles said.

It seemed that everyone was entering into the spirit of boys having fun—performing for one another, impressing one another, competing with one another, in the hope of shining brightest in the company.

I reflected that select societies at Oxford were, in a sense, the playground of "the gang" or "the chaps," and that the chaps had no doubt got their training at their public schools and were continuing their high jinks at university. They would probably carry them on into afterlife, sustained by the old-boy network. Grammar-school boys, like Peter, and foreigners, like me, were co-opted into the gang if we were deemed to have style; in fact, if we wanted to get ahead in English society we would have to take on the colors of chaps. Yet, I suddenly realized, the members of the Leonardo hardly fitted the mold of chaps. Snedden was the only member who was from a top public school—Winchester.

"It's midnight," Snedden suddenly announced, and the meeting was adjourned.

Looking back, I remember few antics in the proceedings of the Leonardo but, rather, excellent papers and discussions on such topics as the divorce of art from science, Oxford's so-called golden years (1910–30), T. S. Eliot's political and religious ideas, different kinds of myths, H. G. Wells, the art of wine tasting, the defense of prejudice, and classics as the best form of education—and such distinguished dinner guests as Helen Gardner, W. H. Auden, and C. P. Snow.

"YOU'RE very lucky to have these rooms, sir," Daniels, my new scout, said. "They were Mr. Macmillan's rooms." Harold Macmillan had become Prime Minister nine months before.

It was the start of the Michaelmas term of my second year, and the college authorities, perhaps realizing that I needed more space to work with readers and amanuenses, had given me some of the most sought-after accommodations in college. They were in Staircase X, in the eighteenth-century part of the college, and were warmer. I had the luxury of a separate bedroom, and it had a washbasin in it, while the sitting room was large enough to accommodate a dozen people comfortably at lunch. (In those days, one could have people to lunch in one's rooms at the price of seven and sixpence per head, excluding spirits and wines.) Yet, perversely, I rather missed my old room in Staircase XVI, in the nineteenth-century part of the college, with its window on the main quadrangle and with George as my scout and Jasper as my neighbor. (Jasper had got himself a large, quiet room in the front quadrangle.)

Daniels was standing and waiting for me to say something.

I made suitable noises of pleasure but couldn't help adding, "Last year, I lived in the sitting room of Gerard Manley Hopkins." Jasper had lived in what had been the poet's bedroom.

"Was he in the Parliament?"

"He was a poet, a great poet," I said.

"Not everyone can sit in the Parliament. Nothing to touch being Prime Minister of England, sir." Not even the college scouts are free of the Balliol prejudice that men in public affairs are better than men of letters, I thought.

As a conversational gambit, I remarked that my old scout was George.

"I know, sir. But he's not a freeman of Wolvercote Common, like I am." Wolvercote Common was a big piece of land in the village of Wolvercote, to the northwest of Oxford. "As a freeman, I have the right to put a pony to graze there for tuppence a year, or keep twelve geese there free."

Daniels left the room—brusquely, it seemed, as if he didn't approve of a former colonial's being given the Prime Minister's rooms and being served by a freeman. Actually, I was wrong in my surmise. Daniels, although somewhat temperamental, was as devoted a scout as George.

I did, however, at first feel slightly awkward rattling around in Macmillan's suite. I'll have to distinguish myself in college somehow if I am really to deserve these rooms, I thought.

A few days after moving in, as I was slumped on a couch in my sitting room, with my bare feet stretched out on a chair, and was dictating an essay to my amanuensis, Helen Hookey, there was a rap at the door and Harold Macmillan walked in, accompanied by the Master. I had just grasped the fact that he wanted to see his old rooms when he started backing out, almost before he had entered. He must think that the college has gone to the dogs, I reflected.

🌸

Most of us structured our lives around the Oxford year— short, concentrated terms for enjoying everything the university had to offer, and vacs for reading and travel. (Some undergraduates spent part of their vacs with dons in remote country houses and chalets, conducting "reading parties," which combined group study and discussion with outdoor activities like walking and hiking.) Hardly anyone at Oxford had a television; a don wouldn't be caught dead with a television aerial sticking up from the roof of his house. Nor did pubs have television. In fact, the pub culture hadn't yet arrived in full force. Some of us might go to a pub for lunch, or walk along the river in the summer to the Trout—a pub in the village of Godstow—and sit in the garden over a Pimm's No. 1 cup, an iced, sweet, bubbly, fruit-filled drink, with the very taste of summer in it. But no one spent the evening just drinking in a pub, and women undergraduates certainly didn't go to pubs much. Undergraduates generally spent their free time acting, rowing, beagling, hunting, playing cricket or rugby—when they weren't reading papers to societies, dining together, or debating. (Since I had one of the best suites in the college, the Leonardo Society now met in my rooms.) We were able to crowd so much into an Oxford term because we were all young and frisky, with a lot of animal energy, and possibly because studying at Oxford meant that one was thrown back on one's own resources, to make of them what one would.

Most undergraduates took their first set of university examinations, Prelims, at the end of the first two terms, after which they were officially matriculated into the university. (Those of us who came up to Oxford with a degree matriculated without Prelims.) Subsequently, there was no university examination until the end of their time at Oxford, when they sat for Schools. Since most of us took three years to complete our degrees, the second year afforded a sort of license for slacking off from work and pursuing other interests; there was always the third year for buckling down to books and getting a respectable degree. I was determined to get a First, because I thought of myself as a scholar and felt that I would end up being an academic, but most undergraduates were not deeply concerned about the results of their Schools, provided they thought they could get a Second. (Unlike Cambridge, which made a distinction between a high and a low Second, Oxford at the time awarded an undifferentiated Second, and it was considered quite respectable, since in those days, unless one wanted to go on to do research and become an academic, no one inquired how well one had done on individual papers.) In fact, most undergraduates didn't worry about what they would do after Oxford; being there was its own justification.

I remember once, early in my first year, walking down past Christ Church and into the Christ Church Meadow and suddenly having a wave of feeling that I couldn't bear it if I were not at Oxford. In reality, my first year had been full of problems and bewilderment. After my free life in California, the cloistered existence of an Oxford college seemed like life in a boarding school. Moreover, it took me until my second year to meet most of the people I found congenial, or even to discover that they were there.

IN the beginning of the Michaelmas term of my second year, Jasper Griffin and Murray Forsyth, who was now my tutorial partner, were elected to Arnold and Brakenbury, a college debating society with about thirty members. Named after Matthew Arnold, who was at Balliol in 1840 and 1841, and Hannah Brackenbury, a benefactress of the college in Jowett's time, the

A. and B. had been two separate societies—the former serious and intellectual, the latter frivolous and social—until a year or so earlier; then the two, having, in different ways, found themselves in difficulties, had placed a wedding announcement in the *Times* and had got married, dropping the "c" out of the bride's name somewhere along the way. Although the merged society tilted toward the Brakenbury end of things, some of its members who also belonged to the Oxford Union, the university debating society, claimed that the Arnold and Brakenbury standard of debating was higher than that of the Union. That seemed like an exaggerated claim, since the Union had long been recognized as the nursery of Parliament. (Its ex-presidents, Lord Hailsham among them, had been dazzling Parliament and the world at large with their speeches for decades.) But the claim could not be dismissed out of hand, since in the politically fractious fifties the Union had lost some of its lustre when it came to elegant speaking. (In my time, an Indian friend, Rudolph Demelo, who was known more for his political passion about things Indian than for his mastery of the English tongue, was elected the Union president, after a divisive campaign in which his race seemed to be the main issue.) It was said that the Arnold and Brakenbury was a forum for formal but irreverent and ironic speeches by Balliol men, who were known for a commanding presence, for a tongue-in-cheek style, and for scorching wit in general. It certainly seemed to me, from hearing the Arnold and Brakenbury members carry on in hall, the J.C.R., and the quadrangle, that they, even more than other undergraduates, delighted in word play—in puns, in verbal fancies, in literary allusions, sometimes in versification of the commonest daily occurrences. I set my sights on joining the Arnold and Brakenbury, thinking that, whatever my English speech lacked in polish, I stood a chance because I had some skill in debating.

Though I was sure that it was bad form to let on to anyone that I was at all interested in joining the Arnold and Brakenbury, I asked Michael Meredith, one of my few student readers and a

Balliol man who had been a member of it for some time, how one got chosen for it.

"You have to be taken as a guest to one of its biweekly meetings, and make a humorous speech, and then the membership votes on you," he said. He suddenly added, as if reading my thoughts, "Why don't you ask Griffin or Forsyth to take you as a guest?"

"They are new members—would that make a difference?" I asked.

"Perhaps," he said. "Then you can come as my guest to the next meeting." He seemed to have immediate second thoughts about his invitation, because he went on to say, "Your candidacy may not fly at all unless your speech sets the society on fire. I should tell you, it's an almost impossible audience to speak to. Everyone drinks too much port, and does everything possible to throw the speaker off balance. I remember that when I had just launched into my speech as a guest Robert Oakeshott emerged from under the table on all fours, at my feet. Robert stood up right in front of my face and, breathing whisky at me, shouted 'Who are you?' Hecklers shouted from the floor 'Answer the honorable gentleman!' and 'Who are you? The honorable gentleman is waiting for your answer!' People from the floor started singing 'My Father Knew Lloyd George.' The whole idea was to derail me, but I pressed ahead full steam. I didn't miss a word of my speech. I went on talking, above the clamor."

The society met in the Massey Room every second Tuesday after dinner, and it was now the Thursday before the next meeting. I can't write out my speech in Braille, I thought. Reading Braille is too slow for speaking. In any case, it seemed to me that Braille notes would sink my candidacy, for clearly the whole point was to come across with panache—to seem effortlessly witty and self-confident. I decided I would go without anything specific in mind to say, and depend on the inspiration of the moment to carry me through.

"What is the motion for the next meeting?" I asked, swallowing hard.

"Too much hedging leads to ditching," he said.

❧

THE evening I was taken as a guest to the Arnold and Brakenbury turned out to be Ladies' Night. We undergraduates were so used to performing for the benefit of male society that we almost forgot that there were ladies in the real world and that men down the ages had preened themselves, strutted, and waxed eloquent for the benefit of the opposite sex. (In those days, the word "woman" was considered coarse.) Moreover, because of the drawing power of the Arnold and Brakenbury members, some of the most glamorous Oxford female undergraduates were on hand. I felt even more tongue-tied than I would have otherwise, but I managed to insert myself between Michael Meredith and Jasper at a table where three other guests—Michael Mockridge, Robert Walters, and James Hughes—were already seated. Also at the table were Dinah Brooke and Kathleen Halton. They were not technically at Oxford—they were studying at St. Clare's, an outpost of London University in the town of Oxford—but their presence was easily accounted for: they were judged to be two of the prettiest girls around and were known to be the toasts of every society.

"What are you doing here?" Dinah asked me from across the table. She had a gentle, dreamy way of speaking, which went straight to my heart. James Hughes, who was her beau, laughed. He had the air of someone who had just got off the sofa in the J.C.R. Hughes was always red-eyed, with stubble on his cheeks, and often gambled late into the night in a room at the bottom of my staircase.

Dinah was waiting for an answer.

"I'm a guest," I said.

"No! You're not going to make a speech to this crowd!" Dinah said. "They'll tear you limb from limb. You don't know what the English public-school boys are like." Her remark all but unhinged me, despite the touching softness about her.

"But I'm a fighter," I said weakly. I had trouble getting my words out.

"Order! Order!" Snedden, the president, shouted from the head table, and my heart started racing, as if I had already been called to speak, though in fact guests were not given the floor until the proponents and opponents of the motion had had their say.

All the speeches were read, and they all possessed an elegant style, if little content. They were shot through with farfetched quotations and foreign phrases, and there was a lot of posturing and exhibitionism in delivery, as if the speakers had been drilled in oratory at school.

The atmosphere was very much that of a mock House of Commons. People spoke "on paper," and there were "proposers" and "opposers" of the motion. Everyone was referred to by surname and with a handle like "the honorable," "the right honorable," or "my distinguished opponent." The officers of the society were invariably referred to by their titles, some of which, like "leader of the house" and "constable," seemed to be straight out of the House of Commons, while others, like "ex-president," "extreasurer," "joint rotating president," "senior honorary member," and "both auditors," seemed to be takeoffs on the titles in the House of Commons. The speeches were frequently interrupted from the floor with "Hear, hear!" and "Shame, shame!" and thumpings on the table. Several ladies gave rousing formal speeches on paper under the rubric of "non-members"—not to seek admission into the A. and B. but to make a splash at Balliol. Men made several arch references to the silver tongues of "lady nonmembers," who could pour out "withering corn" with the abandon of their sex. It was not difficult to distinguish the Arnold types. They made more serious speeches, even if there was quite a lot of foolishness in them. Whether the speaker was a woman or a man, the more cutting the verbal thrust was, the more elaborate was the courtesy employed. Throughout, the decanters of port were kept circulating, clockwise, and there was a lot of drunken heckling of the speakers.

After the formal speeches, the leader of the house opened the debate from the floor.

I leaped up onto the table. If Robert Oakeshott can crawl under the table on all fours, I can stomp around on the table, I thought. What is public school if not a high-wire act carried off on the strength of bravado?

Walking among glasses and decanters of port—people scooted them out of my way as best they could—I harangued those assembled on the narrowness of English male society, invoking the romantic dating custom of American campuses. "There ditches are used for trysts rather than for men in a drunken stupor to fall into, as here in England," I said.

The stunned silence of the first couple of minutes of my antic gave way to heckling.

"Do your home run on the ground!" someone shouted.

"This house doesn't believe in American corn!" someone else cried out.

I walked up and down the table, challenging the hecklers to stop me, but none of them interfered, perhaps because, having seen me around the college, they knew that I was surefooted. I carried on—or, rather, the port in my blood carried me on. "Hedge not!" I cried. "Take your lady into the ditch!"

There was thunderous thumping of the tables, and "Hear, hear!"

In later years, it seemed to me that one of Jowett's unfortunate legacies to Balliol was his emphasis on symbols of worldly success—holding political office or entering the Civil Service—rather than on symbols of private fulfillment, like writing poetry or novels. But, walking on the table, on which glasses danced with the thump-thump of the hecklers, I imagined myself a member of the Indian Parliament, with the Prime Ministership within my reach.

When all the speakers had finished, there was "summing up" and "division of the house," as in the Commons. People were asked to raise their hands to signify whether they were for the motion or against the motion, and for abstention or for non-abstention—whatever that was. The votes were counted and tallied, and Snedden announced, "The match is lost by the proposers, ten points to seven, with ten abstainers and seventeen non-abstainers." No doubt, the term "non-abstainers" was part of the parody of voting in the Commons. Once the results were announced, the house stood adjourned.

Two days later, I got a formal note from the secretary—again, it was Ockenden—saying that I had been elected a member of the society. Mockridge, Walters, and Hughes were also elected.

Subsequently, the A. and B. debated such motions as "This House would rather bask in the sun than cry for the moon," "This House would rather be married to the Arts than be a Bachelor of Science," "This House prefers headlamps to footlights, though all the world's a stage," "This House would rather go to sea in a sieve than be sold down the river," and "This House would rather have died in the Middle Ages than lived to be middle-aged." Every term, in addition to the biweekly meetings, the society dined in style in the Massey Room—once, on two suckling pigs named after its eponymous hero and heroine. Every term, it held a champagne breakfast in the room of a member. (At one point, the breakfasts were almost banned after the treasurer, Hugh Pritchard, fired a champagne cork out the window and accidentally knocked the hat off the Master's wife.)

❦

IN the Hilary term of my second year, Ranald Nicholson, a graduate of Edinburgh University who was doing a D.Phil. on Edward III and the Scots, came up to me in the quadrangle one afternoon and said, "We've elected you to the Thistle Society."

Since the Thistle Society was a college dining club exclusively for Scots, I was surprised, and I said as much.

"We got around the fact that you're not a Scot by making you burgess of Berwick-on-Tweed," he said. Berwick-on-Tweed lies on the border between Scotland and England. Traditionally, both the English and the Scots had claimed it—indeed, had fought wars over it—so by making me a burgess of it the club was apparently saying that I was not a Scot and yet I belonged to Scotland. In any event, the Thistle Society was the brainchild of Ranald, and he could probably define the boundaries of its membership as he liked.

I thanked him for the honor. As a rule, students doing postgraduate work didn't enter the stream of Oxford clubs and societies, perhaps because many of them were not naturally gifted at parrying blows with wit and learning. Postgraduate students of the college's Scottish tribe, however, were a little different. Many of them had done their undergraduate work at ancient Scottish universities and felt no awe of Oxford, in contrast to ex-colonials, like Indians, Canadians, Australians, and, indeed, Americans. In hall or in the J.C.R., the postgraduate Scots tended to sit together and self-confidently exchange Scottish stories and jokes. They seemed to feel that they had a special claim on Balliol. After all, the college was an ancient Scottish foundation, and the Master himself was a Scot.

Ranald certainly gave the impression of enjoying Balliol as if the place had been designed for him. He was rotund and magis-

terial, with a booming Scottish voice and a judicial English manner. Though he was almost twenty-seven, he seemed to delight
in the adolescent antics of English undergraduates, who came up
to university straight from school. He was apt to make good-
natured but scathing remarks about the dour Scots and dull Glas-
wegians in college. He himself was from Edinburgh.

A few days before the dinner of the Thistle Society in the
Trinity term (it dined once a term), Ranald stopped by my rooms.
"Your attendance at the dinner is *de rigueur*," he said.

"I had no intention of not coming," I said.

AFTER we took our seats along the tables in the Massey Room,
the bard of the club, Eric Anderson (later the Headmaster of
Eton), saluted the assembled by cocking a snook at Chaucer,
declaring:

> Although in number they were but fifteen
> Yet each alone noteworthy could have been,
> So wise they were, so temperate and so able
> They would have graced even Balliol's high table.
>
> As we went on I learned of their professions,
> Their likes and hatreds, follies and obsessions.
> A Puritan there was, and eke a Priest,
> A Boxer and two Sailors at the least,
> An Engineer, a Writer, and a Host,
> A Merchant from the far Atlantic coast,
> A Lawyer and Musician did I see,
> And eke Classicist and Burgesses three.

From this distance, I cannot recall who every one of those
was, but the puritan was Bill Wilkie, an especially earnest chap

who was reading Greats, and the priest was Geoffrey Finlayson, who, in contrast to some stodgy Scottish members, was lively, energetic, and amusing. The engineer (as it turned out, "engineer" was the bard's version of the knight) was the Marquess of Douglas and Clydesdale, Angus Alan Douglas Douglas-Hamilton, and, as such, the person of highest rank not only in the Thistle Society but also in the college; an Etonian and a car enthusiast, he was reading engineering. The host was, of course, Ranald; the lawyer was John Thomson, a great talker; Eric himself was the writer; and I was one of the burgesses.

As soon as Eric had finished his poem, which ran to what sounded like fourteen or fifteen stanzas and was entitled "First Epistle of Ariel to the Thistle" (along with Chaucer, it seemed, St. Paul and Shakespeare had been Eric's muses), there were cries of "More!" and "Encore, encore!" As if he had anticipated the popular demand, he launched into a second poem, this one entitled "MacGonagall's Address to Oxford":

> O Oxford, O Oxford with your dreaming spires
> Where all the youth of England after learning enquires . . .

The members of the Scottish tribe often complained about how expensive Oxford was—and, of course, they were celebrated for parsimony. But that evening no expense was spared for the dinner, and as a main course we were served haggis. I felt like the skeleton at the feast. The mere thought of eating sheep entrails and suet revolted my Hindu body. Some atavistic notion of what was fit to eat seemed to take hold of me, and, do what I might, I couldn't swallow a single forkful of haggis, even for the sake of decorum. The scout, noticing my plight, obligingly piled up potatoes and vegetables on top of the delicacy, and I was able to maintain a pretense of eating the main course without actually eating it. The more everyone around me exclaimed at the perfection of the haggis, the more of an outsider I felt. Indeed, everything about the evening—or, rather, the night, because the dinner didn't end until about six-thirty in the morning—had a surreal feeling.

Soon, however, I grew to relish my status as an honorary Scot and enjoyed enormously dining each term with the Thistle Society.

❧

AT one point, I became a member of a newish Oxford club called the Voltaire Society. Its purpose was to promote the anti-clerical, anti-establishment ideas of Voltaire. The members prided themselves on not following any of the normal procedures of an Oxford society, such as keeping minutes. In fact, many of them were postgraduate foreigners, who were not members of any other Oxford societies, and even most of its English members were aggressively irreverent. They seemed to consider themselves too high-powered to hear papers from their kind, and preferred to be addressed by eminent philosophers and literati. I knew that as a member I would be a square peg in a round hole, but I could not resist the blandishments of an American friend, Paul Noyes, who was determined that I should not only join the Voltaire Society but help him run it. I then prevailed upon Jasper to join it.

Early in my tenure as an officer of the society, I invited E. M. Forster, whose acquaintance I had made during visits to Cambridge, to come and speak. My hope was that Forster would add literary grace to the society and so deflect it from its self-consciously intellectual course. Paul and I and the two other officers received him at the train station and took him up to wash and unpack in a room we had reserved for him at the Bear, an inn at least five hundred years old. While we were still there, standing around awkwardly, he opened a little attaché case and fussily arranged his pajamas, a couple of military hairbrushes, a hand mirror, and shaving things around the room. He seemed very vulnerable, and more like a elderly aunt than like a world-famous writer.

At the inn, he only picked at his food. Afterward, at the meeting, he did not so much address the society as talk informally about his sinecure at King's College, Cambridge. When he finished, an undergraduate philosophy type got up and asked, "Forster, why haven't you written a novel since 'Passage to India'?" I could have throttled the fellow for his arrogance, but Forster replied, in the most charming way, "One day, I woke up and the world I knew and understood had disappeared. A novelist can only write about the world he understands." I found the answer disarming and also affecting, but the members of the society went after him as if he were a penny-a-liner rather than a great novelist. The more concrete his answers, the more abstract their questions: What did it mean to live in a world and not understand it? Didn't a writer need to justify his life, like any other workingman? Wasn't historical truth better than fictional truth, anyway?

I was furious, and remained so, although Jasper said that if Forster wasn't I shouldn't be. I resigned my office, and Jasper took over my responsibilities.

❧

THE foregoing account of undergraduates' pastimes may give the impression that when we were not seeking amusement, drinking like fish, or talking volubly, we were vainly struggling with abstractions beyond our years. That may be so, yet the struggles helped us to think on our feet, to sharpen our wits, to develop a certain lightness of touch, and to cement friendships, while also providing us with some relief from the tensions of living and studying in a closed, essentially male society. Writing about these goings on from this distance is disconcerting, because they seem childish and silly, yet at the time they were enthralling, and not just to me but to my most sophisticated English contemporaries. Evidence of this fact is that every last detail of the members' activities is meticulously set down in the minutes of the societies (except, of course, the Voltaire Society), and those minutes are preserved for future reference in the college's muniments room. (I've had recourse to them as a check against my memory.) I doubt if any of the members, whether they are now members of the House of Lords or the House of Commons or are eminent civil servants, ambassadors, priests, or professors, would be embarrassed by the thought that a record of their youthful antics has been preserved. The truth is that, though most of them were in their late teens or early twenties, and many of them had had experience of the world only in school, they conducted themselves in the manner of worldly men of affairs, as if Balliol and the societies were a stage where they could rehearse for their parts in the real world.

VII

BEGINNINGS,
VISIONS,
DREAMS

I N THE MAGICAL DAYS OF MY SECOND YEAR, I BECAME
for a time a member of a loose literary circle centered on
a prodigy of a poet, Dom Moraes: time and time again,
he brought us together. Indeed, if we met, it was likely
to be because Dom had stopped by and made us drop
whatever we were doing to go to a pub or a party, or
simply to call around on other friends—for most of us knew him
better than we knew one another. I first heard about Dom from
a friend at Jesus, Dom's college. "I was in the porter's lodge a
year ago or so, collecting my post, when I noticed a copy of

Botteghe Oscure with poems by Dom Moraes in it," he told me.
"The name looked exotic, and I wondered if 'Dom' was a title for
a member of a priestly order, or something. Then I caught sight
of this beautiful, sylphlike, thin boy, who had a dark complexion, dazzling, luminous, doe-like eyes, and raven hair. He cleared
his throat shyly and asked me, in a barely audible but perfectly
English voice, 'Do you know where the Second Quad is? I think
that's where my room is.' I found his room for him. He told me
that his name was Dom Moraes, and immediately invited me to
a pub. While I nursed one beer, he downed four or five double
whiskies. You have to meet him to believe him."

Dom came up in the same year I did, but I didn't meet him
until we were halfway through our second year. Then, one day,
soon after my book was published in England and, to my cha-
grin, picture posters announcing it were plastered in Oxford
bookshop windows, someone walked into my room without so
much as a knock, as if he had never known a door to be closed to
him. I didn't recognize his footstep.

"Yes?" I said, rather distantly, without turning around. I
didn't welcome the interruption. I was absorbed in dictating a
tutorial essay, and my time with my amanuensis, Mrs. Hookey,
was precious.

"Dom," the intruder said. The voice resonated like a bell. It
was as if royalty had descended upon me—he was already a legend. "Vedkins, what about a tiny drinkkins?" Dom said.

I hurried Mrs. Hookey out.

"What would you like?" I asked. I made a movement toward
my array of bottles and glasses.

"No, ducks, tiny pubkins, if you don't mind."

I soon learned that this was Dom's way of speaking: he pre-
fixed "tiny" to certain words, added "kins" or other diminutive
suffixes to many, and used endearments like "ducks" or "ducky,"
in the manner of theatre people. From anyone else, that kind of

speech would surely have sounded precious or affected, or even disingenuous, but he had such a gentle voice and such an unassertive manner that it sounded merely cozy. In fact, I soon noticed that some of his friends had taken it up, and before long I was using it myself, but only when I was in his company. Anyway, in the Oxford setting the speech didn't sound ludicrous. It seemed that every gang from a great public school had a private language of its own.

As a person, Dom seemed different from other people. He had a lemur-like quality. He was very lithe, very smooth-moving. Everyone was taken with his extraordinarily delightful looks. He drew friends to him strongly, perhaps because he seemed to have so many simultaneous ways of being. He could be nervous and shy, or witty and deft. He could be withdrawn and invincible, or lost and helpless. He could be very playful—not in the sense of boisterousness but in that of a limberness of personality which allowed him to behave in different ways at different times, or even at the same time. In a gathering of strangers, he hovered unobtrusively at the edge of the room, as if he had removed himself into a private world. But in a gathering of friends he was the center of attention—telling stories and creating merriment. He was engagingly restless, always flitting from thing to thing. One felt that one could never get a fixed impression of him. Every impression would be only a glancing view.

❧

Dom's mother was an Indian, and his father, Frank Moraes, came from the Portuguese colony of Goa, near Bombay. Moraes, himself an Oxford man, was the best-known Indian journalist, and had recently become editor in chief of a major English-language newspaper, the *Indian Express*. Since he spoke and wrote only English, he was the first port of call for British or American visiting men of letters. Before Dom was fifteen (the age at which I left India for the first time, to go to America), he had travelled with his father to half a dozen countries. When he was sixteen, he met his father's friend Stephen Spender, and Spender helped him to get a place at Jesus. Dom spent the next year travelling through Europe and came up to Oxford to read English when he was eighteen. In 1957, when he was nineteen, he published his first book. It was a little volume of poems entitled "A Beginning."

The poems were rather small-scale, fine things, almost like light pencil sketches—tentative and provisional. They had a limpid beauty—an extraordinary felicity of word, phrasing, and rhyme. Quiet but lush, unformed but smooth, honest but confused (if beautifully so), they often conveyed a childlike wonder about grown-up experience. A lot of them were about romantic love. At times, they were overtly sexual and at other times so innocent that they conveyed a sense of almost virginal surprise. Many of them were exotic; his frame of reference was not only India but North Africa. They could be shocking, too. One poem about Auden conveyed attraction and reverence but also distaste: "He missed one day in spring his time to die." The book was a literary sensation, and critics were soon comparing him to Rimbaud, to Yeats, to Dylan Thomas.

We all enjoyed hearing Dom recite his poems. He had an entrancing voice—delicate, sensuous, and full of feeling. It conveyed a lovely mixture of childish eagerness and writer's diffidence.

Dom seemed to know everybody who was anybody, not only at Oxford but also in London. That was partly because of his father and partly because of his own success as a poet, but mostly because he simply turned up everywhere unannounced and made a great impression. In fact, at Oxford, Dom floated in and out of All Souls, in and out of the houses of dons and of heads of colleges. Almost every door seemed to be open to him. Because of him, we in Dom's group, as we came to think of it, met all kinds of people we would never have met on our own.

Dom's group was our answer to the tightly knit clique of public-school men—and, in a neat contrast to it, our group was constantly changing. People would be part of it for a while, then drop out, and other people would join it. Insofar as Dom's group had a core, it was made up of Gillian (Jill) Thomas, Del Kolve, Quentin Stevenson, Julian Mitchell, John Fuller, and Peter Levi.

Jill was a compassionate, Lawrentian woman, who had a rich, deep contralto voice. There was a quality of the universal mother about her. She was generously bosomy, with long golden hair, which was always coming undone. In fact, she always looked as if she herself were about to come undone, through an explosion of sheer energy. She was an only child. Her father had been a solicitor's clerk, but he had vanished from her life when she was four; she had grown up in the town of Street, Somerset, where her mother was a schoolmistress. Jill had gone to a school there that favored country girls. In 1954, she had come up to St. Anne's, Oxford, to read English, and she had got a First. She was staying on and doing a B.Litt.

Jill met Del Kolve, an American Rhodes scholar, soon after he arrived at Oxford, in 1955, to read English at Jesus. Many Rhodes scholars tended to be either beetle-browed or rowdy, but Del was something of an aesthete. Most Americans were rigid, but he was easy and nimble, eager to explore new paths. He had taken his degree in two years and had got a First. He was staying at Jesus for a third year to teach and to do research under J. R. R. Tolkien. (Eventually, he did his D.Phil. at Oxford.) Jill immediately fell in love with Del. As she used to say in later life, therein lay her woes. For two whole years while she was in love with him, neither of them realized that his sexual preference was for men. Del says that in a sense he had always known that—in the past, he had been attracted to men in America—but had never allowed himself to think that homosexuality could be a life choice. He says that in Wisconsin, where he grew up, there wasn't enough of a visible homosexual life in his day for a naïve, innocent idealist, which he was, to think that it was possible to live like one. Jill, for her part, says that it had not occurred to her that a man she loved and who loved her could prefer men.

In fact, for many of us at Oxford the notion that anyone at the university might be a homosexual was unthinkable. After all, in England the practice of homosexuality was then a crime, and people were prosecuted for it; consequently, to imagine that there were homosexuals in college was rather like imagining that one was living among criminals. (In 1957, the government adopted the Wolfenden Report—a document drafted by the Departmental Committee on Homosexual Offences and Prostitution, under the chairmanship of Sir John Wolfenden—which made homosexuality among consenting adults legal in Britain for the first time. It was a first legal step toward accepting homosexuality as a way of life, and, of course, people's attitudes were much harder to change than the law.) Yet there were clearly a lot of contrary sexual currents running beneath the surface of people's behavior; one simply didn't think much about them. For instance, there was a particular friend of ours, a heroically self-confident college figure, who was in the A. and B. and the Leonardo, and was the director of the Balliol Players, which performed at various schools during the summer vac. He had a manner that would now be immediately recognizable as camp—exaggerated gestures, a thumping, aggressive walk, a slightly effusive way of speaking, and a limp-wristedness that seemed like a comic affectation—but one took it for granted that all this was just because he was an actor. The assumption that he—and everyone else—was a heterosexual was rather like the assumption that it was good to be tall. There was a body of agreement on such things, and, if some didn't agree, others were, to say the least, surprised. People who were "gentlemen" (or wanted to be) had a set of stereotyped opinions. They were happy with things the way things were; they didn't protest. There was a certain complacency, part of that effortless superiority of being at a seven-hundred-year-old college—indeed, at a seven-hundred-year-old university. The vision of many such chaps was so narrow that they didn't realize that their experience was very different from everyone else's. (An extreme example was Ray Ockenden, who was shocked to discover that there were lots of children up and down the country who hadn't taken A levels, and even more shocked to learn that there were also vast hordes of children who hadn't even taken O levels.) Throughout my undergraduate years, I couldn't accept the fact that anyone I knew might be a homosexual. Actually, I secretly harbored a fear of homosexuality, and even of forceful women like Jill. It was only much later that I realized that Del, or anyone else I knew, was a homosexual.

By the time I was part of Dom's group, Jill and Del had broken off, but I didn't know why, especially since they remained very close. In fact, Jill seemed to be still in love with him, if in a hopeless way. Del, for his part, seemed to enjoy being mothered by her.

Jill later told me, "There was this terrible irony that was being played out while Del and I were in love. The Wolfenden Report allowed Del to begin living according to his sexual preference. All the time, Wolfenden's own son Jeremy, who was up with us, was overtly homosexual. He had a brilliant career at Oxford, only to end up committing suicide—or, at least, dying under mysterious circumstances. It was an odd conjunction—the Wolfenden father and son with Del's and my love."

When I got to know Quentin Stevenson, he was enjoying the distinction of having his first book of poems, "The Succession," published by Oxford University Press. He was keen and dashing, and, as I later learned, was, unlike Del, always conscious of being a homosexual. Still, even he had got engaged when he was very young.

Julian Mitchell, who also turned out to be a homosexual, used to pedal furiously through Oxford, his spectacles sliding down his nose. He had come up to Oxford the same year I had, and, like me, was reading Modern History, but in Wadham College. He had a sharp, authoritarian, brush-off, upper-class manner, but it was so exaggerated, and had such a humorous edge to it, that one was never sure whether he actually came from a well-established family or was just affecting to have such a background. His bluster was a little like that of Colonel Blimp—an affectation of the archetypal Englishman. While Julian was at Oxford, John Lehmann, the editor of *London Magazine,* was impressed with an article of his in *Cherwell,* an undergraduate publication. That helped launch Julian on his literary career. He told me once, "If you have any spark and you're at Oxford or Cambridge, you will be of interest to the London literary or theatre world." He proved to be a perfect example of his theory.

Sometimes John David Caute was part of the group around Dom. He had just had his novel "At Fever Pitch" accepted by a London publisher. Like Julian, he was a historian at Wadham. Provocative and iconoclastic, he saw everything through Marxist eyes. At one time, Patrick Garland was also in the group, because, though he was an actor, he had literary aspirations. Before coming up to Oxford, he had spent a year pretending to be a teddy boy (a youthful street rowdy affecting Edwardian dress) at a seaside town, where he ran a ride or a shill game at a fair. He was reading English at St. Edmund Hall, a college utterly without social pretensions. A protégé of Neville Coghill, he played leads in many plays put on by O.U.D.S., the Oxford University Dramatic Society, and he became its president. (One imagined that Garland was going to be a great actor, but he ended up being a distinguished director.) John Fuller—son of the poet and solicitor Roy Fuller—and his girlfriend, Prue Martin, were sometimes around, too. They seemed to be always holding hands and silently looking into each other's eyes, even when they were at parties. They were close to Dom, but I never got to know them well. (John Fuller later became Fellow and Tutor of English at Magdalen College, Oxford.)

And then there was Peter Levi, who was around near the end of my time at Oxford. He was a lean, urgent-eyed Jesuit who wrote poetry with a religious flavor. He had an extraordinarily intense quality about him. When I met him, he was almost twenty-seven—older than just about anyone else in the group. He had gone to Beaumont, a distinguished Catholic school; had become a Jesuit when he was seventeen; and had come up to Oxford in 1954, when he was twenty-three, to read Greats at Campion Hall, where Jesuits who were up at Oxford lived. He took Mods in the Hilary term of 1956. That autumn, he was forced to give up reading Greats (he eventually did a Pass B.A. degree—one not classified—in Classics), because of an accident. By the time I met him, a couple of years later, he had turned the accident into an absorbing, if excruciatingly painful, story. (We all turned everything that happened to us—good or bad—into a story, as if we thought that our stories were what made us interesting to our friends.)

"I took a long walk with my friend Denis Bethell," Peter told us when he resurfaced after a couple of years' absence. "We walked along the river and then up onto Boar's Hill, and then left the wooded path for the main road in the hope of catching a bus back. It was almost dusk by then. An old woman was driving a car. She was looking down at Oxford—not at its spires or towers but at its lights. The poor thing was so distracted that she all but ran me over. My only memory is of her frightened face and her saying, 'I didn't mean to do it.' I thought of saying, 'I bloody well hope not,' but then I lost consciousness. Denis didn't get a scratch, but I had a concussion and was in the hospital for a long time. When I got out, I went across the country to Eastbourne to see my father, who was dying. It was all very nasty, because he wouldn't go to the hospital, and when he died there was a lot of blood. After that, I started having fits of weeping that went on for months. Every now and again, I would collapse and have bad headaches. I couldn't concentrate on anything, I couldn't get out of my chair."

He paused, and people asked "Was there no one to take care of you?" and "Didn't the Jesuits send someone to look after you?" and "Why didn't you ring up? We would have all come down."

He said, "No. I wanted to be alone. I didn't think of getting in touch with anybody."

Even as he told the story, he was almost laughing, as if he didn't want us to feel sorry for him in any way but, rather, wanted to amuse us. I thought that that was very English of him, and was impressed.

"Of course, I couldn't go to Campion Hall and confess once a month to the Chaplain, as I was required to do," Peter said, resuming the story. "The Chaplain is a small man, physically and spiritually, and he reported me to the Provincial, saying that I was behaving badly. The Provincial sent for me. I was very rattled by the interview. He told me that I was not to go back to Oxford for my studies; instead, I was to see a psychiatrist in Harley Street. I was very depressed and went back to Osterly, near London, where I was staying at the time. My room there had lino on the floor, and a sputtering gas fire, and was really quite dreadful. I sat down and started reading Euripides' 'The Cyclops' in Greek and suddenly felt perfect tranquillity and happiness. I find that that always happens to me when I sit down and read Greek."

We knew people who now and again checked themselves into the Warneford Hospital, the local mental institution, especially if they were undergoing a crisis during examinations—occasionally, people took Schools at the Warneford—but we had no idea what a psychiatrist did or what a meeting with one would involve, so we asked "Did you go to the psychiatrist?" and "What was the psychiatrist like?" and "What did he do to you?"

"He was terribly funny," Peter said. "His first question was 'When did you last masturbate?' I said, 'What? When did I what?' He said, 'Come, come. Was it Tuesday? Wednesday? Thursday?' "

There was laughter all around.

"I said, 'I only did it a long time ago when I was a small boy.' I told him that I thought I was getting better, because I was writing again. He said, 'Let me see your writing.' I showed him an unfinished poem I'd just been working on. He read it, and said, 'Clearly, it's about your desire to kill your father. That's why you can't finish it.' I said, 'No, it isn't finished because it's a very tight poem. It's a sonnet and it depends entirely upon the final rhyme and there is no word in the English language for the rhyme I want.' He insisted that I couldn't finish it because I had wanted to murder my father and felt guilty about his death. I refused to have anything more to do with him."

"The fellow sounds as if he should be a patient in the Warneford!" we cried.

"That's right, and he's not alone. After him, I saw many other doctors for my nervous breakdown and religious crisis, but the only one I really connected with was a neurologist in Harley Street, and that was because he and I discovered that we had a common interest in beagling."

Everyone laughed, and swore that psychiatrists were fools.

In 1977, Peter resigned from the priesthood—he had been ordained some twelve years earlier—and from the Jesuit order, and married Deirdre Craig, the widow of Cyril Connolly, taking on her several children. The last time I saw him, he was Professor of Poetry at Oxford, with a dozen volumes of verse to his credit, and had become a plummy gent, with theatrical gestures. The transformation was truly remarkable.

❦

OFTEN I felt out of my element in Dom's group. I was part of it only because of Dom himself, my fascination with him. Without my fully realizing it, he was introducing me to a whole new way of living, thinking, and feeling. Also, his mere company seemed to confer on me a special status: people had only to look at him to be drawn to him, and anyone who was with him was illuminated by his halo. (With me, I felt, it was the other way around: people, if they were drawn to me at all, had to look past appearances.) All the same, I wondered why I would jump up, drop everything, and run after him, like a child after the Pied Piper any time he played on his pipe. Why wasn't I more like Tylor, who, come what might, sat in the same chair in the Senior Common Room, had the same few friends, went out regularly for dinner and bridge with Puggy and the Crosses. (Cross was married to a woman who was a solicitor at a very good London firm and also acted as his reader, secretary, research assistant, and adviser.) Or why wasn't I more like Manohar Sondhi, an Indian friend at Balliol, who was always with other Indians, all of whom, like him, prayed regularly and ate no meat. Not even other members of our group ran after Dom as I did. But then, perhaps because of my blindness, no matter how far afield I wandered, I always had the feeling that I was fenced in, that if I could just get over to the other side the grass really would be greener. And Dom seemed always to be leading me to fields greener than any I had imagined.

Still, Dom didn't occupy much of my time or energy. Many of us had separate, extremely ordered lives, in contrast to the quixotic goings on of Dom's group. All of us had close friends who had never met him and never knew any members of his group. With them we had more conventional undergraduate friendships. After all, most of the time we were confined to the precincts of our own college. We had to be in by a fixed hour. We weren't allowed to spend the night away without an explanation and permission. We weren't allowed to do this and we weren't allowed to do that.

All those rules and constraints applied to Dom, but he didn't take any notice of them. He would disappear for days at a time, or whizz off to London whenever he felt like it. He was always in trouble for not turning up for tutorials and for not writing his essays. He had an atmosphere of vagrancy about him. Indeed, he seemed to occupy a country of liberty all his own, even as he emanated an aura of mystery.

I admired and envied him for his freedom, but I was incapable of emulating him. My life was hedged in with readers and schedules. If I stood a reader up, I risked losing his or her help. In any case, I was obligated to pay for the reader's time. Also, I could study only when I had a reader, for practically no history book I was required to read was available in Braille or on tapes. Unlike other people, I could not stay up half the night and catch up on my work. Compared with Dom's carryings on, my drudgery and studies seemed boring. I did my best to hide from him the mechanics and the problems of my life, so that I could be worthy of his company. My circumscribed mode of existence made Dom's life seem particularly romantic and glamorous, and his attention particularly flattering.

Anyone other than Dom would have been sent down for any one of a number of infractions of the rules, but his tutors were so fond of him that they were constantly making excuses for him, not only to themselves but also to the principal of Jesus, John Traill Christie. A punctilious Scot, Christie felt he needed to keep a decorous control of the college, but he loved poetry. A part of him seemed to know that one good poet was worth all the broken rules. He had taught at Rugby and Westminster, public schools in the first rank, and, perhaps as a result, he took a tolerant view of boys' misbehavior. Anyway, Christie had a soft spot for Dom.

I also found Dom very touching, for I sensed that he was not without his sorrows, even if he spoke of them so lightly that it was hard to know exactly what they were. In fact, he often turned his sorrows into stories, as though they either belonged to someone else or lay in the misty past. His stories—incandescent and nearly always amusing—seemed to me to be his way of finding solace, whether he knew it or not.

Once, when many of us were gathered around a table in a pub and were chatting, he announced, "My mother died last night."

We gasped.

Dom went on to tell a long, complicated story about the circumstances of her death. Only when his autobiography, "My Son's Father," was published, some ten years later, did I realize that Dom had invented the whole story of her death. Looking back, I imagine that he told the story about his mother because he wanted us to be particularly nice to him that evening—that on the spur of the moment he had just come up with it. On the whole, one would think of such a story as the last coin one would produce, but he merely dropped the remark into the general talk like any other conversational ploy, and he went on to embellish the event, dwelling on the matter of being motherless. I remember he gave some convincing particulars; if he hadn't, the group, knowing Dom's talent for fantasies, wouldn't have been taken in.

What was so strange was that not only in this instance but in many others there was a vast out-of-scaleness about his fugue of fantasies and the possible benefit he could hope to derive from them. The fact is that they often caused us to doubt him. They made us wonder, for instance, if his riveting stories about going, as a small boy with his father, on dangerous journeys to the borders of Red China were true. In his case, one never knew what was true and what wasn't. His inventions, however, had less to do with his trying to escape the consequences of events—although they had something to do with that, too—than with what seemed to be the relationship of his mind to reality. His imagination always tried to make everything more interesting than it actually was; it was as if the worlds inside his head were more exciting than the world outside. I was convinced that his imagination, along with his tenuous hold on reality, was integral to his poetry. In a typical Oxford manner, I set such store by being interesting myself that I never felt emotionally cheated by his inventions. Besides, sometimes they even helped to explain his poems, which were otherwise lost on me. I fancied that he had a literary imagination, that his inventions were the stuff of literary men, and that I would always be a stranger to their world now that I was reading history.

Years later, when Dom turned from poetry to journalism, people very quickly got the idea that what he was writing had more to do with dreaming than with waking, and his inventions, for all their aura of novelty and charm, were read with, at the very least, a wry smile.

ONE day, Dom came back from London and told us that he had met two young American poets and had invited them to give readings at Oxford.

"Who are they? Are they any good?" I asked.

"No," he said. But then he said that about practically all his contemporaries, unless they were his friends. "They're quite odd," he went on. "Allen Ginsberg and Gregory Corso know how to make a splash."

I'd never heard of them, but Del said he had. He thought he'd seen something about them in *Time*—about their doing something odd like going along streets talking to fire hydrants, and saying, "You have bigger tears than I do."

"How bizarre!" we exclaimed, laughing.

I remarked that it was unusual for popular magazines to feature poets.

"Ginsberg and Corso are perfect foils for popular publications, which have little use for serious poetry," Del said. "It's par for the course if they can show up a couple of poets doing ridiculous things like talking to fire hydrants."

Everyone wanted to know what they were really like.

"You see, in the middle of this rather posh party Allen took off his clothes, jumped up on a table, and started reading a long poem called 'Howl,' " Dom said.

"Next, you'll tell me that Corso bit off Ginsberg's nose," Julian said.

I somehow felt that Dom was telling the truth. In any case, I wanted to hear the rest of the story, so I asked, "What in the world is 'Howl'?"

Dom chose to answer me rather than Julian. "It's his poem, my dear."

"What is it about?" Jill asked sternly.

"I couldn't hear everything, there was so much noise. But it had something to do with the best minds of our generation groping around naked in various places in America trying to find a drink or some marijuana. But no one paid Allen any attention until he shouted, 'Man, I'm going to be reading "Howl" on the BBC, on the Third Programme!' Of course, everyone gathered around the table, but then poor Gregory felt left out, so he jumped up on the table, too, and started taking off his clothes, yelling, 'People who wear clothes are creeps! Flowers don't wear clothes!' Well, my dear, you might say there was pandemonium."

"You're making it all up, Dommy," Julian said.

"I am not," Dom said, a bit truculently. "I've invited them to Oxford, and you will all meet them. In fact, they seem very left wing, so I've arranged a reading for them at the Labour Club."

"You haven't!" Quentin said.

DOM and a small group of us went to receive Ginsberg and Corso at the Oxford railway station on the evening of their reading. Ginsberg, who was in his early thirties, had brown, owlish eyes and wore horn-rimmed eyeglasses. Corso, who was in his late twenties, was a small, dark, shaggy man. Both of them were dressed in bluejeans and checked flannel shirts. I was struck by how friendly they were, and how eager to please. Ginsberg actually came across a little like a salesman, except that he seemed to make a point of being unkempt and unwashed. Corso seemed to delight in being Ginsberg's sidekick. Every time Ginsberg said something, Corso would come out with some such enigmatic remark as "Allen, don't let them shoot the wart hog," or "America is full of creeps, but here they're crazy like daisies, man." To such effusions Ginsberg had his own peculiar responses, like "Baby, we're the wildflowers."

We rushed them to the Labour Club meeting and found that there was quite a crowd. Either Dom had done a very good job of spreading the word or Ginsberg and Corso were better known than I had thought. I was barely able to find standing room in the back.

A Labour-type undergraduate introduced Ginsberg, ending with a flourish: "Who says that the left doesn't produce good poets?"

Ginsberg thereupon began reading from his poem entitled "Over Kansas":

> "Starting with eyeball kicks
> on storefronts from bus window
> on way to Oakland airport:
> I am no ego."

In Oxford, where writing and conversation had high polish, his verse sounded particularly unformed.

From somewhere, a woman shouted in a broad Northern accent, "Whatever this is, it's devoid of content or metre!"

There were catcalls and murmurs from various parts of the room.

"If such buffoons can become poets, then everyone is a poet," someone said.

Ginsberg boldly sailed through the poem without stopping or hesitating, as if he were used to hecklers.

"I'm going to read a poem called 'Bomb,' " Corso said, in a boyish, enthusiastic voice.

The crowd seemed to settle down, no doubt expecting a poem in praise of the Campaign for Nuclear Disarmament, a cause dear to the heart of practically every member of the Labour Club.

"Budger of history Brake of time You Bomb
Joy of universe Grandest of all snatched sky I cannot hate you."

"The fellow is praising the bomb," said a man somewhere near the front. "I've worn out my feet marching against the bomb, and this chappy calls it a 'joy.' "

There was such a hubbub that Corso had difficulty continuing over it.

"Man, Gregory is just praising the *shape* of the bomb!" Ginsberg yelled.

"What shape?" the man asked.

Corso pressed on with his reading, his boyish voice full of the wonder of his own words:

"Do I hate the mischievous thunderbolt the jawbone of an ass
The bumpy club of One Million B.C. the mace the flail the axe?"

"It's a disgrace to have an American imperialist—"
"How dare he praise the bomb in the Labour Club!"

Corso, perhaps with the best of intentions, had touched a raw nerve of Oxford undergraduates, who were as passionate about politics as they were about anything else in life.

Someone near me threw a shoe in Corso's direction. Soon shoes were flying through the room in the same spirit in which their wearers had marched in protest against the bomb. The intention didn't seem so much to hit Corso—the shoes were aimed at the wall behind him—as to make a political statement.

"All man hates you they'd rather die by car-crash lightning drowning
Falling off a roof electric chair heart-attack old age old age O Bomb."

Corso valiantly continued with the poem, as if he liked having the clatter and thud of high heels, sandals, and walking shoes as a background to his reading.

People were standing up, looking for their shoes, putting them on, and trying to get out of the room.

"Who thought of getting these chappies to speak at the Labour Club?" somebody asked the room.

Came the reply: "Dom."

GINSBERG and Corso stayed with Dom in his digs for several days. He took them with him wherever he went—to pubs, to the rooms and houses of friends, many of whom were dons. He showed them around the colleges, and showed them off to anyone and everyone. They became a source of endless amusing stories, which were embellished with each telling. One story, which is still told at Oxford, is of what happened when Dom took them to meet Auden.

At the time, Auden, who in the previous year had been made Professor of Poetry, was very much around. In the morning, he was often to be found at the Cadena Café, where a Viennese-type string orchestra sometimes played, and there anyone could go up and talk to him. With certain people, and especially with women, he was shy, but with most undergraduates who had some literary interests he was extremely forthcoming. Dom would regularly turn up at the Cadena and regale Auden with stories, and Auden would laugh and laugh. He would sometimes bring Auden to my rooms. I was so much in awe of him that I couldn't think of much to say, but Dom would just get going on his stories.

It was said that Auden was somewhat put out at Dom's bringing the two scruffy American poets around. He didn't know what to do with them, but eventually took them to Christ Church, his college, and showed them its cathedral, with Dom in attendance. Auden walked them all around the cathedral, reading inscriptions in Latin and translating them, telling them the names of cathedral dignitaries commemorated there. "Gentlemen, this is St. Lucy's Chapel," he said as he shepherded them about. "In this aisle there are many monuments to Cavaliers killed in the Civil War. . . . This, gentlemen, is the north transept. Up there is a window which dates from the sixteenth century, and this is the tomb of James Zouch, who was the canon of the priory, and who, as you see here, died in 1503. . . . These are the bays between the fourteenth-century Latin Chapel, where services were held in Latin into the late nineteenth century, and the thirteenth-century Lady Chapel, which houses the beautiful fragments of St. Frideswide's shrine."

Ginsberg and Corso trooped along behind Auden like good schoolboys, listening respectfully and asking appropriate questions (How old was the Cathedral? How big was it? How was it connected to his college?) and making appreciative noises at his explanations. Indeed, they were on their best behavior, as if they thought that by making a good impression on Auden they might somehow get a leg up in the literary establishment.

At the end of the tour, Auden walked his guests out of the

college, and started to take his leave, saying, "Gentlemen, it has been a pleasure."

Ginsberg thereupon got hold of Auden's tie and started shoving it into his mouth, while Corso grabbed Auden by the knees, and both men cried, "Maestro, maestro, don't leave us! Let us be your servants and students!"

Auden became extremely flustered, but the more he tried to extricate himself, the more tightly he was held by the neck and knees.

After Auden finally got away, Ginsberg said to Dom, "The prig!" And Corso said, "Yeah, man, who cares about all those nuns and monks? What has that got to do with the price of hashish in Tangier?"

Dom and many of us dined out on this story for some time. Years later, I asked Auden about it, and he neither confirmed nor denied it. He simply laughed, and said, "That's typical Dom. Anyway, those fellows had no manners, and I never understood why Dom should have brought them to me."

ONE of the most striking aspects of Dom's life in Oxford was that he lived openly with Henrietta Bowler, who had been married and divorced twice and had two small children. In fact, Dom's relationship with her was perhaps the oddest part of our group's Oxford experience, for the fifties were a period of sexual innocence. It was before the Pill, before couples lived together openly out of wedlock. Certainly at Oxford men conducted themselves as if chivalrous devotion to women were still the prevailing code, and most women arrived at Oxford as virgins and left as virgins. I remember that at one point Jill shared a flat with Virginia Kent, who was both extremely attractive and clever. Virginia later told me that young men were always falling at her feet and proposing marriage to her but no one ever made a pass at her. Women looked down upon other women who had "steady" relationships. Their idea was to meet a lot of men and to have "the Oxford experience." They saw their virginity as contributing to their freedom and independence: to yield to a man, it seemed, would shackle them in frightening dependence, and so preserving their virginity was the only way for young women to complete their studies at the university. In fact, few women one met at Oxford were attached to any one man. Most of them saw different men at different times. (The attachment of John Fuller and Prue Martin, which was deep and permanent, was an exception.)

Dom had met Henrietta in London when she was working as a secretary to his publisher, David Archer, who had founded the Parton Press from the York Minster Pub in Soho. Archer had initially run it as a one-man show, for he was a publisher without any books to publish. He was a man of such modest means that he was always trying to cadge money from his friends and acquaintances, claiming that he had expectations from a nice elderly aunt in Canada, and that his ship would come in one day soon. But he and Henrietta used to have drunken lunches at the York Minster Pub, and in time she persuaded him that he needed a secretary. Archer took on Dom soon afterward as the first author whom he actually published, and Dom started lunching with them. Before long, Dom moved in with Henrietta and set up housekeeping in her studio flat, at Apollo Place, in Chelsea, near the Embankment. (I later learned that the flat had been left to Henrietta by the painter John Minton, who had killed himself. He had been devoted to her and in love with her former husband.) Dom thereupon began leading a double life, in Oxford and London. He was nineteen and was in his first year; she was twenty-seven.

Since Henrietta was older than the rest of us, and we were all very inexperienced and of an age when we exaggerated age differences, she seemed to us to have attained the sort of slap-happy adulthood that we saw as so distant. She was provocatively sexy, and liked to challenge men. By turns blowzy, boisterous, flighty, and hoity-toity, she was always either making jokes or making trouble, as if she found life without drama boring. We all liked her, at the same time that we were overwhelmed and frightened by her. (Even Jasper, a placid person of equable temperament, was fascinated by her.) When she was not around Oxford, Dom was always talking about her and her flat. He would take off for London to see her and be gone for weeks at a time. The whole situation was extremely exciting to us, not only because she belonged to another world but also because our own lives were so tightly governed by the rules and regulations. The two of them lived as if there were no tomorrow.

Henrietta was a stunningly handsome woman with burning eyes and brilliant-henna-colored hair. Her laugh was full and noisy, almost to the point of being hysterical; it would go up and down several octaves. Part of what made her so attractive was that her personality was shot through with contradictions. She was dazzling, destructive, and volatile—more fun to be with than anyone else when she was in a good mood, but also someone you couldn't wait to leave when she was in a bad mood. She was terrifically worldly, and yet had a kind of open, helpless, childlike immediacy. Sometimes she would brush one off like a fly; at other times she would enjoy the moment with such glee that one's spirits would soar. Sometimes she was girlish and coy with Dom; at other times she treated him as a mother might treat a child—but a cross mother, one who would slap her children. Both her marriages had been unhappy, and, perhaps because of that, there was something quite rancorous about her. She could hit out at people and shower them with spite and venom. She and Dom seemed often to be spatting, she indulging in good-natured histrionics and bullying, and he mostly talking back in monosyllables—"But," "Yes," "No"—and with little laughs.

Henrietta was about the only person who could keep up with

Dom's drinking. Dom would have a double whisky as an eye-opener at half past ten and would be drunk by noon. When he was flush with money, he would stand drinks to practically anyone and everyone in a pub. He would throw money around the way he would drink. We accepted his drinking—and everything else about him—because he fitted our notion of the poet, right down to the toes. The fact that he was sometimes incoherent and feckless seemed to us a mark of his general gaiety and genius. He and Henrietta went through at least one bottle of whisky a day each.

We felt that it was right for Dom and Henrietta to live in a carefree manner—do things the rest of us would like to do but were not able to, perhaps because we were not, among other things, sufficiently daring. My own feelings were more complicated. For reasons I could scarcely have put into words at the time, Dom and Henrietta seemed like family, and I found it very easy to be a third—and a weaker, dependent—member of the menage. The more independent and competent I was when I was on my own, the more inadequate I felt in company, and, consequently, the more I tended to adopt the role of a child when I was with a couple, as if, because of my handicap, I could not lay claim to many of the things that most adults took for granted—that Dom certainly took for granted before he was out of knee pants. Oddly, none of the dons or the Oxford grandees—to say nothing of the undergraduates—were openly disapproving of Dom and Henrietta, possibly because their relationship was outré. Even if some people were disapproving, that didn't stop them from having Dom and Henrietta to lunches and to drinks. Far from being ostracized, Dom and Henrietta were seen as glamorous. It was the glamour of an artist's life—the idea that just down the road there was a world of talented eccentrics.

As if Henrietta's frequent presence weren't enough, her children, too, were in the picture. I remember that one of the first times I saw Dom he had been landed at Oxford with Joshua,

Henrietta's four-year-old son, so that Henrietta could fly off to the Continent. As it happened, his college had just suggested that Dom move out, and he had taken digs near Christ Church, on St. Aldate's. They consisted of a room next to Del's, over a shop selling milk and cream, and opposite Christ Church's Memorial Garden. Contrary to all the rules, Dom and Henrietta used to live in the room. (An undergraduate was sent down from Trinity for having a woman spend a night in his college room. Similarly, a woman from St. Hilda's was sent down for having a man spend a night in her college room.) Dom looked after Joshua for the better part. of a week, taking him to friends' rooms, to lectures, and even to pubs. He also inveigled Jill into looking after the boy for long stretches.

To see Dom, the dreamy poet, going around with Henrietta, a "woman of experience," was to feel that Dom was rather like a rabbit in the grip of a hawk. She had an intense way of looking at him, as if she wanted to eat him up, and she radiated instant hostility toward any other female. There was an unmistakable feeling of physical violence even between her and Dom. Often there was also an air of violence among the friends who gathered around them, and it was quite disturbing—although I myself never actually saw any fights break out. The atmosphere of violence was especially pervasive among their friends in London, where Dom and Henrietta would start drinking in a pub—say, York Minster. Friends—occasionally including some of us from Oxford who happened to be in London—would drift in and join them. They would all spend hours there, and then Dom and Henrietta would buy a couple of bottles from an off-license shop and take everyone home. The band of friends would sit and talk and drink in the studio flat until the drink was all gone. Often streams of people would arrive with more bottles. Regulars included the poets Stevie Smith, David Wright, David Gascoyne, and George Barker; the novelist Colin MacInnes; the playwright Frank Norman; the painter Francis Bacon; the editor Francis Wynd-

ham; the photographer Johnny Deacon, who was always around
the York Minster taking photographs of writers and hawking
them to fashion magazines; and, of course, Archer. Some of these
friends, like MacInnes and Norman, were known for having a
violent streak. Others, like Wyndham, were so pacific that one
almost feared they might be beaten up.

ONE day, Frank Moraes turned up at Oxford. Everyone was
instantly drawn to him, not only because he was Dom's father
and an Oxford man but also because he seemed to be a constant
and secure presence in Dom's turbulent life. Moreover, much like
Dom, he had an aura of romance, as someone who had been
everywhere and met everyone, who was a man of the world and a
grand figure in his own right. Like Dom, he had a quality of
merriment about him, and a touch of sadness, too, and, if possible, he drank even more than Dom, but he retained control. I
had my own reason for being drawn to him: here was another
Indian father visiting his son at Oxford. But the contrast between
their father-son relationship and my father's and mine could not
have been more marked. They talked about each other's mis-
tresses, like upper-crust English people, as if they were beyond
the normal moral code of the middle class. I would have been
mortified even to mention to my father an affair of the heart if I
had had one. (I didn't have one.) Dom's father also had an appropriate air of affluence to go with his sophisticated manner.

He took Del, Julian, and me out for an expensive dinner at
the Mitre, the celebrated Oxford Inn, dating from the fourteenth
century. He plied us with food and wine, and the one smoker
among us with cigars, and told us at one point that Dom's relationship with Henrietta was costing him thousands of pounds a
year and was keeping Dom in drink and in trouble. He said he
was determined to break up the relationship, and talked as though

he would cut Dom off without a penny if he continued to see Henrietta. He asked for our help.

Del and Julian took sides against Henrietta and succeeded in breaking up the relationship, but only temporarily. Henrietta refused for a time to have anything to do with Del. When she finally did talk to him, she said, "You betrayed me but I forgive you." (Eventually, Dom and Henrietta broke up of their own accord, but Dom's personal life remained tumultuous for some time.)

❧

TOWARD the end of my second year, in June, 1958, it was announced that a committee consisting of C. V. Wedgwood, Lord David Cecil, L. P. Hartley, C. Day Lewis, and V. S. Pritchett had awarded the Hawthornden Prize to Dom. The prize was intended for the year's best work of imagination published by a writer who was under forty-one. Graham Greene and Robert Graves had won it when they were young, but by now it had not been awarded for some fourteen years—not since the death of its founder, Alice Warrender.

The announcement created a sensation, not only because Dom was twenty but also because "A Beginning" was privately published and had sold a mere four hundred copies, and the Parton Press was now on the verge of going out of business. (A literary prize traditionally honored both an author and his publisher.) Moreover, Dom was really known only to his father's London friends and a coterie of Oxford literati.

A prize-giving ceremony was to be held in the Arts Council's house, in St. James Square, in London, on the tenth of July. Dom, who was eager for his close friends to be present and celebrate his day of triumph, imagined the ceremony as a momentous theatrical event, like the début of a great actor or opera singer. Henrietta's view of it was, if anything, even grander. "Everyone who's anyone will be there," she told me. "If you're not there, everyone will know you're a nobody. It would be like living in England in the twenties and missing the début of John Gielgud or Laurence Olivier." Still, I grew fearful of walking into a room full of London society, and perhaps being ignored by my literary friends, including Dom, who might find me a drag, and I was not altogether happy about Dom's getting all the attention.

It happened that two or three days before the ceremony I was rushed to the hospital with pain in both my jaws. I was examined and was told that I had four impacted wisdom teeth. As luck would have it, a bed was available, and within hours surgery was performed, with general anesthesia.

I got out on the day of the ceremony. My face was so swollen that I could scarcely talk, smile, or eat, but I went. I couldn't bear the thought of being a nobody.

I was afraid that I would scarcely be able to find Dom, or perhaps he would be too busy to take notice of me. I could imagine myself, were I in his place, neglecting old friends, out of my own sense of insecurity. But hardly had I walked in the door when Dom rushed up to me, and he stayed at my side for much of the afternoon. As we walked around the room, which was chock-a-block with practically all the day's leading poets, writers, and editors, and, of course, the members of the committee, and all Dom's friends from Oxford, from the York Minster, and from Chelsea, it was hard to take a step without being greeted by the likes of Auden and Spender and Louis MacNeice and Walter de la Mare and Kingsley Martin.

Lord David Cecil, who was presiding at the ceremony, called the meeting to order and presented the Hawthornden medal and a check for a hundred pounds to Dom. There were no speeches. It was as if Dom were an established poet, and people should know who he was. The atmosphere was like that at English parties, where no one was ever introduced. Not even Dom spoke. It was as if the medal and the check were part of his birthright. I was so impressed by the English way of doing things—of assuming intimacy in the middle of the anarchic world—and so delighted with Dom's deserved success that I all but forgot my anxieties and my swollen face.

My pleasure—and everyone else's—at Dom's triumph was only increased by barbs of criticism that were soon aimed at him, like one in the *Times Literary Supplement* the next day; after all, he was being taken seriously. The article said:

He has the usual fault of a very young poet of a romantic temperament, an innocent sentimentality. We may be put off by the very first stanza in his volume,

> "Dying is just the same as going to sleep,"
> The piper whispered, "close your eyes,"
> And blew some hints and whispers on his pipe:
> The children closed their eyes. . . .

The two off-rhymes and the two rich rhymes there tell the reader that this is a contemporary poet. . . . But later on in the poem we find (the italicized words show it) a determined freshening up, ironical, enlivening, of traditional romantic idiom. . . .

> He blew a wavery *quittance* on the pipe,
> Then *honked* with thumb and finger at his nose
> And *shuffled off* to find a place to sleep.

This is not a poem that wholly "comes off," but what is encouraging about Mr. Moraes's talent is the delicacy, the avoidance of crudeness, in these no doubt rather contrived variations of verbal tone and texture. . . .

And without having anything new or striking to say, Mr. Moraes has the one quality which Mr. Empson once described as the sole quality which a clever impostor, today, cannot fake: supple confidence in the handling of rhythm.

In due course, Dom got a poet's Third and enjoyed a certain notoriety for having invented in Schools convincing quotations from "The Canterbury Tales" and "The Faerie Queen." (I saw him a few years ago. He was married, and was living and writing in Bombay.)

In April, a couple of months before the Hawthornden ceremony, Edward Weeks, the editor of the *Atlantic Monthly,* and his wife came to London. The previous summer, as an editor of Atlantic–Little, Brown, he had published "Face to Face," my account of my childhood and adolescence. Indeed, he had nursed me along for several years as I wrote it, and had published a couple of excerpts from it in the *Atlantic.* I had come to think of him as my mentor, and I now looked to him to help me consolidate my position as a sort of hanger-on in the literary world. Being around Dom and the Oxford literati had begun to work its magic on me, making me think that I wanted to continue to be around good writers and poets, even if I could not be one of them.

Mr. Weeks was on a publisher's scouting mission, and he and his wife took up residence at the Stafford Hotel, in St. James Place, for three weeks. They invited me there for tea and dinner. At the appointed hour, I presented myself at the hotel, and found Mr. Weeks, who had just come from his London tailor and was wearing an elegant new suit, full of enthusiasm and good cheer, as usual. We had a festive dinner in the dining room with Mrs. Weeks. Although I had not previously met her, she talked to me about the children—they had a son and a daughter—as if I were an old friend. For the first time, I felt like a literary man, fussed over by my editor and taken into the family fold.

"The good book goes on selling in all parts of the country, my boy," he said after Mrs. Weeks retired and we settled down to a round of brandy. He cleared his throat. "The couple of installments in the *Atlantic* and your radio and television appearances gave it a real sendoff."

His reference to the "book"—never mind his seeming to rank it with the Good Book—was mortifying. I still couldn't bring myself to refer openly to what I'd written as a "book"; in my letters and conversations I referred to "Face to Face" deprecatingly as a "narrative."

"Not a week goes by that we don't sell at least a couple of hundred copies," he continued. "Our treasurer will soon be mailing you the latest royalty statement, with a sizable check."

I mastered my base impulse to ask him what the size of the sizable check was.

"Another round, my boy?"

"No, thank you," I said. I was beginning to feel a little tipsy, but, pretending to be more of a man of the world than I felt, I appreciatively swirled the golden liquid in my glass, sniffed it, and took the smallest sip I could politely get away with. I didn't like the aftereffects of brandy: it always woke me up at dawn with a headache. But it felt good to bask in the company of an American—particularly one so warm-hearted and given to encouragement. Even his plain business talk seemed refreshing after the intellectual fencing that went on unremittingly at Oxford.

"What is your next book—some more autobiography?" he asked.

The mention of autobiography gave me a turn. Not only did I then regard the genre as a low form of literary activity but I also felt that when I wrote "Face to Face" I hadn't known how to write—that it was only after I got to Oxford that I had begun to learn how. In fact, I felt that everything in the way of reading and writing that I'd done before Oxford was tawdry.

"When can we look forward to your next book?" Mr. Weeks asked again.

"I'm a one-book man," I said. "Everyone has one story inside him."

"I understand, my boy," Mr. Weeks said, almost too quickly.

If I don't write a new book, Mr. Weeks won't be interested in me any longer, I thought. I won't be a literary man anymore.

"At the moment, I'm enjoying being just an undergraduate," I said. "Maybe when I go home, after finishing at Oxford, I can write a piece for the *Atlantic* on how the young people in India are going about the task of building a new nation." I made my suggestion sound as pompous as possible, thinking that that was what would appeal to the *Atlantic's* editor.

"That's a grand idea," Mr. Weeks said, rising to the bait.

I suddenly felt rebellious. "I actually do have an idea for a book—I will be the editor," I found myself saying, as if I were in competition with him.

Mr. Weeks became extremely attentive. I had just got the idea, with the help of his brandy, and I had to improvise on it, like a jazz musician who hits a note by mistake and has to turn it into a figure.

"I've never met more interesting people than I'm meeting at Oxford," I said. "I'm sure I can get ten or a dozen undergraduates to write essays about the disturbing political and social situation in the West, and make a very interesting book out of it."

"But will disparate voices, no matter how brilliant, really make a book?" he asked.

"Have you heard of 'The Declaration'?" I asked. He said he hadn't, and I savored for a moment the Oxford triumph of one-upmanship as I told him about it—that it was a sort of manifesto of angry young men in England, probably inspired by John

Osborne's "Look Back in Anger," and that it had been hailed as a tract for the times.

My tongue loosened by more sips of brandy, I was soon telling him about my friends in the A. and B. and the Leonardo and in Dom's group, and saying that, for all I knew, they might be the future Audens and Einsteins. I went on to describe a dazzling new friend I had just made—Alasdair Clayre, who, in his second year, was already being spoken of as another Isaiah Berlin. Sir Isaiah, the All Souls luminary, was a friend of Mr. Weeks's, and had contributed a celebrated article on Winston Churchill to the *Atlantic.* In fact, Mr. Weeks had introduced me to him, and, as a result, I had had several scintillating teas with Sir Isaiah at All Souls. I thought that my reference to a new Berlin would go down well with Mr. Weeks—clinch the argument in favor of the book. "Another Isaiah—what an exciting prospect," Mr. Weeks said. "But the book simply must have unity."

"That will be for me to make certain of as the editor," I said, a little severely. "I'll build the book around a particular theme. It's bound to be of interest to an inquiring mind. I can guarantee you that it'll be better than 'The Declaration,' which got a huge amount of attention here."

That fact seemed to fire his interest. "It sounds like a book that will appeal to the young and to the old and to the Americans and to the English," he said, suddenly doing an about-face and running away with the idea. "I'm lunching with your English publisher, Billy Collins, next week. Maybe the *Atlantic* and Collins could publish the book jointly and make it into a transatlantic sensation. I'm sure there will be several pieces in the book which the *Atlantic* would want to run. Sunday papers here would be falling all over themselves to publish them, too." His enthusiasm was exhilarating, especially since Mark Bonham Carter, my editor at Collins, had lost interest in "Face to Face"—and, for a time, in publishing—about a month earlier, after standing for a seat in Parliament as a Liberal and winning it. In any case, I now saw myself becoming a well-known editor, like Mr. Weeks, one day—discovering talent and bringing it to the notice of the world.

"I think we should draw your contributors not only from Oxford but from Cambridge, too," Mr. Weeks was saying.

"Of course," I said. I knew that he had spent some time at Trinity College, Cambridge, and was very proud of the association. Besides, I thought that the book could only profit from expanding the pool of talent to include Cambridge.

"I'll be going up to Cambridge, and I'll mention your project to my friends," Mr. Weeks said. "I'm sure Noel Annan could be enormously helpful in rounding up the undergraduate talent there." Noel Annan was the provost of King's College.

I thanked him, and said that after he had prepared the way I would make a scouting trip to Cambridge myself, and that I also had some contacts of my own there. In my wish to impress him, I mentioned Sylvia Plath, having got to know her when she was at Wellesley and I was at Harvard summer school, and having run into her again, with Ted Hughes, in Cambridge.

"I could see her being a contributor to an anthology of poetry but not to a book of essays, like yours," Mr. Weeks said.

He said that whenever he came to London he also visited Oxford, to call on Sir Isaiah Berlin and to make a pilgrimage to Boar's Hill to see John Masefield, the Poet Laureate. "I'll be coming to Oxford on May 9th and 10th, and would like it very much if you were to accompany me to the Masefields'—they have quite an establishment," he said.

Oh, to be a literary man, I thought. I said that I would be delighted, and that I would like to give a party for him (Mrs. Weeks was returning home from London soon) at Balliol to meet friends of mine who might contribute to the book.

"I'd very much like to meet the future Audens and Einsteins," he said.

We spent some time chatting about various friends of mine whom he would be meeting, and when I left him it was nearly midnight.

❦

HARDLY had I settled back in Oxford when I received a letter from Mr. Weeks, dated April 22nd. He wrote, in part:

I had a most agreeable luncheon with your publishers, Billy Collins and Mark Bonham Carter. . . .

They asked what new project you had in mind, and when I sketched in your suggestion for ten or a dozen essays from the young undergraduate leaders in Oxford and Cambridge, their misgiving was plain to be seen. They said that a collection of papers—even if they were fired by the fervor and intellect which we hope for—would be a very hard book to sell. "Tell him," said Collins, "that the project would have a good deal more promise if he could do the writing entirely himself; if he could draw and elucidate the several characters showing us what they stand for, the book would have a unity, and it might have a compulsion, which it could not possibly have if it were done by a dozen different hands."

You may remember that this was my own initial reaction, for long experience has taught me to be wary of books which are essentially a composite.

I was disheartened, but only momentarily. I shot off a reply saying that I planned to go ahead with the project anyway, in the hope that a more literary house than Collins might take it on. I said that I thought I could persuade my friends to take the risk that I was willing to take personally.

My letter had its intended effect, for Mr. Weeks wrote back, "That's the spirit! You go right ahead and scout the possibilities of the Eloquent Twelve. You and I will discuss the lineup of the writers and their different fields when we meet on May 9th."

The weekend at Oxford with Mr. Weeks went off like a dream. We lunched at the Mitre on a couple of trout, which he had caught himself and had got the hotel chef to cook. I had him around to drinks with Dom and the group and an assortment of Leonardo and A. and B. friends.

The high point of Mr. Weeks's visit was going to see the Masefields, on Boar's Hill, a wooded area on the south side of Oxford, with large houses and gardens, where Robert Graves, Robert Bridges, and Edmund Blunden had established their homes, and which had been made famous by Matthew Arnold in his poems "The Scholar Gipsy" and "Thyrsis"; indeed, it was from Boar's Hill that he saw "that sweet city with her dreaming spires." Masefield himself, who was now in his late seventies, turned out to be like no other literary figure I had ever met. He had not gone to university, and had no connection with Oxford or Cambridge, and he had the air of a self-made, self-reliant person— almost that of a lighthouse keeper. There was a certain kind of informality in his household which I had associated only with Americans. Within moments of arriving, Mr. Weeks had rolled up his sleeves and was working at the kitchen sink on another of his trout, which he had brought them as a present, while Mrs. Masefield, John Masefield's wife of over fifty years, hovered about. In answer to some rather American-style questions from me (since I was with Mr. Weeks, I was behaving more like an American myself), Masefield said that he had run away to sea when he was a boy, that the sea had been his muse ever since, and that he had earned his livelihood at menial jobs in America and later working as a journalist in England. Salt and sea seemed to pervade his talk and his house.

I asked him at one point how he felt about being Poet Laureate, and he said, "Oh, that. I was made Poet Laureate in 1930. Everyone has long since forgotten that." He has written hundreds of plays, poems, novels, and articles, has been accorded the highest honor his country had to offer, and yet feels forgotten, I thought. What hope is there for lesser mortals? Still, being entertained by the Poet Laureate—the Masefields extended their hospitality to me as if I were already on a par with Mr. Weeks—went straight to my head. It confirmed me in my determination to become a man of letters—without, however, doing much writing myself.

Not long afterward, wearing the hat of an editor, I made my scouting trip to Cambridge, put out the word to university publications, consulted dons and undergraduates at both universities, winnowed my list of likely candidates, and sent out invitations to prospective contributors, asking each one for his or her "credo," in the form of an essay of about five thousand words.

I was soon deluged with letters and essays. They kept on coming throughout the summer. I was up to my ears in paperwork—reading draft upon draft of essays, suggesting revisions, editing copy. Every day, the postman would deliver a pile of envelopes for me at the porter's lodge, and every day I would take another pile to the post office. I felt I was running a cottage industry. Some of my prospective contributors not only were big noises at the universities but had already made names for themselves in London, and I had to contend with their idiosyncrasies. I feared that my editing had given offense to Andrew Sinclair when he failed to reply to my suggested revisions of his essay. But then he wrote to say that he had been travelling in Spain and had not seen his post for two months. The Oxford people, by and large, were much more forthcoming—no doubt because many of them were friends—but they, too, presented problems. Conrad Russell, a brilliant historian, who had just taken a First in Modern History, initially wrote me a letter about publishing his contribution anonymously. (He was not on good terms with his father, Bertrand Russell, who had left his third wife, Conrad's mother, some years earlier to marry a fourth. At that time, Conrad was just fourteen and Russell himself was eighty.) Subsequently, he wrote to say that if it was important his name could be used after all, but using it would require some changes in the manuscript.

By prodding contributors, sifting the contributions, and collating different versions, I finally had what I thought was a respectable volume, with essays by Dom, Del, Jasper, and Andrew Sinclair; Garry (Hon. Walter Garrison) Runciman (heir of the second Viscount Runciman of Doxford), a recent Cambridge graduate who was as brilliant as he was rich; John Charap, a mathematician and postgraduate theoretical physicist at Trinity College, Cambridge; Richard Drakeford, a composer at Worcester College, Oxford; and Sheila Abercromby, an undergraduate reading English at St. Hugh's. The collection included several anonymous essays as well. (Alasdair Clayre was unable to deliver an essay.) Jasper and I came up with what we thought was both an accurate and a commercially promising title for the book— "Young Men's Dreams"—from this verse from the Book of Joel:

And it shall come to pass afterward, That I will pour out my spirit upon all flesh, And your sons and your daughters shall prophesy, Your old men shall dream dreams, Your young men shall see visions.

My own essay, "Orphans of the *Sturm*," which led off the volume, centered on a beatnik American tourist, Ruth, who had turned up at Oxford and whom I'd got to know: it dealt with the attraction of the Beat Generation and its nihilist values, which were especially unsettling to me just then, as I was thinking about returning home, and perhaps even helping to build the new Indian nation. Dom titled his essay "The Forked Island" and in it recounted poetically his childhood experiences in Bombay ("I found if I imagined [the beggars] were plants . . . I could walk past indifferently, like someone in a rose garden, even brushing the heavy-handed flowers with my legs as I went by") and affirmed his belief in love. Sinclair's essay, "The Space of the Now," which was embellished with such memorable verbal infelicities as "cock a quirk" and "part of my hopings," put forward the idea that people should assume different personae in the course of their lives, on the ground that "civilisation was built upon lack of candor." "Time Off to Think," by John Charap, narrated succinctly and fascinatingly his background as a Jew brought up in the Anglo-Jewish community of London's East End, described his disaffection with Judaism and discovery of a love for science, and wrote of abstract intellectual pleasure in a way that rendered it aesthetically, and even sensually, appealing. The writer of an anonymous essay, "From Sleep and from Damnation," about standing on the threshold of religious faith, conducted an exceptionally mature and serious dialogue with himself, examining, among other things, the claim of logical positivists that ethics are the reflections of instinctive wants, and pointing out that a perversion of this idea has become a justification for materialistic popular cultures; inspired by the lives of the saints, he saw in the love of God an opportunity for spiritual self-discovery which was not available to him through, say, humanism. Richard Drakeford, in "The Discordant Music," was singular in shunning autobiography (he said he didn't find himself interesting) and concentrating instead on the nature of musical composition and its place in the life of the spirit. In another essay, an undergraduate who asked that her name not be used—at least, not until she'd found a husband—contained such Miltonic bombshells as "University should, I think, now try to teach girls that they will be happiest in domestic circumstances," "There are few women, I think, who can wholly satisfy their creative instinct in any way other than making babies," and "Women's creative powers are so channelled as to make them incapable of greatness and genius in the arts." In "The Luxury of Attitudes" Garry Runciman wrote about the problems of being brought up rich and said he found that when he adopted liberal skepticism his only deeply felt wish was for mutual tolerance; recognizing the vagueness of such a creed, he concluded, "My summary, in a sentence, is that we should all think straighter, act nicer, understand better, and feel less." Jasper's essay, "The Individual and the Absurd," was an intellectual autobiography, describing a childhood marked by a love of learning, which was followed by an early schoolboy socialism (largely a product of maternal influence) and then by an adolescent questioning of attitudes, still going on. "I was sixteen when I stopped to think; I sank at once, well out of my depth; and I am not yet properly emerged," he wrote.

The volume was ready in October, just before the Michaelmas term of my final year. I had the edited copy typed and sent to Boston, and returned to my books.

I didn't hear anything from Mr. Weeks until the new year. Then I received a two-page letter, which kindly but firmly rejected the manuscript, on the ground that the essays were "highly introspective, too dependent on vague generalities, forbiddingly earnest, and dull." His silence had made me fear the worst, and I had for some time been bracing myself for a rejection. I wanted to be an editor like him, but I had no confidence in my judgment; in fact, almost immediately after the volume was posted I had begun to worry about my selection of essays—about my failure to give contributors clear directions, about my editorial work, about my choosing so many contributors in the light of their academic reputation rather than their ability to speak for our generation, about the vein of negativism in the book. As it happened, his letter had arrived when I was sick in bed and was feeling overwhelmed by the pressures of my final year. Nevertheless, I found it hard to wash my hands of the project, and I allowed my American literary agent, Elizabeth Otis, who was handling the volume, to submit the manuscript to McGraw-Hill. Its editor in chief, Edward Kuhn, Jr., also rejected the manuscript, but on business grounds:

All of us who read the book were impressed with it in its own right, but I'm afraid it bears too much resemblance to the *Life* article of a year or so ago on Princeton men, and the Rinehart book that followed the article. This is a particularly unfortunate coincidence of similarity since, as the Princeton book contains the reflections of American students, it not only takes the edge off this idea, but points up the comparative remoteness of Mehta's book as well.

Kuhn enclosed the Rinehart blurb for the Princeton book, "The Unsilent Generation," which was edited by Otto Butz:

The Unsilent Generation
An anonymous symposium of eleven college seniors' view of themselves and their world which reveals—far more truly than statistics or surveys could do—the temper, the moral attitudes, the credos, and the aspirations of young people today. Here are the surprisingly frank autobiographies of eleven articulate members of the generation which has been called silent. Are they our sons? You be the judge.

I got hold of the book. It read much like its blurb, and made me realize that my project could have had no chance in the commercial world, which prized affirmation, positive thinking, and outright enthusiasm.

I now faced the dreaded task of getting in touch with all the contributors, thanking them, and giving them the news that our effort had come to nothing. But when I told Dom he said, "Don't worry, Vedkins. We will all write our own books—and a lot of them, too. And they'll be so good that they'll set the world on its ear."

VIII

IN THE FORCE
AND ROAD OF
CASUALTY

W HILE I WAS AT OXFORD, MOST OF MY FRIENDS AND I
felt that we were living through some of our happiest
years. One reason for this feeling no doubt had to do
with the nature of Oxford itself. It was small and intimate, and yet very worldly. Practically every scholar or
man of letters we studied, it seemed, had gone to Oxford
or Cambridge. It had a mystique: even its spires were said to be
"dreaming." Another reason had to do with our youth. However
confident a persona each of us put on, our inner lives were full of
Sturm und Drang. We craved certitude and order, and Oxford

gave us both. All those of us reading in a particular school studied the same prescribed texts, often the same books. (I remember that some of my friends found their fathers' notes helpful, if their fathers had read the same subject.) Furthermore, it seemed that some of the best minds in Britain and the world beyond had been gathered at Oxford and Cambridge by a process akin to natural selection. Everybody had survived one open competition after another from childhood on. Indeed, there was a hierarchy among British schools, which competed for places and scholarships at Oxford and Cambridge, and a hierarchy among Oxford and Cambridge colleges, which, in their turn, competed for the best schoolboys, and the boys were awarded scholarships according to their performance on the entrance examinations. There was a similar hierarchy among undergraduates, who competed for the best degrees. (It was understood that one who got a First became a scholar or went into the Civil Service or the Foreign Office; one who got a Second went into a profession or became a writer or a journalist; one who got a Third settled for business or one of the other greasy trades.)

As we grew older, we discovered, of course, that many of these supposed certainties did not always hold true even in England, to say nothing of the larger world. Moreover, there was a definite closing in of options for clever men, and one could sense a creeping gloom among top undergraduates as they approached the end of their Oxford years; it sometimes made them reactionary in politics and out of sympathy with the mass culture that was taking shape around them. (Now that the mass culture has arrived, some people at Oxford speak of it as the New Dark Age.) They felt that they were misfits in their own country and culture. Many of them settled for an academic career, doing so not because they were natural teachers or because they felt there were certain books that had to be written but because there was nothing better to do out there. In contrast, like many good students from America, I had come to Oxford in the hope of perhaps becoming an academic, but I was beginning to doubt my abilities. I felt I could never be as good as, say, the Greats men, because I had long since missed the bus for learning the ancient languages thoroughly. Nor could I comfort myself with the thought that I was as knowledgeable about Indian culture as they were about Judeo-Christian culture. I did not, for example, know Sanskrit. Almost all my education had been in the West. If I ended up living in the West, I felt, I would always be a second-class citizen. At the time, in my heart of hearts I wished that I had been born an Englishman and that I had all the intellectual equipment, with the accompanying symbols of privilege and power, of the best of the English.

Yet in later life I could never forget the fact that some of the best undergraduates I knew came to have troubled lives. I am thinking here especially of three of my friends: Roger Scott, who came up in my year as a scholar to New College to read Greats; Alasdair Clayre, who came up, also in my year, as a scholar to Christ Church to read P.P.E.; and my Balliol friend Richard Snedden, a scholar a year ahead of me, who was also reading P.P.E. They had all been scholars at Winchester College, which in my time was spoken of, together with Eton, as the best public school in Britain. In their time, there were some five hundred boys at Winchester, of whom about seventy were scholars—the academic crème de la crème—and lived in what was known as College, an austere, monastic six-hundred-year-old building.

I once asked Maurice Keen what Roger, Alasdair, and Richard had been like at school. Maurice had been at Winchester with them, but he was a bit older than they were and had come up to Oxford to read Modern History a couple of years before I did. (A star pupil of Southern, he later succeeded him as Fellow and Tutor of Medieval History at the college.) He was a friend of all of us.

"Roger, Alasdair, and Richard were all head boys," Maurice told me. He went on to explain that a head boy was always a scholar in his last year of school, chosen by the headmaster in consultation with the second master. Such a boy was supposed to represent the highest values of the school—indeed, of public-school education generally. He had to be an all-round golden boy—not only have academic abilities of the highest order and be good at sports but also enjoy the esteem of both the staff and the other boys. In addition, seniority could play a part. If someone sufficiently qualified stayed on for an extra year—generally boys were at Winchester for five years—he would be preferred as head boy to someone a year below him, however "golden" the younger aspirant.

"Were you a head boy? Could Jasper have been one at his school?"

"No. Neither of us is any good at sports."

I asked him how Roger, Alasdair, and Richard had all managed to become head boy.

"They were a year below me, and theirs was, by any standard, a golden year. I left after five years, but, as it happened, one of my contemporaries, Leo Aylen, stayed on for a sixth year and was head boy for all of it. If he had not stayed on, Roger and Alasdair—but not Richard—would, by all contemporary reckoning, have been strong contenders for the office. Anyway, both of them decided to stay into a sixth year, I suspect partly because each quite fancied the head-boy entry on his curriculum vitae. Roger became head boy for that Autumn Term, then left school. Alasdair succeeded him for the Spring Term, then left. Richard had also stayed on for the sixth year, less surprisingly, because he had come into the school unusually young—at twelve and a half. He decided to stay the whole year, and therefore was next in line for the office when Alasdair left, and so became head boy for the Summer Term—no doubt keeping out of office the most golden of the next year down, whoever that may have been. After Winchester, Roger and Alasdair went on to spend two years doing their National Service before coming up to Oxford—just as I had done—while Richard came straight up from school."

At Oxford, Roger, Alasdair, and Richard all seemed to be destined for great things. Yet the later lives of all of them were sad. I was left wondering whether the turns in the fate of all three were a coincidence or were in some way a consequence of their fast-lane education. It certainly seemed to me that their almost overbred intelligence could have developed only in the milieu of a British public school and the Oxford and Cambridge of the day. (Even people who had stable afterlives in a way my friends did not, seemed to have been oddly affected by their school experience. One Balliol friend was so shy that during a conversation he would actually try to climb the wall—hoisting himself up onto a mantelpiece or the top of a bookcase, and perching there like a frightened bird. He did other odd things, too, like walking up to a piano in a room full of people, striking one key, and then looking around to see what effect the "ping" had had on people. He had come up to Balliol just after he turned eighteen, and it seemed that his mind had been forced far ahead of the rest of him.) Nevertheless, they mastered their shortcomings sufficiently to become distinguished scholars, even if they never managed to—and, it may be, never wanted to—overcome a certain unworldly, eccentric attitude toward life.

OF the three, Roger was perhaps the handsomest and had the most dignified bearing. The legend of his school glory had preceded him to Oxford, and when he arrived he was taken up by several prominent Winchester dons, like John Sparrow, the Warden of All Souls. However, they soon realized that he was not what they had thought he would be. He was oversensitive, fragile, and ruthlessly honest, and he seemed to be in constant spiritual turmoil. Perhaps because I had come from America, at Oxford these very qualities drew me to him, but some of the high-powered Winchester, or Wykehamist, dons saw them as a social handicap, and dropped him. He took their rejection of him very hard, and he left Oxford after a year or so, in the middle of his studies. I remember thinking at the time that talented people everywhere have difficulty, and perhaps take longer than ordinary people to make their way in the world.

Hardly anyone saw Roger after his departure. In 1970, he published a novel called "Downfall."

Alasdair was an especially close friend of mine at Oxford, but I didn't see much of him after I came down. One of my vivid early memories of him is an evening at the Royal Opera House, in Covent Garden. The father of one of my readers, Rose Donaldson, had just become a director of Covent Garden. Rose, a jolly, well-connected young woman, had the opportunity to take a couple of friends to a production of "Boris Godunov" and had invited me to go. As bidden, I dressed in my dinner jacket and met her at the Oxford railway station. I was enormously delighted to find that her other guest was Alasdair, a man who would have stood out in any company. He had fine, well-defined cheekbones, dark hair and eyebrows, and, always, a lively, interested expression. He made the air sparkle with his conversation.

Alasdair entertained us all the way to London, talking about operas he had seen and singing snatches from them; the other passengers in the compartment fell as much under the spell of his gaiety as we did. At one point, he launched into "Boris Godunov," singing the part now of the scheming monk, now of the distraught czar, now of the chorus of peasants, and also singing the ringing of church bells. Sometimes his imitations fell flat, but he pressed on, totally unself-conscious. He had a lovely lilt to his voice.

At Covent Garden, we were seated in the Royal Box; Rose explained that this was one of the perquisites of a director when royalty was not present. The box was a spacious room with heavy curtains on the stage side. When we arrived, they were closed. Here Rose's parents, John and Frances Donaldson, presided over a dazzling party, which included Sir Isaiah Berlin and several people I didn't know—a merchant banker and his wife, and another couple, who, it seemed, had an estate near that of the Donaldsons. I was so intimidated by the company that I could scarcely find my tongue. Alasdair, however, went right up to Sir Isaiah and started talking to him. I was struck by the similarity of their voices: both were energetic and quick off the mark.

As an undergraduate, Alasdair was often compared to Sir Isaiah, as if people expected the younger man to lay claim one day to the older man's mantle. Like Berlin, Alasdair enjoyed chasing ideas and attaching them to thinkers, and puzzling out why those men had thought and acted as they had; like Berlin, he was a natural synthesizer. (Berlin, it seemed, couldn't mention Kant without mentioning Fichte and Hegel, as if he always saw connections among thinkers.) Like Berlin, he was passionate about music. And then there was Alasdair's shout, which sounded as if he had picked it up from Berlin. When I first met Alasdair, I thought that it was part of the hearty English manner, and imagined that many people at Oxford shouted like him. Later, I heard it said that Alasdair had learned his particular shout from Berlin, who, in turn, had learned it from Sir Maurice Bowra, another great Oxford figure. But the differences between Alasdair and Berlin were equally striking. Berlin seemed to have a sombre side, while Alasdair always seemed to be in high animal spirits. Berlin seemed set in his ways, while Alasdair was free.

As we were all standing and chatting, champagne glasses were pressed into our hands, and the waiters kept topping them up. A dinner table materialized, complete with damask cloth, silver, and crystal. There was still some time before the beginning of the opera, and the Donaldsons seated us as if we were in their dining room, Alasdair and I being on either side of Rose. We were served a smoked-salmon course—with very special white wine—and demolished it to the sound of the orchestra tuning up. Just before the curtain rose, the table and the dining chairs were carried out and comfortable armchairs carried in, transforming the private dining room into a ringside parlor, and the thick curtains of the box were drawn back.

Between acts, over more courses, with appropriate wines—and appropriate switching of furniture—almost everyone commented volubly on the voices of the singers and the quality of the sets; on Boris Christoff, the lead, and Rafael Kubelik, the conductor; on this production and others that people had seen. I knew the opera only from a set of records I owned. Although that allowed me to follow the story and the singing, more or less, I felt that if I opened my mouth I would only expose my ignorance, yet it would not do to continue to be silent. I resorted to the time-honored American technique of posing questions, asking at one point how Mussorgsky's opera was different from the Pushkin drama on which it was based, and whether anyone knew the differences between the earlier and the later versions of the opera.

Berlin was fast with answers, but Alasdair was not far behind. He was able to hold his own with Berlin on the subject of Pushkin. Indeed, I was floored by his knowledge and erudition. He was a year and a half younger than I was; I already had an American college degree, obtained while he was doing his National Service. How, I wondered, had he managed to learn so much? Was it Winchester or the English culture? I told myself there was no way to explain the springs of talent. After all, Pushkin, perhaps the greatest Russian poet, had died at the age of thirty-eight.

"What a silly way for Pushkin to go," I said now. "If Pushkin hadn't died in a duel—"

"The 'if's and 'can's of history!" Alasdair broke in. "What if Marlowe hadn't been stabbed to death in a tavern? We might have had a poet as great as Shakespeare."

The dining chairs were almost pulled out from under us, so that the parlor could be reassembled for the last act.

SINCE Alasdair and I were in different colleges, we didn't run into each other as a matter of course. We would arrange to meet by sending each other notes through the colleges' messenger service; there were several pickups and deliveries per day, so we could write to each other in the morning and meet a few hours later. He would usually come by Balliol, and we would go around the corner to Cornmarket Street and either lunch at La Roma, a cozy Italian restaurant, or have morning coffee or afternoon tea at the Cadena Café, to the strains of a live orchestra. (Auden's patronage added a touch of poetry to the atmosphere.) Alasdair was quite a university figure, yet there was nothing patronizing or pretentious in his manner. Almost from the start, he made me feel like an old friend, although there were a number of people he knew better, from school, from National Service, and from P.P.E. studies.

One recurrent topic in our conversation was Oxford philosophy, and whenever we talked about it I felt particularly sad that I wasn't a philosopher. In the nineteen-fifties at Oxford, the linguistic analysis of many chestnuts in the philosophical fire was causing a revolution in Western philosophy. Being an Oxford undergraduate at the time and not taking part in this revolution was a little like being a worker in Paris in 1789 and sitting out the storming of the Bastille. I relied on Alasdair to bring me up to date on the latest bulletins from the barricades. Not only was

Alasdair a regular at the lectures of J. L. Austin, Elizabeth Anscombe, Gilbert Ryle, Stuart Hampshire, and other Oxford philosophical luminaries but he also saw many of them socially; his natural brilliance, his good nature, and his charm attracted dons and undergraduates alike. Many of us saw our dons outside lectures and tutorials—Oxford fostered the feeling that we all belonged to a community of equals—but Alasdair got more out of such friendships, because he had both the Winchester passport and the intellectual ability. (In due course, as everyone expected, he became a colleague of his former dons.) He was also light-hearted, even to the point of being a marvellous gossip. It was as if his high-minded principles found release in animated chitchat. After all, Oxford undergraduates and dons were like a big family, whose quirks, preoccupations, and habits were a perpetual source of amusement and entertainment to its members. To hear Alasdair talk about the philosophers was rather like being the proverbial fly on the wall and watching them wrestle with their ideas.

Some years later, I found myself writing a book much of which concerned Oxford philosophers, and I realized that a large part of what I knew about them I had absorbed from my conversations with Alasdair. Like a good teacher, he had imparted knowledge to me in such an informal way that I had the impression I'd picked it up on my own. I wanted to acknowledge his help in the book, but didn't want to embarrass him by associating him with it and making him a party to what might be controversial or might ruffle the feathers of the people I was writing about, who were his friends and were now also his colleagues. When the book came out, I fully intended to thank him, but I never did. I expected him to say something about it, but he never acknowledged its existence. Almost without knowing it, I took his silence to be a sign of disapproval, and felt wounded. Rather childishly, I responded to his silence with a silence of my own. From a distance, he seemed so successful in the intellectual world that I felt as if our relationship of equality had ceased with my Oxford years. Sustained silence was so out of keeping with our easy undergraduate rapport that I was confused. The thread of our friendship was broken, and the explanations I gave myself for that—for instance, that it was difficult to maintain a friendship from opposite sides of the ocean—were insufficient. Years went by before I realized that his judgment of the book had nothing to do with my gratitude to him. By then, it was too late. On January 10, 1984, around eleven o'clock in the evening, he killed himself by jumping under an oncoming train in the Underground station in Kentish Town, North London.

I remember that when I heard the news I thought of many things, and especially of the death of Anna Karenina, for the novel was a favorite of both of us, and we'd often discussed it. But there could be no comparison between a death near midnight in a gloomy station in the Underground and the death under the wheels of a pounding nineteenth-century Russian train, in a bustling, crowded provincial railway station—and, more important, no comparison at all between Alasdair hurling himself out of this world without abiding faith and Anna crossing herself and begging God's forgiveness with almost her last breath.

The tremor that Alasdair's death created in the English intellectual community is still palpable. In fact, whenever his friends meet, they—that is, we—are apt to remark upon his absence and fall to discussing his manifold gifts, seeing in one aspect or another of his life a reflection of our own. Perhaps I should mention that one of his friends, Peter Jay (a former British Ambassador to Washington), who had been a scholar at Winchester and Christ Church a year behind Alasdair, still refuses to accept the idea that Alasdair committed suicide. He maintains that Alasdair probably fell under the train in a drunken stupor. (In later years, Alasdair was drinking a lot—wine, whiskey, just about anything.) Suicide, however, was the finding at the inquest, where the motorman, who was sitting at platform level, testified that he saw Alasdair actually throw himself under the train.

❦

ALASDAIR was born on October 9, 1935. He was the youngest son of John Clayre, a doctor in Southampton, whose original surname was Christianssen, and who was Danish by birth. For several generations, the Christianssens had been doctors and lay missionaries, and it was by way of Australia that John Clayre had come to live in England. He seems to have had a great love for the Scots—for their robust yet puritanical character—and he gave his children, three sons, names with what he thought was a Scottish flavor—David and Ian, in addition to Alasdair. Dr. Clayre died when Alasdair was eleven, and the children were brought up by their mother, Doris, who settled near Winchester.

Alasdair was particularly close to his mother, a forceful, energetic, inquisitive, determined woman, who, like many women of her generation, hadn't received much formal education. Apparently, because he was both the youngest and the cleverest of her children, she favored him, and after he became a scholar at Winchester she invested ever more pride in his achievements, although his brothers were also intelligent, even if they did not win scholarships to great public schools. (David did engineering at Cambridge and has settled in Canada. Ian is a schoolteacher in Denmark.)

At Winchester, Alasdair was a great favorite of the headmaster, Walter Oakeshott, and, as it happened, Oakeshott left to become the Rector of Lincoln College, Oxford, a couple of years before Alasdair came up. Because of Oakeshott, when Alasdair came to Oxford, after doing his National Service, he had a leg up, and quickly got to know many dons of various colleges. He soon became well known at Oxford in his own right, however, through a column he wrote for *Isis,* an undergraduate weekly. Even people who sneered at the pretensions and frivolities of the "rag" looked out for what Alasdair had to say. In fact, there was a marked disparity between Alasdair's thoughtful pieces and the silly headlines the editors put on them, such as "Clayre Soup" or "Clayre Out." The pieces had a certain kind of intellectual seriousness and political engagement, without the doctrinaire left-wing ideas so characteristic of undergraduate publications then. As a columnist, he seemed to enjoy manipulating abstractions, and forming moral judgments upon the whole social spectrum of England. In one column he attacked the language in which the social sciences were couched. In another, instead of adding his voice to that of the Campaign for Nuclear Disarmament in purely emotional and moral condemnation of "the bomb," he advocated an empirical approach to British unilateral nuclear disarmament, inviting those who airily espoused pacifism to consider its consequences: it might involve renouncing "our trade, our standard of living, our position in the world, our political independence, even our lives." In a third column he reviewed Roy Jenkins's book "Sir Charles Dilke, A Victorian Tragedy," and discussed the Victorian moral code, which if it was publicly violated could spell the ruin of an eminent figure. (Dilke's career was ruined, just when he was on the verge of coming into a high office, by charges of adultery levelled by a self-proclaimed mistress; she was probably prompted to make them by Dilke's apparent actual mistress, who, as it happened, was her mother.) In a fourth he reflected upon the relative uselessness of writing and thinking, his particular métier, compared with the usefulness of building bridges and manufacturing goods, the job of the worker. In looking up the pieces recently, I was pleasantly surprised to find how clearly I recalled them.

IN 1959, Alasdair was awarded a congratulatory First in P.P.E.—that is, his papers were so brilliant that the board of examiners specially commended him in person—and that autumn he was elected one of the two new prize Fellows of All Souls. As its Fellow, Alasdair became one of the then sixty select, self-electing, self-governing, self-perpetuating Fellows of one of the richest colleges at Oxford, which had no students—indeed, no obligations of any kind. At All Souls, he was ensconced in rooms, panelled in mahogany, that are some of the most comfortable in Oxford, and in a setting that is, in its way, as exquisite as that of Winchester or Christ Church—indeed, of any in England. The college, which was founded in 1438, has great physical beauty. Its northern quadrangle, designed by Nicholas Hawksmoor and completed around 1730, ranks as one of the finest examples of eighteenth-century architecture in Britain, and on a clear day its high twin towers and, beyond them, the outlines of the Radcliffe Camera, a library in the shape of a rotunda, and the spires of the Bodleian Library provide a striking vista. It was here that Alasdair was left alone to think and write. In "A Room of One's Own" Virginia Woolf, while bemoaning the social exclusivity of British higher education, says, "Intellectual freedom depends on material things." Alasdair was now provided with those material things as a result of his success in a series of competitive examinations, beginning, in effect, when he was eleven. (Competition, like flogging, had, of course, been one of the principal values that built and sustained the empire.) He used to say that as a sinecure for intellectuals All Souls had few, if any, equals anywhere in the world. An All Souls Fellowship was an unparalleled passport to almost any establishment position. Indeed, traditionally, many of the Fellows had not gone into academic life at Oxford but had held such positions in London—in the Civil Service, in banking, in publishing, in Parliament—and had visited the college only on weekends. Over the years, the college had played a very important part in British politics. Between the wars, for instance, it boasted such London Fellows as Curzon, Chelmsford, Halifax, Simon, Dawson, and Sir Arthur Salter. Some of the most important, if misguided, decisions of the period were substantially made in its common room: not to bring down Mussolini, not to help the Republicans in Spain, not to collaborate with Russia, not to defend Czechoslovakia.

In the early years when I saw Alasdair at All Souls, he seemed to take to the college as if it were his birthright. (I remember one garden party he gave at the college as perhaps the most dazzling Oxford party I ever went to.) The passionate, outspoken Marxist from Dom's group, John David Caute, was elected the same year as Alasdair, but he soon began to bridle at the old-fashioned comforts of the place. In fact, he and some other young fellows took it upon themselves to try to reform the college and bring it into the modern world, by making it, at least in part, into a graduate school—with actual students, and a new building to house them. Their plans eventually fell through, and Caute was so indignant that he resigned his Fellowship and made a public issue of this life of privilege by writing an article about it in the British monthly *Encounter*. In his article Caute fastened the blame for the failure of the reforms on Sparrow, charging that the Warden was clearly offended by the atmosphere of modern intellectual life, since he preferred gentlemen amateurs to professionals, classical discipline to practical subjects, bachelor dons to married dons. (Once, it is said, Sparrow quipped that nowadays young fellows were giving up "All Souls for one body." He himself was a bachelor.) Caute also charged that Sparrow found distasteful such notions as a college's accountability to the state and the opening up of higher education to greater numbers. Caute was silent about which side Alasdair had taken in the affair, and Alasdair was too discreet to violate All Souls' code of secrecy, which was so strict that Caute could not have written the article and remained a Fellow. I do remember, however, that Alasdair was torn by the row, and his distress made me think he might have had a foot in each camp. Caute, like Alasdair, had been brought up by his mother, had gone to a public school, and had garnered certain marks of Oxford success: as an undergraduate, he not only published "At Fever Pitch" but also got a First in Modern History. Sparrow, like Alasdair, had been a Winchester scholar, and, unlike Caute, was a pillar of the establishment: he had read Mods and Greats at New College, taken his mandatory Firsts, been elected to All Souls, been called to the Bar, and become an important figure at Oxford. Alasdair seemed to see their clash as a family feud, and to be pained by it.

At All Souls, Alasdair took advantage of the international standing of the college, and the social and intellectual groups it opened up to him, but he never settled down to any particular line of work. While most of us marched purposefully toward a goal, he was constantly jumping from one thing to another, picking up things, making a success of them, and dropping them, as if he were trying to prove himself in different fields—in effect, continuing on the road of competition. One sensed a certain tension in him, as it seemed that he was increasingly drawn out of the cloistered, cozy world of Oxford, an extension of his Winchester life, into the larger, glamorous world of London.

Perhaps taking a cue from the philosopher Wittgenstein, he worked for a time as a gardener for the writer Richard Hughes, who was a friend of his. He took up architecture, and was awarded a scholarship to study the subject at the Architectural Association in London for five years, but he abandoned it within a year. He tried his hand at fiction, publishing a novel, "Window." (The *Times Literary Supplement* review of the book began, "Mr. Alasdair Clayre has written a book about faith, hope and love. He is not able to cope with these high themes in terms of character; and there are difficulties of feeling that he does not approach.") He also published a volume of verse, "A Fire by the Sea, and Other Poems." He produced television programs and delivered lectures over the air for the Open University—a non-residential university for students of all ages (often employed), in which television is used a teaching aide. He wrote a book, "Work and Play," in which he considered the ideas of philosophers on work; borrowing an analogy from Simone Weil, that the worker is like a rejected lover, he discussed the value of work that is fulfilling, and, drawing upon verbatim quotes from workers, he argued that the problems posed by repetitive industrial work can be solved not by more pay and fewer working hours, as is generally assumed, but by less industrialization, since tedium kills enthusiasm for leisure. At one time, he fell for Scientology, and was taken with its idea that one could maximize one's production and creativity by joining the community of its adherents; he was especially attracted to the commune style of living that some of its adherents had adopted. Members were required to turn over their money. Alasdair had no money to give, and after a few months the scales dropped from his eyes, and he escaped. Escape proved much more difficult for friends of his who had followed him into the movement; one of them had made over a good part of his substantial wealth.

For a while, Alasdair was a folk singer. He published a collection of his songs, and performed them on a couple of records. The liner note on one record was written by the novelist Iris Murdoch, the note for the other by the writer and critic John Wain; he described Alasdair's songs a little in the manner of Polonius—as in turn "lyrical and elegiac," "purely satirical," "satirical with an undertone of pathos," "argumentative-satirical," and "philosophical and lyrical." Actually, his songs were often fatalistic and had about them something of the troubadour, perhaps his most famous being "Adam and the Beast," in which Adam asks God, "Is it among the hunting beasts that I belong?" Some of Alasdair's songs were also recorded by a Persian folk singer, a young woman named Susha Guppy, who had immigrated to England from Iran.

I met Susha once. "I was introduced to Alasdair in the late sixties or early seventies," she told me. "In those days, he and a friend were running a very successful night club. I did an evening of singing there, and that launched my career in Britain. Alasdair's songs were perfectly all right—as a typically sixtyish poet's songs. It was as if he were trying to be Bob Dylan, but the songs were not as good as Bob Dylan's, so he thought that they were no good."

Like his professional life, his private life was turbulent, and was notable more for its conquests than for its stability. "When we were undergraduates, I once saw Alasdair near the sports field," David Pryce Jones, a friend of both of us, recalls. (Alasdair had always been very good at both cricket and football.) "As I was driving away, I saw Alasdair just hustle a girl into a ditch. I can still see her little feet going up into the air. This was the first time I had seen such an approach to courtship, and I think it was symptomatic of the way he set about things with women—I mean, he simply got on top of them. In the early years after we came down from Oxford, when Clarissa and I were living in our little matchbox of a house, in the Knightsbridge area"—David was among the first of us to get married—"at least four broken-hearted girls must have come to the house to talk to Clarissa. All of them had been much shattered by their experience with Alasdair. I remember having a conversation with him when he had got two of them pregnant at the same time. He was ashamed of it, but also proud of it. You see, he was a great moral figure, but had something wolfish about him, too. As he grew older, he got hold of younger and younger girls. Sometimes the wives of his close friends had to worry about the virtue of their daughters. He was a little like the Minotaur waiting for the next shipment of virgin flesh from Greece."

Alasdair's mother began to fret that her son would never get married and settle down, but Alasdair seemed unconcerned about the delay. He was the first to admit that he had trouble committing himself to one woman. And he once pointed out to me, "After all, Isaiah didn't get married until he was forty-seven." In October, 1974, however, when Alasdair was thirty-eight years old, he married Felicity Bryan. They had been living together for two years. Felicity, a literary agent, was the twenty-nine-year-old daughter of Sir Paul Bryan, a Conservative member of Parliament. (He represented the constituency of Howden from 1955 to 1983.) The wedding took place in the crypt of the Houses of Parliament, another of the old and beautiful settings that had formed Alasdair's experience. Their marriage lasted six years, during the last two of which they lived apart.

❧

ALASDAIR'S final piece of work was a twelve-part survey of China, for television, entitled "The Heart of the Dragon," and an accompanying book that bore the same title. The series, in a sense, had its origin in his friendship with Peter Montagnon, his former boss at the Open University and a longtime, distinguished producer for the BBC, whose credits included the series "Civilisation," with Kenneth Clark. In 1979, when Channel 4, a new commercial station, first began broadcasting, Alasdair and Montagnon formed a television-production company and called it Antelope—because, Montagnon explained, "we thought the animal smelled good and it was able to run pretty fast when required." One of the few conditions of the partnership was that sometimes Montagnon would be the front legs and Alasdair the back legs, and sometimes they would change ends; another was that they would work only with people they liked. Although it was clearly in Alasdair's interest to work with Montagnon, it was not so clear why Montagnon wanted Alasdair as an equal partner. He once said that he thought of Alasdair as heir to the late poet Louis MacNeice, and as being in the tradition of the Third Programme, for which MacNeice had done some of his best work. The BBC's highbrow Third Programme had carried the banner for international high culture in Britain until 1970, when it was discontinued, to the accompaniment of an enormous storm in the British cultural establishment. Montagnon, while recognizing that Alasdair would be an anomaly in popular television culture, apparently looked to him to bring to it a touch of the Third Programme.

Alasdair wrote the proposal for the China series in consultation with China scholars, to whom he had access through his All Souls connections. On the basis of that proposal and Montagnon's reputation, Channel 4 funded the entire project. Alasdair then scouted for locations—a job that meant travelling extensively in China, ahead of the film crew.

In the course of the work on the series, Montagnon often found Alasdair an extraordinarily joyous and extroverted collaborator, as is suggested by this entry in his diary, dated October 23, 1981, which he shared with friends after Alasdair's death. It was written when they were in Turfan, in western China: "Last night there was a grand party given by the chief of 'the Foreign Office' in Turfan. He comes from a minority group; a Vega. Alasdair saved our bacon; we had to perform after the local girls and the local bands had just given over with their dances and songs. He was fast asleep in the front row. We dug him in the ribs, and whispered 'Alasdair, you're on.' He leapt up and into the breach, and sang two of his own songs brilliantly, then topped it by doing a Scottish reel, much admired by us, the locals and a visiting herd of American tourists." At other times, it seems, his work habits showed a different, rather anxious side of Alasdair. According to Montagnon, he would often stay up all night, going through a couple of dozen drafts of a chapter, and in the morning his colleagues would find him unshaven and surrounded by the debris of a sleepless night.

Alasdair spent three years on the series and the book. They dealt with China's history, culture, and economic conditions, and, together, perhaps constituted his longest-sustained piece of work.

The date of the publication of the book was January 10, 1984, twenty days before the first installment of the series was to be broadcast. As publication day approached, Alasdair's friends noticed in him signs of anxiety; it seemed to them that he didn't want to expose himself to the criticism of reviewers, as though that would interfere with his sense of perfection. It was on that day that he killed himself.

A MEMORIAL service for Alasdair was held in February, 1984, in St. James's Church in Piccadilly. It fell to Felicity to organize it; neither his elderly mother nor his brothers living abroad knew who his friends were. The task was none too easy for her, not only because she had remarried and had three small children but also because since the divorce many of Alasdair's closest friends had ignored her or seemed embarrassed to acknowledge her. "It is very frustrating to run into people you know—at the opera or the theatre—and have them simply pretend that you don't exist," she told me.

Among those attending the service were some of the most notable figures in British intellectual and social life. David Pryce Jones, Peter Levi, and Peter Montagnon—three of Alasdair's close friends—spoke, with Levi giving perhaps the most moving eulogy. "He was in the tradition of Diderot and Voltaire, except that he was shouting with laughter," Levi said. "He made philosophy as comic as it was serious. . . . He made a walk across a quadrangle feel like a wild intellectual adventure. . . . He even made All Souls sound like an endless opera by Mozart—not a usual view. . . . Alasdair was one of the few moral philosophers who understood the fundamental importance of pleasure, and, of course, its tragic nature. He did as much as anyone to infect our entire generation with liberalism, a love of liberty. . . . He was one of those minor characters in Shakespeare who make the whole play live. He died after weeks of severe strain, in a moment of desperation, by an unconsidered act of desperate courage. 'Against the leaf, that is violently taken with the wind, thou showest thy might, and persecutest dry stubble.' "

❧

FELICITY now lives just outside Oxford with her second husband, Alex Duncan, who is an agricultural economist. In 1988–89, when I was a Visiting Fellow at Balliol, my wife and I saw something of them; they came to us, and we had dinner with her and Alex at their house, in the village of Kidlington. Naturally, one of our topics of conversation was Alasdair. In fact, she and Alex had become romantically involved when Alex was working in Gambia and she went to visit him for the Christmas of 1980 to recover from the final breakup of her marriage to Alasdair. (She and Alex had first met almost ten years earlier, when she was twenty-six and he was twenty-two, after her mother died and her father married Alex's mother.)

One day, Felicity came to lunch at the college, and we had coffee in my room. The subject of suicide was very much on my mind. That Michaelmas term, two undergraduates had committed suicide—one, Darran Walters, by taking cyanide crystals, and the other, Adam Lal, by jumping out of a fourth-floor window. It was reported that Oxford and Cambridge had higher suicide rates than any other universities in Britain, and, apparently as a precaution, many gas fires in college rooms had long since been replaced by electric ones.

"Was Alasdair prone to depression?" I asked Felicity.

"Not in the early years of our marriage," she said. "His troubles had more to do with his fear of settling down, and his wish to remain perpetually youthful. When he wasn't running around

after very young girls, he was often involved with quite aristocratic, fashionable women."

"Were the two of you happy together?"

"We certainly had a very sociable life. In the early years, we
had a lovely time. We travelled a lot. Though we did once go to
America, and once to Denmark, to visit Alasdair's relatives, who
were very jolly, we mostly went on little jaunts. On Friday, he
would get the idea of going to France for the weekend, and within
minutes we would be on the road on his motorbike. He was
deeply committed to his motorbike, had it long before he married me. He liked it because he could go anywhere with it—put
it on the train or ferry. We would go to Waterloo, take the train
to Southampton, and go over to Le Havre, and we'd be in France.
We would stay in a small hotel in Paris, look at things, have
good meals, stay up late talking and drinking, and come back on
Sunday. Then, in London, too, we were always going to parties
on the motorbike. It made him feel fancy free. There was a bit of
the gypsy in him. Alasdair was a very interesting mixture of the
reclusive and the gregarious. He preferred dinner parties to cultural evenings, but we did go to some plays, and I used to drag
him along to operas—I'm a great opera fan."

"Alasdair couldn't have been a very easy person to be with,"
I observed.

"When we first got together, he was trying to write for six
months of the year; for the other six months, he was working for
the Open University. I think it's a difficult thing for an agent to
be married to a writer, and particularly a writer who doesn't feel
he's doing very well, so we didn't share our work, and that made
things easier. He never wanted me to read his writing. I never
even read 'The Window.' "

"That's surprising," I said.

"I suppose he didn't feel proud of it and therefore didn't want
me to read it. We did do a lot of work together, though, getting

his records off the ground. We also used to sing a lot together. He had a lovely tenor voice."

"As you know, I didn't keep up with him during the years you were married," I said, "but it seems that he found settling down to a particular kind of work very difficult."

"Yes, though he was always involved with the media—especially television. At one point, he left the Open University and started working for the BBC in Manchester on a sort of television magazine program. He saw it as a chance to get out of academic television and do something more general, but the program was not a success, because it was the first time he had had to work like a reporter, and he didn't come off very well. He tried to go back to the Open University, but he'd lost his slot there. Then, he worked for the *Economist* for a time. He had done some long essays for the magazine, and the editor, Andrew Knight, had the inspired idea to have Alasdair do a political column. He tried his hand at it, but it wasn't a success, either, because it meant that he had to hang around the lobby of the House of Commons and talk to politicians. Reporting just wasn't his line."

"I wonder why he didn't stick to the academic life," I said. "He was so well suited to it."

"He did, of course, have his room in All Souls, in the tower, as part of his Fellowship, and he would disappear there. But he didn't seem to have any really close friends there of the sort he could confide in. Anyway, Englishmen of his upbringing often have trouble talking about their feelings, particularly with other men. In fact, I think that's why some of Alasdair's closest friends were not English. Also, he was fearful of judgment by his All Souls colleagues. He felt that he had already let down so many people who had put a lot of faith in him. You see, he felt he was a failure. While we were married, 'Work and Play' came out, and he didn't enjoy its publication at all—he was so fearful of reviews."

"You lived mostly in London?"

"Yes. We lived in a flat, which he had bought before I knew him. It was on Mill Field Lane, half way up Highgate, West Hill, and from its roof terrace one had a lovely view of the Highgate Ponds, on the Heath. Alasdair was very much attached to it, because it was unusual and out of the way. It was a delightful walkup for a bachelor, but it had only one big room, and that doubled as his study and our living room. As far as I was concerned, it wasn't an appropriate place for a couple. Moreover, it was isolated and inconvenient. The entire time we were married, I tried to get him to move to a house—get more settled, have children—but he resisted the idea."

"Was that why you broke up?"

"Yes, although the immediate cause was my finding out that he was having an affair. He continued to have the affair, and was very much involved with the woman, but he couldn't see why that should get in the way of our marriage. We went to a marriage counsellor who was a Jungian analyst. I think she was recommended by Montagnon's wife. I found the whole process of therapy incredibly tearful and difficult. The hour would completely knock me out. Then Alasdair and I would have lunch together, and have a bright and jolly time, but there was no way to save the marriage, because he wouldn't have children. Just before I remarried, he invited me round to a splendid house he had bought in St. John's Wood. I couldn't stop crying. It seemed to me extraordinary that he should have got this big house—just the sort of house I'd always wanted for us—after I left him."

"Still, you kept in touch after that?"

"He came to see me at our house in Oxford just after we moved there, in 1983. I'd recently had Max, my second child, and Alasdair had just returned from China. I was eager to hear his impressions of China, but he kept saying, 'This could have been us. This baby could have been ours.' He seemed to want to start the marriage over again. I imagined that it was seeing me with my baby in our beautiful old Oxford house that had upset him. I tried to change the subject to 'The Heart of the Dragon,' but he kept saying that he was very, very lonely—that an American girl he was involved with had left him and gone back to the States. 'But how is the series going?' I persisted. He said that he wasn't sure how it would do—he considered it a secondary, rather than an original, work and dreaded the prospect of seeing it reviewed. All kinds of people were against him, he said. He sounded very paranoid. Toward the end of his life, he was telephoning me regularly. Generally, he would stay on the line for about an hour. There was no way I could calm him. One day, he called me and he just went on and on, and I put the phone down on him. I'd just had Ben, and I was breast-feeding him. I was very tired from having had three children, one after another. He phoned back. Alex picked up the phone and said, 'Alasdair, will you please stop phoning Felicity—it upsets her too much.' After that, we didn't speak until the Christmas before he died, when he phoned me at the office to say that he had lost his driver's license. He said that he had been caught speeding by the police and discovered to be over the alcohol limit. He thought he was going to be sent to prison. I assured him that he wasn't—that he had only lost his license. That was the last time I spoke to him."

"Did he talk about anything else?"

"He talked obsessively about money problems. That was ironic, because he died quite well off. After all, he owned the flat and the house, both substantial residences. And then Antelope went public some time after he died, and did extremely well. I often felt guilty about that last telephone call, and I often thought of him, but I didn't really mourn him until I got the news that 'The Heart of the Dragon' had won the Emmy—it was really extraordinary that an English television series should have won the Emmy. I burst into tears, and for a whole week I found myself thinking of him and crying. I felt that the Emmy was a symbol of success that would have meant a great deal to him, that would have given him self-esteem."

"But he had so many symbols of success much grander than the Emmy."

"But he needed a new one each time he did something."

❦

RICHARD SNEDDEN, the third of my Winchester friends and the only child of Sir Richard and Lady Snedden, came up to Balliol a year before I did, when he was twenty years old, as a scholar. In contrast to Alasdair, Sned was a self-contained chap, who epitomized a certain kind of conventional British attitude and attention to style. He seemed to be comfortable only in his gang of public-school men, and for him people were either "in" or "out." Because he had gone to Winchester and was a scholar, I imagined that he would end up in the exclusive Foreign Office. As an undergraduate, he was particularly interested in holding offices— in societies, in the J.C.R., in anything at all. He seemed to be fascinated by the trivia of the elections, like a child with an all-consuming hobby. In my first year, he was elected treasurer of the J.C.R., a student office outranked only by the offices of its president and secretary. The next year, he stood for president against Peter Davison. Peter was an outsider—he was a Canadian, and the only undergraduate at Balliol reading Theology— and he was very personable. Sned was perceived as a stiff, establishment candidate, and he lost. (Sometimes it seemed as though Americans and Canadians were the only people who could get elected to any office, because the public-school and grammar-school boys wouldn't elect each other.)

The only reason I got to know Sned at all was that both of us were members of the Leonardo and the Arnold and Brakenbury. At most other colleges, I probably would not have been taken into such select societies, and would never have crossed the path of someone like Sned. But Balliol had a tradition of nonconformity and openness, which threw people from different worlds and backgrounds together. At meetings of the Leonardo, when a paper was being discussed Sned was usually silent, or would let drop an enigmatic remark about extrasensory perception, or, if he did not like something someone had said, would groan—"Ugh." He shone only in private meetings. There he would be free with pranks and suggestions. Once, he proposed that the Leonardo invite Lord Hailsham, who was then the Deputy Leader of the House of Lords, as a guest speaker from London. People protested that such a grand personage would not deign to journey up to Oxford just to entertain fifteen self-important undergraduates. Sned maintained that if one summoned "the fellow" by telegram, rather than the usual formal letter, he would grasp the importance of the invitation, and hotfoot it to Oxford. Sned, on his own initiative, did send the telegram, but Hailsham never appeared.

Sned really came into his own in the frivolous A. and B., where he held many offices, in addition to that of president. He once made a speech on the subject of his habitual silence, and punctuated it with long pauses. Another time, he somehow got hold of a deck chair, brought it into a meeting, stretched out in it, and conspicuously fell asleep. Someone surreptitiously set a match to the canvas from underneath. Sned awoke, crying out "Dean! Call the Dean!" The president, Christopher Fildes, ordered Deputy Constable Jake Broadley to extinguish the smoldering fire. John Albery was singled out as the culprit, but, upon his expressing contrition, was forgiven. The president then called upon Toby Jessel, who held the office of both auditors, to help. The meeting concluded with Toby pretending to rock Sned in the charred chair while crooning Brahms' "Cradle Song." Sned took great delight in all the commotion.

Ray Ockenden, in his valedictory speech as president of the A. and B., mocked two of Sned's conspicuous habits—feigned napping and secret telephoning. He was always rushing off to make a telephone call at the porter's lodge. We imagined that he must be telephoning his parents overseas—Sir Richard Snedden was a big wheel in shipping and travelled a lot. Ockenden's speech was in the form of rhymed couplets:

> And who's this, creeping wanly from his bed
> Well, well, well, if it's not me old mate Sned.
> Like all great diplomats a firm believer
> In enigmatic phone calls to Geneva.

The Arnold and Brakenbury and the Leonardo Society were anathema to the sporty types, like football players, who affected such working-class customs as eating fish and chips off newspaper; to Christians in the college, like the members of the Oxford Inter-Collegiate Christian Union, who were against all societies that were not religious; and to socialists, who thought public schools and public-school ways antediluvian and deeply corrupting. Yet Oxford was full of select societies, many of them steeped in romantic lore. In the university at large, there was the Bullingdon, which had no fixed premises, and whose membership was restricted to twenty, but which was renowned for its bluest-of-the-blue members, who went on to play important roles in British society. They would hunt once a week, and in the evening, after riding their horses to the club's livery stable, would try, as one member at the turn of the century put it, "to crack their hunting crops on undergraduates in the Quad"—usually unsuccessfully. Perhaps even more famous was the Gridiron, which was exclusive—at one time or another, the Prince of Wales, the Crown Prince of Norway, and Prince Paul of Serbia had been members—but boasted past intellectual members, among them Aubrey Herbert, Ronald Knox, and Harold Macmillan.

Within Balliol, there was the Annandale Club, which had no intellectual pretensions but was notorious for its upper-class excesses. For instance, one of the after-dinner amusements of the club's members some fifty years earlier had been to throw large quantities of college crockery down the hall steps in a ritual waterfall. Their high spirits were matched only by the tolerance of the authorities, who simply billed the members for the damage the morning after. But if those members—many of them Etonians—were wild, they also included some of the most brilliant Balliol men ever. Even A. D. Lindsay—their contemporary, who later became Master of the college—though he was repelled by their debauches, admired the natural brilliance of some of them, like Aubrey Herbert, who was perhaps identified even more closely with the Annandale than with the Gridiron, and who, though he was rusticated from the university for a time, went on to get a First in Modern History and to play an adventurous role in Parliament and in the First World War. (John Buchan used Herbert as the model for the hero of his novel "Greenmantle.") The Annandale members of my day—they included Snedden, Christopher Fildes, and Denis Cross—had style, if a prodigal style. They would get dressed up in tailcoats with silver facing on a gray collar (the club colors were black, silver, and gray) for no other purpose than to dine together in the Massey Room. And there were no more than ten Annandale members at any one time.

"What goes on at an Annandale dinner?" I once asked Sned.

"We have ananas Annandale."

"What's that?"

"A pineapple with its insides scooped out, and filled up with pineapple, ice cream, and kirsch."

"What else happens?"

"We hold a sweepstakes on the number of leaves on the pineapple, and the president usually wins. Our sconcemonger is called upon by a member to sconce the president for some failure or solecism in dress, like not wearing shirt studs in the club colors." In hall, if anyone commented on the silver or the paintings, or quoted Latin, or mentioned the name of a woman, he could be sconced—that is, given a flagon of beer or wine, which he had to drink down. If he drank it all, the challenger, or sconcer, had to do the same, and so it went until one of the two fell down. The point of the ritual was to teach unmannered louts the art of polite conversation. "As part of the Annandale sconcing ritual, the president is brought a large silver pot of champagne, and he does his best to drink it," Sned went on. "The silver pot is then passed around, and the members become considerably rowdier. It's not all that different from A. and B., except that we do a little throwing about of things, in such a way that the Dean will ban the club for a term or two. But why are you asking? Dining societies only suit Englishmen of a particular kind. They are not for you wogs and frogs."

There was more jest than insult in his last remark, and I couldn't help smiling, reminded, as I was, of the Duke in "Zuleika Dobson," whose club was so exclusive that he could tolerate only himself as a member.

I didn't tell Sned that, even as the puritan in me disapproved of dining clubs, the bon vivant in me was envious of the members of every last one of them; that I, as an outsider, found Annandale members fascinating, and felt they were almost visionaries, in the sense that they imagined the real world to be like the Annandale, with rigged sweepstakes and with champagne on tap, as it were; and that it seemed to me that to be a foreigner in England and not to belong to at least one dining club was like missing out on the elixir of the English experience.

Still, my own friendship with Sned was unexpected indeed. At the time, I could not have explained it, but in later years I thought of many reasons for it. He was part of a group that one would immediately have picked out as being among the most interesting of the college groups. Though he himself did not put out much energy, I was drawn to him anyway, because he and his group had a certain style, natural elegance, and air of superiority, because I saw winning their acceptance as a kind of challenge, and because I wanted to feel that I was fully in the stream of English life. Besides, I not only was drawn to eccentrics, which

I imagined Sned, among others, to be, but also believed in eccentric relationships, which I saw ours to be.

Sned and his handful of hard-drinking, poker-playing, hell-raising Annandale cohorts perpetuated certain antiquated college traditions. One of their capers was to get "tight" at the club dinner, dash over, in their tails, to the east wall, which separated Balliol from Trinity, a college known for its social pretensions, and make a spectacle of themselves. They would line up at the wall, urinate on it, and belt out the old anti-Trinity song, competing to see who could sing the loudest:

> If I were a bloody Trinity man,
>   I would, I would,
> I'd go into a public rear,
>   I would, I would,
> I'd pull the chain and disappear,
>   I would! I would!
> Bloody Trinity! BLOODY TRINITY!

One could hear them going back from the wall to the Massey Room singing "I Would Honor Yet the School I Knew" or "Lloyd George Knew My Father." No doubt when Lloyd George was Prime Minister one's father's being known to him must have opened all kinds of doors for one, but now those doors were supposed to yield only to merit. It was one thing to sing this song, a staple of all college dining societies, in the privacy of the Massey Room but quite another to sing it in the quadrangle, in the hearing of undergraduates, who, by and large, disapproved of privilege.

SNED got a Third in P.P.E. People had expected him to do better in Schools, but then again members of his particular set generally aspired either to a First or to an even rarer Fourth, which was just above failing—to either extreme, as opposed to a middling result, which was the lot of most undergraduates. After going down, he spent two years in the R.A.F. There he was assigned to the Department of the Air Ministry, and worked as a scientific adviser. Afterward, he got a job with the Bank of England. We thought he was selling himself short, since in those days an Oxford graduate from a great public school who was going into finance would have been expected to go into the much classier world of merchant banking. After a couple of years at the bank, Sned left it and started working for I.B.M., U.K. He eventually became product planner for the company in the Netherlands. In the late sixties, he returned to England as the company's market coördinator, and went to live with his parents, in the village of Boars Head, in Sussex. They lived in a Victorian house called Aldwick Grange, built in 1873.

Sned had always felt inadequate beside his distinguished father. Sir Richard, born in 1900 and educated at George Watson's College in Edinburgh, at Edinburgh University, and at Middle Temple Inn, had been called to the bar in 1925. He served as a director of numerous companies, like Consolidated Gold Fields, but his main interest was shipping. In 1929, he had joined the Shipping Federation, a business organization of shipowners, as assistant secretary, and by 1957 he had risen to become its director. He was by then well known as a labor negotiator, perhaps because he was ruthless to anyone who opposed shipping interests but, at the same time, was sincere in his concern for the sailors' welfare, and so enjoyed the confidence of both the shipowners and the leaders of the seafarers' societies. In 1951, he had been knighted for his work in industrial relations. As a person, he was said to be delightful and amiable, quick and shrewd. Though he was a quiet speaker, when he thought that right was on his side both his material and his delivery could be devastating.

On Friday, March 6, 1970, Sned, then thirty-four, came home from work seeming confused and upset. He had been depressed for some time, and particularly since the death of his mother, at the age of sixty-nine, about six weeks earlier. He had been very close to her, and in recent years had confided to his friends that his father mistreated her. It was hard to tell whether his perception was correct, especially since he himself had a history of psychiatric disorders, dating from at least 1965. In that year, his mother had found him with a loaded gun between his knees, as if he were intending to shoot himself, and he had spent three months in a mental hospital.

Father and son passed the weekend of March 6th together. Whatever Sned's own feelings of inadequacy, his father was very proud of him. Indeed, there was said to be a bond of deep affection between them.

But, as it was later reported in the newspapers, on Monday morning Sned went to the garage, got an axe, and walked into the drawing room where his father was sitting, reading a book. With the axe, he struck his father two heavy blows across the forehead, fracturing his skull.

Then he went into the dining room with the axe, and said to Miss Winifred Lyall, who had been the family housekeeper for twenty years, "I couldn't stand Daddy worrying about me anymore. I hit him with this. You can kill me now."

Miss Lyall screamed. She feared that he was going to kill her, too.

"It was the right thing," Sned said, putting down the axe. "You're all right. You can kill me."

Miss Lyall told him to call the police. He dialed 999, the police emergency number, and said, "I think I have killed my father." He couldn't continue.

Miss Lyall took the phone from him and told the police what had happened.

When the police arrived, Sned gave himself up, saying, "Oh

God, what have I done? He was suffering because of me. I wanted to kill myself as well—but I didn't have time. I have been a burden on my father for a long time. I thought I would end it all, killing him and then killing myself."

Sir Richard was found slumped in his chair, a book in his lap. He was rushed to Pembury Hospital, near Tunbridge Wells, in Kent, and he died there that same day.

The murder made headlines not only in the popular tabloids but also in the intellectual papers. On March 10th, at a special Magistrates Court in Mark Cross, in Sussex, Sned was charged with murder and remanded into custody. On May 14th, he was tried at Lewes Assizes, in the county. He pleaded not guilty by reason of insanity.

Mr. Basil Wigoder, Queen's Counsel, who was prosecuting, gave an account of the circumstances of Sned's crime, from which it emerged that on the day before the patricide he had decided to go back into the mental hospital, and had consulted the family doctor, John Elliot, about it. He had told Dr. Elliot that he might harm himself, and that, because this would worry his father so much, he might also do him harm. During the meeting, the Doctor had noticed that Sned's moods fluctuated from deep depression to euphoria, but thought that he had calmed down. After extracting a promise from Sned not to do any harm to either himself or his father, Dr. Elliot had felt sufficiently reassured not to commit him immediately to the hospital.

Dr. Jack Hobson, senior physician in the department of psychological medicine of Middlesex Hospital, who had visited Sned in prison, testified that for a period after his father's death he was certifiably insane, and said of his mental condition at the time of the murder, "Snedden did not know . . . he was doing wrong. He felt it was the only right thing to do."

Sned was acquitted by the jury of the murder of his father, and the presiding justice said that, by court order, Mr. Snedden should be "detained in a hospital specified by the Home Secretary." He was thereupon sent to Broadmoor Hospital.

The British law that a person who has committed murder or manslaughter cannot benefit from the estate of his victim does not apply when that person is found to be insane. Therefore, Sned inherited nearly a hundred and forty thousand pounds. His inheritance was administered for his benefit by the family solicitor, Arthur Prothero.

Sned survived his father by only a little over five years. I thought of visiting him in Broadmoor, but I was not sure he would want to see me. After all, I was not a school friend or an Annandale friend, and I had not met his parents or received his confidences about them. In fact, I later learned that hardly any of his friends visited him. By his heinous act, it seemed, he had put himself outside the pale. His Annandale cohort Christopher Fildes was an exception. He went to see Sned both in jail before the trial and in the hospital afterward. "In jail," he told me after Sned's death, "it was just like Evelyn Waugh's 'Decline and Fall,' when the chaplain comes to see Captain Grimes and asks him if he is all right with God: ' 'Course I wasn't, told the fellow so.' That was just the kind of meeting I had with Sned. At Broadmoor, we had only a brief conversation. I seem to remember he was wearing the standard scruff order of an undergraduate—an old tweedy jacket, flannel trousers, a soft shirt, and a tie. 'Fildes,' he said. 'You know what? My friend over there and I went to the management yesterday and complained that the radiators were talking to us. We made quite a song and dance over it. Then James, a party to our practical joke, broke in, saying, "Don't pay any attention to *them,* they're both absolutely out of their minds. It's ridiculous for them to say that the radiators were talking to *them,* because they were talking to *me.*" You see, Fildes, you have to do something to keep sane in this place.' Even in Broadmoor, old Sned had style."

IN "The Merchant of Venice," Aragon, one of Portia's suitors, delivers a memorable speech while examining the golden casket. He rejects it as the choice of

> . . . the fool multitude, that choose by show,
> Not learning more than the fond eye doth teach;
> Which pries not to th'interior, but, like the martlet,
> Builds in the weather on the outward wall,
> Even in the force and road of casualty.

I was one of that "fool multitude" who didn't always find it easy to look beneath the surface glitter of Oxford, or, as Anthony Trollope put it, in "The Bertrams," to look beneath the eating of much pudding and the making of much noise at the young heart. But the casualties, no less than the victors, of the complex system of British education were witnesses to its enigma.

IX

A LASTING
IMPRESSION

W HEN I CAME UP TO OXFORD, I BECAME FRIENDS AT FIRST
with almost anyone who was friendly and outgoing: with
Christian evangelists, who tried to rush me into their
society, the Oxford Inter-Collegiate Christian Union; with
visionary socialists, who went out of their way to be nice
to students from underdeveloped countries; with self-
proclaimed philistines, including one charming fellow who hailed
from Blundell's School, in Devonshire. (As a result of an agreement made in 1615 between the estate of Peter Blundell, a Devonshire merchant, and Balliol, Blundell's School was guaranteed
two closed scholarships to the college for its boys—a sort of permanent sinecure. Men from Blundell's, a minor public school,
were famous for living it up at Oxford and getting Fourths.) But
soon I gravitated toward people whom I admired. I sought out

people who were intellectually striking and provocative, and I became snobbish in a certain way. I was especially drawn to the Greats men, who seemed to me among the cleverest of the undergraduates, and I fell under the spell of one of the most dazzling of them all—Jasper Griffin.

It seemed that at Oxford no matter how good someone was, there was always someone better, and Jasper was no exception. There were Greats men at Balliol who excelled him in some things. Martin West was more scholarly, in that he could, for example, apply himself to a text with seemingly limitless energy; Jasper was better at hard thinking than at hard work. Roger Tomkys was more well rounded, being not only scholarly but also a top-notch cricketer; Jasper had no interest in sports. Anthony Leggett had more intellectual stamina. Gerald Toomer, a second-year Greats man at Corpus Christi, was fabled in the university at large for having a recondite knowledge of antiquities unmatched by any other undergraduate since the beginning of the war. Still, Jasper seemed to me to be the most impressive, perhaps because he was both brilliant and sensitive; Oxford undergraduates tended to be only one or the other.

He had red hair and a red beard, which he must have grown as soon as he left school (in Italy, where he once spent a holiday, people had called him Barbarossa), and was tall, slim, and angular; his elbows and shoulders seemed to stick out. He had a towering presence, and a deep, large, overpowering voice. His speech, perhaps partly because it came through his beard, had an authority that made him seem far older than his age. He struck me as so self-contained and reserved when I first met him that I found him extremely intimidating.

I used to like to drop into the J.C.R. when Jasper was having tea there; he had a passion for food, and he spent a good deal of time in the J.C.R. over tea, sandwiches, and cakes. Undergraduates would gather around him, as if he were the Pied Piper. He went in for a certain amount of hamming. He used words like "forsooth," and spoke so exquisitely that one sometimes felt one was listening to formal prose being read aloud. He had a stunning facility for quick repartee; he talked the way people snap their fingers. His memory was phenomenal, containing, it seemed, everything he had ever read, and he was never at a loss for an apt quotation.

Not everyone was susceptible to Jasper's magic. Some undergraduates—especially those who had gone to grammar schools—considered him a reactionary public-school chap. But that was an impression based on superficial observation and on things like Jasper's opinion of the untidy table manners of a fellow-undergraduate I'll call Toby. Toby was an artist and had an artistic temperament, and, having been brought up in an intellectual left-wing household, he had relaxed ways. For him, eating a piece of lettuce meant starting at one end and letting the rest of it hang out of his mouth. "Eat up that lettuce, Toby!" Jasper would bellow, in a spirit not so much of laying down the law as of upholding standards of behavior. Toby would laugh, the lettuce would drop to his plate, and the unsightly process would begin over again. Toby knew that Jasper had a fierce manner but an affectionate nature, and I can't remember his ever taking offense at anything Jasper said.

Not even Jasper's friends were always up to his ironic wit. One evening, when he and I walked into a room where Ralph Spence, Bob Walters, and some of our other friends were sitting over coffee, they all fell silent, as if they were none too pleased to see us. We were rather nonplussed—we had been prowling around looking for some amusing company. Later, I asked Bob why they had been so unwelcoming, and he said, "We had been talking about something serious, and we knew that if we let you two into the conversation you would just disrupt it." Far from taking umbrage at that explanation, I was delighted to find myself so closely identified with Jasper.

I often wished that, like Jasper, I had had a classical education; so much of the English literature I read seemed to be influenced by the classics. I had a conversation with him on the subject not long ago. "Until the twentieth century, anyone in England who had any kind of education at all had an education in the classics," he said. "Until the university reforms of the eighteen-seventies, all education at Oxford and Cambridge was in that tradition. And, yes, it is true that a lot of English literature is influenced by the classics. Dr. Johnson wrote poems in Latin. Marlowe translated big chunks of the Aeneid, and his 'Dido, Queen of Carthage' contains bits out of its fourth book. Milton wrote a lot of poems in Latin, and the whole style of 'Paradise Lost' is really unintelligible unless one knows Latin and is familiar with Latin epics. Dryden and Pope were the greatest of translators from the Latin and Greek. Pope made his name and fortune translating Homer, and his best poems are explicit imitations of classical poets. He wrote these marvellous poems called 'Imitations of Horace.' People like Wordsworth, Coleridge, and Shelley were all very keen on Greek. Keats was perhaps an exception. He wasn't a gent—he was mostly self-educated—but he picked up as much Greek as he could. In fact, it may have meant more to him because he learned it himself. Tennyson was tremendously keen on Virgil and wrote a very fine poem on him. Arthur Hugh Clough wrote English poems in hexameters. Matthew Arnold was a considerable scholar of the classics, and Gerard Manley Hopkins wrote poems in Latin, which you have no doubt seen in the back of the collected poems. Eliot knew the classics pretty well, too. He was very much interested in Heraclitus and Virgil. There's not much Greek and Latin in his poems, though—there's more French. Louis MacNeice read Greats at Merton. The truth is that if you want to study English literature at all, even that of the twentieth century, you have to know some of the classics. It is really extraordinary how there is a sort of symbiosis between English literature and the classics. In fact, people who don't know the classics are sometimes quite baffled by things English poets say.

The classics are also important for German, French, and Italian literature. People like Schiller wrote poems about Greek gods which could be Greek poems, except that they are in German. Goethe, in 'Klassische Walpurgisnacht,' brings in all the characters from Greek mythology. That was the European culture. The fact that poems made references to the classics went with the fact that buildings had Greek columns, that music included works like 'Orpheus and Eurydice' and 'Dido and Aeneas,' that paintings had nymphs—and all the rest of it. That was the culture that everyone in Europe had in common. One could say that America, too, was part of that culture. The people who made the American Revolution were not very different from English gentlemen, and the whole idea of the American government— the Capitol, the Senate, checks and balances—was based on an interpretation (or, in some instances, a misinterpretation) of the Roman constitution. Some American writers, like Edgar Allan Poe, were very keen on the ancients, and people who went to posh American schools automatically got a certain dose of Greek and Latin. Of all the great writers, the one who is least visibly indebted to the classics is, of course, Shakespeare—though his Roman plays show an extremely perceptive understanding of ancient Rome. We are told by Ben Jonson that Shakespeare had 'small Latin and less Greek.' Still, it isn't clear what Ben Jonson is saying. Does he mean less Latin and Greek than he himself had? Ben Jonson was quite learned."

My friendship with Jasper made me feel included in British society for the first time. I had previously felt that I was on the outside looking in. As it happened, one of the most talked-about new books in our first year was Colin Wilson's "The Outsider," whose thesis was that all great artists and writers were outsiders. I read the book avidly, but it only slightly weakened my wish to be an insider; for one thing, it seemed to me that the British reviewers who extolled the virtues of being an outsider were themselves, in one way or another, insiders. I had thought that by coming to Oxford I would become an insider, but being at Oxford had made me feel more like an outsider than ever. Nothing in my reading had sufficiently prepared me for the reality of the British class system, which at every level seemed to have firm, if unspoken, rules of exclusion. Class distinctions were so rigid for people born in Britain that foreigners didn't come into the picture at all. "Wogs begin at Calais" was an adage that was still around, and I couldn't simply laugh it off, as many other foreigners did. Jasper, however, belonged to the public-school élite at the college. He could hold his own with people of every stripe. His intelligence was luminous, and he was at home in European culture. In the heady early days of our friendship, I wondered why he had chosen me as a friend. Was it the mere accident of our living next door to each other, or did I lend a certain exotic touch to his English life? When I came to know him better, I discovered that he himself was an outsider. That discovery shocked me, and it also deepened our friendship.

His parents came from the ranks of the working class, Jasper told me—or, rather, the upper working class. His father was the son of a policeman, and his mother was the daughter of a cabinetmaker. Both were born in 1909, in East London—his mother actually within the sound of Bow Bells, which is where, by the popular definition, true Cockneys are born. Both came from large families: his father was a twin, and the twins were the youngest of seven children; Jasper's mother was the next to youngest of eight. Jasper's parents were both intelligent people—in fact, his mother passed the eleven-plus, a standardized examination that all English children were required to take at the end of primary school—but they were members of a generation that didn't get the education it deserved. Both had to leave school young to go to work—his father at fourteen and his mother at fifteen—and both ended up in the transmitting section of the Post Office. They met there, and married in 1933.

Jasper's mother loved poetry. When she was pregnant for the first time, she walked around reciting poetry, in the hope that her child would grow up to be a poet. That child, born on May 29, 1937, was Jasper. She had one other child, Geoffrey, born two and a half years later. When the boys were small, their parents read to them books by writers like H. G. Wells and George Bernard Shaw. They did so because they believed that education was important, and also because, like Wells and Shaw, they believed that a socialist society was better, both morally and practically, than a capitalist one. Jasper's parents held left-wing views; indeed, for a time his father was a member of the Communist Party. Because of his views, he was several times passed over for promotion in the Civil Service.

When the war came, Jasper's father enlisted in the Navy. Jasper's mother and the boys were evacuated from London early in the war, and as time went on they were moved repeatedly. They were sent initially to the West Country, and there they were quartered first in a house in Bath, then in a minute cottage in Bristol. Next, they were packed off to Northumberland to live as lodgers in Wallsend. Jasper recalled the war as a dour, cold, and bleak time. Of course, everything was rationed—even hot water. Jasper remembered the paint mark five inches up—indicating the maximum level of water allowed—in all the bathtubs he got to use. There were frequent blackouts, and long queues for rations; his mother would leave him to stand in one queue while she stood in another. He remembered that once when he was walking with his mother he saw some long, curved yellow things hanging in bunches outside a greengrocer's shop and asked her what they were. She said, "They're artificial bananas, for show. You'll get some real bananas when the war is over."

After the war, his father again took a job in the Post Office, this time in its telephone department, and he settled the family in Sydenham, a lower-middle-class section of Southeast London. Jasper, who during the war had gone to a series of state-supported primary schools, was now enrolled in a state-supported church school. He sat for his eleven-plus there in January of 1948, when he was ten and a half. The eleven-plus examination, set separately by each school district, was used to separate the children who were thought to be promising from those who were not. Those who scored high were put in the academic stream; they went on to state-supported grammar schools or privately supported public schools, and, in time, had a shot at going to Oxford or Cambridge or one of the few other universities in the country. The rest were put in the non-academic stream; the schools they went to concentrated on the teaching of practical subjects and technical skills, with a view to equipping their charges with the means of earning a livelihood. (In the seventies, the eleven-plus examination, which had often been attacked for perpetuating the aristocratic British education system, was phased out.)

From some sample papers that I read in Oxford during one of the many controversies in the newspapers over the eleven-plus I gathered that the examination could be quite difficult. It generally consisted of several forty-five-minute papers, in English, arithmetic, and "intelligence," which was actually a reasoning paper. The English paper included this sort of assignment for a composition: "Imagine you are an insect, such as an ant, and wish to crawl across your garden. Describe the difficulties and adventures you might have." There were also tests of reading comprehension, which presented the children with extracts like this:

"What are you doing up there?" called the stranger.

"We're living here," said Dick, moving farther down the branch. "At least Jean and I are. The others are just visiting."

"These woods are private."

"We're allowed to play here," said Jean.

"Who says?"

"I don't know, but we always have done."

"Come down," said the stranger. "That's what I say, come down. These woods are private."

"We can't," Peter said in a squeak. "We're marooned." He leant over the sitting-room wall to have a better look at the stranger, knocking his sister's acorns off the dining-room table, and in his efforts to save them kicked Miranda out of the nursery so that she fell to the ground among the acorns.

The stranger put Miranda in his pocket. "These woods are private," he said. "Come down."

"We can't," said Jean, "really we can't. Father's coming back at dinner-time with the ladder. We asked him to take it away so that we should really be marooned. It's the floods, you know. The water is thirty feet deep all round this tree. We're living off the acorns we pick from its branches."

"Please throw up my acorns," said Patsy. "They're very precious, and Peter can't come down for them."

"And Miranda," said Jean. "Peter and Patsy are taking her home tomorrow and she must have a bath before she goes."

The stranger seemed at a loss, as if the children were talking a language he knew only imperfectly. But he dug his hands into his pockets and repeated the one thing he understood. "These woods are private."

Questions followed, such as "Suggest two reasons why the stranger kept saying the same thing again and again," "Give one thing said by Jean which was true in the children's ordinary life," and "What do you think 'marooned' means?" The children were also asked to continue the story for ten lines.

The arithmetic paper had about twenty-five questions, such as "Multiply 7 cwts. 3 qrs. 16 lbs. by 13" and "Change 3 9/10 to an improper fraction." The intelligence paper set the children mathematical puzzles on this order:

From A to B is 5 miles by road, but only 3 miles if you go across the fields. Frank and Edward both set out from A at nine o'clock to go to B. Frank went by road, and Edward went across the fields. Both walked at the rate of four miles per hour. Edward got to B one hour before Frank. How much time did Frank waste on the way?

And this paper had more questions than even the brightest students could ever get through.

Jasper's eleven-plus consisted of the usual three papers. He took the English paper in the morning, the arithmetic paper in the afternoon, and the intelligence paper on the following day. The results were announced after two months. Children at his school who did well in the eleven-plus generally went on to a local grammar school, but he had done so well that his schoolmaster advised him to try for a public school. (It conferred prestige on a primary school to get one of its boys into a good school.) At the time, there was an arrangement between the London County Council and certain public schools—St. Paul's and Christ's Hospital, for instance—which was designed to give boys from less privileged backgrounds a chance at a public-school education: boys who did especially well in the eleven-plus could take a scholarship examination for one of those schools. Jasper's parents wouldn't consider sending him to an upper-crust, grand school like St. Paul's (most of the boys there, as at Winchester, came from well-heeled families and paid their way, so that those who were on scholarship felt at a disadvantage), but they were talked into letting Jasper try for a scholarship at the less grand Christ's Hospital—about thirty miles away from their home—by a schoolmaster who believed in the place. Jasper was successful.

CHRIST'S Hospital came much closer to fulfilling the original spirit and function of public schools than did its grander counterparts, or so it appears from "The Christ's Hospital Book," which was published in 1953, on the occasion of the school's four-hundredth anniversary. To speak very generally, public schools were founded in order to educate poor boys and orphans, and many of them were initially attached to religious houses. After the dissolution of the monasteries by Henry VIII, the monastic properties were looted by members of the royal court, who had no interest in charitable work. The cause of schools was then taken up by church leaders, merchants, and well-off citizens.

Christ's Hospital was established on the site of a dissolved Greyfriars monastery in London's Newgate Street, in 1552. A celebrated sermon urging the rich to help the poor was given by Nicholas Ridley, the Bishop of London (the same Ridley who, three years later, was burned at the stake near Balliol as a Protestant heretic), and as a direct result of his sermon the school received a royal charter from Edward VI. The funds to support the new school were raised in part by appeals to the London citizenry from the pulpit. In 1582, the school was put on a solid financial footing when London's Court of Aldermen gave it the responsibility for licensing and controlling all carts and carters in the City, and it carried on those operations almost continuously until 1838.

Originally, the school's curriculum was rudimentary, and its pupils were generally prepared only to be apprentices to London merchants. But within a few years some of its pupils were going on to university and making contributions to letters. Its alumni during the reign of Elizabeth I included Edmund Campion (Elizabeth made him a martyr, and later, in 1886, he was beatified), the historian and antiquary William Camden, and the poet and dramatist George Peele.

In 1666, many of the school's buildings burned down in the Great Fire of London, and they had to be gradually rebuilt or renovated. In time, Christ's Hospital prospered.

By the nineteenth century, many public schools had abandoned any thought of charitable work and had become socially select boarding schools serving the upper classes, for high fees. Christ's Hospital continued to cater to poor boys of all abilities, however, and to provide them with a subsidized education; a few boys paid no fees at all. The funds to support the school came partly from inherited wealth—built up from the licensing of carts and from benefactions—and partly from various patrons. Some patrons were individuals who made benefactions and, in return, received the right to present a boy for a place. Others were charitable societies, like the livery companies—the guilds of London—which were so named because their members once wore the distinctive dress of their trades. The livery companies had lost their raison d'être over time, but, because they had once enjoyed a monopoly on one trade or another, they were rich, and they functioned as dining societies, with their own buildings, ceremonial silver, and heads, or masters, and with a new-found purpose, which was doing charitable work. Christ's Hospital was unique in that it had the characteristics of both an orphanage and a grand public school. Charles Lamb, who attended the school from 1782 to 1789, writes of it in his essay "Recollections of Christ's Hospital":

It is, in a word, an institution to keep those who have yet held up their heads in the world from sinking; to keep alive the spirit of a decent household when poverty was in danger of crushing it; to assist those who are the most willing, but not always the most able, to assist themselves. . . .

For the Christ's Hospital boy feels that he is no charity-boy; he feels it in the antiquity and regality of the foundation to which he belongs; in the usage which he meets with at school, and the treatment he is accustomed to out of its bounds. . . .

The Christ's Hospital or Blue-coat boy [the boys wore a cleric's blue coat as part of their uniform] has a distinctive character of his own, as far removed from the abject qualities of a common charity-boy as it is from the disgusting forwardness of a lad brought up at some other of the public schools. There is pride in it . . . and there is a *restraining modesty*. . . . His very garb, as it is antique and venerable, feeds his self-respect [the uniform in Lamb's day was identical to what Jasper wore except that it also included a round blue cap and a yellow waistcoat]; as it is a badge of dependence, it restrains the natural petulance of that age from breaking out into overt acts of insolence. This produces silence and a reserve before strangers, yet not that cowardly shyness which boys mewed up at home will feel; he will speak up when spoken to, but the stranger must begin the conversation with him. Within his bounds he is all fire and play; but in the streets he steals along with all the self-concentration of a young monk. He is never known to mix with other boys, they are a sort of laity to him.

The school seems to have been an extremely austere place then. Samuel Taylor Coleridge, who was at Christ's Hospital at the same time as Lamb, recalls that his master, the Reverend James Boyer, who was also the headmaster, upon finding him in tears on the first day of his return from the holidays, said, "Boy! the school is your father! Boy! the school is your mother! Boy! the school is your brother! the school is your sister! the school is your first-cousin, and your second-cousin, and all the rest of your relations! Let's have no more crying!" Boyer was as rigorous as an abbot. Coleridge reports that Boyer flogged him when he was about thirteen for having confessed that he was a non-believer and therefore didn't want to be a clergyman.

In those days, the students' diet was no better than that at Winchester. Coleridge writes:

Every morning a bit of dry bread and some bad small beer. Every evening a larger piece of bread, and cheese or butter, whichever we liked. For dinner—on Sunday, boiled beef and broth; Monday, bread and butter, and milk and water; Tuesday, roast mutton; Wednesday, bread and butter, and rice milk; Thursday, boiled beef and broth; Friday, boiled mutton and broth; Saturday, bread and butter, and pease-porridge. Our food was portioned; and, excepting on Wednesdays, I never had a bellyfull. Our appetites were dampened, never satisfied; and we had no vegetables.

And it appears that hunger wasn't the boys' only affliction. Coleridge writes about the boys' getting cramps from the cold:

When I was a little boy at the Blue-coat School, there was a charm for one's foot when asleep; and I believe it had been in the school since its foundation, in the time of Edward the Sixth. The march of intellect has probably now exploded it. It ran thus:

> Foot! foot! foot! is fast asleep!
> Thumb! thumb! thumb! in spittle we steep:
> Crosses three we make to ease us,
> Two for the thieves, and one for Christ Jesus.

And the same charm served for a cramp in the leg, with the following substitution:

> The devil is tying a knot in my leg!
> Mark, Luke, and John, unloose it, I beg!—
> Crosses three, &c.

And really, upon getting out of bed, where the cramp most frequently occurred, pressing the sole of the foot on the cold floor, and then repeating this charm with the acts configurative thereupon prescribed, I can safely affirm that I do not remember an instance in which the cramp did not go away in a few seconds.

The education was traditional in manner. About his studies with Boyer, Coleridge recalls:

I enjoyed the inestimable advantage of a very sensible, though at the same time, a very severe master. He early moulded my taste to the preference of Demosthenes to Cicero, of Homer and Theocritus to Virgil, and again of Virgil to Ovid. He habituated me to compare Lucretius, (in such extracts as I then read,) Terence, and above all the chaster poems of Catullus, not only with the Roman poets of the, so called, silver and brazen ages; but with even those of the Augustan era: and on grounds of plain sense and universal logic to see and assert the superiority of the former in the truth and nativeness both of their thoughts and diction. At the same time that we were studying the Greek tragic poets, he made us read Shakespeare and Milton as lessons: and they were the lessons too, which required most time and trouble to *bring up,* so as to escape his censure. I learned from him, that poetry, even that of the loftiest and, seemingly, that of the wildest odes, had a logic of its own, as severe as that of science; and more difficult, because more subtle, more complex, and dependent on more, and more fugitive causes. In the truly great poets, he would say, there is a reason assignable, not only for every word, but for the position of every word; and I well remember that, availing himself of the synonymes to the Homer of Didymus, he made us attempt to show, with regard to each, why it would not have answered the same purpose; and wherein consisted the peculiar fitness of the word in the original text.

In our own English compositions, (at least for the last three years of our school education,) he showed no mercy to phrase, metaphor, or image, unsupported by a sound sense, or where the same sense might have been conveyed with equal force and dignity in plainer words. *Lute, harp,* and *lyre, Muse, Muses,* and *inspirations, Pegasus, Parnassus* and *Hippocrene* were all an abomination to him. In fancy I can almost hear him now, exclaiming "Harp? Harp? Lyre? Pen and ink, boy, you mean! Muse, boy, Muse? Your nurse's daughter, you mean! Pierian spring? Oh aye! the cloister-pump, I suppose!"

Early in this century, Christ's Hospital, like some other London public schools, moved from the congested, unhealthful city to the country. It sold its old site in Newgate Street and, with the profits realized from the sale, bought a lot of cheap land just outside the little town of Horsham, in West Sussex. The buildings it put up there were mainly of red brick with touches of white stone, the central buildings being long, some with cloisters or end towers. The architecture of the buildings was in some ways reminiscent of the Tudor origins of the school. In London, most of the teachers had lived away from the school, with the result that its pupils had had to be cared for by resident matrons and beadles. In the country, the teachers and pupils all lived together in a single well-knit community, the teachers doubling as housemasters, and the pupils enjoying the healthful, open setting of a boarding school.

❦

ONCE when I was discussing with Jasper the history of his school, he observed that the origins of my Arkansas school must have been very different from those of Christ's Hospital.

"There is not much to tell about my school—it had more in common with Dotheboys Hall in 'Nicholas Nickleby' than with Christ's Hospital," I said. "It was the brainchild of a partially sighted Baptist minister from Louisville, Kentucky. He had gone to the Perkins Institution for the Blind, in Massachusetts. He gathered eighteen or so boys and girls around him and set up a school in 1859 in Arkadelphia, a backwater in southwest Arkansas. Arkansas itself is one of the most backward states. Four years later, around the time Arkansas got involved in the Civil War, the good minister ran out of money. He sent the children home, packed his belongings in a wagon, and trekked back to Louisville. After the war was over, some three and a half years later, he returned to Arkansas and started up the school again, this time with the help of state money. Within two years, he was in need of more money, and, with his consent, the state took over the school and moved it to Little Rock, the capital of Arkansas. The school's alumni generally made their living by caning chairs, by making mops and brooms, or by taking up piano tuning or gospel singing. No doubt many simply hit the street with a tin cup. Just before the Second World War, the school moved to a new site in Little Rock. That is where it was when I attended it. It was still so poor and backward that I was the only one in my class of seven who even thought of going to college."

Jasper, who was not one to dwell on unpleasant facts, had listened to me with growing unease. "Yes, I see," he said, and added, a little ironically, "That school is not without its exotic interest."

"I don't know about that," I said, and I asked Jasper what his life at Christ's Hospital was like.

"It was a very Spartan existence," he said. "When I first saw my school bed—wooden boards laid across a frame, with a very thin mattress on top—I thought, I won't be able to sleep on it. I had a soft bed at home. But after the first night I never gave the school bed a thought. I was so tired at the end of the school day that I was scarcely aware of how I slept. Of course, I arrived at school in the winter of 1948—really a very Spartan time in our national history. One imagined that this was the way the world had gone on—in those days it didn't occur to one that things could be any different from the way they were—and one just fitted into it. Anyway, in winter and again in summer I was at school for three solid months without a break, even for a weekend at home." The winter and summer terms lasted thirteen weeks apiece, and the spring term lasted eleven weeks. "I found everything about school strange—I had never been away from home before," Jasper added. "One felt totally cut off from the world. It was like being put on a ship and sent off to sea. But then all public schools were like that. That's why the school one went to played such an important part in one's life. It was the most intense experience one had."

Jasper, a naturally reticent person, was not very forthcoming about his school, but from what he told me piecemeal over the years I was able to build up a picture of his life there. The school consisted principally of a large quadrangle on which four buildings faced. One was the dining hall, another the chapel; a third contained the assembly hall and classrooms, and the fourth laboratories for science classes. A road ran through the north end of the quadrangle like a hair through the center of a postage stamp, and lining the road just outside the quadrangle were sixteen three-story houses—eight on each side of the quadrangle—in which all the boys were quartered. A music block, metal- and woodworking shops, a cricket pavilion, a gymnasium, a swimming pool, a working farm, and a bird sanctuary were scattered about the school grounds.

Fourteen of the houses were occupied by some seven hundred boys in the senior school, who ranged in age from eleven to nineteen, and the two other houses by about a hundred boys in the prep school, who ranged in age from nine to eleven. The houses were grouped in blocks of two, and each block was named after an illustrious "old boy." Jasper was put in a block named after George Peele; his house was known as Peele A, and the other as Peele B. He quoted to me a charming poem by Peele that was a favorite among the boys in his house:

> His golden locks Time hath to silver turned;
> O Time too swift, O swiftness never ceasing!
> His youth 'gainst time and age hath ever spurned,
> But spurned in vain; youth waneth by increasing:
> Beauty, strength, youth, are flowers but fading seen;
> Duty, faith, love, are roots, and ever green.

A dormitory at the top of Peele A was for boys between the ages of eleven and fourteen; a second dormitory, on the middle floor, was for the older boys. The ground floor was given over to a day room, at the front, and a changing room, at the back. Peele A had two housemasters—a senior one, who was married and had children, and a junior one, a young bachelor. (The school's junior housemasters tended to be young, and there was a quick turnover.) The housemasters were in general charge of the boys, but six monitors—older boys, appointed to the office in each of the dormitories—kept them in order and enforced the daily regimen. There was no ambiguity about when one had to do what: everything had to be done *now.* The boys in each dormitory were often together from the moment they got up to the moment they went to bed; they moved, sat, ate, and played together, as if in a phalanx. There was no room or corner into which a boy could retreat to be alone.

"Boys at school were more intensely together than people are as married couples," Jasper recalled. "Since we were, in a sense, shut up in the house, the possibility of being close chums with someone in a different house didn't really exist. When I first got to school, my house was not a particularly intellectual establishment. The tone of the house was set by the elders, as we thought of them, and it was a rather breezy, unreflective, sports-playing, ball-kicking heartiness. The tone of the house is, of course, a transient sort of thing. It depends very much on what sort of boys happen to enter at a particular time. By the time I was at the top of the house, it was a nest of highbrows, because it happened that the boys who came in with me were all destined for Oxford or Cambridge. So, in a sense, my generation changed the character of the place."

Christ's Hospital offered both academic education and vocational training. (The school regularly admitted boys for considerations other than academic.) The object of the former was to get as many boys as possible into Oxford or Cambridge, which was where most of the masters had been educated; the object of the latter was to prepare boys for a trade. The "academic" boys were able to specialize not only in classics but also in history,

English, mathematics, modern languages, or the sciences, and the "vocational" boys in pottery, woodwork, metalwork, mechanical drawing, or farming. In their early school years, the academic boys did some manual work and the vocational boys took some general subjects. Throughout, the two groups lived together and ate together.

Every morning at five to seven, when the bell sounded, Jasper got up, washed, took his school uniform out of his settle (each boy had a settle, or small trunk, standing next to his bed), and dressed quickly in the cold. (The entire school was supposed to be centrally heated—and, indeed, there were radiators and steam pipes everywhere—but it nevertheless always seemed to be chilly.) Standing by his bed, he put on a coarse but comfortable collarless white shirt; a starched linen band, which he attached to the shirt at the throat with a safety pin (and which looked, he said, like an oversized bus ticket); pepper-and-salt knee breeches; a thick dark leather belt with a silver buckle; bright-canary-yellow knee socks; and black shoes. Finally, he put on an ankle-length blue coat with silver buttons down to the waist. (In the summer, if the weather was hot he wore ordinary flannels and a blazer, a white shirt, and any socks he liked.) Whatever a boy's age or family background, he wore this "cleric's" uniform—the same garb that Lamb had mentioned.

Jasper, along with the other boys in his dormitory, was marched out in the cold to the dining hall for breakfast: "Right turn! Quick march! Left, right! Left, right!" When the boys reached it, they sat on a long bench at a long table. The food was dished out by some of them. (All the boys took turns doing various school jobs.) The daily fare was tea and toast and marmalade, with porridge or cornflakes added on alternate days. Sausages were a treat, served perhaps once a week. The boys who lived in a block close to the dining hall could dawdle over breakfast, but Peele was a quarter of a mile away, so Jasper had to hurry through breakfast and, as he said, "scoot back in a jolly slippy fashion."

Then he made his bed, cleaned his shoes, and got ready for school. At eight-thirty, the boys were marched out to chapel. There, in a big room, with an echo, they sang a couple of hymns, listened to a reading, and said a few prayers. They were out at ten to nine, just five minutes before the first class period began. Jasper had classes until lunchtime, which was at one, and again from four-thirty until suppertime, which was at six.

Every academic boy was started out on Greek at the age of eleven. Boys who, like Jasper, were going to do classics began Latin a year later. (The school took the rather eccentric view that if boys were going to learn only one classical language it should be Greek; most schools started children out on Latin, on the ground that it was fundamental to European languages and culture in a way that Greek was not.) Along with Greek, every academic boy was also started out on a modern foreign language, either French or German. Boys who didn't seem particularly clever were generally put in classes for German, because it was thought to be more like English. Jasper was put in a class for German. (Later, he felt that it had not been a good choice for him, because he learned the language more quickly than most of the other boys.) In the first year, in addition to Greek and German he did mathematics, English, history, geography, and divinity. He found mathematics difficult at first, because the class jumped into trigonometry without enough preparation, but eventually he found his footing in it. (By the time he was fifteen, he had completed differential calculus.) In English class, the boys started out reading the comedies of Shakespeare. They didn't understand every word of what they read, but the plots carried them along. The master would analyze the plays in class, and the boys would write little essays about them during prep (homework hour). The master made the boys learn poems by heart. "I would just be told that I had to know 'The Ancient Mariner' or 'Kubla Khan' or sections of 'The Prelude' by the next day, and on that day I would be called upon to recite part of it," Jasper said. "Memorizing poems was one of the most valuable things I was made to do at school." In history, there was just "the book." It was written in a narrative style, because the idea was to give the boys a chronological framework on which to hang everything. They were expected to read "the book," meditate on chunks of it, and then write essays two or three pages long. For the first year or two, they concentrated on the Middle Ages. "By the third year, we were doing nineteenth-century history," Jasper said. "By then, I had developed a full set of left-wing views, so I took a keen interest in the rise of the Chartists and the start of the labor unions, and came to know more about nineteenth-century social and economic history than most of the other boys." The teaching of geography was completely divorced from concepts of economics—from the ideas of trade and exploitation. "From geography I mostly got the impression that the world contained hot plains and very high, cold mountains," Jasper said. "The books had colorful pictures of strange-looking people clambering around in tea plantations in India or in coffee plantations in South America. I remember one picture of a man in Malaysia, in Malaysian dress, extracting rubber from a rubber tree. Exotic pictures in books made a great impression on me, because I had never seen people like that, and in those days television was unheard of. Somehow, geography never seemed to apply to Europe."

Geography was given such short shrift because its concerns were thought to be the most practical. So strong was the academic masters' aversion to anything practical that arts men did very little science, and among the sciences mathematics alone enjoyed prestige, because its concerns were deemed to be the most theoretical. The school had broadened its curriculum but still labored under the centuries-old belief that a man had only to know Greek and Latin to be educated—to be a cut above the rest of humanity.

Divinity was one subject that all boys were required to do throughout their school years. "We went through the Old and

New Testaments, reading the stories aloud in class and later meditating on them," Jasper said. "That was not a very advanced criticism of the Bible but a sort of moral education." Some boys were extremely pious, but Jasper, perhaps because his mother had always been outspokenly disbelieving, didn't accept any part of Christianity. He argued a lot about religion with other boys in Peele A.

Sports were taken only a little less seriously than divinity. Every day between two-thirty and four, a boy was required to play a game. Jasper wasn't good at any of the games. He was excused from cricket, because it was so boring for good cricket players to have bad players like him on the pitch, but he was made to play rugger. "Moreover, everyone over fourteen had to be in the Cadet Force for at least a stretch, unless he was a conscientious objector," Jasper said. "The Cadet Force drill took the place of compulsory sports on Friday afternoons. The Cadets, dressed up in military uniforms, paraded with rifles—and even fired them occasionally—under the direction of the drill sergeant major, who was an ex-Army character. Boys who wanted to go into the Army as a career took the drill very seriously, but I found it to be a tremendous charade and a piece of buffoonery, and did it only under duress."

Jasper went on to say, "We were leading a physically strenuous life and growing a lot. There wasn't a moment in the day when I wasn't thinking about food. I remember I was permanently hungry. I think everybody was." Lunch was a hot meal, but supper was usually a plate of cold cuts, and bread and jam. Even sweets were rationed until 1951. The boys usually got sweets for school when they went home for holidays, but, even though the sweets were stored in a locked tuck cupboard and doled out a few at a time, they were gone in the first two or three weeks of term. There was a sweet shop on the premises, but, as was true for all shops, everybody had to have a ration book to get anything there.

In the evening, there was a quiet time, when boys sat in the day room and did prep. When Jasper was eleven, prep was only half an hour; for older boys, it was longer. At bedtime, there was a reading from the New Testament, followed by a couple of short prayers. The younger boys were supposed to be asleep at eight-thirty. Older boys went to bed at nine-thirty. Monitors could stay up in the day room until ten-forty-five, but then all lights had to be out.

On Saturday, there were regular classes in the morning and, in the afternoon, a round of informal games and activities in the day room. Boys could play Monopoly or table tennis, read a book, or simply talk to their friends. On Saturday evening, older boys who were members of the Literary or Debating Society might meet, and give short talks on literary topics or argue about the issues of the day. On Sunday, everybody was allowed to sleep until seven-forty-five. The day was structured by morning and evening religious services. The boys were also required to do things like divinity prep and writing letters home.

There were all kinds of punishments for boys who didn't keep to the schedule of studies and games. If someone was laggardly in marching to breakfast, he might be ordered to do a run in a set time, or made to do an extra drill on the orders of the drill sergeant major. If his work was not up to the mark, he might be made to sit and do an extra composition on Saturday afternoon. Punishments were a tiring and tiresome business, which most boys naturally tried to avoid. Jasper succeeded; he didn't receive many punishments.

"I'm sure your school day at the Arkansas school was just as full," Jasper said.

I was taken aback by his bringing up the subject of my school again; I would have preferred to be silent about it. My school had as little to do with Oxford as a bullock cart with a lorry. Still, it was Jasper asking the question.

"We were certainly kept busy from morning to night," I said.

"But, as I look back, it seems to me that we didn't learn very much—or, rather, we learned meaningless things. For instance, a lot of energy was spent on teaching us social adjustment. In our English-grammar class, we didn't even get to the point of parsing sentences. People in Arkansas knew no language except English, so no one thought of having foreign languages in the curriculum. After a great deal of agitation, I got the school to introduce French, but we hardly got beyond learning the names of the suits of playing cards." Even as I said this, I recalled how the de la Chapelles had gone about teaching us Oxonians French, but then, of course, they were not running a school.

"Playing cards!" Jasper exclaimed.

"I think for a whole year we played cards in French class every day," I told him.

"I knew that strange things went on in American schools—but not that!" he said, with a hearty laugh. He seemed to be horrified as much as amused.

JASPER told me that the boys found the Greek alphabet rather easy, and were quickly moved on to Greek grammar. Greek had—or appeared to have—much more complicated grammar than English. There was an elaborate, precise system of cases, genders, tenses, and so on. One of the first days that grammar was taught in Greek class, he opened the grammar book to a page that had two columns, one headed "sing." and the other "plur." He imagined that "sing." had to do with music and was a verb; he couldn't think what "plur." might be. He was soon busy memorizing the cases of nouns—singular and plural—and the inflections of verbs. For the first couple of years of Greek, Jasper was just memorizing grammar. Then he started writing sentences—turning English sentences into Greek, and Greek sentences into English. Later, he did the same with Latin.

Derek S. Macnutt, a Cambridge man in his middle fifties, was the head of the Classics Department. To Jasper he was an intimidating figure. Besides teaching Greek and Latin, he set cryptic crossword puzzles in the *Observer,* under the nom de guerre of Ximenes. The pseudonym was borrowed from Francisco Jimé-nez de Cisneros, a sixteenth-century inquisitor-general of Spain, and, indeed, Macnutt fancied himself a bit of an intellectual inquisitor. In class, he was prone to explosions of temper, his characteristic bellow being "Get it right!" The boys who didn't "get it right" were liable to get a clout on the head—especially those boys who sat in the front row. Macnutt was a stout man and couldn't pass between the benches, so the boys in the back were safe. "In those days, 'Get it right' was the way everyone taught Greek and Latin," Jasper said. "That made learning them a little like learning a code with one-to-one equivalences." The schoolmasters laid down rigid rules of Latin and Greek grammar; it was as if the rules were fixed, like the movements of the stars, and had been obeyed by all classical authors—as if Greek and Latin had never been living languages, spoken by living people. But the rigid system of teaching served the boys well. It trained their memories, inculcated in them a respect for accuracy, and daily stretched their minds over difficult material. Jasper had the cast of mind for that form of education. He would generally "get it right"; indeed, he was always at the top of his class. Even so, he found not only Macnutt but all the schoolmasters intimidat-ing, perhaps because he saw them with the eyes of a child. In reality, he eventually came to see, many of them were kindly, well-meaning, dedicated men, with children of their own. Since university, they might not have reread anything beyond the basic texts, but then to be good schoolmasters they didn't have to know all the latest fancy scholarly footwork, such as the discovery of a new Greek poem on papyrus, nor did they have to develop whim-sical notions about certain classical passages, as dons did.

"In the beginning, our masters would find something for us

to read that was not too difficult," Jasper recalled. "We were started out reading artificial bits that someone had doctored and patched together in a later period. The trouble with real authors is that sooner or later they say something difficult. After all, they were not writing with a view to being read by English schoolboys two thousand years later. After three or four years of Greek and Latin grammar and composition, we were finally able to read a bit of the real classical stuff and start analyzing it. We read chunks of Ovid and Cicero, and so on. I remember we read aloud Ovid on love. I just got the idea of an entertaining world of bright colors and pretty people. When I was fifteen, we read a whole play of Euripides, and soon we were reading a lot of real authors, like grownups. It was strange stuff, and we didn't receive much help about the texts beyond the way the grammar worked. No one made any comment on their aesthetic value. We spent a lot of time trying to imitate the styles of the real authors, in Greek and Latin."

Certain comedies and other works had indecencies in them that the schoolmasters sometimes thought were not suitable for young boys to read aloud in class, so they dished out decent bits of texts to be read in class and left the boys who were scholarly or simply curious to read the indecent bits in private. Jasper remembered that he found some of the indecent bits in Martial and Petronius, for instance, quite repulsive; even though he thought that some of Martial was amusing, he concluded that there was a coldheartedness in the poet, which was off-putting. From the readings that Jasper did on his own, he got the impression that the Romans had a bent for certain kinds of obscenity, such as subjecting their women to oral practices. He imagined that they went in for "sex as power" and showed hostility to women. (He had a similar impression of Americans, based on a little reading.) Some of what he read in the classical authors, however, he found enticing. For one thing, they alluded to the fact that women naturally enjoyed sex, and took the line that if women enjoyed sex too much, then one had to be "jolly slippy" with them or one would have a problem keeping them faithful. All this was a revelation. Also, there were a number of references to homosexuality in some of the texts. Such aspects of classical texts were never discussed in class—or, indeed, among the boys. Jasper now chuckles over such anomalies of classical education as the fact that some of the great classicists of the past skirted the issue of homosexuality in the texts. For instance, Jowett's introduction to his celebrated translation of Plato's "Symposium" talks about everything else but omits the fact that the dialogue is about homosexual love, which Plato holds up as a higher form of love than heterosexual love.

Jasper was in the fast lane for Oxford and Cambridge. By the time he was sixteen, his Latin and Greek were so advanced that he was allowed to skip those subjects on the O levels. He did take O levels in subjects like English, maths, and history. Because Jasper did so well, he eventually became one of two senior boys in Peele A who were privileged to enjoy some privacy: he was given a little individual study with a coal fire. He was also assigned a fag, a junior boy who was supposed to light the fire in the morning and keep it supplied with coal. In addition, the fag was supposed to make Jasper's bed and keep Jasper's shoes polished. He was so inept that Jasper often ended up doing those chores himself. The tradition of fagging is notorious, of course, for encouraging master-slave, bully-coward relationships at public schools, but at Christ's Hospital, according to Jasper, fagging was a pretty innocuous business.

After O levels, Jasper was "awarded his buttons." The bestowing of this honor was a school institution, which dated from the days when only a few boys stayed at school after they were sixteen, and was known as "being made a Grecian." Charles Lamb speaks of Grecians as "the solemn Muftis of the school," from whose time eras were computed: it was said that "Such or such a thing was done when S— or T— was Grecian." The Reverend W. M. Digues La Touche, who was at Christ's Hospital from 1864 to 1870, writes, "The Grecians were quite a class apart; very superior persons indeed. We never dreamed of addressing one of them; if one spoke to us it was considered to be an honour. I remember . . . being awed by what I imagined was their deep and profound learning, on seeing two or three of them walking along a cloister with black portfolios under one arm, foolscap paper peeping out here and there. They had a special gait as they walked, known as 'spadging'; a longish stride with a dip of the whole body in the middle of the pace." In the nineteenth century, only boys who did classics were made Grecians, but in Jasper's time there were Grecians in all areas of academic work.

Jasper found being a Grecian very grand. For one thing, it meant that he could do Greek and Latin all day long, and was excused from the other school subjects, except for English literature, which was deemed to be related to the classics, and divinity, which no one was allowed to drop. It also meant that in addition to A, or advanced, levels—which tested students' competence in fewer subjects but in greater depth than the O levels did—he took S, or Special, levels, which were considered even more advanced than A levels. He had a lot of freedom to get on with his work and pursue his classical interests. And Jasper was now taught in a special, gentlemanly room set aside for Grecians. He no longer sat at a desk—as he had for every class from the day he arrived at Christ's Hospital—but in a chair at a table, like a grownup. In other respects, however, he continued to be treated like a schoolboy. During his last year at school, he and a friend went to the headmaster one Saturday and asked him for permission to go and see a highbrow film in town. The headmaster said, "It would be so easy for me to say yes. Therefore, I will say no."

When Jasper was eighteen, he took a special entrance examination for Balliol, which involved an interview and a week's worth of morning and afternoon papers, designed and marked by his future tutors at the college. On the strength of his performance, he was awarded a Domus Exhibition. He missed the grander and somewhat more remunerative Domus Scholarship in classics, which in his year was won by Roger Tomkys.

"In my four years of college in America, I don't think I came close to getting the kind of preparation and education that you got at Christ's Hospital," I said.

"Why was that?" Jasper asked. "You always give the impression of working hard."

"Oh, I always worked hard, but, somehow, American colleges end up spoon-feeding one with lectures and textbooks. At college, a lot of time is wasted on taking courses in things that here one would be expected to learn on one's own. I mean, courses in how to read novels intelligently, how the government works—things that people here pick up themselves from reading books and newspapers."

"Quite right," Jasper said. "People here go to school or university only to learn things that they can't learn on their own. But then a system like ours couldn't possibly work for mass education, which is, of course, what you have in America."

"One thing I can say about American education is that one learns about life in the real world at a much earlier age—or, at least, I did."

"That's right," Jasper said. "I have noticed how Americans coming to Oxford find us English so innocent."

❧

AFTER Jasper finished his Greats degree, at the age of twenty-three, he went to Harvard to do research in early Latin poets. "This is not a lovable spot," he told me when I saw him there in 1960. At that time, I happened to be at Harvard, too, working toward a Ph.D. in history. "Socially, it is a rather glacial place. It is not a place I would like to spend all that much time in."

I told him that my experience of Harvard was a good deal like his, except that I also thought that it was like Hollywood, full of intellectual stars, and that the election of Kennedy as President had only encouraged the tendency.

"There's not so much glamour in Harvard classics," he said. "But I can see what you mean."

After a year at Harvard, Jasper returned to Balliol, and he has been there ever since. In 1963, he was elected Fellow and Tutor in Classics—one of the most important permanent jobs in classics in England—though at the time he didn't have a D.Phil. and he hadn't published an article or a book. (He has never got an advanced degree, and he published his first book, "Homer on Life and Death," only in 1980, when he was forty-three.) He was elected to the position on the strength not only of his performance in Schools but also of his university prizes and scholarships in Greek and Latin—both the language and the literature—which he had won through competitive examinations. One of my strongest memories of Jasper in our undergraduate days is of his sitting for those examinations—gladiatorial contests of the mind—year after year.

In the Michaelmas term of our first year, when we had hardly settled in at Oxford, Jasper sat for the Ireland and three Craven Scholarships. The examination was an ordeal of ten papers (Oxford papers are generally three hours long, and are taken on consecutive days, one in the morning and one in the afternoon) and was widely regarded as the most formidable in the university. That year, Gerald Toomer walked away with the Ireland. Although Jasper did not get a Craven (the Cravens were the runner-up scholarships), he did get mostly betas and beta-plusses. That was a good enough showing for him to be encouraged to try for the Ireland again, the following year. In the Trinity term of that first year, he sat for the Hertford and de Paravicini Scholarships, which consisted of six papers. Once again, Jasper lost out on the top prize, which was the Hertford—this time to Martin West, who was a year senior to him—but he got one of the two de Paravicinis, the secondary prizes. In the Michaelmas term of our second year, he again tried for the Ireland. This time, Martin West won it, but Jasper got the first of the three Craven Scholarships. In the Trinity term of that year, he again tried for the Hertford, and he got it. In the Michaelmas term of our third year, he sat for the Ireland for the third time, and he won that, too. In the Hilary term of his fourth, and final, year (the Greats degree was a four-year course), he sat for and won the Passmore Edwards, a comparative-literature prize. By the standards of the Ireland and the Hertford, that was a short examination; it consisted of only three papers. Although it was designed primarily to test a candidate's knowledge of English literature, people had to know a lot of Greek and Latin to compete for it. That same term, he sat for and won the Jenkyns Exhibition, a college examination consisting of six papers; it was a sort of dry run for Schools in Greats, and every final-year Greats man at Balliol was required to take at least some of the papers.

Of course, in addition to all those examinations for university prizes Jasper had to sit for the two major examinations required for his degree. In the Hilary term of our second year, he sat for the thirteen papers of Honour Moderations, or Mods—a sort of Part I of Greats Schools—and in the Trinity term of 1960 he sat for the ten papers of Greats. (He got alphas in all the papers of both Mods and Greats.) I once calculated that as an undergraduate he sat for no fewer than seventy-five papers, or some two hundred and twenty-five hours of written examinations.

I remember that when he was sitting for examinations he would sometimes get urticaria, especially around his eyes, and his voice would acquire a strained edge, as if he were trying to sound normal but couldn't quite manage it. The mental exertion was as impressive to me as his choice of the half line from Horace, "quid si prisca redit Venus" ("suppose the old passion is returning"), that he once used as his signature on an examination paper.

(The examiners required that a candidate use a motto for his signature, so that his identity would be unknown to them during the marking of the papers.)

When Jasper won a prize, he would be flush with money for a few days. He would splurge on a dinner at the Capri or the Elizabeth—the two most elegant restaurants in Oxford—or he would buy a vase or a figurine for his room. The money was never very much. The Ireland awarded fifty pounds a year for four years, the Craven forty pounds a year for two years, and the Hertford a one-time payment of sixty-five pounds, and many other prizes were less. (The award amounts had been set at the time the prizes were originally established—one of them was three hundred years old—and had not been increased very much over the years.) Jasper was on a state scholarship, so every extra bit of money was welcome.

In later life, I once asked Jasper how the Ireland and Hertford papers differed from those of Mods.

"The Mods papers were set so that ordinary chaps could make some sort of showing," he said. "The Ireland and Hertford papers were suitably harder—off the beaten track and very recherché. Those papers were meant to give the candidates a chance to display their learning and demonstrate that they were well rounded in the classics."

"You must have had a vast body of knowledge in Greek and Latin language and literature on which you could be examined."

"I don't know about that, but the Ireland and the Hertford papers were both comprehensive and abstruse. In the critical papers we might be asked to discuss the metres in two anonymous passages—one Greek and one Latin—or to comment on the style of several anonymous Greek and Latin extracts and identify them by author or period. We would have to write essays on minor authors and on subsidiary literary forms. What I found most challenging and enjoyable in the Ireland was the translation papers—especially the Greek Verse and Taste paper and the Latin Verse and

Taste paper—because of the breadth of knowledge in both modern and ancient tongues one had to have to do them at all. I remember that we had to do things like turning the prose of Johnson or Swift into Greek, or, alternatively, the Greek of Plato, Homer, Euripides, Alexander Aetolus, or Lucian into English, and turning the Latin of Cicero, Pliny, or Apuleius into English, or, again, authors like Shakespeare, Shelley, Hume, and Matthew Arnold into Greek iambics or Homeric hexameters, and the like, or, alternatively, verses from Terence, Cornelius Severus, or Lucan into English verse. Whenever we were turning verses from one language into another, we had to translate them in the appropriate style and metre. We didn't always have the background, so it required a certain amount of bluff."

"What kinds of things did you have to do in Mods?" I asked.

"In Mods, there were papers on set books, on a special subject, on unseen translations, on verses and prose passages, and the like. There was a textual paper on manuscripts, which was a bit of a business."

"How reliable are the ancient manuscripts that are around?" I asked.

"In the case of these ancient works, we have only copies that are very far removed—a thousand years or so—from the originals. It's a universal fact of life that if you have to copy out a page of something you will introduce at least one mistake in doing so. If a copyist kept a whole line in his head while copying it, the end of the line would tend to be a bit less accurate than the beginning of the line. Or, again, if he was copying three lines of verse where the first line and the third line began with the same word, he might just drop the middle line, because his eye would have picked up the same word in lines one and three. Anyway, to someone copying out Aeschylus a thousand years later the Greek would have been ancient Greek. It would be rather like an ordinary English-speaking person today copying out Chaucer. The tendency of a copyist who didn't understand some of the text would have been to change it in the direction of something he did understand. As the process of copying goes on, it introduces corruptions progressively, with each copyist, no doubt, adding some of his own stuff somewhere along the line. Furthermore, the bottom of a page might get torn and mislaid. And so on. You can imagine the fearful problems one has in dealing with ancient manuscripts, and the only way around them is through knowledge and understanding of the period. For instance, all poetry in ancient Greek is strongly bound up with religion, so knowing a lot about the religion of the ancient Greeks can help you to weed out the corruptions. Also, it helps if you know a lot about the way they spoke the language. For instance, the style of Aeschylus is grand and exalted, rather like that of Christopher Marlowe. In dealing with copies of his texts, one has to ask, " 'What is the limit of his grand style? Where would Agamemnon have stopped speaking in the grand style in order not to sound ridiculous to the audience?' It would have been easy for Greeks living in Aeschylus' time to tell, but it's very hard for us. Still, we have to try to come close to telling the limits of that style. The encouraging thing is that a lot of very clever people have applied their minds to the ancient texts and made many brilliant discoveries. They have made wonderful guesses, and sometimes those guesses have been confirmed by the discovery of another manuscript, with what appears to be a more nearly correct version of the text. Even so, some corruptions are so deep that there is no way to correct them."

I had come to fancy myself something of an amateur literary historian, and had always been fascinated by different surviving versions of a literary work. We talked for a while about how various scholars had devoted their whole lives to studying the printing presses of Shakespeare's day, trying to reconstruct the movement of the typesetter's hand in order to get at the corruptions in Shakespeare's folios.

Then I said that after all the various ancient-language-and-literature papers the final Greats papers must have come as a relief.

"Reading for the Greats part of the degree was really very different," Jasper said. "When we were preparing for Mods, each of us went to the tutor alone with an exercise, like turning Tennyson into Greek in the style of a particular author. The work was a continuation of what we had done at school. But with Greats we had new subjects—Ancient History, and Ancient and Modern Philosophy, none of which we had ever done before. We went to our tutors in pairs—I went with Roger Tomkys—and we read our essays on alternate weeks. Writing essays continuously was something very new—something I had scarcely done before. The thing about ancient history is that a lot of it is detective work—it's a matter of evaluating meagre evidence and drawing some conclusions from it—and the essay form lends itself to that very well. In the Greats examination you tend to get questions like 'How much evidence is there that the standard of provincial government was improved under Augustus and Tiberius?' and 'What specific contribution do the tribute quota-lists make to our interpretation of Athenian policy between 454 and 446?' "

As Jasper talked on about his Ancient History papers, I realized, with pleasure, that we had done similar things. Of course, in my History School there had been less detective work, and the material had been different, but, like him, I had been constantly interpreting evidence and trying to draw conclusions about men and events from a mass of details.

"As you know, for philosophy, those were the heady days of Oxford philosophy," Jasper continued, "and the philosophy and logic papers were full of questions like 'Is being reliable compatible with being a free agent?' and 'Could my body have housed your mind?' and 'When a frightened man trembles, is his trembling caused by his fear?' and 'Is butter a universal?' and 'Can what was probable become certain, or vice versa?' and 'Is it our duty to assist the revolutionaries of another country when we think that their cause is just?' "

"Do you think that all those examinations were a good test of your abilities?"

"Certainly Oxford exams encourage a certain amount of glibness. To do well, one has to encapsulate a neatly rounded answer to a question in three-quarters of an hour. There are a lot of intelligent people taking the exams who plan to be scholars and academics. Many of them barely get going in three-quarters of an hour. They suffer. Most people who do well are able to adapt themselves to the system and are very quick. Sometimes it is said that the point of doing those kinds of exams is to fit you for being a high-powered civil servant. The idea is to show that you can quickly get on top of a varied body of material and produce a nice, coherent statement."

WHEN Jasper and I were in our second year, Miriam Dressler, an American classicist from Brooklyn, came to Oxford. Soon after she arrived, Jasper saw her in a seminar on Euripides that they were both attending. The seminar was taught by Eduard Fraenkel, who had been the Corpus Christi Professor of Latin since 1935 and Emeritus Professor since 1953. Miriam was reading Greats at St. Anne's College. I was with Jasper when he and Miriam met for the first time socially, toward the end of the Michaelmas term. It was in Walton Street, at the digs of a classicist; among other friends, Peter Gregson and Roderick Allison were there. Miriam had come there with Jay Kayser, another American at Oxford. He had a free manner, and was very likable, but people in the room were put off by his casual dress. (Jasper later remarked to me, "The chap didn't even have socks on.")

I had a flicker of interest in Miriam, and tried to talk to her about America, but she paid no attention to me, and none to Kayser, either. Instead, she concentrated her whole attention on Jasper, as if she already had a crush on him from Fraenkel's seminar. She seemed to be in awe of Jasper, and talked to him the way a pupil talks to a teacher.

"I have come here with a B.A. from Barnard and an A.M. from Radcliffe," Miriam said at one point. "In America, I was a top student in the Classics Departments, but here I find that my classical education is inadequate for an Oxford Greats degree. Classics here are too specialized. Everyone seems to start Greek and Latin much earlier than we do in America. Seminars and lectures are pitched too high."

"You are probably getting a jaundiced view of classics at Oxford because of Fraenkel's seminar," Jasper said kindly. "Gerald Toomer and Martin West are not your ordinary classics chaps here."

Miriam was not reassured. "I'm very much taken aback by the quality of the work here," she said. "I keep on asking myself, 'What kind of place have I come to?' "

"Do English classicists think well of any American classicists?" I asked. "People say that, according to Fraenkel, only Wendell Clausen, a professor at Harvard, is competent to edit a classical text."

"There is a certain feeling at Oxford that American classicists simply don't know their texts—that one has to go through an education in a British public school or a German *Gymnasium* or a French *lycée* in order to be a good classicist," Gregson said. He himself had gone to Nottingham High School, a grammar school.

"Fraenkel has simply got it into his head that American classicists are dumbos," Jasper said. "You know, he wrote this terrible review of the Harvard Servius. Servius is a vast ancient commentary on Virgil, written at the time that Christianity was taking hold. A whole team of people at Harvard—about ten people, under the direction of Edward K. Rand—set out to edit the text. Editing a text like that presents great problems. They produced their first volume. Fraenkel wrote this devastating review of it in the *Journal of Roman Studies* which was so long that it had to be in two parts, separated by a year. The first part came out in

1948 and the second in 1949. He crucified the team. He said that the work showed every conceivable kind of ignorance—ignorance of the manuscripts, ignorance of Latin, ignorance of antiquity, ignorance of religion. The effect was so shattering that in the last nine years or so no more volumes of this work have appeared. That means that all the people at Harvard who worked on it—Rand's people, classics professors here and there in America—hate Fraenkel and wouldn't dream of having him near them."

"Anyway, Fraenkel has never gone to America," Gregson said. "He has no desire to go."

After that meeting in Walton Street, Jasper and Miriam started seeing each other as a couple. Jasper, a secretive person, never talked about her, but all of us who were his friends knew that he was smitten, because soon after meeting her he shaved off his beard. Once, I remarked to Jasper on how lively Miriam was, and asked, "Is Miriam your first woman friend?"

"No, second," he said reticently. "I saw a woman a few times last year, but nothing came of it."

In 1960, Jasper and Miriam both took the Greats examination. They both got Firsts, and that summer, when Jasper was twenty-three, they got married, in New York City.

WHEN we were up, the classicists used to speak of Eduard Fraenkel as perhaps the greatest classicist in Britain, or even in Europe. Every year, he gave a seminar, alternately on a Greek or a Latin author. Any classicist could go to it, but ordinarily a student wasn't put on to it by his tutor unless he was judged to be able. Jasper went to the seminar for three years, when Fraenkel was teaching, successively, Catullus, Euripides, and Petronius, and I often used to hear him discuss the seminar with other classicists in it. Fraenkel's method of teaching appeared to be to parcel out little chunks of the text, maybe twelve lines, and to ask the student to go through the text, translate it, explain it, and, on occasion, say what the text must have been like before the accretion of corruptions. With a bit of Euripides, for instance, the student might say that the surviving text implied the existence of a particular cult of the gods which was not known at the time Euripides was writing, so the mention of the cult reflected an interpolation from a later time. The student had to expound upon the text—discuss it in all its aspects. "After a student had finished, Fraenkel would either tear him to pieces or give him, as it were, a pat on the head," Jasper told me. "It was a very intimidating experience. In the seminar, he seemed absolutely strung up. There were explosions of rage sometimes, though he was also capable of great enthusiasm—of lighting up. You got the feeling that this man really cared about the subject. For him, it was not just a job or a way of passing the time. When I first started going to his seminar, he was sixty-eight and was retired, but he was still carrying on with the seminar as he always had. That is how intensely he cared about things."

Fraenkel was equally at home in Greek and in Latin, with special expertise in early Latin, and he was very keen that Greek and Latin should not be dealt with separately. He also knew a lot about the history of classical scholarship in all the major European languages right back to the Renaissance, and spoke Italian better than he spoke English. (His mother tongue was German.) A student might be treated to a disquisition on what happened in the Byzantine monasteries when manuscripts were copied, or on what sixteenth- or nineteenth-century scholarship had to say about them. What the student was made aware of was that a great many people had contributed to the elimination of corruptions from the text, and that eliminating corruptions was a long, long process. "What made him so awe-inspiring as a teacher was that he knew a colossal amount about Greek and Latin," Jasper said. "And he was very intense about what he knew. Years after the seminar, Fraenkel told a student that every week before it he would throw up, out of tension."

In the twenties and early thirties, Fraenkel, a Jew born in 1888, had been a professor at the universities of Berlin, Kiel, Göttingen, and Freiburg im Breisgau. He lost his professorship in 1933, when the Nazis started their racial persecution. At the time, a great many Jewish professors were being dismissed, but no German university made so much as a gesture of protest. A significant number of the Jewish scholars, largely through the efforts of Gilbert Murray, then still the Regius Professor of Greek at Oxford, were brought to England. Quite a number of them ended up at Oxford. Fraenkel was one of the few who really became integrated into the Oxford system. In 1934, he applied for the Corpus Christi Professorship of Latin, and got the chair. That caused a great rumpus, with people writing letters to papers, and so on, wanting to know "What does it say about English classical scholarship that there isn't any Englishman who can qualify for this chair?" But Fraenkel turned out to be a very good choice, for he came to Oxford not just as a German scholar but as an extraordinarily learned scholar. For his part, he must have thought, with some justice, that classicists in England, however brilliant, were not learned enough, and must have conducted his seminar as he did in order to show the English how much there was to know if you really took things seriously.

Fraenkel's magnum opus is "Aeschylus Agamemnon," a three-volume study published in 1950; it is a work of mammoth learning on a play of seventeen hundred lines. Fraenkel spent twenty-five years on the book. (In my day, people used to say that it had taken him more than twice as long to go through the text of "Agamemnon" as it had taken Agamemnon to capture Troy.) In it Fraenkel reviews and considers all the known commentaries ever made on the text, all the articles that had been published in obscure places—who had said what through the centuries—and he even quotes personal letters written by the scholars who wrote the commentaries. That Aeschylus' text merited the years of labor and attention that Fraenkel lavished on it is unquestioned, because the text is very complicated and the textual tradition—the way the text has been passed down through the ages—very poor. Still, even the greatest classical scholars have probably not read Fraenkel's book in its entirety but only dipped into it; the book is overwhelming, and it contains no pointers to suggest what it is working toward.

Fraenkel received the greatest behind-the-scenes support in his scholarly endeavors from his wife, Ruth, whom he married in 1918. She died in 1970. On the same night, Fraenkel took his own life. Apparently, he had always intended to do so if he survived her.

The best scholarly estimation of Fraenkel was written by Jasper's tutor for Mods, Gordon Williams, in 1972, in the *Proceedings of the British Academy.* In his article he goes into considerable detail about Fraenkel's wife but doesn't so much as mention Fraenkel's children: Fraenkel had four children—two sons and two daughters. One reason might be that Williams did not want to mention the suicide of one of Fraenkel's daughters, who had killed herself when she was in her twenties.

FRAENKEL'S suicide was seen by many of his colleagues as a rational act. After all, he was an old man who didn't want to go on living without his wife. Anyway, the Romans certainly took the view that suicide was a man's right, and Shakespeare also expresses this view. He makes Cleopatra say:

> What's brave, what's noble,
> Let's do't after the high Roman fashion,
> And make death proud to take us.

And Shakespeare has Gloucester in "King Lear" say:

> Alack, I have no eyes.
> Is wretchedness deprived that benefit
> To end itself by death?

At Fraenkel's memorial service, however, Roger Mynors, who was then Kennedy Professor of Latin at Cambridge, electrified the congregation, which included many scholars who had come from the Continent, by saying from the pulpit, "He took his own life, and we must all be prepared to say that that was wrong."

Jasper, who was in the congregation, says that at the time he thought it was entirely Fraenkel's business whether or not he wanted to go on living in those circumstances, but that eleven years later he had second thoughts, because in 1981 a man who had been one of his own first pupils, Colin Macleod, killed himself in a very gruesome manner. He was thirty-eight, and was a student at Christ Church—as tutors there are called—at the height of his classics career. He had been a particular favorite pupil of Fraenkel's, and before he killed himself he talked a lot about Fraenkel's suicide. "It wouldn't have crossed Fraenkel's mind that killing himself would become a factor in his pupil's death," Jasper told me. "No doubt it would have broken Fraenkel's heart if he had thought so. But then you cannot know the results of your actions. Anyway, Macleod was very high-strung, and he might have killed himself regardless of Fraenkel."

Still, Macleod's suicide was especially disturbing to Jasper, because just five weeks earlier Jasper's former tutor, Robert Ogilvie, in what appeared to be a passionate act of despair, had shot and killed himself at the age of forty-nine.

When Jasper and I were undergraduates, we imagined that few people at Balliol, or in the university at large, could have fulfilled the Oxford dream of a Renaissance man better than Robert Ogilvie, who became Fellow and Tutor in Classics at Balliol in 1957, when we were in our second year, and, consequently, became, along with Gordon Williams, Jasper's tutor for Mods. Robert had gone to Rugby and had come up to Balliol in 1950, when he was eighteen, as an exhibitioner—a status between that of scholar and commoner, which is based on the results of the college's entrance examinations. He had got a First in Mods and Greats. Before returning to Balliol as a tutor, he had been Director of Studies in Classics at Clare College, Cambridge, for two years. His father, Sir Frederick Ogilvie, who had also read Classics at Balliol, had been Principal of Jesus College, Oxford, until his death, in 1949, and, when we were up, his mother, Lady Ogilvie, was Principal of St. Anne's College, Oxford. For all Robert's varied accomplishments and his social position, he was apparently a little wary of teaching Jasper. "Tutorials with him are a bit like shadow-boxing," Jasper told me at the time. "There is a bit of a feeling that Robert and I are circling around each other." Robert's wariness may have been due to the fact that, the previous term, Jasper had won the de Paravicini. Robert himself had not tried for any of the university prizes or scholarships, although, even in the Oxford setting of keen competition and competitive examinations, he was known to be unusually competitive. It was said that he must have decided early that he would be an elder statesman of the university, and passed up trying for them for fear that he might not win. But his need to win may also have had something to do with the death of his elder brother, James, in a mountain-climbing accident on the Matterhorn in 1948, when he was twenty-three. The Ancient History tutor Russell Meiggs used to speak of James, also a Balliol classicist, as having been even more brilliant than Robert; in fact, he used to refer to James as "the one and only Ogilvie." When I first heard that remark, it unsettled me. Can't people be good in different ways and at different things, I wondered.

Robert was a young bachelor who lived in college, and he was therefore much in evidence. He was a regular at the meetings of the Arnold and Brakenbury, of which he was elected a "senior honorary member," and at the meetings of the Leonardo. During a debate or a discussion of a paper, he was sure to deliver himself of some highly polished, brilliant, ironic remark that made us feel he was at once one of us and superior to us. He was often in the Buttery, talking to dons or to successful or well-connected undergraduates—dispensing his intellectual or social approval. I remember that he would always offer dons whisky and selected undergraduates sherry. The rest of us, if we happened to be standing around in the Buttery, were ignored as though we didn't exist. I didn't mind that. To me he was like a Greek god, and it was right for him to cavort with his own kind and to be admired by mere mortals.

The truth is that we were very much in awe of him. He seemed to have everything one could wish for. As a classicist, he was at the top of the Oxford hierarchy of scholars. As Fellow of Balliol, he had tenure for life. He came from an old Scottish family, and so was born into the governing class. He had brilliance and energy. People thought that he would end up as the head of an Oxford college or a top public school, or as a Minister in the government, if not Prime Minister.

In the fifties, it was still believed that a First in Greats equipped you to do anything in life—teach, run an industry, govern a country—especially if, like Robert, you were a member of the upper class and had gone to a top public school. In fact, in an earlier time, when Britain had its empire, Robert might have held a grand position and run a colony. The Greats education system still prepared people to do things like that, but, of course, there were now virtually no colonies to run.

After I came down, I continued to encounter Robert occasionally. In 1959, he married Jennifer Roberts, an Oxford graduate; in time, they had two sons and a daughter. For some years, Robert and Jasper were colleagues and neighbors. The Ogilvies and the Griffins lived in adjacent college houses, and had rigged up a mechanical device that was turned on if one couple was out, so that the other couple could listen for that couple's children. Since I often stayed with the Griffins when I visited Oxford, I could have got to know Robert and Jennifer better than I did, but he simply seemed too grand.

In 1965, Robert published his big book, "A Commentary on Livy": it made his scholarly reputation. In 1970, he resigned his fellowship at Balliol in order to become the Headmaster of Tonbridge, a well-known public school. After that, I didn't see much of him, but I continued to get intermittent news of him. In 1975, he became Professor of Humanity at St. Andrews University, in Scotland.

Six years later, when Robert killed himself, there had been no warning that anything was seriously wrong. It is true that reports had reached his friends that he had lately been drinking heavily, but then people in Britain, and especially Scots, are known for their heavy drinking. If it was a burden for him to be the son of two heads of Oxford houses, or if he felt that he was living in the shadow of his brother James, he never gave any sign of it. Rather, he carried off his position with a great deal of aplomb. Indeed, on the face of it he seemed an extremely secure, self-confident, capable person. No one who knew him had an inkling of the demons that must have driven him. But after his death I did remember something that Ray Ockenden told me after going down. "One afternoon, we were sitting on top of a Scottish mountain," Ray said. He had been an undergraduate at the time, and had been a member of a reading party with Robert in Scotland. "Robert suddenly asked me if I would be the best man at his wedding. That struck me as very strange—I scarcely knew him. At the time, Robert was surrounded by so many friends, and I pictured him to be such a worldly don, that it didn't even occur to me that, deep down, he might feel lonely."

᭄

ALTHOUGH the Griffins and I have lived on opposite sides of the Atlantic for most of our adult lives, we have remained close, managing to see one another at least once a year. Not only did I stay with the Griffins whenever I was at Oxford but also, in 1988, when I was elected a Visiting Fellow at Balliol, my wife and I moved into a college house near theirs, and we saw them often. One day during that time, over tea in my college room, which I used as a study, Jasper and I were talking about classicists, and I asked him if he thought that a classical education might have any ill effects.

"It's very hard to say, you know," he replied. "One has a certain set of qualities, and whether they are due to a certain kind of education or not is hard to tell."

"Does it make people élitist?"

"Not necessarily. In fact, there are really many classical scholars in England who are very progressive. There is, for instance, Kenneth Dover. He is a rather Bolshie type of character. One of the most eminent Marxist historians in England is Geoffrey de Ste. Croix, who has written a great book about class struggle in the ancient world. He went to Poland when the liberalization process began, and harangued people about how their government misunderstood Marx. Dover and de Ste. Croix might represent a minority strain, but that strain is not negligible."

"Is there nothing, then, that is common to classicists?"

"One thing we all have in common is an interest in words. My mind is very much triggered by words, just as there are people whose minds are triggered by figures. This interest of the classicists gave a rather literary character to the English culture in the old days, as if people were doing endless crossword puzzles—quoting P. G. Wodehouse, quoting Shakespeare, being interested in Dr. Johnson. You simply did not become good at Greek and Latin if you weren't like that. The classics pushed you in that direction."

I mentioned one or two of our brilliant classical friends who had not fulfilled their promise, and said I wondered if one effect of a rigorous, regimented school life at an early age might not be to slow you down in later life.

"There is no way to tell something like that," Jasper said.

I recalled that many of us who had come from less brainy, more dilettantish American schools and colleges had found our English contemporaries at Oxford intellectually much older than their years but emotionally much younger. Some of them seemed to have got stuck in childhood prejudices that ill became their adult lives. Many of them had not seemed to know what to do with themselves when there wasn't anyone telling them what to do. They had had trouble coping with the freedom of English university life. Certainly Jasper and I both knew people who seemed casualties of high-pressure schooling. A few of them had fallen apart in later life, like my three Wykehamist friends. "Did boys at your school ever break down under pressure?" I asked.

"As far as I could tell, the boys adapted to school very well," Jasper said. "Most boys are happy in a pack, and will put up with extraordinary miseries. I think the gang is the natural unit for boys. It imposes uniformity. With a lot of young boys, that is actually the thing they like. So strong is the influence of public opinion when one is young that boys don't like to be different. But there was really no way for me to know for certain how anyone else felt. Boys just don't talk about how they feel."

"I wonder if there are not unfortunate emotional consequences of pushing children when they are so young," I said, again thinking of my three Wykehamist friends. (Jasper really knew only Snedden.)

"I think people tend to imagine that the English-public-school type of education cripples people emotionally, but the truth may be that most children are emotionally robust."

"Did people generally take to the school with enthusiasm?" I asked.

"I think some people take to a particular kind of schooling, and it becomes very important to them, as it did to me. Other people go through exactly the same schooling and come out of it untouched, as if out of a swimming pool without getting wet. I would wager that education has less impact on most people than theoreticians like to think it has."

"Have you kept up with your school contemporaries?"

"I haven't kept up with most of them," he said. "I think I would have if this college had not become such a thing in my life. One of those in your life is enough."

I mentioned a couple of the commonest charges brought against public schools—that they send forth boys with an undeveloped heart and that they encourage homosexuality.

"Critics say that intellectual pressure applied at that early age may tend to burn people out," Jasper said. "It's very hard to say how far that's true. No comparative studies of, say, someone having a classical education and someone not having a classical education exist—and probably none can exist, because you can never isolate the significant factors. The business about an undeveloped heart sounds obvious, but, again, it is not so easy to establish the truth of such a claim. And there are plenty of boys who went to public school who are not homosexual, and plenty of boys who didn't who are homosexual."

"Would you say that the regimented school life had any ill effect on you?"

"I have thought a lot about it," Jasper said. "Would I have been very different if I had not been at that school? If, having gone to Christ's Hospital, I had turned out to be homosexual, people would have said, 'That's very understandable. His father was away in the war, then he went to this kind of school without any girls, and anyway he was rather an aesthetic kind of chap—

it all forms a pattern.' But it's not as simple as all that. It certainly was a very strange upbringing—it threw you on your own resources. At one time, I thought it made me withdrawn and self-sufficient. But several people have since told me how openly emotional I am."

"I can't imagine anyone thinking you withdrawn or self-sufficient. I would say you are self-reliant."

"I suppose the effect that a school like that should have had was to make one fairly self-reliant emotionally—in the sense not so much of denying one's emotions as of not indulging them. Whether it did have that effect on me, I don't know. Perhaps it didn't. The fact that both my brother and I got married so young may have something to do with our not having been so emotionally self-reliant after all." The circumstances of the marriage of Jasper's brother, Geoffrey, were different, and tragic. Geoffrey, who was two and a half years younger than Jasper, and who possessed that transient beauty of youth which poets sing about, had contracted bone cancer just after he took Mods from Queen's, and had died at the age of twenty-two. He and Anne Menzies, an undergraduate at St. Anne's, had married with full knowledge of his impending death.

Jasper and I finished up tea and started out for home together. We lived in North Oxford—a ten-minute brisk walk away.

"What lasting effect do you think the school did have on you?" I asked.

"That's hard to say. But I do know that I don't care so much what people think of me. You see, in that school you wore this extraordinary kit, and whenever you went to town or took a train everyone stared at you. Well, you got used to that. If you compare me with some other academics, I am apt to be much more of a ham than they are. I'm not so afraid of performing, of coming across as a little vulgar."

"Did you find the school a strain in any way?" I asked. "Did you have trouble doing your lessons, concentrating, meditating? You were so small when you went there."

"Oh, one could have done much more than one did," Jasper said. "At that age, one could have done almost anything. One could have learned several more languages, for instance. In the early years at school, I had a lot of time, when I did things like reading 'Tom Jones' and 'War and Peace.' In the later years, I worked hard. It was worth it. Studying Greek and Latin, talking about Shakespeare—doing things like that—transformed me. Many people just chugged along thinking that studying is one of those things one does at school. But I took to the classics."

"Do you think that a public-school kind of education discourages creativity?"

"If you read the autobiography of Evelyn Waugh, about being at Lancing, you would conclude that the school was set up to stop anyone from being interested in any of the arts. Yet not only he but many of his school contemporaries became writers. The thing about artists is that they come from all different kinds of backgrounds—often from quite unexpected backgrounds."

I brought up something that when I was an undergraduate had filled me with awe of the Greats men at Balliol—their seemingly unlimited ability to versify in ancient tongues. In contrast, some of us had trouble scanning a poem in our own tongue. "I remember that when we first arrived at Oxford you were doing a lot of Greek verses—turning a lot of T. S. Eliot into Greek," I said.

"That was a showoff," Jasper said. "The form of contemporary poetry—the pace of contemporary poetry—just doesn't lend itself easily to translation into Greek or Latin verse forms. Normally, therefore, one translated Shakespeare or eighteenth- and nineteenth-century poets, because they go into classical forms much more easily. After all, we have tragedies in English and tragedies in Greek; we have epics in English and epics in Latin. Poets like

Milton and Matthew Arnold are very close to the ancient authors, whereas poets like Eliot are not—there is no form like 'The Waste Land' in ancient literature."

"Yet I remember that you could recite any number of poems by Eliot, Auden, Yeats."

"I've always been interested in modern poetry."

"How was it that at the age of nineteen you seemed to know all the well-known poems in Latin, Greek, and English by heart? How did you train your memory?" I asked.

"You must realize that from the time I became a Grecian we did things like translating Shakespeare into Greek and Latin verse. Verse composition was a thing I spent a great deal of time on between the ages of seventeen and nineteen. And when you do that you have to memorize a lot of poetry. Of course, we did a lot of prose composition, too. But prose composition is not as hard as verse composition, which involves things like turning English poems into Greek iambics or Latin elegiacs."

"What was the point of doing such composition?"

"The thing about translating into Greek and Latin verse is that it's exceedingly difficult, because the ancient verse forms are really so different from those of English. Greek and Latin verse is full of rules. French verse—that is to say, translating English verse into French—gives you a bit of an idea of rules, but Greek and Latin verse is much more complicated than that. When you first try to do it, it appears that the rules have been so designed as to make it impossible. I remember that at school boys would take two lines of English verse and spend a whole day trying to turn them into Latin and still not be able to do it. Most boys, even those who were quite able, didn't acquire any facility at all for doing verses. But those of us who were able to do them got a good deal of insight into how the ancients actually wrote and thought. Doing them gave us extreme sensitivity to literary forms. It gave me a particular insight into English literature—the considerations of euphony, for instance. Of course, doing them was a remnant of nineteenth-century education. At that time, everyone had to do verses whether he had the talent or not. Boys had to do them before breakfast or get flogged. In fact, boys got flogged every time they made a metrical slip—something that is terribly easy to do. Swinburne and Shelley had a rough time of it at Eton. Yet, ironically, Shelley was stoned by his peers just because he wrote poetry."

"I suppose flogging was simply part of education in that period," I said.

"Clearly, public schools in the early nineteenth century were like the ships of the time. They were governed by force, and frightful things happened there. Boys were sometimes flogged by their masters into unconsciousness. But then the rest of society was like that, too. Even in my day, I was lucky I was good at classics, because I was exceptionally bad at things like sports, in which the other boys excelled. You see, the kind of classical education I was given continued to put heavy emphasis on Latin verse composition. In fact, that's why I became very conscious of the literary echoes of words. There are now books of reference available—word indexes, special grammars, special bibliographies—in which scholars can look things up. But the people in my day were given a training that enabled them to take a piece of highly wrought English, a piece of Macaulay or Milton, or whatever, and turn it into Greek—and not just Greek but Greek of a particular style. That training gave one a consciousness of what is particular about any author's style, and helped one to develop one's own conscious style."

The rush-hour traffic on Woodstock Road was horrendous. Buses, lorries, European cars with noisy motors were roaring past. Jasper was walking with his usual big strides. Although now a large, substantial figure, weighing some two hundred and ten pounds, he still walked at a fast clip, just as he had when we were undergraduates. I had trouble not only keeping up with him but also hearing him over the traffic. I waited for an especially noisy lorry to go by, and then said, "I'm sure force was never used at your school."

"No one was physically punished," Jasper replied. "But doing verses was very much a continuation of the nineteenth-century aristocratic system of education—very extravagant in its use of the time and energy of the schoolmasters, who expected a lot of the pupils. It was also very much along the lines of the philosophy of the First World War generals. You have the enemy's machine gun firing away. You throw a thousand men at it. Nine hundred and ninety-three of them will be killed, and four will be wounded. But three will get through."

"How would you go about defending such an extravagant and harsh system of education?" I asked.

"I think that when one is young it's important to be made to do things with intensity. Not absolutely everything, and not all the time—or you would crack up—but something. Children may from moment to moment say that they would rather take this easy and the next thing easy and the next thing easy, but actually, when it comes down to it, they don't want to. Though there's an increasing tendency to make education intellectually very easy, I firmly believe that if you don't acquire the ability to do something difficult when you are young you will never have it. Doing things like memorizing poetry and learning skills for maths can be done with great ease when one is a child. Then the mind is like a blob of sealing wax. If you hit it while it's still hot and soft, you can make a sharp, clear, lasting impression. If you wait too long, it's cold and hard. To put it another way, a good classical education will produce a mind that is capable of stretching itself. A less rigorous education will produce a less elastic mind. Another justification is that the ancient world was a whole world in itself, which existed for a thousand years. It was a complete, complex society that underwent many changes. It had history, philosophy, literature, geography, yet it was very different from ours. Studying that world is bound to be educational, because most people are imprisoned in the tyranny of the present; they imagine that things must always have been the way they are now. Of course, there are a number of societies that could serve the same educational purpose—India, China—but it happens that the ancient Greek and Roman world is more accessible to us in the West, because it is connected to us directly. Anyway, a lot of clever people have gone through this system of classical education and benefitted from it. That was certainly true when I was doing Mods and Greats. How long that will continue to be true no one can say."

"Are people still doing classics the way you did it?"

"In my day, the education was much more linguistic. We just had to do Greek and Latin, and we got our heads clumped if we got it wrong. It turns out that I was a member of almost the last generation to do verse composition. It was the most serious thing we did in the final years of school. At Oxford, in my first five terms, when I was preparing for Mods, I scarcely wrote an essay. I spent most of my time doing Greek and Latin verses and prose, or doing textual criticism on ancient authors—that is to say, talking about manuscript corruptions and emendations, and suggesting alternative kinds of readings of them. It's all very different now. Undergraduates nowadays don't really have that kind of linguistic background. They are unaware of literary forms, and so on. In fact, no undergraduate now does textual criticism in the first five terms, and the number of people who can do verse composition is very small. I hardly get one person in two years who would like to try it—though now and again one of them can make a few lines scan. I am lucky if I get one student in three years who can actually do some. The number of papers in the Ireland and the Hertford has had to be sharply reduced, and the requirements have had to be tailored to what people can do. Also, the prose compositions my undergraduates do now are not nearly so difficult as they were in my time, nor do they have the same panache. The ability to do verses and prose was developed through years of application, and people simply do not get that kind of training anymore. Instead, there is a new interest in literary criticism and literary history. So what undergraduates are now doing for Mods is writing essentially literary-critical and historical essays. That goes back to what they are doing at school. Schoolboys are no longer boning up on all this detailed grammar, or translating Matthew Arnold's 'Balder Dead' or 'Sohrab and Rustum' into Latin verse, and so on. Rather, they are doing things like reading secondary literature on ancient writers. There is generally more freedom at school, and boys have more options. Nowadays, if you want to recruit boys to this rather difficult option of doing classics you have to be nice to them. And the classical degree at Oxford has become more like what people do in the English school or the Modern-Languages school."

We turned in to Staverton Road, where Jasper lives, and suddenly everything was quiet. We were walking in the gentle air of Oxford again, away from the traffic and turmoil of the modern world. "Are you saddened by this change in the study of the classics?" I asked.

"No, because it is not a uniform record of loss. When I was young, we only read the texts and thought about them as texts. One never said what a text meant or what was good about it. We were just supposed to pick that up. We didn't read secondary critical literature. We didn't even have the vocabulary to discuss the content. The idea of there being any kind of theory about texts was unknown. It took all one's energy simply to finish translating the texts—to go through the minefield of grammar, metre, dialect, not to mention the corruptions in various surviving manuscripts. Nowadays, people are incomparably more sophisticated in a literary sort of way. That is a gain. But there is also a loss—the study of the classics is on the decline everywhere. The number of people who are embarking on Greek and Latin is shrinking all the time. The way the whole society is now turning, it seems to be turning away from the study of ancient languages and literature, even away from the study of medieval history, or, indeed, of foreign languages or foreign history. In the old days, classicists made a perfectly respectable living by teaching their pupils and, beyond that, restricting themselves to editing texts and doing things of that kind. But that's no longer possible, partly because many texts have now received very good editions. Classicists are now writing general books about Virgil, about Sophocles, and so on. It's not clear that most of these books are necessary, but we are all under enormous pressure to publish. Nine-tenths of what is published in any field is probably without much value. People publish not because they have something to say but because they've got to. In this respect, what has happened to us classicists is partly what has happened to all academics in the Western world. It's just a situation we've got ourselves into. In my view, it has had terrible results. Take the study of English literature. Professors of English literature and professional literary critics do not have any classical background, as their predecessors did, so they are naturally not interested in classics, and don't consider it important. They are interested much more in critical theory. I think this is an essentially one-sided, perhaps even perverse, way of studying literature—especially poetry. Such an approach puts too much emphasis on having ideas about a poem, rather than attending to its sound, for instance. Anyway, there is a frightful pedantic tendency to do literary criticism with footnotes and bibliography and theoretical apparatus, and such an approach ends up substituting something else—the secondary literature—for the text as the focus of interest. To enjoy a poem is really not as difficult as we now seem to pretend. Of course, to write good literary criticism and good literary history is difficult, but I think that writing mediocre literary criticism is the easiest of all activities. There is almost no human being who can't do it."

We reached Jasper's house, and he invited me in for sherry. We looked into the kitchen and greeted Miriam and Julia, the oldest of three Griffin daughters, who was doing a postgraduate degree in English literature at Oxford. They were busy cooking. All three daughters—Julia, Miranda, and Tamara—had gone to Oxford High School, a girls' school that is run by a private trust with help from the state and has a national reputation for getting a very high proportion of its students into Oxford and Cambridge. Because Jasper and Miriam are so well known as dons at Oxford—Miriam has been a Fellow and Tutor of Ancient History at Somerville College since 1967—all three of the daughters had chosen to go to Cambridge for their undergraduate education. Julia had read Classics and Miranda Modern Languages; Tamara (though a professed atheist) was currently reading Theology.

After a few minutes in the kitchen, I followed Jasper up the familiar stairs to the first floor of the house, and settled myself in one of his capacious armchairs while he handed me a glass of sherry.

"I myself think that, of all the arts, literature is the most akin to magic," he said. "The most interesting thing about a text is its magical element."

"Few people think that anymore," I said, taking a sip.

"Well, that's right. Even when I became a don, there were dons teaching English literature who were not under the spell of words. They couldn't quote anything from memory. There was a don who taught English—excellent person, very good scholar, knew a lot, but never quoted anything. He said he never remembered poetry. I also now have colleagues who teach Latin who are like that—they never quote from memory. Well, as for me, I wouldn't have become a literary person if I hadn't been able to remember words. What is important to me is that it is all in my mind."

X

FRIENDS APART

M Y FRIENDS TENDED TO BE DRAWN FROM DIFFERENT
worlds, and I was constantly trying to mix them. But
my Oxford parties were often failures, for it seemed that
the only thing my friends had in common was their
friendship with me. If I had Jasper, Vijay, Dom and
Henrietta, and Alasdair over for drinks (not to mention
several other eccentric friends I grew close to in my third year),
they would set each other off: Dom would become more incoherent, Henrietta more belligerent, Jasper more ironical, Vijay more
silent, and Alasdair more competitive, if subtly so. The party
would not jell. As the attempts to bring my different friends
together continued to fail, my feeling of being an insider at Oxford
was gradually dissipated: it seemed that any one of my friends
could touch only a part of me, and that my lot was always to be

an outsider and an expatriate, marching to a jumble of discordant tunes. But I am getting ahead of myself.

One evening early in the Michaelmas term of my third year, while I was in my rooms having drinks with some English friends, my Indian friend Moni Malhoutra, a Rhodes scholar who had come up to Balliol that year, walked in. With him was an Indian I'll call Hari, who had also come up that year. Hari, a tall, retiring fellow, was one of the most charming Indians at Oxford. Indians liked him, and many of them felt protective toward him.

"We have something to tell, but we can't say it in front of the white sahibs," Moni said in Punjabi, with undisguised irony.

I downed my sherry quickly, and my English friends took the hint.

"Moni, you tell," Hari said, in a barely audible voice, as soon as we were alone.

Whenever Moni—a hearty, inquisitive, affectionate fellow-Punjabi—waited for me in my room while I was out, there would be unmistakable signs of him. A cushion or two might be flattened, the books and magazines on the table might be shifted, the cards on the mantelpiece, from various clubs and societies, might be out of place, the sleeve of some new record might be lying about. He made himself at home like family. By comparison, Hari, even when he sat around with me having coffee, left no trace of ever having been there. He was a little like a ghost, or perhaps like a furtive Indian in a Victorian novel who is there one minute and gone the next.

"No, Hari, you tell," Moni said. They sounded like two little boys with a secret.

"Yes?" I said, trying to sound interested but not too interested. I felt I had to tread carefully. Hari was as secretive as he was sensitive.

"Hari thinks he has got syphilis!" Moni burst out, with a big laugh. He was so good-natured and laughed so easily that no one—not even Hari—could take offense.

"No!" I exclaimed. "It's not true."

"I don't *think*, I *know*," Hari said.

"How do you know?" I asked, trying to absorb the news.

"I was having coffee at Christ Church with some English undergraduates, and an obviously loose girl came and sat on the arm of my sofa," Hari said.

He had trouble going on, and, partly to prompt him, I asked, "How did you know she was loose?"

"She kept her legs apart in a very sluttish manner—anyone could tell she was a prostitute." He swallowed hard and fell silent again.

"Come, Hari," Moni said. "Out with it. You wouldn't take my word for it, but you said you would listen to Ved."

"She bent over me, and breathed in my ear, and asked me if I'd like sugar in my coffee," Hari said. "What could I do? I said, 'Yes, please.' She took the spoon from her own cup, wiped it with her rumpled handkerchief, and then used it to serve me sugar and stir my coffee—with the very same spoon." He stopped as if that were the end of the story.

"So?" I said. "Then what happened? What did she do?"

"Don't you understand?" Hari cried. "She seduced me."

"How? Where? You were sitting among a group of your friends, weren't you?"

"Her arm was on the back of my sofa. She was leaning over me. She was watching me, so I had to drink the coffee."

"Poor Hari," Moni said.

"But what happened?" I asked.

"I left as soon as I could and rushed over to Moni's room. I've got her pregnant. I've got syphilis."

Moni let out his big, rich Punjabi laugh. "I've told him that's impossible, but he won't believe me. You tell him, Ved."

"No, I've got syphilis," Hari protested, his voice quaking. "I'm sure of it. I can feel it. My whole body seems to be falling apart."

I finally caught on, and chided myself for having been so slow. A South Indian Brahman like Hari, who had been brought up with all kinds of extreme notions of purity and pollution (until recently, in that part of the country an Untouchable was not allowed to walk on the same public roads as other Hindus, much less enter their homes), could easily imagine that one caught syphilis as one did typhoid or cholera—from sharing a spoon with a carrier. But I still failed to understand how Hari could imagine that he'd got the girl pregnant.

Moni and I started explaining the "facts of life" to Hari, as if he were a small child. We both thought that we would have more success explaining the concept of procreation than differentiating between kinds of infection. But he had grown up with such strongly held beliefs that he resisted us, as if we were trying to undermine his religion. We couldn't even get him see that for his sperm to enter a woman's body an insertion was required.

"How do you suppose, then, that women get pregnant?" we asked.

"Don't you know sperm flies through the air?" Hari demanded.

Moni let out a howl, and I couldn't help joining him.

"Sperm is just like millions of germs and bugs that fly around," Hari said, getting even more agitated. "That's why Jains walk around with cloths over their faces, so they don't swallow any."

We told him that sperm was different. We tried to get him to picture Hindu temples—the representations of lingams, for instance—but there was no way to get through to him. He had got syphilis, and a prostitute was carrying his child.

By the end of a long evening, we had calmed him down somewhat. But for weeks thereafter he fretted about the girl and the spoon. He consulted many other Indian friends on the subject. Some of them were as innocent as he was, but they all tried to console him. He'd be reassured one moment and be near hysterics the next. He got so carried away that he had a sort of nervous breakdown. It took hospitalization in the Warneford to get him back on his feet.

❦

SOME time after the Warneford episode, Hari took me to meet Raghavan Iyer, another Indian Rhodes scholar, and his wife, Nandini. "They are the most successful Indians around," he told me as we walked toward their house, on Winchester Road, near St. Antony's College. They had both got Firsts in P.P.E.—Raghavan in 1953 and Nandini in 1955.

I was indeed impressed. English schoolboys were trained almost from the time they were seven to succeed at competitive examinations and to land a First in Oxford Schools or Cambridge Tripos. Few foreigners—particularly foreigners like Indians, for whom English was a second or third language—could ever manage to equal the best of them. In fact, only a handful of Indians had ever got Firsts; it was so rare a feat that "First" was used almost as a handle to their names.

"I think they're the only Indians since the war who've got Firsts," Hari said.

"No, that's not right," I said. "V. K. Ramaswami got a First." Ramaswami, who had read P.P.E. at Balliol, had got a First in 1949, and was a Fellow of the college now.

"But Ramaswami is a bachelor, and Raghavan is married to someone who also has a First," Hari said. "In the history of Oxford, there have never been two Indians with Firsts who married each other. Between them, they're bound to have twice as much intelligence as anyone else."

I had to laugh. It was typical Hari logic—perhaps even typical Oxford Indian logic.

"Raghavan is the future Radhakrishnan," Hari said, unfazed by my laughter. Sarvepalli Radhakrishnan, who had been the Spalding Professor of Eastern Religions and Ethics at Oxford until the early fifties, was a scholar of both Eastern and Western philosophy and a Fellow of All Souls. He was currently serving as the Vice-President of India, and was expected to be the next President—as he indeed eventually was. "Like Radhakrishnan, Raghavan will be a philosopher king."

"No doubt because he's a Brahman, like you," I said, only half in jest, for it was within the realm of possibility that someone who was as well placed in Oxford as Raghavan Iyer was could rise to the top of India. "What is he doing now?"

"He's a Fellow of St. Antony's."

When we reached the Iyers', a gathering was in progress. They apparently held regular gatherings of acolytes, the purpose of which was to enlighten the assemblage on theosophy—on its notion of man's perfectibility, and on its sources in both Eastern and Western thought.

Raghavan, who was presiding, was explaining how his father, a theosophist, had taught him that evil in the world was a result of man's desires, and that good in the world was partaking of the divine being. Nandini was making the rounds with coffee. Both of them were so strikingly handsome that they could have passed for movie idols. Although both spoke beautiful English (Raghavan had been president of the Oxford Union), they were dressed in traditional Indian clothes—he in a long buttoned-up coat, which other Indians at Oxford wore only on formal occasions, in place of a dinner jacket, and she in a sari. Their house also seemed to be a blend of East and West: it held a lot of books on Western political philosophy and Hindu religion, and there were scents of both incense and cologne in the air.

"Some of you here are newcomers, and would want to know what theosophy is," Raghavan was saying. "It is an attempt to find the common core of belief and meanings in different religions before they were institutionalized and reinterpreted. You see, the myths of different religions are similar in structure, and theosophy combines the tenets of all of them. But theosophy is not religious in a ritualistic sense. Rather, it is a search for self-knowledge and for self-perfection. For its principal goal is to help one rediscover and reëxpress the full extent of one's own divinity. A soul is perfected not only through a cycle of reincarnations, and through spiritual exercises, but also through the cultivation of proper attitudes. I hope that you will all discover for yourselves the path to self-perfection. You will find that it is illuminated by the example of great souls, or mahatmas, and there is a good chance that it will be further illuminated when we find and decipher a certain theosophical work, containing occult secrets, that is now lost somewhere in the Himalayas. In the meantime, psychic vibrations can help you to cultivate proper attitudes. You need discipline and training to be able to feel them, however." He talked on in this vein, casually alluding to Greek thinkers and Buddhist, Vedanta, and Christian mystics.

Raghavan paused and turned to his wife, who was now sitting down. "Do you have anything to add, Nandini?"

Nandini, in a few well-chosen words, corroborated his points, but also gave her own interpretation of theosophy, and ended by remarking that she had become a theosophist after meeting Raghavan. Her participation from the audience somehow heightened the aura of veneration around him. But, of the two, she seemed to be of the more scholarly bent, while he came across as something of an evangelist.

I felt that Nandini, shy, reserved, and extremely thoughtful, complemented Raghavan beautifully, and that they had reached some kind of perfection in their lives and their marriage. Like Hari, I could even imagine Raghavan being a second Radhakrishnan. I envied him—envied his having had the best of both Eastern and Western education, and his being married to a woman who was not only a fellow-Oxonian but also one who had got a

First, and who had such an impressive social presence. With someone like her at my side, what couldn't I do, I thought. Undergraduate that I was, I began dreaming not only of getting a First but also of marrying a beautiful Indian woman who would also get a First.

After that meeting, I often encountered Raghavan on Oxford streets or in Oxford societies. He was always dressed in a long Indian coat, and he was always trying to proselytize people—urging them to come to his conclave and to join the Theosophical Society. I found that he was taking charge of the lives of his followers. He actually arranged a marriage for an Indian friend at Balliol to an Indian woman who was doing an extramural course in social work. The more I saw of him, the more he reminded me of Hindu holy men who used to come calling on my mother and prescribe remedies to restore my eyesight. The general Oxford attitude of skepticism and irony set in, and a few other Indians and I would bait him a little. I remember that we once asked him what someone like Radhakrishnan had that lesser mortals like us didn't have.

"Someone like Radhakrishnan is steeped in the philosophical traditions of the world, and so he is wise in a way that academic brilliance in itself cannot match," he said. "You see, a very clever and intellectual person can be manipulative. In contrast, a wise person is divine."

"Do you have such qualities?" one of us asked mischievously.

"People say I do—not just Indians but also the English," he said with a straight face.

I stopped wanting to be Raghavan, but the ideal of getting a First and marrying a First—an Indian First—stayed with me. (As it happened, Raghavan proved to be a fish out of water at Oxford; he eventually went to California to teach at the university in Santa Barbara. He and Nandini still live there, and his body of followers has continued to grow.)

ONE morning during the Trinity term of my second year, I got a letter in the post with a coronet engraved on the envelope. Inside was a little note that said, "I adored reading your book 'Face to Face' and I long to meet you." Along with the note there was a formal invitation:

Lord Oxmantown
at home
Peck Quad, the House,
six o'clock.
Sunday, 20 April

The House was a nickname for Christ Church. The Peckwater Quadrangle was framed by the college library and by several Georgian buildings that had some of the grandest rooms at Oxford. The rooms were reserved for the sons of some of Britain's noblest families, who had traditionally favored Christ Church. Although Oxmantown was clearly a fellow-undergraduate, I'd never met the chap, and while I was still wondering how I should respond to His Lordship's invitation I received another mysterious letter, in the afternoon post, in a fancy but almost illegible hand. It was from a woman, Shireen Mahdavi. She introduced herself as a Persian student at the London School of Economics. She, too, said that she had enjoyed my book and would like to meet me. She offered to accompany me to drinks at William's.

William must be Oxmantown, I thought, and was confirmed in my conjecture when I looked him up in *Who's Who,* in which he was listed as Lord William Clere Leonard Brendan Wilmer Parsons Oxmantown, the heir of the sixth Earl of Rosse.

Although I had accepted Oxmantown's invitation, I feared I

would be out of my class, and I fully intended to catch a diplomatic cold. So I wrote back to Miss Mahdavi politely declining her offer. But on the day of the party I received letters from both Shireen and William, pressing me to come, as if they had guessed that I would try to back out. I put on my best suit, took a taxi to Christ Church, and arrived at Peckwater Quadrangle at the appointed time.

As I entered Oxmantown's rooms, an extremely dashing but rather impish fellow decked out in a well-cut boating jacket with Irish Guard buttons rushed away from a group he was talking to and came dancing toward me, pitcher in hand, as if I were a long-lost friend. Practically the first words out of his mouth were "Mmm, a Pink Lady for Ved." He was William Oxmantown.

I was so nervous that I all but put out my arms to embrace whatever lady he was offering me.

William pressed a chilled glass into my hand, and tinkled an iced drink into the glass from the pitcher.

"I simply adooored your book," he said. He had a way of stretching out a word by adding a sort of extra chord to it.

Almost before I'd taken a sip of my drink, I was surrounded by women, one of whom was Shireen. "I loved your book," she said, half embracing me, as if to make it clear that she was offering me her friendship but knew she was being a little forward. I was touched by her warmth and delicacy.

The party was my first encounter with any contemporaries who seemed to take an interest in me because I was an author. Dom and other friends of mine tended outwardly to adopt my dismissive attitude, whatever they might have felt inwardly. Even as I resisted the praise, I found it exciting to be admired.

Shireen introduced me to Anne Cathie, who kept switching effortlessly between our conversation and one in French, behind us (it turned out that she was reading Modern Languages at St. Anne's), and to Priya Adarkar, who, though she was a Hindu, seemed to have been brought up mostly in England. She had a perfect English voice, but was wearing a sari and sandals, like a traditional Indian girl. She was always laughing, but at the same time tended to hang back, as if she were nursing a secret sorrow—a combination of traits that made her extremely attractive to me. Either because she was included in such a grand English gathering or because, starved as I was for female company, I was impetuous, I immediately began thinking of her as another Nandini. I was excited to learn that she was reading English, because that meant she could help me with my writing, and that she was in her first year, which meant she was younger than I was. (She was, in fact, eighteen years old.) Also, she was soft and very relaxed, and she was about four inches shorter than I was—just the right height for me. I could easily imagine my parents trying to arrange my marriage to her.

Priya, Shireen, and Anne all seemed open and outgoing, very different from the débutantes and intellectual women I generally met at parties. The three had known one another for many years: Shireen had been sent to England for education when she was twelve, Priya when she was eleven, and all three had been in the same class at Channing, a boarding school in Highgate, in London.

While I was talking to them, William was flitting about with the pitcher of his special gin mix, saying, "Mmm, what about another Pink Lady? You simply must have another." He spoke in an extraordinary singsong, clipping bits of words in his lower register and almost hooting the ones in his upper register, and, at the same time, dropping in an odd French word or phrase—his voice full of laughter. Much to my confusion, he kept bringing people around to meet me, as if I were the guest of honor. Many of the men he brought around were intimidating: they were tall and elegant, and all of them seemed to have gone to Eton or Harrow; they talked about going beagling and hunting, and had names like Robert Fearnley-Whittingstall.

I was flabbergasted by William's attention but also elated by it. No one who has not lived in England can possibly know the glamour of the upper class, I thought. It makes the world feel lighter and airier, with limitless possibilities, as if one were still a child and could go in any direction. William was my first friend who actually had a title. In his company, I felt that I was at the Oxford I had read about in books. He could have been a character in "Zuleika Dobson" or "Gaudy Night" or "Brideshead Revisited." I didn't have a sou to my name, and was probably condemned to the life of a drudge. But how I wished that I had private means, as he must have, so that I could live like a gentleman aesthete—avoiding the vulgar activities of working and producing, and instead cultivating art for its own sake.

At one point, William introduced me to his roommate, a very serious Scotsman named Colin. I thought I'd finally met a kindred spirit, but then William said, "Colin actually believes that all wogs start at Calais. He even disapproves of us Irish, because we have our Pink Ladies on Sundays."

There was much laughter all around, with Colin himself joining in, if in a restrained way.

"I'm glad that wogs are no worse than frogs," I said, to show Colin that I understood that William was having him on.

William was very much the life of the party, and yet he himself was not quite of it. There was something out of the ordinary about him—a certain sweetness of nature disguised by a pixie-like, mischievous demeanor, which seemed to set him apart from most of the people in the room.

It was getting late, and the party was thinning out.

"Mmm, a little dinner at the Capri," William said, coming over to me.

The Capri was one of the two best restaurants in Oxford; the other was the Elizabeth, and both restaurants were steps away from Christ Church. My friends and I, when we wanted to splurge, tended to go to the Elizabeth, which was smaller and more staid;

we found the Capri a little too chichi, just right for the Peck dandies.

William rounded up Shireen, Priya, Anne, Robert Fearnley-Whittingstall, and a boisterous fellow named Brian Stone, and we went across to the Capri, where the headwaiter, Romeo, seemed to be waiting for us.

"Right this way, m'lord," he said, escorting us to a big table that was set up to accommodate us.

The restaurant had a festive air. Its waiters were Italian, young, and just a touch offhand and arrogant, and they added to its atmosphere of Continental chic.

Everyone took a long time studying the menu and ordering. There were a lot of complicated individual orders, but practically everyone wanted the crêpes Suzette for sweet.

Before we were very far into the dinner, Shireen turned to me—I was seated at her end of the table, with William—and asked, "Do you think I'm a scheming foreigner?"

"Not at all," I said, taken aback.

"William's mother thinks so," she said. "She thinks I'm a grasping Persian in search of a British title, and she's awfully worried, because she wants William to marry a rose from the English aristocracy."

I felt a guilty twinge; after all, I'd started scheming for Priya, who was sitting across the table, between Brian and Robert, openly laughing at their jokes and wonderfully holding her own.

"No, Mummy simply adooores Shireen," William said, also to me. I seemed to be a pawn in a long-standing flirtatious game. "She thinks Shireen is a very good influence on me."

"But, contrary to Lady Rosse's suspicion, I wouldn't marry William if all of Ireland were offered to me on a platter," Shireen said. "All I want to do is to be friends with William and develop William's social conscience. All he likes to do is drive fast, give parties, and go to balls. Anyway, I'm going to go back and put my education to good use, helping the poor of Persia."

"But, Shireen," William said, "Mummy really *does* approve of you. She thinks you're making me serious and responsible."

"No, William," Shireen said, in her turn dragging out his name, almost adding an extra syllable to it. "She thinks I want to be a titled lady, the chatelaine of your Birr Castle."

"But, my dear," William said. They both laughed, William squealing and Shireen snorting. Her laugh, her voice could have been straight out of the English upper crust. It was easier to imagine her living in Britain as the wife of a lord than returning to Persia to work in the slums. And yet beneath her very polished manner there was an unmistakable sincerity.

William suddenly said to me, "You must come to Birr." The very name sent chills down my spine. Some ancestor of his must have shivered to death there, I thought.

"How did the castle get its name?" I asked.

"The town and the castle have the same name—it means 'the place of springs,' " he said, and added, "Mummy would simply love to meet you."

"Me!" I exclaimed.

"She and my father simply adore scholars and intellectuals," he said. "When my father was up at the House, all his friends were super-intellectuals. Harold Acton, Evelyn Waugh, Roy Harrod—people like that. He also knew a few Indians who wore smashing maharaja clothes."

The wine was going around faster and faster, and everyone seemed to be flirting with everyone else. From across the table, Brian was now flirting with both William and Shireen.

This is how the upper classes live, I thought. They have no inhibitions. Far from being an intruder, I felt I was being lifted up, into a stratosphere, and I was especially pleased when William did some adept switching of places and I found myself sitting next to Priya. She's so different from most other Indian women at Oxford, I thought. She's neither superficially Westernized nor rigidly Indian. She has the depth of an Indian woman and the mental clarity of an educated Western woman. Listening to her cultured voice and open laugh, I was more taken than ever with the idea of getting to know my first Indian girl who, like Nandini, might be at home in both England and India. The idea was thrilling, and I felt extremely grateful to William.

WILLIAM began inviting me to a party practically every Sunday; Shireen could come up from London only on weekends. I could never work out why I was wanted. Was it because William was trying to follow his father in cultivating "intellectual friends" or "maharaja friends"? Was it because Shireen saw in me a means of developing William's "social conscience," or because she was drawn to other people from the East? Was it simply because I gingered up their relationship? Shireen, who with most people was rather aloof, in the way that only extremely beautiful women can be, was always flirtatious with me, and her flirting seemed to make William only the more passionate about her. (In those days, I often ended up being a third party in relationships.) If he was in fact torn between his love for Shireen and his mother's idea of an English rose, my presence seemed to draw him closer to Shireen. It was impossible for me to entertain the idea that the two of them might like me for myself. I compared myself unfavorably to practically anyone. How could I hold a candle to a lord and a Scheherazade? As much as I enjoyed William's parties, I always felt that I cast a shadow on their gaiety, and therefore a part of me wanted to turn down his invitations. Another part of me, however, always wanted to go, because there was a good chance that Priya would be there. I had sent her several notes, asking her to lunch with me at a pub or to come around to my rooms for tea, and she had politely but firmly declined. Yet she was so friendly when I saw her in a group. Can it be that she is an Indian girl at heart, and so is afraid of compromising herself by seeing me alone, I wondered. Or is she so social that she has too many engagements to fit me in? Or does she simply consider me unsuitable? Anyway, before William's parties Shireen would materialize in my rooms, and, however definitely I had resolved not to go, I would give in.

Whether Priya was there or not, going to William's parties on Sunday evenings added a new female dimension to my life. Since women were a minority at Oxford, they were far outnumbered by men at most parties, but at William's it was the other way around. There were smart Oxford girls, London débutantes, Irish lasses, and their voices ranged from horsy to operatic, from music-hall to blowzy-barmaid; I got the same thrill from listening to their voices that other people got from looking at their faces. Women seemed to float in and out of William's rooms, apparently taken with the idea of marrying a lord, the heir to an earldom. William flirted like mad with every one of them, chatting them up with talk about fast cars, and ski slopes in Switzerland, and London balls; he often raced off to London in his sports car to see his aunt, Lady Bridget Parsons, or his half brother, Tony Armstrong-Jones, who was working as a society photographer and cutting a great figure in both artistic and social circles. (In 1960, Tony married Princess Margaret.)

Shireen, Priya, and Anne were always around William, like three priestesses of libation—Priya, oddly, always in a silk sari, her long black hair either loose or in plaits.

Of the three, Priya came from the best-educated and most professional family. Her father, a diplomat, had gone to Cambridge, and her mother was a doctor, and they had always wanted Priya and her brother, Dilip, to have an English education. Dilip had already finished at Kings College, Cambridge, and was studying in America. For all practical purposes, Priya had been brought up as a non-Indian. The first experience she had of Indians came when, after finishing at Channing, she went to Hong Kong, where her father was posted as a High Commissioner, and she met Indian officers. As the daughter of an Indian government official, she had a certain status in the Indian community and wanted to present herself as Indian. She started wearing saris, which, because she tended to be plump, were more flattering to her figure than Western clothes.

Unlike Priya, Shireen, who was Muslim by birth, was very conscious of Western fashions and wore only the latest Western styles. She came from a very rich, well-connected merchant family in Persia. Her mother was related to the most recent wife of the Shah, and her father had served as governor of several provinces. Not only was she strikingly beautiful but everything she did or said seemed to accentuate her exotic quality; she worked as a volunteer in the East End in London, and took every opportunity to describe her social work to socialites. I was astonished that anyone who was not English could have such poise and self-confidence. Although she studied at London, she was in some ways more Oxford than anyone at Oxford; she had been crushed when she hadn't won a place there.

A little like Shireen, Anne had a way with men and a lot of poise, but, unlike her friend, she was from a poor family. She was at Oxford on a state grant. She seemed determined to make her social mark with intellectual prowess and came off as something of a fighter, if slightly cold. Clearly the brainiest of the three (she got a First), she boasted that she could go to four college drinks parties a night and it would not affect her studies. (The phrase had perhaps come to be used because spirits were so expensive that many undergraduates invited people for coffee or tea instead of alcoholic drinks.) At a party, she seemed to make a beeline for the most elegant blade. As I came to know her better, I found her not so cold as I had first thought her. Her father, who was a regular soldier, had been killed in the Second

World War when she was four years old, and she had been brought up by her mother, who had been helped by various charities for war widows and had worked as a secretary. When Anne was seven, she had been badly burned. She was wearing a taffeta dress and had been careful to keep her distance from the fire, but hadn't realized that the dress could be sucked into the flames. She had been hospitalized for several months, and she still had a few scars on her arms.

As I came to know William better, he also seemed quite unusual. "Eton was a disaster," he once confided to me, without any prompting. "I hated it. Because I liked to play the piano, I was considered effeminate. Everything artistic was considered sissy sissy feminine and was beaten out of one. Then a doctor found that I had 'a patch on the lung,' a euphemism for T.B. That resulted in my being in bed for six months in Birr, after which I was sent off to the Alpine pastures in Switzerland, and I studied at Aiglon, an international school. My experience at that school gave me the feeling that all peoples of the world were equal and there was no reason that my closest friends should be of the same color or country or creed that I was. But my parents made me go back to Eton, and I was there for another term. That was an even greater disaster. I just wasn't cut out for Eton. I didn't get on with the people there. I didn't naturally conform to the British patterns of educational behavior. After that, I spent some time at Grenoble University. And then I spent some time at a horrible crammer in the Lake District before coming up to the House. Luckily, the Scotch nationalist who ran the crammer had three daughters."

In different ways, knowing a bit about the past difficulties of my glamorous new friends touched a sympathetic chord in me. I saw them in a different light from their party personae. I myself, of course, was a really damaged piece of goods, but they, too, had their private hurts.

❦

AT William's parties, Shireen had only to stand in a corner, and men swarmed around her. I still felt shy with her, and would try to get away from her to another part of the room—I usually wanted to seek out Priya anyway—but Shireen would come and find me. This meant that I was always in the circle that included William, who so doted upon her that he could hardly bear to have her out of his sight.

When William was not at Shireen's heels, he was rushing around with his pitcher of Pink Ladies, topping up glasses and trying to get people tipsy.

"Who wants another little Pink Lady?" he might call to the room right after he had topped up all the glasses.

"Brian's is getting low!" Robert Fearnley-Whittingstall might call out, or Brian might shout, "Robert is getting besotted with Pink Ladies—it's time for some din-dins!" Brian had a stentorian voice that threatened to rattle the windowpanes.

At the end of the evening, William would organize his close friends to go out to the Capri. We men would share the bill and pay much more for dinner than I, at least, could afford. Still, I never resented the expense. William and his friends were becoming my friends, but, sadly, my attempts to introduce my other friends—Jasper, Dom, or Del, say—to him were, by and large, failures. I was able to run, as it were, with either the hare or the hounds, because I had no fixed identity and could fit myself to whatever company I happened to be in.

❦

ONCE, I managed to persuade Priya to have tea with me alone in my rooms. I had bought a very special rich chocolate cake in honor of her coming. I pressed some on her, but she adamantly refused it.

"I have to watch my diet," she said simply. "My mother is diabetic, and I've always had to be careful."

My heart went out to her, and I didn't know what to say. She's soft and guileless, I thought. Artifice may be necessary in relationships between men, but it is refreshing to be with a woman who is so honest.

Generally, I was unsure of myself, but when I was confronted with difficult social situations I took an aggressive tack.

"I think you're avoiding me," I said, even before she had taken a second cup of tea.

"No. Why do you say that? We have so much fun chatting at William's."

"Do you like me?" I pressed.

She shifted in her chair, apparently in discomfort. "What an odd question."

"But then why do you always decline my invitations? We've known each other upward of six months. But this is the first time we have sat down alone. I'm sure you have lunches and teas with Robert and Brian. I know Shireen and Anne do."

"It's not that I don't want to come and see you but that I'm so often at Cambridge," she said. "In fact, I just get back in time for William's. That's why I arrive there so bedraggled."

"What's in Cambridge? How can you go there in term time?"

It was a common complaint that Cambridge was one of the most difficult places to get to from Oxford. There wasn't a good road or a good bus connection between the two towns, and people often had to go the long way around, via London. The trip was so arduous and time-consuming that there was less contact between undergraduates at the two universities than one would have expected.

"You do ask a lot of questions," she said.

I could tell that she expected me to stop, and was eager to change the subject. But I persisted, saying, "I must know."

"Why must you know?" she asked—a tiny bit coquettishly, I thought.

"Because . . ." I didn't know exactly how to say what was in my mind. "Because I dream about you."

She became very thoughtful, and after a silence she said, "As you know, Dilip was at Kings, and I have a lot of friends there."

"But you have a lot of friends here," I said. "There must be a reason you're not telling."

"Well, if you must know, I go to see Amartya Sen."

"Who is he? Are you romantically involved with him?" I stopped, but she didn't say anything. I felt bold and reckless. I felt that if I didn't press my advantage now I might not get another chance. "How can you be? You are from Maharashtra, and it's clear from his name that he's from Bengal." Even as I spoke, I knew I sounded stupid. Priya and I, just like Raghavan and Nandini, were from two totally different linguistic regions of India, and so could communicate with each other only in English. Clearly, the constraints of India, where people from the same linguistic region, the same caste and community, married, did not apply to Oxford or Cambridge people. In fact, in India the whole idea of a "love marriage" was considered immoral.

"I don't know what you're talking about," she said. "But I think of him all the time. He's like no one else."

"Is he an undergraduate?"

"No. He's an economist and a Fellow of Trinity College."

The disclosure took my breath away. For an Indian to be a Fellow of Trinity, a preëminent college, almost a university within a university, where the likes of Newton and Bertrand Russell had gone—it was unheard of. Amartya Sen must put Raghavan Iyer in the shade, I thought. What could I be to him? What chance do I stand against him? How could I compete with him?

Writing this today gives me an odd sensation. How could all of us have taken such a closed and stratified view of success? But we did.

"Are you engaged to him?" I now asked Priya.

"It's not like anything you think," she said. "We just enjoy each other's company, that's all. But no one can ever mean as much to me as he does—and it's all one-sided, it's all hopeless."

It is all hopeless, I thought. She's like me—a soul full of total devotion. She has all but admitted that she loves Amartya, and she'll probably never look at anyone else for the rest of her life.

Indian that I was, I imagined that once a relationship was formed it was as stable as a rock. Even if I recognized, intellectually, that people got in and out of relationships, emotionally a woman's involvement with another man seemed to put her beyond me, as if she were already a wife and mother, and so, in a sense, sacred.

"Oh, well," I said swallowing hard. "But you will come and have tea sometimes, won't you? We can still be friends."

She grew thoughtful again.

"You could tell me about Amartya," I said. "I'd like to know all about him."

"It's true there is no one I can talk to who understands the Indianness of it all," she said.

So it was that I started seeing Priya on her own—not as a prospective suitor, as I had hoped, but as a confidant. For hours at a time, I would hear about Amartya: that he was a member of the Apostles, the crème de la crème of the Oxford and Cambridge societies; that he had written his doctoral thesis in one year flat; that he had already been a professor in Calcutta for two years; that Trinity had been so keen to have him as a Fellow that it had held the position for him until that spring; and that he was not even five months older than I was.

Most of the time, I listened and was filled with admiration. Sometimes, though, I switched off and wondered why I was being

such a martyr. But then I would tell myself that at least I was
with Priya.

❦

"MY parents would like you to come to our little pad in the
bog," William said as he was leaving for the Christmas vac. It
was my final year, and I had planned to stay in Oxford for the
entire vac and study, but William's invitation to Birr was tempt-
ing. Among other things, I had never stayed with a British family—William was Anglo-Irish.

"If I come, could we spend some time in Dublin?" I asked.
"I would love to visit the haunts of Joyce, Yeats, and Sean O'Ca-
sey."

"Of course," he said. "We can go pub-crawling all the time.
We have a lot of friends in the city."

I decided to take a week off from my studies and visit William. When I arrived in Dublin, in the late afternoon of a cold
January day, he was at the airport to receive me.

We bundled ourselves into William's plush, chauffeur-driven
car and set off for Birr. I'd imagined that the castle was near
Dublin, convenient to the pubs, but it turned out to be two solid
hours away, deep in the country.

"How will we go to and from Dublin?" I asked when I realized that Birr was not just around the corner.

"You'll simply adooore Birr," William said, in his charming
falsetto, blithely evading my question. He went on to say that
the original part of the castle, a gate tower, was medieval, and
that when his ancestors took it over, in 1620, they had added
two flanking towers for defensive purposes. Over the centuries,
the castle had been built up around the towers.

"How big is Birr?" I asked

"The castle has about a hundred rooms, and we have about
nine hundred and ten hectares."

I was staggered. The Rosses also had establishments in London and Yorkshire where they spent a good deal of their time. "Who lives in all those rooms?" I asked.

"My parents love to have little house parties when they're at Birr. Just now, they have about forty people for a shoot."

The prospect of meeting forty new people, without question many of them peers of the realm, was so daunting that I wished I were back at Oxford, quietly curled up in my chair. "You must have a big staff," I said.

"Just the usual footmen, cooks, scullery and sub-scullery maids, and, of course, the housekeeper and the butler."

The castle sounded like a world unto itself, and I was afraid that once I got inside it I would be trapped there, like a bird in a golden cage. "When will we go pub-crawling in Dublin?" I asked.

"Any time—any time at all," he said, with his musical laugh.

"You knew all along that we wouldn't be able to go to Dublin," I said.

"You'll adooore Birr. My parents are sooo looking forward to meeting you."

"It must be very cold and damp," I said, dreaming of the blazing fires in cozy little pubs where Joyce might have warmed himself.

"Nooo," he said. "The castle is centrally heated with oil. It's the only one in all of Ireland that is. It's as warm as toast."

"Blarney," I said, mimicking an Irish brogue. "You're having me on."

"Not at all. My father decided to put in central heating after the war. It took years to complete the work. Since there were no drawings of the plan for the castle, when the workers started drilling holes in the walls—some are fifteen feet thick—they never knew what they might hit or where they might come out. At one point, they were boring holes and discovered a lot of bones. At first, we thought they were animal bones, but my father sent them to the museum to be analyzed. They turned out to be human bones, dating, probably, from the medieval period. What the bones were doing in the wall, of course, no one had any idea."

❧

MY room was in a Victorian suite, where, as Connors, who brought up my luggage, informed me, the Rosses had started out their married life. My particular room was named the Conroy room, after Sir Edward Conroy, who had eloped in 1837 with Lady Alicia Parsons, the sister of the then Lord Oxmantown. Armed with pistols, His Lordship had pursued the runaway couple all the way from London to Gretna Green—the village on the Scottish-English border famous for quick marriages—but to no avail.

The occupant of the other room of the suite looked in. He was Lord Talbot of Malahide, a bachelor in his late forties, who had served as Her Majesty's Ambassador to Laos. After we exchanged some amenities about my education and his—he was a Wykehamist who had been at Trinity College, Cambridge—he left.

"Would you like to change for dinner, sir?" Connors asked me, in a whisper.

"Why?" I asked. I was wearing a suit and tie.

"I've just laid out Lord Talbot's dinner jacket," he said discreetly.

"Oh!" I exclaimed. "Do we have to wear dinner jackets for dinner?"

"Yes, sir. We always change for dinner at Birr."

Thank goodness I brought along my dinner jacket, I thought. At Oxford, I had asked William if I should bring especially warm clothes for Ireland. "No, we'll see to it that you're kept warm with little Irish lasses and Pink Ladies, and such," he had said.

"But we'll be pub-crawling," I had said. "I believe Dublin is fiendishly cold."

"Oh, you must bring your dinner jacket."

"Dinner jacket? Why, I'm sure Joyce never owned one."

"In some pubs, they're *de rigueur*," he had said, with a laugh.

Now Connors took my dinner jacket out of the suitcase and busied himself in the dressing room—it was between my room and the bathroom I shared with Lord Talbot—laying out my clothes and putting my cufflinks and studs into the buttonholes of my shirt.

After Connors left, I stripped down to my shorts and made a dash for the bathroom to take a quick bath, only to find that the door from my room into the dressing room had been locked from the other side. I gathered that His Lordship was taking a bath, so I patiently waited. After a while, I heard through the door what sounded like heavy snoring. God, His Lordship has fallen asleep in the bathtub, I thought. I rattled the door. There was some stirring in the bath, and I heard His Lordship shuffling about and going off through the door between the bathroom and his room. I rattled the dressing room door vigorously, but he didn't seem to hear. I decided to get back into my clothes and go around and try to get into the bathroom from his room, but discovered that while my back was turned Connors had whisked away all my clothes, no doubt to brush and press them. The only clothes I could find in the room were my pajamas, which had holes in them. I waited, cursing in turn His Lordship and Connors, until Connors reappeared and rescued me.

By the time I had got into the dressing room, changed, and gone downstairs, the entire house party was seated in the huge dining room. I was placed at the right of William's mother, who was wearing a tiara and was covered with jewelry. I was flabbergasted. Of all the people of varying quality and degree gathered in the dining room, I was certain to be at the bottom. If I'd been an artist of great repute, perhaps I could have taken precedence over the noble company, but what claim could I have to the honored seat at Her Ladyship's right hand, except that I had been befriended by William? Also, the boiled front of my shirt was very stiff and perhaps longer than it should have been. It stuck out in front of my chest, making me feel even more self-conscious and awkward.

"You're one of William's intellectual friends—you're such a good influence on him," she said.

Ah, so intellect was my passport to the honored seat, I thought. I decided to act the part and talk like a revolutionary. "Lady Rosse—"

"Call me Anne," she broke in emphatically.

"Anne, then—I'm a socialist," I announced. It was an aggressive conversational ploy, but then I was trying to master my acute discomfort.

"So am I," she said, with a hearty, unladylike laugh. "I believe in champagne for everybody in the world."

I had to laugh. I soon forgot myself.

I asked Anne if this was the dining room where they ate when William was a child.

"Yes, whenever we were at Birr. But there is a special entrance from the back staircase for the children and their nanny, and they processed in here for the third and fourth courses."

"We had to sit with our nanny at the children's table and behave," William called from somewhere down the table. "I thought we'd never grow up and sit at this grand table."

"They were impossible when they were small," Lady Rosse said. "The nanny had terrible trouble keeping an eye on them, with the hazards of battlements, the moat, the river, the lake, the ravines all around. They were forever escaping her eye and hiding, in the dungeon and the torture chamber and God knows where else."

"Poor nanny—she was always going around the castle, calling 'William! Martin! Tony!' " William's younger brother, Martin, piped up from another part of the table, mimicking a frantic woman's voice.

Lords and ladies I knew only from my history books. They always seemed remote and august, their society as far beyond my reach as the moon. In my year at Balliol, there was the Marquess of Clydesdale. I had imagined that to people like him and William I must appear a little like an aboriginal in the Indian hills. Why I had such exalted notions of the British upper classes I was never able to work out. I had merely to hear an impressive British voice to crawl into my shell and begin feeling unworthy. But here were the Rosses, talking like any other family, and the other conversations I could make out through the hubbub were equally mundane. The subject matter is different, but the concerns and aspirations are the same, I thought.

For coffee and port, we moved into what was called the saloon, perhaps the most beautiful room in the castle—in the Gothic style, with floor-length windows that overlooked a rushing waterfall beyond. By the end of the evening, especially after we had circulated—William was often at my side—I had got acquainted with many of the guests, most of whom insisted that I call them by their first names. In addition to Milo (Lord Talbot), there was his sister, the stylish Rosie (the Honourable Rose Talbot); Lord and Lady Mount Charles (an Etonian in his mid-thirties, who was called simply Mount and seemed to have an eye for pretty girls, and his fun-loving wife, Eileen), and one of William's parents closest friends, Roderic More O'Ferrall, from Kildangan, where he had an estate. There was also Nick Bolton, a friend of Martin's, who said things like "My father is just the Bank of London, you know." Martin and William had also invited three girls each. Martin's guests included Coral Knowles, whom all the young men ostentatiously flirted with; William's guests included Belinda Brady, whom his parents very much disapproved of, but whom William had smuggled into the castle, pretending she was an Honourable, and also a rather petite girl named Angela Colhoun, whom William called Princess Margaret behind her back, perhaps because his parents preferred her for him, much as they preferred the real Princess Margaret for his half brother, Tony, who was not there.

Around midnight, all the older people went to bed, and a new party got going, with a batch of local girls somehow arriving, as if on cue. Martin put on some Elvis Presley records, and everyone started dancing. William put up Coral and Angela in turn to ask me to dance, and I tried my best to shake a leg with them, saying little but putting on a bold face. It was not easy, because the songs were fast-moving numbers. As I was slipping out to go to bed, William informed me over the thumping music, as casually as if he were telling me the name of the chambermaid, "The shooting breakfast will be at seven-thirty."

"Am I expected to come down for it?" I said. "It's past two."

"Of course," he said, with his impish laugh. "Everyone is going to the shoot."

In the morning, Connors woke me, and I hurriedly got dressed and rushed downstairs. The gathering was as noisy as if it were a continuation of the dinner party—as if the guests had never really turned in. People were serving themselves from a sideboard where ham and all kinds of game were laid out. I allowed myself to be served by Angela, feeling ridiculous in my city suit and shoes; everyone else was in tweeds and boots, the women sporting Hermès silk scarves and the men plus fours. William's father, Michael, a man with a grand manner, came over and sat next to me. Like William's mother, he had been extraordinarily solicitous, so I found myself confessing to him my total ignorance of shooting or hunting.

"What would you like to know?" he asked.

"For a start, what sort of game are people out for?" I asked.

"Every gun will be trying for woodcock," he said. "They're the most elusive bird, partly because they're small and partly because they follow a zigzag flight pattern. But I'm sure everyone will manage to bag a few pheasants. We raise ten to fifteen thousand pheasants for the shoot each year. Woodcock and snipe can't be reared, but they have a gamier and richer taste. Woodcock is my favorite."

"It must be quite a job to furnish the land with the birds," I said.

"Not really. The landscape at Birr has a lot of cover. There are glens, with a lot of rhododendron and hazel, and eskers, with a lot of oak and ash. The undulating character of the woods makes them very good for the shoot, and the good shot especially appreciates the high eskers, because the birds rising from them are easy to aim at. The eskers at Birr are relics of the Ice Age."

It was the first day of a cold spell, and we all put on our mufflers and coats, got into cars for the shoot (I was put in a car full of women, again next to Lady Rosse), and were driven to a "beat," called the Long Orchard, a couple of miles away on the Rosses' land.

The air was filled with the sounds of gun and beaters.

All the men trudged off for the shoot. I alone was left sitting with the women, like a child.

"It's very much a driven shoot," Lady Rosse said.

"What's that?" I asked.

"As you can hear, the beaters are flushing the birds from under the cover, and driving them toward the guns."

There was rapid fire, almost like a machine gun.

"Gosh," I said. "Who do you suppose that is? It sounds as if he had brought down a whole flock of birds."

"I think I know who it is," Lady Rosse said. "He's a garrulous gun, and I'm certain he hasn't bagged a single bird."

Eileen, who was sitting on the other side of Lady Rosse, laughed, as if she also knew the identity of the "garrulous gun." "It's the mostly silent gun who aims before he shoots—that's the gun that will put birds on our table," Eileen said.

For want of anything better to say, I was about to ask who among the company were the "garrulous" guns and who the "silent" ones, but Lady Rosse anticipated me.

"It's very unsportsmanlike to know who gets the birds," she said.

"It's not the birds but the enjoyment of the shoot that matters," Eileen chimed in.

Even as they were chatting, I felt like switching off. I wanted to be anywhere but there—under the eyes of women schooled to observe every look or gesture for its social implication. How could they fail to notice that I was uncomfortable and bored? I consoled myself with the thought that I was morally opposed to killing game, and savored a moment of superiority to the sportsmen and their lady well-wishers in the car. But then I thought about the meat I regularly enjoyed eating, and grew unsure. In fact, shooting down a bird seemed not as bad as slaughtering a lamb for the table—or, for that matter, hunting a deer. Even the fact that the sport was carried on with a gun didn't seem so very bad, on closer examination. Maybe the "guns" worked out their violent impulses in the sport of the shoot. Certainly the Rosses and their guests seemed more at peace with themselves—at peace with their titles, money, and well-being—than many people I knew. But not being able to hide behind a feeling of moral or intellectual superiority made me feel more exposed than ever. Anyway, there was no hiding the fact that I would have nothing better to do all morning than listen to the women talking in the car and to the sounds of beaters and gun dogs from behind the ridges. While the men tramped about, took aim, and shot, I twiddled my thumbs, unable to help looking blank and restive.

"Are Michael and William good shots?" I asked at one point.

"They've never shot in their lives," Lady Rosse said. "I don't think William enjoys standing around in the cold. But they're both good sports."

"I could have gone with them," I said.

"I thought your Hindu spirit would be offended by the massacre," Lady Rosse said, with a little laugh.

"Oh God," I said to myself. But I suddenly felt better. Given the choice between tramping around in the cold and sitting in the warmth of the car, I had no difficulty in deciding where I'd rather be. Anyway, I was beginning to enjoy listening to the ladies chattering away about everything and nothing.

In the event, the morning passed quickly, perhaps because of various interruptions: the shoot moved from beat to beat—from the Long Orchard to the Larches, then on to the Black Grove and the Brick Grove and the Coolnahinch—the men getting back into the cars for the longer stretches.

The game was cooked with dispatch and was served to us for lunch in the beautiful Georgian Dower House, called Tullanisk, which was surrounded by woods of oak and beech.

Much fuss was made over the "guns"; in addition to Milo, Mount, Roderic, and Martin, they were Eckie Ruttledge, who was something of a tippler, even in that company; a Group-Captain Fairtclough, who was constantly getting bits of his lunch in his handlebar mustache; and a Major Hutton.

"Good shoot, what?" said Major Hutton.

"Jolly good!" said Captain Fairtclough.

"But just a half-day shoot," said Eckie, taking a big swig of his sloe gin.

People were sipping sloe gin and chatting away about the morning's results—twenty-two pheasants, one woodcock, one snipe, two pigeons, and one hare. The size of the bag wasn't anything to write home about, it seemed, but then Eckie reiterated, "Only half a day was shot."

"How long will you be with us?" Milo asked me over pudding.

I had planned to stay a week, but the Birr experience had been so overwhelming that I found myself saying, "I'll be leaving tomorrow. I'm afraid I must get back to my books."

"What a pity," said Angela.

Indeed, despite the protests of William and the Rosses, I left for Oxford the following day. (A few years ago, I returned to Birr with my family and stayed with William, his wife, Alison, and their three children. He had inherited the castle upon the death of his father, in 1979.)

❧

ONE day in October (a couple of months before I went to Birr), there was a hesitant knock on my door, and, as I got up to answer it, an even more hesitant opening of the door.

"I'm Jonathan Kozol," a stranger said, in a quiet, American voice. He walked in and paused, as if he were waiting for a reaction to his name.

I invited him to sit down. Strangers, especially Americans and Indians new to Oxford, often dropped in on me. I had "The Magic Flute" on the gramophone, and I went over to turn it off.

"That's the Queen of the Night aria," he said, perching on an arm of the sofa. "It's my favorite. Could I hear it again?"

I picked up the arm and put it back, and happened to hit the aria just right.

"How did you do that?" He emanated boyish wonder.

"Just luck," I said. "Are you at Oxford?"

"Yes, at Magdalen. I came a couple of weeks ago."

It was the autumn of my last year at Oxford, but his first. I felt benevolent toward him.

"I'm a Rhodes scholar from Hahvahd," he said, pronouncing "Harvard" in an enchanting way. "I've written a novel. It'll be coming out in Britain soon."

I smiled to myself. He's a Harvard man, I thought—something I've long wanted to be. He has written an actual novel—the dream of all potential writers. I offered to make him coffee.

As I busied myself getting water from the basin in the bedroom, putting the kettle on the gas range in the staircase hall, and getting cups and saucers from the bookcase in my sitting room, he followed me around as if he were being introduced to a new Oxford ritual.

I poured him some coffee and asked him what his novel was about.

"About a Harvard romance," he said.

Soon he was relaxing in my room, drinking his coffee and crunching a chocolate biscuit and talking about his novel. "It is the story of a Harvard undergraduate and a Radcliffe girl who fall in love and decide to quit Harvard and go off to Europe."

"To do what?"

"To travel, to make love, to eat pastries in the Luxembourg Gardens in Paris. Ah, Paris! It has a fatal attraction for us American writers."

For all his apparent worldliness, he was, in his own way, as endearingly childlike as Hari. In fact, he made me think of the virtuous characters in Dostoyevsky. It was certainly refreshing to meet him, especially at Oxford, where posturing was part of civilized life, and many people developed a persona like a carapace.

I wanted to tell him that I'd written a book, too, but decided that there was no point in that. After all, he was a real writer, while I was just a one-book man, someone who happened to have a special story to tell.

The record switched off, and there was an awkward silence.

"What's the dénouement?" Even as I asked the question, I felt embarrassed. It was an aggressive, Oxford-type question, at odds with the spell he seemed to cast.

"Oh, on the ship coming home a blond, blue-eyed rich fellow runs off with the girl," he said, eager to explain. "He's really empty-headed, but she doesn't have the wit to know it. Only the lover knows. It's an autobiographical novel—all first books are."

I felt pleasantly heartened. I asked him how he had come to write the book.

"It's not a long story," he said. "Melanie was a Southern belle and an heiress." I have substituted Melanie for the girl's real name. "She and I were the only juniors accepted in Archibald MacLeish's writing class. It was the most select writing class at Harvard. Before the Christmas vacation, MacLeish told me that I wouldn't get an A unless I wrote more." He paused dramatically, like a good storyteller who wants to keep his listeners on tenterhooks.

"Please do go on," I said, thinking what a charming way he had of speaking. He tended either to slur the letter "s" ("classh" for "class") or to drop it ("tory" for "story"), and that made him sound even younger than he was.

"I asked Melanie if she would go away with me to write. To my amazement, she agreed."

Asks a girl on an impulse, she agrees, and they're off, as if on a floating bed—that's how real writers live and write, I thought. What a contrast to Priya, who for six months wouldn't even come across to my college.

"I was behind the wheel, but I wasn't sure where we were going," he was saying. "It was late in the evening, it was cold, there was snow on the ground. We ended up living in a remote cottage on a lake deep in the country. We had to collect wood for the fire, and we didn't have much food. We would write furiously during the day and make love at night. I wrote my novel there. Our vacation became a scene in it, but transplanted to Europe. The boy who took her away on the ship was modelled on a Harvard friend, whom she eventually married. Maybe that was socially right."

"But you finished at Harvard."

"Yes. The powers that be gave me summa cum laude."

I asked what he was reading at Oxford.

"I've had it with being an undergraduate," he said. "Once is enough. You see, before I went to Harvard I spent six years in Noble and Greenough, an Episcopal school in Dedham. I was probably the second Jewish student ever to go there. We got four or five hours of homework every night, and all our masters spoke with English accents. Then, at Harvard, I was at Eliot House, a very anglophile place. Its master, John Finley, was always talking about his time at Oxford. So by the time I finished there I had spent ten years among people who were acting and speaking as if they were English." He was utterly different from me, and yet he seemed to have in his background his own little experience of the British Empire. I felt we had at least that in common. "So I don't feel that Oxford is all that big a change for me. It's true that the cold weather and the formality of Magdalen freeze me. I have a great sense of youth. I am fascinated by everything, but here I feel scared. In fact, I feel somewhat juvenilized. Girls have to be out by seven in the evening, and we are locked in at ten o'clock. At Harvard, we could stay out with our dates until seven in the morning. I may be childish in some ways, but I feel much more grown up than people here."

The more he talked, the more confused I got about his opinion of Oxford.

"What do you intend to study here?" I asked.

"I'm going to do a D.Phil.," he said.

"Have you got a topic?"

"Shakespeare," he said, without a moment's pause. "I'm going to do my doctoral dissertation on 'Hamlet.' "

I caught my breath. "Oxford is a scholarly place. Everything here is very much based on texts. You may have trouble getting the thesis topic approved."

"I did my senior thesis on 'Hamlet' at Harvard with Harry Levin. He thinks my ideas are original and they'd make a very good D.Phil. thesis. Levin is a great man. His scholarship fascinates me. When I was a senior, I used to meet him in Eliot House's Senior Common Room regularly. He would sit under the portrait of F. O. Matthiessen and talk about 'Hamlet.' "

"Have you got an adviser here?"

"Yes. The college has referred me to Helen Gardner."
"Watch out. She is a formidable scholar."

❦

In subsequent days, I saw a lot of Jonathan, in part because
he appealed to my American self—my old self, before it was
touched by Oxford. I took him to the Bombay, an Indian restaurant on Walton Street. I introduced him to Blackwell's. I listened
patiently to his complaints about Oxford. I told him that all
Americans had a miserable first year at Oxford, that I myself had
had a rocky first year, but that if one got through it and made
the effort the place had a great deal to commend it. He was not
convinced. He said he wished that I could have gone to Harvard.
Then, he felt, I would have seen Oxford in a different light. Still,
I was the only apologist for Oxford whom he was drawn to; indeed,
I seemed to be one of the few people he felt at ease with.

Often when I saw Jonathan, he was accompanied by his close
friend Herb Kohl. Like Jonathan, Herb had been at Harvard—
had lived in Eliot House and been a protégé of John Finley. Both
Jonathan and Herb had been big noises at Harvard and complained that at Oxford no one took any notice of them. Herb had
a Harvard Fellowship to New College to study philosophy for a
year. They mostly sought out each other's company, and even
went out together for a time with Oxford undergraduates who
were twins, Nancy and Ruth Leys. Yet Jonathan and Herb were
quite different. Jonathan had the air of a rich kid—he was the
only child of a Boston psychiatrist—who wanted to make it on
his own. Herb's family was from the Bronx; his father was a
contractor, and his grandfather had been a day laborer. In contrast to Jonathan, Herb had gone to public school, and at Harvard he had apparently felt socially somewhat at a loss, much as
he did at Oxford. Jonathan was very intense, and seemed always

to be pushing to get at the "truth" of things. Herb was noisy and turbulent, and seemed to feel comfortable only when he was a little high. He used to buy a fifth of Johnny Walker in the morning and finish it by the evening, but drink didn't seem to have a bad effect on him; it made his mind "loose to play," he used to say. He was boisterous by nature, and drink made him more ebullient, more friendly. With some whisky in him, he would be theatrical and entertaining, and would have surreal flashes of brilliance, pulling ideas together helter-skelter and making unexpected connections between them.

I felt a certain affinity with Jonathan—with his loneliness, with his wish to belong but not knowing how to, with his taking himself seriously. He seemed to think of himself as a Writer with a capital "W," and, although this attitude was very un-Oxford— Oxford people tended to be offhand and self-deprecating—I admired his honesty. Similarly, I was much taken with Herb's animal exuberance—a trait that I felt I shared with him. Moreover, both Jonathan and Herb made me feel that by not getting a Harvard degree I had missed out on the best of American education—made me feel that, however well I did at Oxford, I would have to go to Harvard, so that I wouldn't feel at a disadvantage in America.

I GOT hold of a copy of Jonathan's novel, "Fume of Poppies." The character of its hero was unexpected: he seemed more like a sexual athlete, fantasizing about "the spaces between the toes of his love," than like the leprechaun kind of friend I had discovered in Jonathan. Autobiography and autobiographical novels are not at all the same thing, I thought, and I took up this point with him.

"My book is not all that autobiographical," he said disarmingly. "Rather, I wrote the novel and then tried to live the life described in it."

"No!" I exclaimed.

"Yes. After graduating, I spent a crazy summer hitchhiking across Europe with Lisa." That's not her real name. "She was a girl I met after finishing the novel. I had run out of money, so I had to borrow some from a friend who was in Italy. We travelled through Europe on a shoestring. Lisa thought of trying to come to Oxford with me, but she returned to America instead."

I circulated the novel among my literary friends. If they got past its title, which I thought was poetic but they dismissed as pretentious, their verdict was, in the words of one of them, "Eating and fornicating is fine for American men of letters, but the English demand something more." My attempts to get them to accept Jonathan himself were equally unavailing: they were as uncompromisingly English as he was uncompromisingly American. Even Dom was standoffish with him.

❧

ONE afternoon, Jonathan came to my room quite shaken up. "I've just had my meeting with Helen Gardner," he said. "I told her about my work with Levin and my idea of doing a D.Phil. thesis on 'Hamlet.' 'You've found some new manuscript?' she asked sarcastically. I said, 'Of course not,' but I told her that I thought I had some pretty interesting ideas about the play for my D.Phil. thesis. She asked me, 'What kind of ideas?' I said I'd lately been thinking of comparing 'Hamlet' with Joyce's 'Daedalus.' Daedalus has always fascinated me. She said, 'Look, Joyce is an American subject. If you want to study him, go back to Harvard.' She showed me the door."

I comforted him as best I could, and asked him what he was going to do.

"I don't know, exactly," he said, "but there's certainly no point in going back to her, and I don't think there's any point in looking for another adviser. I don't think anyone else here would be any more receptive to my ideas or to me."

In his place, I would have been devastated. I would have thought of Helen Gardner as an authority figure, and gone back to her, and tried to fall in line with her thinking and the Oxford system. Or, failing in that, I would have thrashed about until I had found another adviser and another topic, and then would have settled into some course of study. But Jonathan had a much greater sense of himself, and appeared to have much more inner confidence. Certainly he was much more sure of his destiny as a writer.

He stuck around Oxford, pursuing his own literary interests. He read writers he liked—Faulkner, Dreiser, Dostoyevsky—and engaged in passionate arguments with another American, who liked much more disciplined writers, such as Fitzgerald and Flaubert.

Near the end of his first term, Jonathan told me that he had been in Blackwell's and had run into Bill Williams. Williams had invited Jonathan to Rhodes House for a drink, and Jonathan had told him that he wanted to give up the Rhodes scholarship and go to Paris and write. He felt that writing and scholarship were incompatible. Williams had sympathized with him, but, like a father, had worried that he might not make a living as a writer. At the end of their talk, Williams had said, "Think it over, but I expect you won't be back after Christmas."

"Give up the Rhodes!" I exclaimed. "Two or three years of free, princely study at Oxford? What can you be thinking of? You could stay here and do a low-level research degree like a B.Litt. and write."

"But I don't like it here," he said. "I want to be in Paris."

In the hope of dissuading him from making what I thought was an unbelievably rash decision, I told him that I had once spent nearly two years trying to get myself merely considered for a Rhodes, and that I still dreamed about my struggle, which had involved the exchange of dozens of letters among American, Indian, and British Rhodes authorities.

"I was as poor as a church mouse," I told Jonathan, "and if it hadn't been for another foundation, which came to my rescue at the last minute, I would have missed out on an Oxford education, which is about the best thing that has ever happened to me."

"It all seems so unfair," he said simply. "I wish you could have my Rhodes."

JUST before Christmas, Jonathan fled Oxford for Paris, to write, and, like so many American expatriate writers and artists, was living on the Left Bank. In the following months, I heard from him often. He said that he had written to Bill Williams resigning his Rhodes scholarship. With the courage perhaps born of youth, and the strength perhaps born of his Harvard novel, he had given up in one stroke Magdalen, Oxford, and the Rhodes. (A Rhodes official told me that he couldn't come up with many examples of people who had thumbed their noses at the prize.) Jonathan's letters were always exciting to read in the cloistered surroundings of Oxford. He stayed at first in one of a warren of windowless rooms on four or five floors of a cheap hotel in the Latin Quarter, on Rue Saint-André des Artes. Then he shifted to a hotel known only by its address, 9 Rue-Git-le-Cœur, near the Place Saint-Michel. The hotel was run by an amazing woman, Mme. Rachou. She ran a most wonderful café in the hotel, only for writers and artists, preferably American expatriates. She was so powerful that she could get policemen to eat out of her hand. Jonathan went on to say that he had inherited Gregory Corso's phonograph and girlfriend, that Bill Burroughs was reading passages of "The Naked Lunch" to him, and that Allen Ginsberg was a neighbor. He added that he had been befriended by James Jones and his wife, Gloria, and by William Styron and his wife, Rose. He spent a lot of time drinking with these people in their apartments or at the Brasserie Lipp. He had begun another "autobiographical" novel, this time about his paternal grandparents. He had fallen into a writer's life. There were times when he was lonely and sad, and missed Magdalen, but he was never coming back. He was off to Tangier for a few days. His life sounded to me impressively foreign and artistic.

*

IT was the Easter vac. I was living in the desolate Colonial Services Club—a sort of lodging house for old colonial servants who came to Oxford for some brush-up study. Now it was Easter Week, and I hadn't had any luck lining up readers, so I couldn't do any work even if I wanted to. I wished I could get away from Oxford—take a break before the ordeal of Schools. But I had no place to go.

Early in Easter Week, I met Herb Kohl walking along the Broad outside Blackwell's and asked him for the latest news of Jonathan. He didn't have any, he said, but he was going to Paris for Easter—would I like to come along?

In England, it seemed to take years to break through people's reserve. Jasper had been my best friend for nearly three years, and I had scarcely visited his house once. When vacations came, my English friends packed up and left, as if our friendship were a book that could be laid down at the beginning of the vac and picked up at the end. And here was Herb, whose temperament bore little resemblance to mine, and whom I really knew only as Jonathan's friend, inviting me to go with him to Paris.

I suddenly felt homesick for America and American ways. I felt sad that Jonathan had dropped out of my Oxford life, and I was filled with longing to see him. I was seized with the wish to know his life in Paris for myself. At the same time, I had certain anxious thoughts about going to Paris with Herb. What would I do there without books and readers? What if Herb and I didn't get on? How would I manage on my own in a mostly strange city? Maybe Herb would want to go to museums and films. I would expose my inadequacies to a person I scarcely knew. But I told myself that Jonathan would be in Paris; he had an understanding heart; he was a friend.

"I'd love to go with you to Paris," I said, trying to sound spontaneous. "When are you going?"

"In a couple of hours."

"Then I can't possibly go," I said. "I have an Indian passport. I'll need a visa."

"I'm going to London first. I can mess around there as long as it takes you to get your visa. I'm going to be staying in a loft there with the brother of a guy I just met yesterday. We can both stay there. I think there are some girls living there. Maybe we can get a couple of them to come to Paris with us."

The mention of the girls excited me. I was becoming an expert on Amartya's life but was making no headway with Priya. "This House would rather be rash than righteous"—that was a motion we'd been considering for a debate in the Arnold and Brakenbury. "Be rash, take a chance, you've got nothing to lose but your pride," I told myself, and I felt a surge of animal exuberance.

Within a couple of hours, I had packed, and Herb and I were on the train to London. I took a taxi straight from Paddington Station to the French Embassy, while Herb went to a bookshop, and by the time we set off for the loft I had my visa and we had downed enough wine to float a toy ferry across the Channel.

I'd hardly got inside the loft before I was introduced to Imogen, the sister of the loft's owner, who was out of town. She was sitting at a table in the smoke-filled kitchen, demonstrating to her school friend Primrose how to open an egg by sticking her thumb in it. (The girls' identities have been disguised.)

Herb struck up a conversation with Primrose, and I asked

Imogen, "What's wrong with cracking an egg with a spoon?"

"That's not art," she said. "Anyway, that's not the way they taught us at Cordon Bleu."

"So you've been to Paris," I said.

"Of course," she said. Her voice was fresh, very English, clear, and upper-class.

As the evening progressed, I discovered that a year or so earlier Imogen's mother had been all ready to present her to the Queen, but Imogen had ducked out of the round of débutante parties and balls. She had spent some months flitting about Europe; besides attending the cooking school in Paris, she had taken in fiestas in Spain and gone sailing in Greece.

At Oxford, I would have shied away from her. I would have been intimidated by her voice and her Englishness, and would have immediately thought of a dashing English friend, like Alasdair, who was more deserving of her attention than I was. At the same time, I would have taken refuge in the thought that she was intellectually my inferior and therefore unsuitable for me. Anyway, at Oxford I mostly forgot my need for the companionship of a woman, and lost myself in my work and in college life—the diversions of dining clubs and witty conversations into the night. But now, sitting in a loft in London, freed from responsibility by having no schedule of readers, with wine in my veins, and with wild Herb at my side, I felt bold and reckless.

"Does the egg-cracking etiquette mean that no Cordon Bleu girl can keep her fingernails long?" I asked Imogen.

"No. I have long fingernails," she said.

"Can I see?" I asked.

She put her hand in mine in a perfectly easy, natural manner. She had long fingers and long, shapely fingernails. I was soon telling her that I imagined she had long, light hair and a strawberries-and-cream complexion.

"You're uncanny," she said. "How did you know?"

Before the evening was over, Herb and I had invited Imogen

and Primrose to come with us to Paris for a few days, and, to my astonishment, they had accepted.

❦

THE following day, we took a boat train to Dover, then a ferry to Le Havre, and then a train to Paris—eating and drinking all the way. There was a lot of group talk, but Imogen and I were also able to have a long tête-à-tête on the deck. Everywhere we went, Imogen's hand was in mine.

In Paris, we discovered that Jonathan was still travelling—in Spain, Morocco, God knew where else. But we traced his steps, almost as if, in some mysterious way, he were guiding us—as if we were characters in "Fume of Poppies." We went straight to 9 Rue Gît-le-Cœur. The hotel was in the Latin Quarter, across from the Prefecture of Police. It had a grubby entrance foyer. Off that, through a glass-panelled door, was Jonathan's café, with a window overlooking the street, and a zinc counter, tended by a small, gray-haired woman. She was Mme. Rachou, the owner and proprietress of the establishment. She was so small that she had to stand on an overturned wine crate to look over the counter.

Mme. Rachou led us up a dark, slippery staircase, which spiralled around an airshaft. Along it were dingy barred windows. The walls were cracked and peeling, and the floors were covered with cracked red tiles. The air was filled with the heavy, cloying odor of marijuana. On the landings were kerosene stoves for simple cooking.

"*L'électricité est seulement pour l'éclairage,*" she said.

What else could it be for, I thought, and almost laughed out loud.

"*Oui, Madame,*" Herb said. "*Je comprends. Pas de hot-plates dans les chambres.*"

"Genius," said Primrose.

How could Jonathan have done this to us, I thought. Imogen

is used to cooking at Cordon Bleu and is worthy of being presented to the Queen, and here I've brought her to a ghetto. We
have to find some other place. I wished that Imogen could speak
Hindi, so I could tell her that we didn't have to stay there.

Madame showed us to two uncarpeted rooms. Each had one
smallish bed, a table, a little basin, and a bidet, and looked out
on the air shaft.

"*Nous voudrons une chambre avec une salle de bain,*" I said.

"*C'est impossible, Monsieur. Si vous la desirez, vous devriez chercher
un autre hôtel.*"

"These rooms are great!" Herb called out from the other room.
"Henry Miller and Hemingway would love them."

"*Où sont les toilettes?*" Primrose asked, coming in.

"*Là-bas,*" Madame said, and she pointed down the hall.

Herb ran down the hall and reported that, although it was
just a hole in the floor, it was adequate.

"What do you think, Imogen?" I asked, trembling from head
to foot.

"It's smashing," she said.

"Fabulous!" Primrose called from the other room.

The airshaft carried the sounds almost as if we were all in one
room.

I asked Madame if there was a bathtub somewhere.

"*Mais oui,*" she said, and she explained that she heated water
for a surcharge.

After putting down our luggage, we followed Mme. Rachou
downstairs to the café. Over wine, we all practiced our bad French
on her, and learned that as a young country girl she had started
working in an inn in Giverny, near the house of Monet, that she
had got to know him there—he would often lunch at the inn—
and that she had had a soft spot for artists ever since.

From her vantage point she had a good view both of the street,
through the window, and of the entrance foyer, through the glass
panel. One felt that if she didn't like someone's looks she could

bar the door against him; her manner, while tender, was also authoritarian.

We told her that we all had literary or artistic aspirations.

Just as if Jonathan had staged the scene, even as we were standing at the bar an official-looking person in a suit turned up and wanted to know who all her guests were. *"Vous avez beaucoup des Americains et Anglais ici,"* he said. *"Il faut que je voie leur papiers. Vous avez leur passports, bien sûr. Donnez les moi, s'il vous plaît."*

Mme. Rachou talked to him in French for some time, mentioning the names of several of her friends at the Prefecture of Police. She got him to accept a glass of Pernod and leave.

"I'm sure the hotel is full of illegal Americans, who must find it easier to slip across the border to Holland or Belgium every three months than to go through the formalities of registering with the 'police of foreigners,' " Herb told us. He was surprisingly worldly wise.

WE spent four or five days in Paris, staying up late and sleeping late. In fact, our day began in the afternoon. We would do a lot of wandering. We would go to the Brasserie Lipp. We would drink wine, but Herb quickly developed a taste for Pernod and drank it as avidly as he used to drink whisky at Oxford. At the Lipp, we would run into some very sleek Harvard friends of Jonathan's and Herb's who were writing or editing, or just living in Paris. We would go shopping, pick up a tie here and a purse there. With Imogen's voice always in my ear, her hand in mine, I felt deliciously happy, as if I were on a drug, without a care in the world. We would pick up some delicacies from a *pâtisserie* and go to the Luxembourg Gardens and eat them. (Herb and I had got both Imogen and Primrose to read "Fume of Poppies.") At night, we would finish off our day by waiting, with truck drivers, people in the food industry, and prostitutes, for Les Halles to open at dawn, and for all the produce to be brought in and put into wrought-iron Crystal Palace–like buildings. At 6 A.M., when the nuns came to collect the leftovers from restaurants, we would go back to the hotel, passing ranks of security forces, which reminded us of the savage Algerian War in progress.

At the end of the week, Imogen and Primrose went off to Turkey in search of new adventures. Herb stayed on in Paris for the rest of the vac. (Although he returned to Oxford afterward to do the final term of his year, I didn't see much of him.) I travelled back to England alone. Sobered up, I settled down to study for Schools.

I continued to receive letters from Jonathan, from Barcelona and Tangier. As he wrote of those places, they sounded even more romantic than Paris. I felt that, no matter how fast I lived, I could never catch up with him. He made much of living like a poor writer. His room was sixty cents a night, he wrote, and he had to cadge meals from established writers. But the romantic spell was broken for me. I told myself that Jonathan's father was a prosperous doctor in Boston, and that Jonathan would never be allowed to starve. I, on the other hand, would have to earn my living every day of my life. I could never afford the luxury of becoming a writer. Anyway, I was not a real writer—I was just a hanger-on. In my years at Oxford, I had scarcely contributed a story or an article to any undergraduate publication. I had set my sights on being a scholar and an academic.

There was, however, the problem of where I would end up settling—in India, England, or America. My wish to return to India had received a jolt from the experience of my first Oxford friend, Vijay Chowdhary.

IN my early days at Oxford, I kept thinking that Vijay found me boring and wouldn't seek me out again. But he often arrived for lunch, usually without notice. I imagined that he came to see me perhaps out of family obligation, or else out of loneliness. He certainly didn't seem to have any friends around. But then he was already an Oxford graduate, and I concluded that many of his friends had gone down after taking their Schools, while he was staying on another year for his postgraduate course. Anyway, postgraduates at Oxford tended to lead solitary lives.

One day during my first term, when we were having lunch at the Chequers, he told me that he was going to India for Christmas vac that year.

I was taken aback, and found myself thinking of my own return home. When I was in America, I had longed to go home. To be out of one's own country for seven years at the stage of one's youth when one is most awake and alive seemed to me a hardship. I had missed my home—longed to see my mother and my brothers and sisters—but, perhaps because I had now seen my mother, the old longing had been replaced by dread: How would I fit in after nearly ten years' absence in America and England? What would we all talk about? Since I left home, Nimi, Umi, and Om had got married, and Pom, Nimi, and Umi had had children, and I imagined that they were preoccupied with the cares of their new families. I felt that I might be in their way.

"Have you ever been to India?" I asked Vijay.

"Mummy did take me to my village when I was ten, but I don't remember much about it. I am planning to go back to my village."

The way Vijay talked on about "my village"—a village in a far-off place, in which he had neither been born nor spent any time—made me think that he imagined it as having a pub, a cricket pitch, a church. I'd grown up hearing stories about other Oxford-educated Indians who, full of romantic notions, had gone home to their villages and had fled from them in horror and disappointment, and I worried about Vijay's return—and my own as well.

"What will you do there?" I asked.

"Does one need a reason to go to one's own home country?"

"Do you know much about it? Have you read much? I wonder if you might not be in for a surprise. I certainly would be."

"I want to experience India. I want to experience it without the aid of memoirs and books," he said.

The remark sounded absurdly incongruous, made while we were standing at the bar, swilling brown ale, in a twelfth-century pub in a medieval English town, with elegant English voices all around us.

❦

VIJAY was gone for the whole of Christmas vac. After he came back, I couldn't get one concrete piece of information from him about his village or his trip. He became so incommunicative that, the couple of times he stopped by, it was difficult to carry on a conversation with him; he couldn't be bothered to make the effort, it seemed. I came to dread his visits, and started wondering whether he didn't want anything to do with India or Indians anymore, and whether he was stopping by only out of some sense of family obligation, or his British idea of friendship. He would stand around in my room for a few minutes and leave without even sitting down, much less having a cup of coffee. Near the beginning of the Trinity term of my first year, he stopped coming altogether. Since I could not go around Oxford by myself, it was not always easy for me to drop by to see a friend in another college, but I got myself over to his college, only to discover that he had finished his course and left Oxford and that he was continuing his medical studies at St. George's, a teaching hospital in London.

When I next went to London, I made a point of going to see him in the hospital. He seemed to be put out that I'd looked him up, so I left after only a brief visit.

That September, my father happened to be back in London, and we went to the Chowdharys for a Sunday lunch. Vijay was there.

"Vijay has just dropped a bombshell," Mrs. Chowdhary told us almost as soon as we'd sat down. "He just told us that he's planning to chuck medicine. We had no idea that he was even thinking of such a thing."

"A man needs a profession, Vijay," Dr. Chowdhary said. "And I can tell you that medicine is a very rewarding profession."

"It's also remunerative," Mrs. Chowdhary said. "And everyone can see, darling, that you are cut out to be a doctor. You have just the right manner and bearing."

They extracted a promise from Vijay that he wouldn't entertain any such thought.

Later, he walked to the station with my father and me, and brought up the subject of his career himself. "I'm almost certainly going to chuck medicine," he said. "I'm just waiting to make sure that I'm not running away from it for the wrong reasons. You see, I find the actual physical process of doctoring distasteful. I can't handle one more accident victim, sew up one more bloody wound."

This was the most coherent thing he'd said in my hearing since he got back from India, and he said it with such conviction and vehemence that even my father didn't try to argue with him. We just let the subject drop.

Not long afterward, I had a letter from Mrs. Chowdhary telling me that Vijay had indeed given up medicine, and had moved back home in order to write and pursue a literary career.

I telephoned the Chowdharys from the porter's lodge.

"Vijay stays in his room and reads," Mrs. Chowdhary said. "Or goes on ten-mile walks alone, and returns soaked to the skin. It has been raining a lot here." She said that he would take his umbrella but wouldn't open it. Dr. Chowdhary had tried to get him to read for the bar, so that he would have a fallback profession, which both parents wanted him to have, but he couldn't be stirred to take an interest in anything. She said that he had even started taking his meals in his room, but most of the time he wouldn't eat, and the tray would come back untouched.

I thought of writing to Vijay—trying to do something for him. But just the thought made me desperate—filled me with a sense of futility. What can I do, what can anyone do, I wondered. I let the whole matter slide. Whenever I thought of him, I felt guilty. I imagined that he and I had more in common, because of our Oxford experience, than Om and I did. Still, left to myself, I would not have done anything about it. But in December my father turned up in London once more, and accepted an invitation for us to have Christmas lunch with the Chowdharys.

When we arrived, Shakuntala greeted us, but her brother was nowhere to be seen. We asked after him.

"He spends all his time in the garden," Dr. Chowdhary said.

"But that can't be all bad," Mrs. Chowdhary said. "He used to hate geraniums, but now, like us, he loves them."

"He's become silent and secretive," Dr. Chowdhary said. "Quite often, he doesn't even leave his room."

We all went out to the garden. Vijay was digging, and he didn't so much as return our greeting; he seemed not to want to acknowledge my father and me, as if the thought of having to deal with guests were difficult for him.

"You're not well, darling," Mrs. Chowdhary said to him. "Look how much weight you've lost."

"But we won't nag you if you'll only start eating something," Dr. Chowdhary said.

"The reason I don't eat anything is that I'm not earning anything," Vijay finally said, distantly.

"That doesn't matter, darling," Mrs. Chowdhary said. "This is your home."

"There's nothing wrong with me," he said. "I just don't want to be a burden on anybody."

"How you talk!" Mrs. Chowdhary said.

Vijay continued digging, and we walked slowly back into the house.

I felt very sad. The time when I would be going home myself didn't seem far off. From my early childhood, my father had tried to send me to England or America for an education, and at each turn the Western educational authorities had rejected the idea by raising the spectre of "cultural maladjustment." The authorities at the Arkansas School for the Blind, which eventually accepted me, had scarcely known where India was. Now here was Vijay, brought up entirely in England, and yet unhinged by a brief visit to India. What could his "cultural maladjustment" be, compared to mine? His life had been centered on Laindon, Brentwood, London, and Oxford, while mine had stretched from India to America and on to England.

When lunch was ready, Mrs. Chowdhary sent Shakuntala out to get Vijay, but in the meantime he had gone up to his room. She returned without him, saying he insisted on taking his meal there.

We shouldn't have come, I thought. And yet our company seems to cheer them. At the table, the Chowdharys did their best to act natural. There was a lot of talk about Mrs. Chowdhary's wish for Shakuntala to have an arranged marriage in India, like a nice Hindu girl from a good family.

"As you know, Doctorji, I recently took her to India," Mrs. Chowdhary said to my father. "But she didn't like any of the boys that we showed her."

"But, Mummy, they didn't approve of me," Shakuntala said. "They thought I was 'ultra-modern.' "

"Arranged marriages for girls who are brought up in the West can be a recipe for disaster, especially if they are going to settle in India," my father said. "To start with, Western girls have difficulty tolerating the Indian heat."

"Why, Doctorji," Mrs. Chowdhary said, "Shakuntala has been

brought up like a good Indian girl. She'll fit in anywhere."

Shakuntala protested. "If it's all the same to you, Mummy, I would rather live in England," she said.

We spent another hour or so with the Chowdharys and then started for London. Dr. Chowdhary wanted to drive us to the station, but my father and I said we would like to walk.

Out on the road, the cold, brisk air cleared our heads, and the walk to the station gave us a chance to exchange our impressions while they were still fresh. I told my father that it was a depressing Christmas lunch all around. "Vijay seems to be"—I dreaded to pronounce the words—"having a breakdown."

"He needs medical attention very fast, I fear," my father said. "I intimated as much to Dr. Chowdhary."

"After what has happened to Vijay, how can they think of an arranged marriage for Shakuntala?"

"Shakuntala is a very resilient child," my father said. "She'll do whatever she likes, and is not likely to bother about what her parents want for her. She'll be all right."

"I don't enjoy eating Indian food on Christmas Day."

"I know. You would have fancied a goose and plum pudding, like a good Oxford man," my father said.

"And it was so odd to rush through the Indian meal to catch the Queen on the radio," I said. "It was so incongruous."

"As you know, I myself belong to the school of thought that says, 'When in Rome . . .' "

"Yes, I know," I said. "But here is Vijay, almost done in by trying to come to terms with his Indian heritage, and there are the Chowdharys, pushing India on Shakuntala."

"And yet it's all so touching and innocent," my father said. "That's the tragedy of it. What happened to him when he went to India?"

"I don't know," I said. "He wouldn't speak about it."

"He's a real sahib—he might have been unsettled by the experience."

Mrs. Chowdhary must have been thinking along the same lines that my father and I were, because soon afterward she sent me a section of her memoir about her first visit home to India, in 1945, after thirteen years in England. In it she described how she had taken ten-year-old Vijay with her, and how, after meeting her family in Bombay, she had gone to the home of her parents-in-law, in their ancestral village of Muradpur Guruka, in the Punjab.

Because we were England-returned, the family somehow got hold of two commodes and set them up out in the open at one end of the flat roof of the home [she wrote]. They were in full view of people on the roofs of neighboring homes. Then I got to know that there was no village scavenger. "Who'll clean the commode?" I asked. "Don't worry," they said. "You're England-returned, we don't mind doing anything for you and Vijay." I wouldn't have it. I insisted on going to the fields as they all did, as I myself had done before I went to England. I don't mind telling you it wasn't easy. I had to sit in a tall, fairly dense sugarcane field with all manner of insects darting about and with my sister-in-law on the lookout for intruders.

I had to carry a large roll of toilet paper because Vijay flatly refused to use water for the purpose. I settled him down in a secluded corner and held his pants and the roll while he tried to oblige. Suddenly he would jump up and shout, "I can see something coming," and so we would start all over again!

How difficult it must have been for Vijay to adjust, I thought. Even most of us brought up in Indian cities would have found village life extremely difficult.

In the letter accompanying the diary Mrs. Chowdhary said that, when they returned from India, Vijay became, if anything, more English in his dress and habits. By the time he entered Brentwood, he didn't want to acknowledge that there was anything Indian about him. Then something happened to him at

Oxford, she wrote. Maybe it was meeting other Indians, or maybe it was that he didn't fit in with the public-school gangs. Anyway, he became determined to go home to his village and come to terms with his origins. Now Dr. Chowdhary was trying to get Vijay into a mental hospital, but they couldn't persuade him even to see a psychiatrist.

I telephoned the Chowdharys occasionally from the porter's lodge. Around the beginning of March of my second year, I learned that they had obtained a compulsory order and forcibly admitted Vijay to Runwell Mental Hospital for observation.

I went to see him in the hospital. He was undergoing shock treatment and was very unhappy. "I've been seized from my own home and incarcerated here without a trial," he said, in one of his more lucid moments. "It has shaken my confidence in my parents and in British justice." Some days after my visit, I telephoned Mrs. Chowdhary. She said that he had begged the family to take him out. "We were so impressed that he was finally communicating with us that we had him released," she said. "I couldn't bear to see him miserable anymore. He was just wasting away."

A few months after Vijay came out of the hospital, he surprised me with a visit to Oxford. "I have decided to shake the dust of England off my feet and go and live in India," he told me. He was packing up all his belongings and books, he said, and would soon be setting off on a P. & O. liner for Bombay. He added that he had some "seed money" from his parents, and a letter from them to Krishna Menon, an old family friend, who was the Minister of Defence in Nehru's government.

When I next heard from him, he was in India, and his account of his journey made it sound more like that of an English tourist than like that of an Indian returning home. He said that one of the books he had most enjoyed reading on the voyage was Sterne's "A Sentimental Journey," and that he had flown from Bombay to Delhi and taken up residence in the Maiden's Hotel, a well-known

British-style establishment in one of the pleasantest areas of Old Delhi.

Some months later, he was back in England, and I went to see him in Laindon. "I hate Indians and India," he said, and then, although I didn't take his remark personally, he apologized. The tone of his conversation alternated between extreme rage and contrition. It seemed that he had counted on Krishna Menon to find him a job and help him settle down. He had delivered the letter to the Minister's office and waited around at the Maiden's Hotel for an appointment for a full two months. When he did get to see Menon, the visit went badly. "After some chit-chat, he advised me to join the Communist Party," he told me. "That appalled me. I happened to tell him that I'd recently formed a romantic attachment to an English girl. He was flippantly dismissive of the attachment. He assumed I wanted to have an 'affair' with her. I was really appalled. He offered to see me again, but I had had enough. I took the next plane back to England."

His shabby treatment by Krishna Menon, together with his feeling that his "incarceration" had been unjust, changed Vijay. He had gone to India to become an Indian. Now he decided to become an Englishman with a vengeance: previously a Liberal, he became a Tory; he first legally changed his name to George Best and then to George Chowdharay-Best, reclaiming his Indian family name in an Anglicized form; he tried to stand as a Conservative from the constituency of Harrow West, but he was defeated. He wrote some articles for newspapers, bought a car, did a whirlwind tour of Europe in twelve days. But nothing seemed to calm his spirit.

LATE in 1959, Dr. Chowdhary died, and the following February Vijay—or, rather, George—was readmitted to Runwell Hospital. The shock treatment recommenced, and he was kept there for about eighteen months. Whenever I was in England, I visited him there. Each time I saw him, he seemed to be in a rage against his forcible "incarceration," against the shock treatment, against his mother for not getting him out. He was emaciated, and was down from his normal weight of a hundred and thirty-three pounds to a hundred. Eventually, in September, 1961, he was released, but within three months he was back in the hospital, and he spent four more months there.

I saw him not long ago. He was living in a nice house in a pleasant part of London, with his elderly mother and his wife, an Englishwoman, whom he had met at a Conservative political club called the Monday Club. They had got married in 1981, when he was in his late forties. He had put on a lot of weight and was very voluble.

We talked, sitting in his mother's bedroom. She was in poor health, but her mind was clear. He had softened toward his mother, and I noticed that he allowed her to call him Vijay, though his wife, who was introduced as Mrs. Chowdharay-Best, always called him George.

I asked him about Shakuntala.

"Shakuntala? She married an Englishman, an airline steward," he said. "The marriage didn't work out. She is now happily remarried to Tony Banfield, who works in the theatre as a set designer—she herself is a probation officer."

"I wish she had children," his mother said, from the bed.

I asked him what he was doing these days, and he said that he spent most of his time in the library, reading, with a view to collecting illustrative quotations for the Supplement to the Oxford English Dictionary.

"Vijay started as a volunteer," Mrs. Chowdhary said, "but he proved to be so brilliant at research that Oxford University Press is now paying him a salary."

"We are all very proud of him," Mrs. Chowdharay-Best said. "His help has been acknowledged in the Supplement."

XI

THE TOLLING
OF GREAT TOM

T HE TIME FOR LEAVING OXFORD WOULD SOON BE AT hand. My fellowship would come to an end, and I would have to go out into the world without a penny to my name. Where would I live? What would I do? In all the confusion, only one thing was clear: my search for education. It had been the guiding struggle of my life. My father had brought us up to believe that education was more important than money, property, or social position—and, indeed, during the Partition we had learned that all those were subject to vagaries beyond anyone's control. "The world has its ups and downs," he used to say. "But a man with a good education can never sink. He can always pick up and start again." Now I was on the threshold of perhaps the most important examination of my life, which, if I was successful at it, would prove to the world that my intellectual attainments were of the very best. I could not afford to bungle that examination. From every direction, "getting a First" began tolling in my head like Great Tom, the most awesome of the Oxford bells.

William Clark, who had recently written a series of articles about India for the *Observer,* and with whom I'd appeared on the television program "Panorama," told me that if I got a First he would introduce me to the paper's editor, David Astor, who could launch me on a journalistic career. Then Tylor came by my room and boomed from the door, "Your tutors expect you to get a First. I don't remember any blind chap getting a First in Modern History. Of course, you must go back to India and help your fellow-countrymen, in good Oxford tradition, but if at some point you wanted to become a fellow of an Oxford college I would be able to put in a word for you—that is, should you get a First." James Joll, a Wykehamist and a Fellow and Sub-Warden of St. Antony's, to whom I had been farmed out for my European-history tutorials, was sure I would get a First and had urged me to apply for a scholarship for postgraduate work at his college. But meanwhile I had met Jonathan Kozol and had decided that my education wouldn't be complete unless I went to Harvard. I therefore applied, if reluctantly, for a postgraduate fellowship at Harvard. Ever since I was a child, as soon as I made a place for myself I had had to leave it and start somewhere else. The thought of beginning again at Harvard was daunting. But my doubts were laid to rest when, in response to my request for a recommendation, I received a letter from Crane Brinton, with whom I'd studied for a time at Pomona, and who was an influential professor at Harvard. He said that I'd been selected as a Harvard Prize Fellow, and that the Fellowship had a generous stipend, which would see me through to a Harvard Ph.D., but that if I got a First I could skip the Ph.D., since he would sponsor me to be a Junior Fellow in the illustrious Society of Fellows, of which he was a senior member. "People here consider election to a Junior

Fellowship the equivalent of a Ph.D.," he wrote. He counselled me to accept the Prize Fellowship in the meantime, and I did so. (It was the same award I had been offered before I decided to go to Oxford.) My father was sure that if I got a First, Prime Minister Nehru, with whom he was in touch, would create a job for me close to him in the government. From every direction—from England, America, and India—people seemed to be telling me I must get a First. They reinforced my own feeling that getting a First would be in some measure like getting my sight back—that my years of rejections and disappointments would be outweighed by an afterlife of acceptance and triumph. Secretly, I didn't even rule out taking a shot at All Souls. If I did well on its Prize Fellowship examination, the confusion of my cultural background might be an advantage, as, of course, my published book would be; All Souls was said to favor candidates with broad cultural experience and a literary flair. And if by some miracle I got into All Souls I would, of course, pass up Harvard.

Yet a discordant clangor would strike in my head when I least expected it—when I was brushing my teeth, putting on my pajamas, or just falling asleep. It would jolt me like a nightmare. How dare I aspire to a First? How dare I think I could hold a candle to Jasper and Alasdair? How dare I aspire to membership in the fraternity that included Dick Southern and Christopher Hill, Isaiah Berlin and A. J. P. Taylor—for when the board of examiners awarded a First to a candidate it virtually invited him to join the ranks of the top academics. I couldn't console myself with the thought that, having completed an undergraduate degree in America, I had a broader education than many of my Oxford contemporaries. Spreading oneself thin could be no substitute for studying something deeply. Yet the more presumptuous I felt my aspiration to be, the more firmly I was persuaded that I could not hold up my head among academics in the world at large without a First. The fact is that I was afraid to measure myself against anyone, for fear of being found wanting. Whether this was because I was blind or because I was an Indian in the West or because of various blows I'd received along the way, I'm not sure. All I know is that my inferiority was, to me, set in stone. The more I tried to compensate for it outwardly with glamour and panache, the more I quaked inwardly. One result of this attitude was that I often did less well than I was capable of doing, or ruined my performance completely, like an acrobat who has the trapeze within his reach but panics and falls flat on his face. Still, I had come to believe so firmly in the fairness of the Oxford system that I longed to go through the fire.

AT the beginning of each term, we had been given collections, or college examinations, by our tutors on the previous term's work, but those were merely a check for our tutors and our college on how well we were keeping up with our studies. The results of the collections—and, indeed, the good or bad opinion of our tutors—did not count a jot toward our degrees: those depended entirely on our performance in Schools. In Modern History, the Schools consisted of ten examination papers, each three hours long; eight were given in the mornings and afternoons of four consecutive days beginning on a Tuesday, the ninth on Saturday morning, and the tenth on the following Monday morning. There were three papers on English history, in which the examiners could ask us about anything from Roman Britain to the First World War; one on documents of British constitutional history (in my case, from 1660 to 1914); two on general history (in my case, Europe from 1871 to 1939); one general paper on the study of history; one on political science, with prescribed texts from Aristotle, Hobbes, and Rousseau; and two on a special subject (in my case, the Commonwealth and Protectorate from 1647 to 1658). There were also optional translation papers, and I thought of tackling the one in French, but in the end I didn't.

During my time at Oxford, I had, of course, watched many friends take scholarship examinations or Schools, and their apparent confidence was beguiling. They had taken a series of national competitive examinations from the age of eleven on, so they seemed—at least, to me—rather like experienced marathon runners, compared with whom I had scarcely learned to walk. I began to dread more and more the physical ordeal of taking Schools. After the Easter vac, the history tutors had conducted a practice run of the Schools, and I had concluded from it that my results depended on how well I'd slept the night before. A good night's sleep enabled me to show myself to best advantage—I could not only summon up the necessary and appropriate facts but also marshal them in support of my own ideas and arguments—while a sleepless night made my head fuzzy with cobwebs and my fingers jittery with anxiety. Generally, I had very little trouble sleeping. I was usually so tired at the end of the long day that I had but to put my head on the pillow and I conked out. In fact, I was such a deep sleeper that at home my older brother and my sisters used to say that they could put me under a tap and I wouldn't wake up, and at Oxford my scout always had trouble getting me started in the morning. Still, just the thought of not being able to sleep during Schools began to haunt both my waking and my sleeping hours. I would wake up from a dream shaking from head to foot. I would dream that I had overslept and missed a paper; that I had gone in to write the exam but my mind had gone blank; that I'd failed and let down my friends at Pomona, my tutors, and my father, who ever since I could remember had been prepared to "sell his soul" to give me the education he felt I deserved; that my amanuensis didn't know how to spell any of the proper names, and so I had to spell out every other word and I wasn't able to finish; or, worst of all, that I'd missed taking Schools altogether. (Under the Oxford system, that would have meant that I would not get my degree.)

I had typed my collections, but found that I would often lose the thread of the sentence I was typing. Also, I was never able to go back and correct anything. Since college collection grades didn't count toward the degree, mistakes in sentences and inelegance of phrasing didn't matter, but my tutors and I both felt that for Schools I should have an amanuensis, who could, if it should be required, read back to me what I had just written.

As I started reviewing my years of work in history and realized how many books I had read and forgotten or else had intended to read and never got around to, I became frantic. I would dip into a book and read a few pages, abandon it, and look for another, more important book, only to abandon it, too, and dip into yet another one. More than ever, I regretted not being able to skim books—indeed, not being able to read books on my own, always being dependent on readers, who worked only for set hours on set days. Perfectly competent readers of yesterday now began to irritate me by their slowness and obtuseness, even by their having their own lives and obligations, which prevented them from giving me an extra half hour. I wished I could drive them, keep them going, night and day, like dumb animals. My skull seemed to press in on my brain and to throb constantly with frustration. Then I would feel guilty for directing my anger at the very people whose good nature and kindness made my work possible, and would lash out at myself. I would scold myself for having wasted my first Michaelmas term, spent essentially in shopping for a subject to read; for the loss of another term reading English instead of History; for using my first long vac to take courses at Harvard in Chaucer and the twentieth-century novel and to promote my book on radio and television. (I'd done half a dozen television programs.)

Nor was that all. Somewhat perversely, the more time I now spent studying History, the more I wished I were reading great literature. From my present vantage point, I am convinced that this wasn't merely a matter of "the grass is greener"; rather, having never really devoted myself entirely to History, I found myself, as time went on, being pulled away from facts and getting more interested in feelings, fancies, and images. (Even as I write this, it occurs to me that I might have been drawn to facts in the first place to prove to myself that, despite my disability, I could master the world around me.) This development was somewhat surprising, if not troubling, since in essence it subverted the values of Balliol and of England, which put men of affairs above artists and statecraft above art.

FROM home, there were intimations that my family's circumstances were changing, in a way that made the need for me to do well in Schools more urgent than ever. In April of the previous year, Mrs. Clyde had surprised my father by sending him a letter in New Delhi saying that she would not be going to Europe very much anymore. Even that year, instead of spending a few months in Europe, as they had planned—they had got their air tickets and had made hotel reservations all across Western Europe—she wanted to spend only a few weeks there. Moreover, she wanted to give up Old Fields, her estate on Long Island; move into an apartment in Manhattan; and travel in the summer only to the American Virgin Islands. In St. Thomas, she wrote, the pollen count was 0.025, compared with 44 in Old Fields.

As long as my father had known Mrs. Clyde, she had always chosen to go to Europe during the hay-fever season. But from her letter it appeared that if she got properly established in an air-conditioned apartment in Manhattan she might not feel the need to leave New York for health reasons at all. Although she stated emphatically in the letter that the change in her program would not affect his remuneration, in all the years he had worked for her she had paid him to be her "court physician" only when they were in Europe, saying that her medical expenses were tax-deductible only when she was travelling abroad, and that in America he could be just her "guest," meaning that she would pay for his round-trip ticket, wherever he was, and take care of his room and board; that was what she did with all her other close friends. But he counted on the few months' salary he earned from her to meet his annual expenses; in fact, that was practically the only income he had. Being her "guest," of course, did nothing to help him support his family. Reading between the lines of the letter, he feared that if she stopped going to Europe she would stop paying him his salary. And, indeed, within two months, she sent him the following note:

27 May, 1958

DEAR MOLAK,

This business letter will, I hope, reach you before you leave India, but I'll send a copy to your bank in London.

For many reasons and after much consideration I have made the following decisions: I. To dispense with the valued services of my "court physician" as of October 15, 1958.

II. To hope for lengthy visits from my ex- "court physician" as a very close friend, and that he will be able to make trips with me as my guest. These invitations include a round trip ticket to and from wherever he may be.

Aloha!

Ethel

To this cut-and-dried "business letter," which was her way of dismissing him, she added a personal request, as if to underscore the point that his status as a close friend was unaltered:

P.S. If you are near a Boots Drug Store in London, will you be so good as to again get me some hair-nets? This time 18 cap shape, fine real hair, medium size, white and graduated mesh, no elastic. I think the name of the brand was "Marquise" but could be wrong about that. Love to Ved.

In other words, he could count on only three more months of salary from her. In 1959 and thereafter, he would be on his own.

That June, I saw him in London on his way to New York—in fact, we picked up Mrs. Clyde's hairnets together from Boots in Piccadilly—and he never stopped talking about how difficult it would be to make ends meet without her. After we parted, and he went on to New York, he helped Mrs. Clyde find an apartment at One Fifth Avenue, renovate it, move into it from Old Fields, and put Old Fields on the market. When I saw him next, in London late in September, as he was on his way back to New Delhi, he said that she had made no mention of Europe or of further employment for him. "Well, son, all good things must come to an end," he said. "And why should we have thought that my job with Mrs. Clyde would be any different? After all, she's nearly eighty. How long could she keep up her hectic pace of travelling around Europe?" He said that he had put out feelers for some lectures in America, but they would be the following autumn, if they came through at all.

Now here I was in May, some eight months later, at the most important step of my Oxford life, without my father nearby to meet and talk with. Furthermore, I would be going home to reduced circumstances, which would probably mean I would not be able to travel around or do very much.

I NO longer remember exactly what drove me to take mescaline. Was it merely that Adam Kendon, who was working on a D.Phil. in psychology, was conducting experiments with the chemical, needed volunteers, and was fascinated by the idea of having me as his guinea pig? (The son of a Cambridge University publisher, he had come to Oxford the same year I did, but I hadn't got to know him until we were about to leave—perhaps because he had come as a postgraduate student from Cambridge.) Or was it that people had just discovered "The Doors of Perception," by Aldous Huxley, which described, among other things, heightened mental awareness and sharpened perception attained through the use of mescaline? (In the revolutionary philosophical atmosphere of the day, mescaline was said to be a scientific way of investigating the nature and limits of sensory data.) Or was it that in some part of my mind I thought mescaline might exhume memories from the time I had sight—long since buried, at least from my conscious life? Or was it that taking mescaline was somehow connected in my mind with taking Schools—putting my mind to a test? Whatever the case, I agreed to help Adam with his experiment.

One afternoon, around the time I would ordinarily break for tea, Adam, equipped with a tape recorder and a small packet of mescaline in powder form, came to my rooms. He dissolved the powder in a glass of water. "This is half a dose, which means you will be under its influence for four hours," he said. "That will be enough for my purposes."

The solution was bitter, but I gulped it down.

"What do you do to relax?" he asked.

"Listen to music. Why?"

"Put on a record, then, would you? It might help us with the experiment."

As a rule, I hated background music, but Adam was, as it were, the doctor, so I went over to my records, picked the first one that came to hand—it was Beethoven's "Appassionata"—and put it on the gramophone, keeping the volume low.

"How long does it take for the reaction to begin?" I asked.

"It varies from person to person—but it won't be too long."

"Do people ever have bad reactions?" I asked.

"Well, sometimes they do go berserk for a while," he said matter-of-factly.

"What do you mean?"

"People may start screaming during the experiments, because they have horrible visions—although they're never unaware that their visions are brought on by mescaline. For example, they might imagine that demons are about to push them off a tall building."

Adam's manner was exasperatingly judicial and reasonable—almost like that of a don, who could not make a statement without following it up with an example, however unsolicited. His voice, I noticed for the first time, had a slightly sepulchral quality—something an undertaker in a Dickens novel might have. I suddenly had second thoughts about my decision. My mind is all I have, I thought. What if I should lose it—become potty? I felt that I was in a plane that was about to crash.

"Will that happen to me?"

"I shouldn't think so. You see, physiologically, all that mescaline does is cut off the supply of sugar to the brain. But psychologically it seems to bring out a person's alter ego. Atheists will start having the visions of a religious zealot; scholars will have the fantasies of a philistine. Why starving the brain of sugar should produce such reactions is what I hope to learn from my experiments."

"Can you stop it? Can I get off it?"

There was a rush of notes from the piano, rather like water falling over a precipice.

"I have here a box of glucose. You just spoon it down as fast as you can, and it will restore the supply of sugar to your brain and you'll be fine. In fact, after that, mescaline will have no further effect on you. It's not supposed to be habit-forming. In my experience, people who have taken it once never want to take it again."

I felt somewhat reassured, but was furious with myself for

not having asked all these questions before I plunged into his experiment. There were times when I would ponder a decision for so long that I would end up doing nothing. There were just as many times when I would leap into a decision as if I were harebrained.

I needed to go to the loo. When I tried to stand up, I felt lethargic and dizzy and sat down again. My limbs felt heavy, as if they'd fallen asleep.

"What are you feeling?" Adam asked, clicking on the tape recorder. The click sounded like a firecracker, and I would have jumped if I could have.

"Tired," I said, dragging out the word, as I might have in the grip of a high fever. I noticed, as if I were observing someone else, that my voice and breathing had slowed down; in fact, my voice seemed distant, almost disembodied, and I wondered if I might be entering a trance.

"I know what you're feeling," Adam said. "You don't want to talk. You want to be left alone to have your private vision, to retreat into your private world. But the point of my experiment is to find out what that world is."

"Stop it!" I was surprised at the vehemence of my outburst, but his talk was obstructing my perception of the girls.

"What are you seeing?"

"Wait. . . . Stop. . . . Don't . . . say . . . anything," I said haltingly. A very odd thing was happening. The normal boundaries of time and space had dissolved. I had no idea how long I had been sitting there, and I could no longer tell where I was in relation to the gramophone. The room and the piano were inside my head, and the notes were so sharp and clear that I was not hearing them through my ears at all: the pianist was hammering the strings of my mind, which was throbbing and pulsating with the music. Everything except the raging music seemed pointless and irrelevant. My head had taken in the entire universe, which was a gigantic piano, played by hundreds of Javanese girls, tripping across the keyboard. If someone had slipped the mescaline into my soup, and I had not known that the vision was chemically induced, I would have accepted it as real. As it was, while one part of me was having the experience another part of me was observing it, albeit in a very delayed manner, and saying, "This is happening because I took mescaline." But the observing mind lagged far behind the melody, which raced ahead like a rocket.

"They're beautiful," I said.

"Who?" Adam asked.

"The girls."

"What are they wearing?"

"They're stark naked."

"Can you actually see them?"

"Yes, but as shapes, not colors—the way I 'see' in my dreams."

The dancing girls were making raging music with their little bare feet, creating a tempestuous storm on the gigantic piano; there were wild eruptions of chords, as if the composer's tortured soul were trying to vent his grief. But I was in the ecstasy of having the girls right inside my head. "Compared to our music, nothing matters," they sang. Nothing I had held sacred, nothing I had ever valued or loved—my family, my friends, Oxford— seemed to matter. The whole world could be wrapped in one small blanket and thrown away. Beethoven, way out there in the yonder, was playing on a piano that was an entire universe. No. It wasn't Beethoven at all. It was hundreds—thousands—of little naked Javanese girls.

"Is it like being drunk?" Adam asked.

"I feel totally irresponsible. But when I'm drunk I also feel irresponsive. . . . But now I feel more responsive than ever. . . . I now understand the mystics—their religious experience." Although my words came out haltingly, in a barely audible voice, the observing part of my mind was astonished by the lucidity of my answer.

"Ah, you're clearly an agnostic and a very responsible person, who has been living like a monk. Your alter ego is religious and irresponsible and likes to frolic with women."

"What did you say?" I'd almost stopped listening, but the other part of my mind knew he was saying something extremely interesting.

"Anything in your experience comparable to this?"

"It's rather like being in a delirium. Everything seems louder and sharper."

"Could you find your way around?"

"No. The boundaries of time and space don't exist."

After the experiment, Adam took me out to dinner. By then, I must have eaten a half a box of glucose, but even so I kept drifting away at the table, and now the experience was frightening. My mind is all I have, I thought. If I lose it, I'm finished. I asked him again about other people he had given mescaline to and what their experiences had been like.

"J. had a screaming fit, and I had to take him to the Warneford, and T. was just sick. But most people reveal their alter egos, as you did."

"Are you sure it doesn't have any lasting effect?"

"None," he said. "I've taken it."

I felt reassured, and, indeed, after a day or so of feeling slightly weak I felt like myself, but I have never gone near any mind-altering drug again.

❧

I WENT to see the college doctor, Alan Richards.

"Bronchitis again?" he said as soon as I had sat down. I had seen him often, always for bronchitis or a bad cold.

"No," I said.

"What is it?"

"Schools." I could scarcely get the word out.

"What about Schools? Are you worried about taking them? You don't seem that sick to me."

"I'm not at all sick."

He stood up as if the consultation were over.

"I want some Seconal." I had never taken a sleeping pill in my life, but I'd read somewhere that people took Seconal capsules when they couldn't go to sleep.

He started writing out the prescription. "What strength?"

"What's the normal dose?"

"One and a half grains? Three grains?"

"One and a half grains," I said. "If I'm having trouble sleeping, is one capsule enough?"

"You can take two if you really want to go into a deep sleep," he said.

"What if I should have trouble staying awake during the day?"

"You could take Dexedrine."

"What does that do?"

"It gives you a lift, like strong coffee."

So I walked away from his office with prescriptions for fourteen Seconal capsules—two for each night of the Schools and two for good measure—and for a like amount of Dexedrine, which Dr. Richards advised me to take each morning of the Schools. I felt exhilarated. No more bad dreams. Every night of Schools, I would have a good sleep and guaranteed alertness for the day. I felt I had my secret weapon against the examiners. (As it turned out, the sleeping pill made me feel groggy for most of the day, while the stimulant did not so much relieve that feeling as give me a false sense of confidence, making me think that even some of my more mundane answers were brilliant.)

THE night before Schools began, my friends Wilson and Beverley Southam had me to dinner at their flat, on Broadmore Street.

Wilson, a Canadian who had come up to Balliol from McGill in my second year to read Modern History, was about the only married undergraduate I knew. (Ordinarily, an Oxford undergraduate who got married had to go down; a Rhodes scholar had to give up his scholarship.) A huge and powerfully built man, bursting with energy, he was a paragon of an athlete. Although I had little in common with him, I found him especially considerate. He had certainly sensed the extreme stress I was laboring under just then, and had invited me for an early dinner, observing, "We'll make sure you don't drink too much, and see to it that you get back to college in plenty of time to get a good night's sleep."

Wilson, offhand, casual, and optimistic, was so self-effacing that in the Oxford atmosphere of one-upmanship he was an oddity. Back home, he had considered himself a cowboy, yet he was one of the few college people who seemed to be truly rich: the Southam family had made a fortune in the newspaper business. (The family's publishing firm was headquartered in Toronto.) Sometimes, in the middle of the day he walked around in a hand-sewn suit from Savile Row and puffed on a corona cigar, as if he were a man of the world instead of a mere undergraduate. And yet, despite his very polished exterior, there was something stormy about him. I remember how shaken I was when, in one of our first conversations, he told me that a few years earlier his father, who had had a drinking problem, committed suicide. After Wilson had been at Oxford for a year, he appeared with a girl on his arm—Beverley Neil, a fellow-Canadian, who was very shy and withdrawn—and introduced her as his fiancée. A more unlikely match would have been hard to imagine. A registered nurse, she was barely four feet eleven inches tall and weighed ninety-seven pounds, while he was almost six feet two and weighed over two hundred. Whether it was that he took pride in being extraordinary or was trying to put the best face on things, he underscored the obvious disparity between them by often citing their heights and weights. Naturally, we all wondered about their courtship, and I once asked Wilson how they had met.

"A year before I went to McGill, I went off a cliff in a ski race," he told me. He was an accomplished skier, hockey player, and bicyclist, and for a time he also raced cars. "I was in pain for two years, and then had to have one of my kidneys removed. Two days after the operation, I was on the floor doing calisthenics when a nurse came into my room. She was Beverley. She was horrified and told me off. She said if I wanted to kill myself there were better ways to do it. In fact, she was so angry that she hated me for quite a while."

It was hard to imagine Beverley as a sort of Napoleonic figure in the hospital, and I said as much.

"That's Beverley, all right," he said.

"So you fell in love."

"She fell in love," he said. "But it was because of her that I made it through one of the hardest years of my life. So marrying her is a small price to pay, don't you think?" He laughed his hearty laugh.

In my last year, Wilson and Beverley got married in the college chapel. The wedding was on January 10th, which was still part of the Christmas vac, and some of his friends who had to come back from home for the wedding asked him why he didn't get married during the term.

"There have been other marriages in my family on January 10th, and they all ended in divorce," he said, with a hearty laugh.

I reflected, as I often did, on the special quality of Oxford which threw people as different as Wilson and me together and made friends of us. Yet at the same time I was a little frightened of him. Not only he but most of his cronies seemed to be prone to accidents. I remember standing with him on the street outside the porter's lodge one afternoon while engineering friends of his, Chris Spender and Nicholas Ouroussoff, were tinkering with his racing car. Spender was changing a valve in the engine, and the clamp that he was using to hold the spring slipped, flew up, and hit him in the face, shattering two of his front teeth. Wilson rushed him to the hospital, and later he told me that several of his own teeth had been smashed—first, while he was drinking water from a fountain as a boy, and another boy pushed his head down, and again when he was playing hockey in high school.

A friend once asked Wilson how Beverley liked to have him racing cars all over England, and he replied that she never complained or seemed frightened for his safety—in fact, he was sure that she enjoyed it very much. The friend suggested that he see for himself how she enjoyed it. So Wilson got someone else to race in his place, wearing his helmet, while he, from a hiding place, observed Beverley. She was weeping. He gave up racing.

Somehow, I convinced myself that there was something propitious in their having me to dinner the night before Schools. It was extremely relaxing. Wilson was a good host and kept my mind off the pending ordeal, and his excellent wine, together with Dr. Richards' magical capsules, enabled me to sleep soundly.

WITH Schools almost upon us, we had all spent a lot of time going over old examination papers. (Since Schools were public examinations, the papers were always published after the event and were available in the library.) There were as many as twenty-three questions to a paper, we found, and it was clear that much would depend on how fast one could absorb them and decide which were the best three or four to tackle. Yet, for some reason, I hadn't stopped to think how Schools would be administered to me. I had imagined that I would get dressed up in subfusc, like everyone else, and would walk across to the Schools building with the other Balliol historians, and while the others took the examinations in the big writing rooms, under the eye of the invigilators, I would be given a little room somewhere with my amanuensis, Helen Hookey. But then I happened to meet Rodge in the quadrangle, and he informed me casually, as if he were commenting on the weather, that the examiners wanted me to take the examination in college itself, and that it would appoint an amanuensis for me.

"Who will be the amanuensis?" I asked, trying not to show my distress.

He jingled the coins in his pocket and said, "The examiners cannot be expected to divulge that, because she will also be your invigilator." (My amanuenses tended to be women.)

"Will she be a university graduate?"

"Can't say, my boy," he said.

What if she has no knowledge of history, I thought. Will I have to spell every wretched name for her? Will she be able to read the questions quickly? Will she understand what she's reading? (If a reader didn't comprehend the material, he or she could make such a hash of the pauses and emphases that often I would not be able to grasp it fully, either.)

"I really think she should be a graduate."

"The college can make that request," he said. He left abruptly.

I was torn by what Rodge had told me. I was loath to ask for any special consideration; one of the things I valued most about Oxford was that people treated me as an equal to such an extent that I often forgot the problem of my physical impairment in my intellectual life. In fact, I felt that all of us Balliol historians in my year were companions, sailing together toward a distant land called Schools. Now we were finally in sight of land, and it suddenly appeared that my destination was different. But what was even more alarming was the business about the amanuensis. As a rule, no matter how good an amanuensis was, it took me several weeks to get used to a new voice and a new hand, and, of course, it took time for the new person to get used to my ways. I had to learn, for instance, to pace my dictation to the speed of her writing. An amanuensis might write with a ballpoint pen, which was so silent that I sometimes didn't know whether she was still writing or had finished. Or she might use a mechanical pencil, which meant distracting noises—adjusting and readjusting it, and so on. Or she might use an ordinary pencil, and have to keep stopping to sharpen it—not to mention chewing on it or tapping her teeth with it. And she could have other distracting habits. In fact, any sound, however small, would make me tense up, even set my teeth on edge, and interfere with my concentration.

The more I thought about the examiners and the nameless, unfamiliar amanuensis, the more I fretted. Yet my pride would not allow me to discuss the subject with Rodge or with anyone else. Besides, I was sure that the examiners would not yield on the matter. No doubt they were following a precedent, and would take the view that an exception could not be made without compromising the validity of previous results. To the English, precedent was as sacred as the law.

ON the first day of Schools, I woke up from the Seconal sleep with a powerful thirst. No matter how much water I drank, my thirst would not be quenched. I won't take Schools feeling like Tantalus, I thought. I gathered up half a dozen small bottles of tonic water and, just before nine o'clock, went boldly to the Old Common Room, where I had been told my examination was to take place.

Waiting inside the Common Room was a young woman so silent that I could scarcely hear her breathing. She introduced herself as Thelma Smith, and told me simply that she had taken the Modern History Schools from St. Anne's in 1954.

"Do you mind if I drink some tonic water during the exam?" I asked, putting on my most confident air.

She hesitated, as if the invigilator and the amanuensis in her were struggling.

"The supply will keep my throat from getting dry from dictating for six hours," I said. "And I'll be happy to share it with you."

She laughed in a warm-hearted way, and, without wasting any time on amenities or on asking me about my method of work, got down to the task at hand. She seemed so quick and efficient that my only distraction was that I couldn't stop marvelling at her. I drew up a chair on her left at the long table where I had sat for my Handshaking at the end of each term, and cleared my throat.

The moment the college clock outside struck nine, she read:

ENGLISH HISTORY
I

Candidates should complete four answers. They should illustrate their answers by sketch maps where appropriate.

Oh God, maps, I thought. At the time, there were no Braille maps worth the name, and, much as graphs had defeated me in my study of economics, maps had impeded me in my study of history. It was hard enough to imagine the world, with its myriad relationships, but at least the geographical map of the world was more or less fixed. Historical maps, however, were constantly changing, and England, in particular, was so small that the boundaries of its estates, villages, and counties were elusive and almost impossible for me to visualize. If sketching a map had been a requirement of the examination, I would certainly have failed it.

She was continuing with the reading:

1. What evidence is there for commerce into and out of Britain before the arrival of Claudius?

2. "From first to last in Roman Britain the main strategical problem was that of the northern frontier." Discuss.

3. It is beyond question that a great victory was won at Mount Badon in about 500 A.D. What may we legitimately assume about the conquering and the vanquished forces in this battle?

4. Has the influence of St. Augustine and his followers upon the civilization of Kent been overestimated?

5. In what ways was Offa of Mercia a greater king than Edwin of Northumbria?

6. "An inspired copyist with a backing of common sense." Was Alfred anything more than this description suggests?

There were twenty-three questions, and it took a good few minutes to read them out. It then took me a few minutes to choose the questions and organize my thoughts.

"Right," I said, and looked at my watch. I suddenly felt reluctant to dictate to someone using pen or pencil. However competent she appeared, I had no way of judging whether we would be able to work well together.

"I think I'd like you to type my answers straight on the typewriter," I said. I had never before dictated to someone typing, and wondered if I could tolerate the noise. But the die was cast, and for the remainder of the three hours she typed like the wind, hardly ever asking me to spell a name. Helen Hookey, with all her experience with me, couldn't have done better than this amanuensis. My only regret was that I hadn't been apprised of her abilities. It would have spared me much unnecessary anxiety.

❦

IN every paper, the problem was always choosing the questions that were most closely related to the topics I had prepared, either with a tutor or on my own, and that, at the same time, gave me the greatest scope for my own ideas. Each question generally required close mastery of specific arguments embedded in books and articles. Yet I could prepare for no more than ten or twelve questions on any one paper—nor could anyone. I was lucky if on each paper there were three or four questions connected with my research; even so, the connection was often so tenuous that I had to reorganize the evidence on the spot, hoping that the examiners would not notice holes in my answer. Yet the last thing one wanted to do was simply to regurgitate facts. In any year, hundreds of candidates took the same Schools, and the examiners, either as tutors or as Schools arbiters, were bombarded with the same facts year after year; on the papers, the questions might be phrased or pointed differently from one year to the next, but, at a deeper level, their thrust did not change a great deal. Schools, therefore, provided a marvellous opportunity to break free of tutors and books, and give one's own meditations, so one tried to choose a question on which one had a fresh angle or point of view, on which one could exercise a certain amount of historical imagination and judgment and do a new analytical turn, as it were— make the examiners sit up and take notice.

At the end of each day of writing, I would be so washed out that it was a relief to walk around the quadrangle or mill about in the J.C.R. with other Balliol historians, pretending that nothing out of the ordinary was going on. But I would eat dinner quickly, take Seconal, and go to bed early, often falling asleep among my stacks of Braille cards for the next day's papers and then dreaming of key words on the cards which were supposed to unlock the storehouse of historical knowledge and theories I had formed.

Whether it was because I was actually able to get through the ordeal or because throughout the six days I was able to keep writing something without getting stuck or blocked, at the end of the week I had a feeling of elation, tempered only by the thought of what had happened in collections, which was that when I thought I had done well on a paper I had usually done badly—and vice versa.

❦

THE day I finished my last paper was a glorious summer day. We Balliol historians who had taken Schools had chipped in a couple of pounds each to buy champagne for a pre-luncheon party in the quadrangle, and by the time I arrived on the lawn corks were popping and people were tossing down the bubbly as fast as bottles could be opened and glasses filled. I'd written all my papers under the strain of being continuously thirsty—despite the bottles of tonic water, which, with the indulgence of Thelma Smith, I had continued to smuggle in. At the time, I attributed my thirst to nerves, but now I'm sure that it was due to the regimen of Seconal-Dexedrine-Seconal. My thirst was made worse by my not having much of an appetite and by my trying to go about my life outwardly as if taking Schools were the most natural thing in the world. After all, my friends took exams all the time. They didn't stop hanging around the J.C.R. or the college, or stop dropping by for coffee or a drink with me. Having tried to be every bit their equal throughout my Oxford years, how could I now behave any differently? As long as Dexedrine was in my blood, I could keep up the pretense. But the artificial stimulus would wear off by evening, and then I would collapse in a heap. Now someone handed me a chilled bottle and a glass.

"Quick! Quick!" people urged me. "Pour it. It's about to run over." I seemed to be feverish from days of accumulated thirst, and was determined to quench it once and for all, and also to get my money's worth, downing at least two bottles of champagne. I theatrically threw the empty glass over my shoulder and put the bottle to my mouth, all but choking as the bubbles whooshed and gurgled down my throat. I kept raising the bottle ostentatiously and gulping down the champagne until I drained it. I dropped the empty bottle on the ground and asked for another.

There was some scattered clapping and laughter. I felt suddenly that the bubbles were rising up from my stomach and I might at any moment foam at the mouth, but I still felt as thirsty as ever.

Priya appeared from behind me and threw her arms around my shoulders. Everyone had arranged to go out with a woman friend for a post-Schools lunch, and I had invited Priya. In recent months, she had scarcely visited Cambridge. In fact, the Amartya business, which she now referred to as "hero-worship," and which had been going very strong the previous spring, seemed to have waned. As a result, we had seen more of each other. She had come to my society meetings, and I had dropped by her room at Somerville for tea and crumpets. We had also been out punting together. Still, whenever we met she would bring up Amartya, but distantly—more as if she were grieving for his loss than hoping for his love. I thought that it was only a matter of time now before her heart would be completely free, and she would be ready to welcome and reciprocate my attentions. The fact that those attentions might have to be pressed from a long distance away—from India and America—didn't daunt me. I even felt that if I got a First I would be on my way to being as attractive as Amartya. (I had always assumed that she—or any woman—could like me only for my mind.)

"You're really finished," she said, turning me around.

I don't think I'd felt as happy since, as a boy, I had a mynah, who used to sit on my shoulder and say "Hello, Sweetie."

I caught hold of her and kissed her on both cheeks, European fashion.

"I have my best sari on for you," she said.

I brushed my hand against it. It was of heavy silk, and elegantly pleated in the front.

"It's blue—your favorite color."

We had had many intimate conversations, but I felt that now, for the first time, she was actually thinking of me.

Soon we were at the center of a group, which included my tutorial partner, Murray Forsyth. Gallant as ever, he opened a new bottle of champagne and poured glasses for Priya and me.

Many of our friends, among them Jasper and Moni, who were passing on their way to lunch in hall, stopped by, and we pressed champagne on them. All around, people were laughing and drinking and talking as if the Oxford party would continue forever. Priya drank little, but I know I got through another entire bottle.

I'd booked a table at the Capri (thanks to my friendship with William, whenever I walked in there I was treated like royalty), and Priya and I almost floated over to the restaurant, her hand in mine, her sari richly rustling above the squeak and flop of her sandals. A little wind had come up, and she would often have to tug at the free end of the sari to keep her left shoulder covered.

Upstairs in the restaurant, Romeo had the best corner table waiting for us, with a bottle of our favorite Chablis chilling in an ice bucket. He had barely opened it and poured some in my glass for me to taste when the ground under my feet began to give way and the table began to tip—silver, glasses, serving plates, ice bucket, and all. In fact, the whole restaurant began to sway and turn.

I reached over and held Priya. "Are you all right?" I asked.

"Yes," she said, a bit taken aback.

"What's happening to the restaurant?"

"What do you mean?"

"It seems to be rolling and pitching like a ship."

She laughed.

I suddenly felt very old. She was in her second year, and had come straight up from Channing. Her life had passed in the protected surroundings of her parents' home and her boarding school, while I had been buffeted about from pillar to post since before I was five, and my path to Oxford had taken me from one wretched trial to the next, whose like she had never dreamed of, much less known. I felt wary, as if I were a corrupter of youth, a little like the aging Humbert Humbert in pursuit of Lolita.

Something has happened to my mind, I thought. I excused myself.

An advantage of going to a restaurant I was familiar with was that I knew my way to its loo: no matter how crowded the restaurant, I could get there easily, without needing anyone to help me. I now stood up and almost ran. No sooner had I got inside the door to the loo than my legs gave way. I stretched out on the wonderfully cool, clean floor.

I woke myself with a snore. Romeo was bending over me and applying ice towels to my forehead.

"What time is it?" I asked, as if I were in my room. "Oh, my God!" I suddenly sat up. "Has Miss Adarkar left?"

"Madam is waiting for you, sir," he said.

"Has she ordered?" I asked, almost drifting back to sleep.

"Madam is waiting for you to order, sir," said Romeo. He got me on my feet.

Priya was standing in the little upstairs lobby. She supported me into the lift—which I hadn't even known existed—and Romeo put us in a taxi.

I lay down in the back seat, nestling my head in Priya's lap, fully convinced that she and I were going by land to New Delhi.

"My taxi! Look what he's doing to it!" the driver cried from the front seat.

"We'll pay," Priya said. "Hurry, hurry to Balliol."

"I'll pay you, Ma'am, to get another taxi," he said. "I'm not going anywhere."

"What is he complaining about?" I asked. "Give him this fiver." I had been holding the note in my hand to give to Romeo for managing our departure so beautifully.

"No, Ma'am, I couldn't take that from him," the pilot said.

"Just as far as Balliol, please." Her voice seemed to be coming from the other side of the ocean.

I slept and woke up. Priya was talking to some strangers through the window.

"He's very sick. Are any of his friends about?"

"Who is seasick?" I asked the cabin.

"Why is everyone running away?" It was a Canadian voice booming from a radio.

"Damn it, Priya," I said. "The fellow has brought us to Canada."

"Will nobody help? Please?" she said through the window.

"What's the matter?" The Canadian voice clapped onto my ear like a blaring radio that wouldn't turn off.

"He's very sick," Priya said.

"Who's sick?" I asked.

"I will not have his brilliant career at Balliol disgraced by having him carried through the college." Why are we stopping to listen to this awful broadcast, I wondered.

"Drive him to my house."

The next thing I knew, I was naked, and a tiny woman with childlike hands had me by my ankles, while a huge man had me by the shoulders in a tight grip. I was sure he was about to put a straitjacket on me.

"Let me go!" I cried, trying to wriggle away.

Diabolically, they dunked me in scalding water, and when I shrieked they dipped me in freezing water. I thought I had been kidnapped and taken to the Warneford by mistake.

"You're torturing me! What have I done? . . . Oh God, Priya didn't get any lunch. . . . I didn't give Romeo a tip."

"Thank your stars you're among the living" came over the radio.

🌣

THE radio in my head eventually turned out to be Wilson Southam. He had taken me to his apartment, and, to revive me, he and Beverley had bathed me in hot and cold water alternately. I would come to, only to lose consciousness again. (Since Wilson had helped me through both the pre-Schools and the post-Schools trials, I blithely assumed that, powerful person that he was, he would take his own Schools in stride. But when his turn came, the following year, he checked himself into the Warneford a month before. In the Warneford, instead of studying he spent a good bit of time making timetables for study or going off to the golf course, which was virtually next to the hospital, to putt and practice his drives. In fact, like some other undergraduates, he took his Schools in the Warneford. He later explained to me, "It was a good way not to add to the Oxford suicide rate, which I read somewhere was eleven times that of the nation." He got a Third.)

On that fateful day, Wilson dropped me back at college around five o'clock. I felt chastened and humbled by all that had happened, and, like a man who has glimpsed mortality in a foxhole, impetuously forswore all mortal pleasures—especially drink—for life. But no sooner had I walked into the porter's lodge than I was practically embraced by my Punjabi friend Moni, the Rhodes scholar, who was as drunk as a lord and was singing away some garbled blend of songs. He must have just come from one of the many after-Schools parties. But he was still in his first year, and it seemed to me it was only yesterday that he had been lecturing me on the evils of alcohol.

"Why are you drunk? What reason have you to be drunk?" I demanded.

"Oh, degradation! Oh, damnation! . . . Does one need a reason to be drunk?"

I tried to get away from him, but he attached himself to me as if I were his only friend, and kept embracing me in the Punjabi fashion.

"Moni, I'm not feeling well," I said. "I've just finished Schools."

"Finished Schools?" he crowed. "You should be happy." He pronounced "happy" as if it were two words.

He followed me right up to my room, and as soon as we got inside the door he started throwing up vigorously on my carpet. I practically dragged him across the quadrangle to his room, on Staircase XXI, on the opposite side of the college.

I somehow got him onto his bed and set his wastepaper basket next to him. Every time I tried to leave, he jumped up, caught hold of me, and asked me to go the Buttery with him for a drink.

Suddenly, Barry Winkleman, a socialist with a strong conscience, who lived next door to Moni, materialized at the door. "England, bastard England!" Barry moaned, wringing his hands. "Look what she does to nice Indians—how she corrupts them."

Moni, thinking that he had been insulted, challenged Barry to a game of tennis.

"Bastard England!" Barry repeated.

"Oh, degradation! Oh, damnation!" Moni retorted.

I slipped away, and left the two of them to their verbal sparring.

Back in my rooms, I thanked God for Daniels, who had tidied up everything in the meantime. I slumped in my chair, my mind besieged by hundreds of thoughts, and waited for the Schools dinner, given by our tutors. The thought of yet more festivities turned my stomach, but I went through them with no more difficulties.

One final duty remained before I could go to bed. It was to beg Priya's forgiveness. I took a taxi to Somerville and practically barged into her room. Her tenderness confirmed everything I had felt about her, and made me all the more deeply attached to her and to Oxford.

❧

Now that Schools were over, I felt liberated, like a man who has been in a labor camp for most of his adult life, is suddenly released, and finds that he has no bearings in the real world. It seemed that until the end of Schools I had not had a single day without a looming examination or deadline since, at the age of fifteen, I went to America to begin my formal schooling. There, during my high-school years, I had first had to learn English, make up for my missed elementary education, and later—for financial reasons, among others—compress the last two years of high school into one by doing correspondence courses in the summer and taking an exceptionally heavy load of regular classes in the school year. At Pomona, I devoted Christmas vacations—and sometimes even Christmas Day—to preparing for the finals given in late January. This was in part because reading books took much longer for me than for sighted students, in part because I was stuck on campus with nothing better to do, in part because I didn't know what to do with myself if I was not working. It seemed that, having spent my childhood in idleness and in longing to go to school like my brothers and sisters, once I had discovered how I could be educated I couldn't stop learning—couldn't be satiated. The summers of my Pomona years I spent in summer schools, learning subjects outside my major, and accumulating credits that I didn't need for my degree. And when I wasn't doing that I was working on my book. I was determined to get to the top of my class, and, of course, to get to Oxford.

After Schools, I settled all my bills with my readers and took each of them for a farewell drink or lunch. When that was done, I entered upon a strange experience—a stretch of time without a schedule of readers and amanuenses or the obligations of class and tutorials. I set about packing my books and sending them off to Harvard, but I felt so light-headed that now and then I thought I might never pick up a book again; in fact, I could scarcely bring myself to read even for pleasure. I felt that I had scaled a mountain and come down in one piece, and I no longer needed to prove to anyone—not even to myself—that I was able to climb.

I now began to be consumed by one thought—that of finally going home. It was nearly ten years since I had been home or known home. Every Oxford vac, I had thought about visiting my family in India, but there had never seemed to be enough money in the kitty. Despite my forebodings about returning, the wish to see my brothers and sisters, instead of diminishing, grew ever more urgent with the passing of each day, and having seen my mother after seven years had only intensified that wish. Nostalgia is not a healthy or productive emotion, but it seems to me that writers can never be wholly free of it. I now realize that during those summer days I was especially in its grip, but secretly so. As the time for going home approached, my gramophone would sing Vivaldi, Bach, Mozart, and Brahms in the light of day, when my British friends were around in my room. But in the dead of night I would put on old Indian records and squat, Indian-style, with my ear to the speaker, trying to catch the notes of the melody, my heart racing with excitement and fear, as if I were indulging a forbidden passion and might be caught at any moment.

Only one thing was keeping me at Oxford—one final obligation, which I thought was really pro forma. No undergraduate could technically go down until the board of examiners of his Schools had posted the list of candidates who were called for a viva voce—a supplementary oral examination. A candidate was generally given a viva if the examiners could not decide among themselves about the class of his degree. The viva could only improve one's marks, not lower them, and people—especially people who were expecting Firsts—were quite cavalier about them,

since the Oxford assumption was that either one was First material or one was not, and no amount of diligence or slogging could
get one a First. After all, brilliance was not something one could
acquire; it was a quality of mind one was born with. Indeed, most
of the undergraduates who walked away with Firsts made a great
show of never working. One did occasionally hear about a bizarre
decision arrived at by way of a viva, but, in the good Oxford
manner, there was always a reasonable explanation. For instance,
sometimes one heard that the examiners couldn't agree on whether
to give a candidate a First or a Fourth, but it was said that this
usually happened in a field that was in turmoil, like philosophy,
in which what one examiner might regard as a work of genius
another might dismiss as lunacy. Also, sometimes a candidate
would do so brilliantly on some papers and so poorly on others
that the examiners were hard put to it to believe that the papers
had come from the same hand. There were even instances of a
first-rate candidate's missing a paper or two altogether, and it
was said that the examiners didn't want to penalize him just because
his nerves had got the better of him, and they would therefore
try to examine him orally on the missed material. The examiners
took their responsibility of classification very seriously, not only
because if someone got an undeserved bad class it would dog him,
just as an undeserved good class would elevate him unfairly, but
also because there was no appeal from their classification. In order
to avoid second-guessing on the examiners' decisions, all papers
were burned.

I MET Rodge in the main quadrangle. I was all ready to tell
him about Glyndebourne, where I had just been—in a rich friend's
Rolls-Royce, no less—to hear "Così Fan Tutti," thinking that he
would be impressed at how I'd learned to do things in style, but
he said, rather abruptly, "You've been called for the viva, Mehta."

Then he started to march past me, jingling the coins in his pocket.

I ran after him. "What does that mean?" I asked anxiously.

"It can only mean that you are going to be viva'd for a First." Jingle, jingle.

"Where will I have to go? When? How long will the viva be?" I was so taken aback by his news that my words were tumbling out in a rush. I suddenly realized that I didn't know anyone who had gone through a viva, and knew practically nothing about how one was conducted. Rodge must have sensed my anxiety, because he stopped short. He explained that the Modern History vivas would begin in the second week of July; that since the examiners went through the candidates alphabetically my turn would probably come a couple of weeks after that; that the board of examiners would examine me in a room in Schools; and that there was no way of predicting how long the viva might take. "Pray for a long viva, Mehta," he said. "A short one is usually a bad sign."

"Will all the examiners be asking me questions?" I asked.

"No. Only those who think you should get a First."

Rodge, as the senior tutor in history, had seen more Balliol historians through Schools than any of his colleagues. Also, as an old-fashioned tutor who had devoted his life to teaching, he cared more than most about the number of Firsts that Balliol got, since they added to the renown of the college. I should have asked him for his advice, but instead, rather impetuously, I asked if I could be moved up to the head of the list of people taking vivas, so that I could go home early. The Harvard term began around the middle of September; if I didn't get to India before August, I would have barely six weeks at home, and who knew when I would be able to get there again?

Rodge started jingling his coins and whistling under his breath. "I'll make the request to the examiners that you should be viva'd first, my boy," he said. And then he was gone.

His calling me "my boy" gave me a turn, for it took me right back to my first year. Lately, he'd always called me "Mehta," as if we were on an equal footing.

I returned to my rooms with a horrible sinking feeling that in advancing my viva I was making a mistake—that an extra couple of weeks would be helpful for reviewing, or revising, as we called it at Oxford. I felt that by the very act of my writing Schools everything I ever knew about history had gone out of my head—that, in a sense, I had already left Oxford for India and Harvard. And, indeed, many of the books and notes I needed for revision were already on their way to the United States. But, at the same time, rather superstitiously, I took solace in the conjunction of having my viva first and getting a First.

I spent the following days seeing friends, punting on the river, drinking Pimm's cups, and having long lunches at the Trout. I certainly didn't chase after my readers for help with my revisions; my goodbyes to them had been as final as my mental departure from Oxford. Of course, I spent some time with Priya, who was about to go on travels of her own. But, since she had another year to go at Oxford and was still recovering from Amartya, about all I could get from her was "Let's keep in touch." In due course, we exchanged some letters, but she made it clear that there was no future for me with her.

The viva was held on the morning of Friday, July 10th. Seated around the table were the examiners. In addition to the External Examiner, S. T. Bindoff, who was a professor from Queen Mary College, University of London, there was an array of formidable Oxford historians: Michael Brock, Daniel Meredith Bueno de Mesquita, K. B. McFarlane, Michael MacLagan, J. M. Roberts, Betty Kemp, and the chairman, Menna Prestwich. I had not met any of them, or even heard them lecture, but I knew most of them by reputation. Menna Prestwich was said to be one of the most intimidating historians around. When historians from provincial universities came to Oxford to give papers, she would quiz them, as a tutor would quiz an undergraduate, on little-known monographs and articles, and expose their deficiencies, even though many of them were well known and had been trained at Oxford themselves. At least one woman historian was said to have been reduced to tears by the Prestwich treatment.

I remember wondering as I walked into the room whether Menna Prestwich would deign to award me a First. She thinks that history can't be done well in the provinces, I thought. How is she going to reconcile herself to a blind Indian doing history? But I had such faith in the fairness and the accuracy of the Oxford system that I dismissed the thought.

Mr. Brock began the viva. He was an examiner on my third English History paper, on the period from William and Mary to the First World War. He gently asked me to amplify one or two points in my answer to the question "Is the repeal of the Corn Laws entirely attributable to the Anti-Corn Law League?" I had worked on the topic on my own and thought I knew it inside out. I started talking overconfidently and with uncharacteristic assurance—almost, surprisingly, in the voice and accent of Christopher Hill. (At Oxford, I had come to deny my Indianness, even my Americanness, and tended to adopt unwittingly the mannerisms and attitudes of the people I admired; I recall Christopher's once observing, with a laugh, "God, you're talking like me!")

I was suddenly brought up short: I was referring to William Cobbett, the journalist, when I meant Richard Cobden, the free trader, and Brock was correcting me. But he was so nice about it that I was not derailed. The viva went on in what seemed like a very pleasant, amicable way for over forty minutes, with questioning by a couple of other examiners. Since my special subject was also Menna Prestwich's field, I expected her to grill me, but she didn't speak until the end, when she said, "Thank you very much." Her voice was unexpectedly gracious and kind, and I read congratulations in it. (Later, I often wondered whether I would have picked up different signals if I had been able to see the faces of my examiners—indeed, whether I would have done better in

Schools if I had been able to go to their lectures, like sighted undergraduates.)

I walked out of the room thinking I had landed my First.

At college, Rodge was waiting in his room to find out how the viva had gone, and when I described the examination to him he, too, concluded that I had been successful. "Now you can go home, Mehta, knowing that you've done well for yourself and college," he said.

I took the first available flight home.

RODGE'S letter hit me as nothing else ever had. I had felt I could overcome virtually everything, but how could I ever overcome the judgment I found here? My mind became a welter. How could I now ever go back to Oxford? How could I now face the porters in the porter's lodge? How could I face Jasper and Alasdair? My mother had often said that the worst thing for us Indians is to lose face, and I now felt that I had been crippled in a way that was much worse than blindness. The new disability was not one I could ever overcome through sheer exertion of will, and it was one I had brought upon myself.

I remembered John Higgins, the defeated blind man I had met in my early Oxford days who had got a Second, and I contemplated suicide. Why struggle on? What for? In an instant, I could put an end to everything. But I was at home, among people who loved me and whom I loved, and I was with them almost constantly. I wished I were in some isolated corner of the world, where I would not be perpetually made aware of their existence. I was determined to take my own life, and to do so without the aid of a knife, a gun, a rope, or a bottle of Seconal. In a moment of clarity, I reasoned that if one of these devices ended my life I would not truly die by my own hand—I would be killed by something other than myself. The thought was enough to give me pause, to make me delay, to wait for tomorrow.

Those were my thoughts as my father read me the letter from Rodge:

Balliol College
Oxford.
6th August, 1959

V. P. Mehta, Esq.,
C-1, East Nizamudin Road,
New Delhi,
India.

My dear Mehta,

I am very sorry that you didn't after all get your First, which, I must confess, after your account of the viva I thought seemed highly probable. There was a good deal of alpha in your work as you see, but your Examiners say, oddly enough, that you had memory but not enough thought, which is not the comment I would have made upon your work. Perhaps you spent a little too much time upon other things, but I think you have found your Balliol career worth while, even if at the end of it all you didn't get the Class which, in many ways, your intellectual qualities seemed to deserve.

I hope you have found all well in India in your own home, and that your future career in America will be what you wish it to be.

It has been a real pleasure to have had you at Balliol; let us know if, at any time, we can be of use to you.

Yours,

Sd / - A. B. Rodger.

English History I $\beta=/\beta$	Political Sciences $\beta\alpha/\beta\alpha$
English History II $\beta\gamma/\beta=$	General $\beta\alpha/\beta++$
English History III $\beta\alpha/\beta+?+$	Special Subject I $\beta++$
Documents $\beta?\alpha$	Special Subject II $\alpha\beta$
Foreign History I $\alpha\equiv$	
Foreign History II $\beta\alpha$	

The welter of my thoughts was, if anything, only exacerbated by a postcard from Rodge that arrived a week or so later—even though it was clearly intended to comfort me. It said that one of the examiners had told him that at the viva it had appeared that I had indeed got a First, but that later, when the board was reviewing the Firsts, it had been decided that only the top seventeen deserved Firsts, and I was the eighteenth.

To be so near and yet so far. I never once so much as hinted at my disappointment to my family, because I considered such weakness unmanly. And yet my father kept reassuring me, unbidden, that it was not the class of my degree but the class of my mind that ultimately mattered.

In mid-August, Dom turned up in New Delhi.

"Vedkins, what about a tiny drinkkins?" he said on the telephone.

Suddenly, Oxford was in India. We spent a month travelling together, meeting writers, poets, painters, musicians, actresses, flying off to Nepal, carousing around in Calcutta. As we were sitting in a restaurant in Calcutta and remembering our Oxford friends, he said, "Who would have thought it? A lot of them got Firsts."

"I didn't," I said, the words almost sticking in my throat. Then, more clearly, "I got a Second."

"Coo," he said.

"I feel quite cut up about it," I said.

"Why, ducks? Housman failed, Wystan Auden got a Fourth, Evelyn Waugh got a Third, and I got a Third."

I don't know exactly why—I was not really like any of them—but the remark made me smile, and I savored for a moment defiant and truculent feelings about the provincial Oxford values. Even within the terms of those values, the Oxford examiners were not always infallible: Jasper himself had been an exhibitioner rather than a scholar.

"Come to think of it, Kenneth Tynan got a Second," I said. Many of us were under the spell of his writing and intellect.

"Who cares?" Dom said.

Of course, I cared, but viewing the results from Dom's perspective began the process of healing.